Myth and Thought among the Greeks

Myth and Thought among the Greeks

Jean-Pierre Vernant

ZONE BOOKS · NEW YORK

2006

Printed in the United States of America.

Distributed by The MIT Press,
Cambridge, Massachusetts, and London, England

First published in French as *Mythe et pensée chez les Grecs*
(Paris: Librairie François Maspero, 1965). The English
translation was originally published by Routledge & Kegan
Paul in 1983. This edition © Editions La Découverte,
Paris, 1996.

Library of Congress Cataloging-in-Publication Data

Vernant, Jean-Pierre.
     [Mythe et pensée les Grecs. English]
     Myth and Thought among the Greeks / Jean-Pierre
Vernant.
          p. cm.
     Includes bibliographical references and index.
     ISBN 1-890951-60-9
     1. Philosophy, Ancient. 2. Mythology, Greek. I. Title.
     B178.N413 2005
     180–dc22
                                        2005042024

Contents

To Ignace Meyerson

Preface to the 1985 Edition

Twenty years have passed since *Myth and Thought among the Greeks* first appeared. It was published in France in 1965 by François Maspero, in the series edited by Pierre Vidal-Naquet, and was one of the books that helped inaugurate the study of historical psychology in reference to ancient Greece.

In 1971, a second, revised and enlarged edition gave a somewhat newer face to the work, which then appeared in two small volumes in the Petite Collection Maspero series. The work was reprinted nine times (three times for the first edition, six for the second), and thus has endured for over twenty years.

In the introduction to the first edition, I expressed a wish that my undertaking would not remain isolated. I hoped that the paths opened by the Hellenist Louis Gernet and the psychologist Ignace Meyerson would lead to further investigations into the internal history of the Greek individual in terms of his mental organization and the changes that, from the eighth to the fourth century BCE, affect the entire picture of his activities and psychological functions: perspectives on space and time, memory, imagination, the individual person, the will, symbolic practices and the manipulation of signs, modes of reasoning and argumentation, categories of thought. My wish has been fulfilled. I could cite many scholars who have carried out brilliant work along these lines. At present, the historical anthropology of ancient Greece has acquired citizen's rights within classical studies as well as among

9

historians, sociologists, and anthropologists engaged in comparative research.

The present edition returns to the format of the first, in that it includes all the essays within a single volume. It enlarges the second edition still further, with the addition of three new contributions written since that time. It seemed clear to me that these essays had their place here as well.[1]

As for the study of Hesiod's myth of the races, its inclusion in this work is in a way self-evident. Hesiod's account provided an example that allowed me to show what I thought the structural analysis of a mythical text could and ought to be. In the second edition, I included a response to some objections that a philologist had made to the essay. This time, I am including a response to Victor Goldschmidt, whose work inspired the study, although I did not follow him in every respect. In his last writings, Goldschmidt returned to our respective readings to provide a general formulation of the problem of structural interpretation in the history of thought. I in turn was led to reflect on my own work and to interrogate the way the modern interpreter, if he wants to precisely situate what Goldschmidt calls "the author's intentions," must bring together and create an intersection, as it were, of structural analysis and the historical perspective. In the case of the myth of the races, new findings in archaeology concerning the appearance and development of the hero cult in the eighth century led me to reconsider my previous analyses and to modify them on some important points.

Since then, the method of structural analysis has been applied with much success, in France and elsewhere, to many other Greek myths or sets of myths by a number of scholars, particularly Marcel Detienne. As for my own work, if I now had to choose the most characteristic example of this interpretive procedure from among my writings, I would gladly refer to my interpretation of the myth of Prometheus in *Myth and Society in Ancient Greece* and, in a more precise and developed form, in *The Cuisine of Sacrifice among the Greeks*, under the title "At Man's Table: Hesiod's Foundation Myth of Sacrifice."[2]

The second study added here traces out the passage, in the plastic practices of the Greeks, from an attempt to figure the invisible to an art that imitates appearances. This study is a direct continuation of the chapter on the psychological category of the double and the *kolossos*. Or, rather, it clarifies the earlier essay by rendering its ambitions and scope more explicit. In effect, it determines the place occupied by the category of the double within a mental transformation leading to the emergence of the image, properly speaking, in fifth-century Greek culture: we move from the *eidōlon* as a phantom double and as the earthly presence of a supernatural reality to the *eidōlon* as an imitative artifice, a false semblance, in the sense put forth by Plato. These two texts are closely connected to a third, first published in the *Journal de psychologie* under the title "Imitation et apparence dans la théorie platonicienne de la *mimésis*," and reprinted in *Religions, histoires, raisons* in the chapter "Naissance d'images."[3] This question, to which I devoted the majority of my teaching at the Collège de France, is particularly important to me, and I hope to return to it at greater length in the future.

The final addition to the volume, "The Origins of Philosophy," sums up the somewhat more meandering approach of Part Seven, "From Myth to Reason," by giving it nuance and partially modifying its orientation.

In this picture of the Greeks and their inner adventure — a domain in which even what seems most assured can only be provisional, as I well know — there are many blank spots and empty spaces. Some of these I have tried, elsewhere and later, to fill in. This is the case, for example, with the question of the will, which is not addressed in this book but which I study in *Myth and Tragedy in Ancient Greece*, written with Pierre Vidal-Naquet.[4] We try to show that in fifth-century Attic tragedy one finds the first hesitant sketches of the man-agent, master of his actions and responsible for them, possessing a will. The problem is taken up again from a more general viewpoint in the article "Catégories de l'agent et de l'action en Grèce ancienne" in *Religions, histoires, raisons.*

From myth to reason: these were the two poles between which, in a panoramic view, the destiny of Greek thought seemed to play out at the end of this book. Since the first edition was published, Marcel Detienne and I have carried out a joint investigation into *mētis*, in which we attempt to follow the avatars of this particular form of cunning intelligence (so typically Greek).[5] Employing every kind of ruse, shrewdness, craftiness, deception, and resourcefulness, it is a practical form of thought that struggles against obstacles and faces every opponent in an ordeal of strength whose outcome appears both decisive and uncertain. For the wise and sensible man, an expert in many twists and turns, *mētis* brings success precisely in situations where at first it seemed impossible. This intelligence put to use in action has its own functional rules, its own ends and purposes, and its own models of operation. From the Archaic period to the Hellenistic Age, it follows a distinct and continuous line through Greek culture, alongside or in the margins of the great theoretical forms of knowledge, including philosophy. Whether one calls it trickery, wiliness, skill, ingeniousness, or prudence, this Greek *mētis* follows a path of its own (with Odysseus as its spokesman and hero), and today I tend to think that it belongs neither entirely to myth nor altogether to reason.

I would like to express my warmest gratitude to François Lissarrague, who corrected and completed the index of this edition.

Introduction

I have chosen to collect these studies in a single volume — even though their subjects may appear to be rather different — because they were conceived as parts of the same inquiry. For ten years, I have attempted to apply to the field of Greek studies the methods in historical psychology that Ignace Meyerson initiated in France.[1] The subject matter for these investigations is material that has been worked on by specialists — scholars of both Greek and ancient history. However, I shall consider it from a different perspective. The material in question includes religion, with its myths, rituals, and illustrated representations; philosophy; science; art; social institutions; and technical or economic data. But whatever we are dealing with will be considered as a work created by humans, as the expression of organized mental activity. By studying these phenomena, we shall seek to understand the individual in ancient Greece, a being inseparable from the social and cultural environment of which he is at once the creator and the product.

The task is difficult because it is necessarily indirect in character, and it runs the risk of being unfavorably received. In dealing with the evidence, the texts, the archaeological data, the realities that we too must use, the specialists are all faced with special problems requiring specific techniques. In most cases, they see the study of the individual and his psychological functions as foreign to their own particular fields. Psychologists and sociologists, on the other hand, are too involved in the contemporary world to be interested in a study of classical Antiquity, so they abandon it to what they take to be the somewhat outdated curiosity of the humanists.

And yet, if there is a history of human interiority [*l'homme intérieur*] to complement the history of civilizations, we must again adopt the slogan first advanced by Zevedei Barbu in his *Problems of Historical Psychology*: "Back to the Greeks!"[2] If we approach the matter from the point of view of historical psychology, there seem to be several reasons why a return to the Greeks is unavoidable. The first is of a practical nature: documentation of life in ancient Greece is more extensive, more varied, and more thoroughly researched than that in many other civilizations. We have at our disposal a large number of substantial and detailed original works relating to the social and political history and the religion, art, and thought of ancient Greece. To this practical advantage can be added more fundamental reasons. The writings that have come to us from ancient Greek civilization embody ideas different enough from those expressed in the framework of our own intellectual universe to make us feel that we are in foreign territory, to give us not only a sense of a historical distance but also an awareness of a change in man. At the same time, these ideas are not as alien to us as are some others. They have come down to us through an uninterrupted process of transmission. They live on in cultural traditions to which we constantly refer. The Greeks are distant enough for us to be able to study them as an external subject, quite separate from ourselves, to which the psychological categories of today cannot be applied with any precision, and yet they are sufficiently close for us to be able to communicate with them without too much difficulty. We can understand the language used in their writings and reach beyond their literary and other documents to their mental processes, their forms of thought and sensibility, their modes of organizing will and action — in sum, to the structure of the Greek mind.

There is one final reason why the historian of human interiority should turn to classical Antiquity. Within a few centuries, Greece underwent decisive changes in both its social and its mental life.

The city was born, and with it, law. Among the first philosophers, emerged rational thought and the progressive organization of knowledge into a body of clearly differentiated disciplines — ontology, mathematics, logic, natural sciences, medicine, ethics, and politics. New forms of art were created and different modes of expression were invented in response to the need to validate hitherto unknown aspects of human experience: in literature, lyric poetry and tragedy, and in the plastic arts, sculpture and painting, conceived as imitative artifacts.

These innovations in so many different fields indicate a change in mentality so marked that it has been seen as the birth of "Western man," a true flowering of mind and spirit in every sense of the term. These transformations do not relate only to progress in intellectual matters or techniques of reasoning. From the *homo religiosus* of the archaic cultures to this political, reasoning individual (referred to in Aristotle's definitions, for example), these transformations affect the entire framework of thought and the whole gamut of psychological functions: modes of symbolic expression and the manipulation of signs, ideas of time and space, causality, memory, imagination, the organization of acts, will, and personality — all these categories of the mind undergo a fundamental change in terms of both their internal structure and their interrelationships.

Two themes in particular have fascinated Greek scholars during the last fifty years: the progression from mythical to rational thought and the gradual development of the idea of the individual person. These two questions are treated somewhat unequally in the present collection. I have approached the first in a more general way, whereas in dealing with the second I have concentrated on one particular aspect. In order to avoid misunderstandings, I feel that I should attempt to explain my position with regard to each of these two problems. The title of the last section of this book is "From Myth to Reason." However, by this I do not mean that I am considering mythical thought in general, any more than I admit to the existence of rational thought in an immutable form. On the contrary, in the closing remarks of Chapter Seventeen, I

15

emphasize that the Greeks invented not reason as such, but a type of rationality dependent on historical context and different from that of today. Similarly, I believe that in what is known as mythical thought there are diverse forms, multiple levels, and different modes of organization and types of logic.

In the case of Greece, intellectual evolution appears to have followed two main lines of development between the time of Hesiod and that of Aristotle. First, a clear distinction was made between the world of nature, the human world, and the world of sacred powers. These categories are more or less connected or intermingled with one another by the mythical imagination, which sometimes confuses the different areas, sometimes operates by slipping from one plane to another, and sometimes establishes a network of systematic correspondences among all these aspects of reality. On the other hand, "rational" thought tends to ignore the ambivalent or extreme notions that play so important a part in myth. Rational thought avoids the use of associations by means of contrast and does not couple and unite opposites or proceed through a series of upheavals. On the principle of noncontradiction and unanimity, it condemns all modes that proceed from an ambiguous or equivocal basis.

Stated in such a general form, the conclusions I offer are provisional, aimed above all at outlining a plan of inquiry. They call for more restricted, more precise studies focusing on a particular myth recounted by a particular author or on a particular body of myth having variants in different Greek traditions. The only way to trace the transformations in mental processes, techniques, and logical procedures is to undertake concrete studies to determine just how the vocabulary, syntax, modes of composition, and choice and organization of themes evolved from Hesiod and Pherecydes through the Presocratic philosophers. Thus the last part of this book should be read with reference to the first. I have carried the structural analysis of a particular myth, Hesiod's myth of the races, as far as I could, in order to describe a manner of thought that is anything but incoherent, but whose movement, rigor, and logic have their own particular character; the structure of the myth depends, both for its overall design and for the details of its various parts, on the balance and tension between the poles of ideas. Within the context of the myth, these ideas express the polarity of the sacred powers, which are at once set in opposition and associated. Thus, in Hesiod's work, we find a "model" of thought in many respects close to the one that, as expressed in the couple of Hestia and Hermes, seems to dominate the earliest Greek religious experience of space and movement.

It may seem surprising that I have not given a larger place in this collection to the analysis of the individual. This is indeed the one area where Greek scholars have been led by the very nature of their investigations to touch on psychological problems. The transformations in the individual from Homer to the classical period seem quite startling, for Homeric man had no real unity and no psychological depth but was subject to sudden impulses and inspirations that were thought to be of divine origin. The Homeric individual was, in a sense, alienated both from himself and from his actions. Then, however, man began to discover the internal dimension of the subject; the body came to be seen as something distinct, psychological impulses were taken to be unified, and the individual (or at least certain values linked with the individual) emerged. The sense of responsibility developed; the agent was seen as more answerable for his own actions. All these developments in the individual have been the subject of inquiries and discussions that have a direct bearing on historical psychology.

I have not sought to present an overall assessment of these studies, partly — but not solely — because one psychologist has already attempted to do so. Barbu has studied what he terms "the emergence of personality in the Greek world" from a point of view similar to my own.[3] While I fully accept many of his analyses and would advise the reader to consult them, I am inclined to express some reservations about his conclusions. First, it seems to me that Barbu rather forces the issue in the picture he paints of the development of the individual. Because he has not taken all the different kinds of evidence into account, and particularly because he has not studied them closely enough, he sometimes imposes too modern an interpretation on them and projects onto the Greek personality certain features that, in my opinion, did not emerge until more recently. Second, although his study is undertaken from a historical point of view, it is not entirely free from normative preoccupations. Barbu's view is that the Greeks discovered the *true* individual. By basing their inner being on a balance maintained between two opposed psychic processes — on the one hand, an "individuation" that integrates the internal forces of the individual around a single center, and on the other hand, a "rationalization" that integrates individuals into a higher form of order (be it social, cosmic, or religious) — they constructed a perfect form and model of the individual. But from a psychological point of view, the work of certain Greek scholars seems to me to raise a number of objections; they have a tendency to underestimate not only the complexity but also the historical relativism of a psychological category such as the individual, with all its many dimensions. They consider the individual a category whose development is now complete and believe it can be defined in simple and general terms, so they sometimes pursue their inquiries as though the question were one of finding out whether the Greeks were aware of the individual or not and at what moment they discovered it. For the historical psychologist, the problem cannot be posed in these terms. There is not, nor can there be, a perfect model of the individual, abstracted from the course of the history of mankind, with its vicissitudes and its variations and transformations across space and time.[4]

The purpose of this inquiry, then, is not to establish whether the individual personality existed in ancient Greece or not but to discover what the ancient Greek personality was and how its various characteristics differed from personality as we know it today. What aspects of it become defined, in greater or lesser detail, at particular moments, and what form do they take? What aspects remain unknown? What features of identity find expression in particular types of works, institutions, and human activities, and to what degree? Along what lines and in what directions did the Greeks develop the functional notion of personality? What groping or abortive attempts were made to grasp it? What blind alleys were followed? And, finally, to what extent was this function systematized? What was its core? What were its most characteristic features?

An inquiry of this kind presupposes that a scholar has isolated from the body of evidence that Greek civilization offers us the facts that are especially relevant to one or another aspect of personality. The scholar must also have defined the types of works and activities through which the ancient Greeks constructed the framework of inner experience, just as, through science and technology, they constructed the framework of an experience of the physical world. Such an inquiry, therefore, has to cover an extremely vast and varied field that includes linguistic facts and the development of vocabulary (especially psychological vocabulary); social history, particularly the history of law but also the history of family life and political institutions; large chapters of the history of thought, for instance, those that pertain to the concepts of the soul, the body, and individuation; the history of moral ideas, for instance, shame, guilt, responsibility, and merit; the history of art, in particular the problems arising from the emergence of new literary genres, such as lyric poetry, tragedy, biography, autobiography, and the novel (to the extent that these last three terms are not anachronistic with reference to the Greek world); the history of painting and sculpture, with the development of portraiture; and, finally, the history of religion.

Since it would not be possible to address all these problems in a short study, I have decided to limit my discussion of them to the evidence provided by religion. Furthermore, I shall consider only the religion of the classical period; I shall not concern myself with any innovations introduced in the Hellenistic Age. The limitations thus imposed on this inquiry from the start are bound to make it all the more demanding. Since it is confined to religion, I have had to draw careful distinctions within this domain. I have had to consider, in each instance, the effect any particular aspect has had on the history of personality, and how far religious beliefs and practices, through their psychological implications, affect the

inner state and contribute to developing identity. As will be evident, my conclusions are in general negative, and I have been led
to emphasize especially the differences and the distance that, in
terms of religious life, separate the fifth-century Greek from the
believer of today.

The greater part of this collection is devoted to psychological categories that, owing to a lack of contact between Greek scholars
and psychologists, have not hitherto been the subject of research
carried out from a historical point of view. They include memory
and time, space, work and technological activity, imagery, and the
concept of the double.

The most fully elaborated chapters are concerned with work
and with space. Work has marked contemporary social life and
contemporary man so deeply that one is quite naturally led to
think that it has always been unified and organized as it is today. I
have attempted to show that, on the contrary, the significance of
work patterns and their effects on the individual and the group
have altered greatly. The case of the Greeks has seemed to me to
be particularly illuminating with regard to a historical study of
space. The scientific thought of the Greeks, as well as their social
and political thought, seems to be shaped by a geometric viewpoint; this is in striking contrast to more ancient representations
of space, as seen in myth and in religious practices. I have therefore taken the opportunity to follow, in relation to what is in
some ways a privileged example, the transformations in spatial
representations. I believe it has been possible to distinguish the
factors that in ancient Greece determined the transition from a
conception of space that was religious, qualitative, differentiated,
and hierarchical to one that was homogeneous, reversible, and
geometric.

The study of the kolossos and the psychological category of the
double should be seen as an initial contribution to a more ambi-
tious study on the subject of the appearance of the image as such,
the emergence of creative activity that produces images (whether
artificial objects of a strictly "imitative" character or creations of

the mind whose aim is more properly "imagistic"), and the development of the psychological function of the imaginary.

In attempting to open up the whole field of Greek studies to the inquiries of historical psychology, I have in no way underestimated the difficulties of such an enterprise, which far exceeds my capability, or the inadequacy of my own findings. My intention has been to forge new paths, to lay out some problems, and to provoke further investigations.

If this study helps promote combined research by a group of scholars comprising classicists, historians, sociologists, and psychologists, if it points to the need for a concerted plan of action to study the psychological changes that resulted from the Greek experience and the turning point this experience marks in the history of human interiority, then it will have served its purpose.

PART ONE
Myth Structures

Chapter One

Hesiod's Myth of the Races:

An Essay in Structural Analysis

Hesiod's poem *Works and Days* begins with the telling of two myths. After referring briefly to the existence of a double "strife" (*eris*), Hesiod tells the story of Prometheus and Pandora. This myth is immediately followed by the myth of the races, which, as Hesiod says, "crowns" the first. The two myths are linked: both evoke a bygone time when people lived untroubled by suffering, sickness, and death; each in its own way accounts for the ills that have since become inseparable from the human condition. The myth of Prometheus suggests a moral so clear that Hesiod has no need to expound it. The myth speaks for itself: Through the will of Zeus, who, in order to avenge the theft of fire, has hidden man's livelihood from him — that is to say, his food — the human race is condemned to toil. Man is obliged to accept this harsh divine law and obtain no respite from his labor or his suffering. Hesiod draws from the myth of the races a lesson that he addresses in particular to his brother Perses (a sorry wretch), but that is equally appropriate to the mighty on earth, those whose function it is to settle human quarrels through arbitration, in other words, the kings. Hesiod sums up this lesson in the dictum "Observe justice (*dikē*); do not allow immoderation (*hubris*) to grow."[1] However, it must be said that if one goes no further than the usual interpretation of the myth, it is hard to see how these instructions can derive from it.

The story tells of the succession of different races who have preceded us on earth, who have, each in turn, appeared and then disappeared. What is there in such a tale to exhort man to justice? All these races, be they good or bad, were obliged, when the time came, to quit the light of day. And among those races worshipped by people long after they had disappeared beneath the earth, there were some who, while on earth, had manifested an appalling degree of hubris.[2] Furthermore, the races appear to follow one another in order of progressive deterioration. They are associated with the metals whose names they respectively bear, arranged from most to least precious, from highest to lowest. Gold comes first, then silver, followed by bronze and, finally, iron. Thus the myth appears to contrast a divine world whose order has been immutably fixed ever since Zeus's victory with a human world in which disorder gradually establishes itself, until the scales are finally tipped decisively toward injustice, misfortune, and death.[3] But this picture of humanity destined to a fatal and irreversible decline hardly seems likely to convince either Perses or the kings of the virtues of *dikē* and the dangers of hubris.

This initial difficulty concerning the relationship between the myth as it appears now and the significance Hesiod attaches to it in his poem is matched by another, which has to do with the structure of the myth itself. Hesiod adds a fifth race to the races of gold, silver, bronze, and iron: the race of heroes, which does not correspond to any particular metal. Since it is inserted between the ages of bronze and iron, it upsets the parallelism between the races and the metals. Moreover, it interrupts the movement of continuous decline symbolized by the scale of metals of regularly decreasing value. Indeed, the myth makes it quite clear that the race of heroes is superior to that of bronze, which precedes it.[4]

Erwin Rohde noticed this anomaly and pointed out that Hesiod must have had extremely powerful motives to introduce into the structure an element that was manifestly foreign to the original myth, particularly when this intrusion appeared to disrupt its logical pattern.[5] Rohde observes that what interests Hesiod most about the heroes is not their earthly existence but their destiny after death. In the case of each of the other races, Hesiod describes, on the one hand, its life here on earth and, on the other, what became of it once it left the light of day. So it would appear that the myth served two purposes — revealing the increasing moral decline of the human race and giving insight into the posthumous destiny of each successive generation. Although the heroes appear misplaced from the point of view of the first aim, it is fully justified from the point of view of the second. Where the heroes are concerned, this subsidiary purpose appears to have become the principal one.

Taking these observations as his starting point, Victor Goldschmidt suggests an interpretation that goes further.[6] According to him, the destiny of the metal races after they have disappeared from earthly life is "promotion" to the rank of the divine powers. The individuals of gold and of silver become daemons (*daimones*) after death. Those of bronze became the people of the dead in Hades. Only the heroes do not benefit from such a transformation, which would bring them what they already possess: heroes they are, and heroes they remain. We can, however, see why they are introduced into the myth once we realize that their presence is indispensable if the list of divine beings is to be complete. According to tradition, apart from the *theoi*, the gods strictly speaking (of whom no mention is made in the myth), the list consists of the following categories: daemons, heroes, and the dead.[7] Thus Hesiod would appear to have developed his account of the myth by uniting two different traditions that were no doubt originally independent, and adapting them to each other. On the one hand, there is the genealogical myth of the races, involving the symbolism of the metals and depicting the moral decline of the human race. On the other, there is the structural division of the divine world, which can be explained by reworking the myth's original schema in order to establish a place for the heroes. In this way, the myth of the ages could be seen as the oldest example of an attempt to reconcile a genetic and a structural point of view. It is an attempt to make the stages of a temporal succession correspond, term for term, with the elements of a permanent structure.[8]

27

Goldschmidt's interpretation has the merit of emphasizing the unity and internal coherence of Hesiod's myth of the races. Whether the myth originally included the race of heroes is a matter of great scholarly controversy.[9] But it is certain that Hesiod rethought the overall mythical theme from the point of view of his own preoccupations. So we must consider the myth as it is presented to us in the context of *Works and Days* and ask ourselves what, in this form, it means.

On this point, one preliminary observation should be made. As far as Hesiod is concerned, one cannot speak of an antinomy between the genetic myth and the structural arrangement. In mythical thought, any genealogy is also the expression of a structure, and there is no way to account for a structure other than to present it in the form of a genealogical narrative.[10] The myth of the ages is not, in any respect, an exception to this rule. And the order in which the races follow one another on earth is not, strictly speaking, chronological. How could it be? Hesiod does not imagine a unique and homogeneous time within which each of the races has a fixed and definite place. Each race has its own time, its own age, which expresses its particular character. This time, just as much as its way of life, its activities, its qualities, and its defects, defines each race's status in contrast to that of the other races.[11] If the race of gold is called "the first," this is not because it arose one fine day, before the others, in the course of linear and irreversible time. On the contrary, Hesiod describes it at the beginning of his account because it embodies virtues — symbolized by gold — that are at the top of a scale of nontemporal values. The succession of the races in time reflects a permanent, hierarchical order in the universe. As for the idea of a continuous and progressive decline, which the commentators all agree is found in the myth, this is incompatible not only with the episode of the heroes (and it is difficult to believe that Hesiod did not notice this), but also with the notion of time in Hesiod, which is not linear but cyclical.[12] The ages succeed one another to form a complete cycle that, once finished, starts all over again, either in the same order or, more probably, as in the myth in Plato's *States-*

man, in reverse order, so that cosmic time is unfolded alternately, first in one direction and then in the other.[13] Hesiod laments the fact that he himself belongs to the fifth and last race, the race of iron, and expresses regret at not having died earlier or *been born later*.[14] This remark is incomprehensible in the context of human time, which is continuously degenerating, but it makes perfect sense if we accept that the series of ages is a recurring renewable cycle, just like the sequence of the seasons.

Within the framework of such a cycle, even without taking into account the case of the heroes, the order in which the races succeed one another does not constitute a progressive decline at all. The third race is not "worse" than the second, and Hesiod never suggests that it is.[15] In the text, the people of the silver age are characterized by their mad excesses and their lack of piety, and the people of bronze by their acts of immoderation.[16] What in this suggests a progressive decline? There is indeed so little progression that the race of silver is the only one whose faults arouse the anger of the gods and that Zeus annihilates as punishment for its lack of piety. The race of bronze dies, as do the heroes, in battle. When Hesiod wishes to make a value judgment about two races, he formulates it explicitly and always in the same way: he contrasts the two races in terms of *dikē* versus hubris. He stresses that there is a contrast of this kind between the first and second races and again between the third and fourth. To put it more precisely: in terms of "value," the first race is to the second what the fourth race is to the third. Hesiod states that the race of silver is "very much inferior" to the race of gold on account of hubris, by which the race of gold is quite untainted.[17] He further states that the heroes are "more just" than the race of bronze, which is also devoted to hubris.[18] On the other hand, he makes no comparative value judgment between the second and third races. The race of bronze is simply described as being "in no way similar" to the race of silver.[19] Thus, as far as the relationships between the first four races are concerned, the text presents the following structure: a distinction is made between two different groups, with gold and silver in one and bronze and the heroes in the other. Each group is divided into two antithetical aspects, of which one is positive and the other negative, and each thus comprises two associated races, each of which is the necessary counterpart to the other and stands in contrast to it as *dikē* does to hubris.[20]

The distinction between the first and second races depends, as we shall see, on the fact that different functions are involved. The two races represent opposed types of human agents, forms of behavior, and social and "psychological" states. We shall have to be more specific on these points, but we can note right away one feature in which they are not symmetrical. In the first pair, the dominant value and the starting point is *dikē*; hubris is secondary, treated as its counterpart. In the second pair, the opposite is true: the principal consideration is hubris. Thus while each of the two pairs has a just and an unjust aspect, it can be said that, taken together, they too are opposed to each other, like *dikē* and hubris. This explains the difference between the two sets of races in their fates after death. The races of gold and silver are promoted, in the strict sense of the term: from being perishable beings they become daemons. As in their existence on earth, they are linked in the afterlife by opposition. The race of gold becomes *epichthonian daemons*, the men of silver become *hupochthonian daemons*, and mortals do honor to both of them: royal honor (*basileion*) for the race of gold, and lesser honor for the race of silver, since it is, after all, "inferior" to the race of gold.[21] This latter is still honor, even though it cannot be justified by virtues or merits, for in their case these do not exist. Its only justification can be that the race of silver belongs to the same category of reality as the race of gold, since it represents the same function, only in its negative aspect. The posthumous fate of the race of bronze and the heroes is quite different. Neither is promoted as a race. The race of bronze's destiny cannot be called a promotion for it is thoroughly commonplace: having died in battle, the people become the anonymous dead in Hades.[22] Most of those who make up the race of heroes share this common fate. Only a few privileged persons from this more just race escape the ordinary anonymity of death and, by the grace of Zeus, who rewards them with this special favor, retain individual names and existences in the afterlife. These few are carried away to the Islands of the Blessed, where they live free from all cares.[23] But they are not in any way venerated or honored by mortals. Rohde was right to emphasize the "total isolation" of their existence in a world that seems quite cut off from ours.[24] Unlike the daemons, the vanished heroes have no power over the living, and the living do not worship them.

These strongly marked parallels show that in Hesiod's version of the myth the race of heroes is not a badly integrated feature distorting the structure of the myth but an essential part of it, without which the overall balance would be upset. On the other hand, the fifth race does seem to present a problem. It introduces a new dimension, a third category of reality, which, unlike the other two, does not seem to be divisible into two antithetical aspects but appears to be presented as a single race. However, it is clear from the text that in fact there is not just *one* age of iron but rather two types of human existences, in strict opposition to each other, one of which acknowledges *dikē*, while the other knows only hubris. Hesiod lives, in fact, in a world where people are born young and die when they are old, where there are "natural" laws (the child resembles the father) and "moral" ones (guests, relatives, and oaths should be respected). It is a world where good and evil are intimately mixed but counterbalance each other. Hesiod, however, foretells the coming of another life, which will be in every way different from the first.[25] In that life, people will be born old, with white hair; the child will have nothing in common with the parent; neither friends nor brothers nor parents nor oaths will be recognized. Right will depend on might alone. In this world, given over to disorder and hubris, there will be no good to compensate for suffering. Thus, one can see how the episode of the age of iron, in both its aspects, corresponds to the preceding themes, so as to complete the overall structure of the myth. The first category, made up of the gold and silver races, was particularly concerned with the exercise of *dikē* (in people's relationships with one another and with the gods); the second, the bronze race and the heroes, was concerned with the manifestation of the physical force and violence linked with hubris; the third, the iron age, is related to an ambiguous human world characterized by the coexistence of opposites within it. Everything good has its evil counterpart there — man implies woman; birth implies death; youth, age; abundance, toil; happiness, misfortune. *Dikē* and hubris, being present side by side, offer two equally possible options between which humans must choose. To this mixed world, which is that of Hesiod himself, the poet contrasts the terrifying prospect of a human life where hubris has triumphed totally, an inverted world where nothing has survived but unadulterated disorder and misfortune.

The cycle of ages would then be complete, and time could do nothing but turn over and run in the opposite direction. In the age of gold, everything was order, justice, and joy: this was the reign of pure *dikē*. By the end of the cycle, in the latter part of the age of iron, everything will be abandoned to disorder, violence, and death: this will be the reign of pure hubris. From one reign to the next, the succession of the ages does not show a progressive decline. Instead of a continuous temporal succession, there are phases that alternate according to whether they oppose or complement one another. Time unfolds not according to a chronological sequence but according to the dialectical relationship of a system of antinomies. We must now indicate some of the correspondences between this system and certain permanent structures in human society and the world of the gods.

There is no doubt at all that the people of gold are royal *basileis* and take no part in any form of activity that falls outside the domain of kingship. Their way of life is defined negatively in two ways: first, they are unacquainted with war and live at peace (*hēsuchoi*), unlike the people of bronze and the heroes, who are dedicated to fighting.[26] Second, they know nothing of labor in the fields, for the earth "spontaneously" produces countless blessings for them — in contrast to the people of iron, who are dedicated to *ponos* and are obliged to till the earth to produce their food.[27]

As has been shown, gold, whose name this race bears, is a

symbol of royalty.[28] In Plato's version of the myth, gold is the distinguishing and qualifying mark of those among the different kinds of humans who are born to command (*archein*).[29] The race of gold existed in the time when Kronos ruled (*embasileuen*) in heaven.[30] Kronos was a ruler god, associated with the royal function, and in Olympia, each year at the spring equinox, a college of priests made sacrifices to him on Mount Kronos. These priests were known as the royal ones (*Basilai*).[31] Finally, the race of gold enjoys a royal privilege (*basilēion geras*) once it has passed away, for its members are transformed into epichthonian daemons.[32] The expression "*basilēion geras*" acquires its full force when it is pointed out that in the afterlife these daemons assume the two functions that, according to the magico-religious conception of royalty, manifest the beneficent powers of the good king. As *phulakes*, the guardians of mortals, they see to it that justice is observed, while as *ploutodotai*, the dispensers of riches, they encourage the fertility of the soil and the increase of the flocks.[33]

Moreover, in Hesiod, the expressions and words used to describe the people of the ancient race of gold are equally applied to the just rulers of the contemporary world. The people of gold live "like gods" (*hōs theoi*), and at the beginning of Hesiod's *Theogony*, when the just king enters the assembly, ready to settle quarrels and restrain excess by his wise and gentle words, he is hailed by all as *theos hōs*, like a god.[34] The same picture of holidays, feasting, and peace amid the abundance generously dispensed by a totally undefiled earth appears twice.[35] The first instance is the description of the happy existence of the race of gold; the second, that of life in the city, which flourishes in endless prosperity under the reign of the just and pious king. In contrast, when the *basileus* forgets that he is the "scion of Zeus" and, with no fear of the gods, betrays the function symbolized by his *skēptron* by straying from the straight path of *dikē* through hubris, the city experiences nothing but calamity, destruction, and famine.[36] This is because close to the kings, mingled among human beings, thirty thousand invisible immortals are watching over the justice and piety of the rulers in the name of Zeus. Not a single transgression committed

33

by the kings against *dikē* is not, sooner or later, punished through the immortals' intercession. And among this myriad of immortals, who are, as the poet says, "*epi chthoni...phulakes thnētōn anthrō-pōn*," we are bound to recognize the *daimones* of the age of gold, who are described as "*epichthonioi...phulakes thnētōn anthrōpōn*."[37]

Thus the same portrait of the Good Ruler is projected on three different levels at once. In a mythical past, it represents primitive humanity in the age of gold; in contemporary society, it is embodied in the just and pious king; and in the supernatural world, it represents a category of daemons who, in the name of Zeus, watch over the royal function to ensure that it is exercised correctly.

Silver does not possess a specific symbolic meaning of its own. It is defined in terms of gold: it is, like gold, a precious metal, but it is inferior to gold.[38] Similarly, the race of silver, which is inferior to the race that preceded it, exists and is defined only in relation to that race. It is on the same plane as the race of gold and is its exact counterpart and opposite. Pious rule is opposed by impious rule, and the figure of the king who shows respect for *dikē* is contrasted with that of the king who has committed himself to hubris. What seals the doom of the members of the race of silver is, in effect, their "mad immoderation" (*hubrin atasthalon*), which they are unable to renounce in their relationships with one another and with the gods.[39] But the hubris that characterizes them applies only to the way they rule. It has nothing to do with the hubris of war. The race of silver, like the race of gold, has no part in military activities, for these do not concern it any more than does work in the fields. The immoderation of the members of the race of silver operates in an exclusively religious and theological context.[40] They refuse to sacrifice to the Olympian gods, and although they may practice *adikia* among themselves, it is only because they do not wish to recognize the sovereignty of Zeus, the master of *dikē*. For royalty, it is natural that hubris should take the form of impiety. Similarly, in his description of the unjust king, Hesiod makes it very clear that this monarch passes unjust sentences and oppresses people because he has no fear of the gods.[41]

34

Because it is impious, the race of silver is wiped out by the wrath of Zeus. As the counterpart of the race of gold, it enjoys comparable honors after its chastisement. The link based on function between the two races is maintained after death by the parallelism, already stressed, between the *epichthonioi* and the *hupochthonioi*. Furthermore, there are also striking analogies between the race of silver and another group of mythical figures, the Titans.[42] They share the same character, function, and destiny. The Titans are the deities of hubris. The mutilated Ouranos reproaches them for their mad pride (*atasthaliēi*), and Hesiod himself calls them *huperthumoi*.[43] Power is the vocation of these proud beings. They aspire to sovereign kingship. They compete with Zeus for the *archē* and *dunasteia* of the universe.[44] This is a natural, even legitimate, ambition, for the Titans are royal. Hesychius relates *Titan* to *titax*, meaning "king," and *titēnē*, meaning "queen." While Zeus and the Olympians represent the rule of order, the Titans embody the rule of disorder and hubris. Once they have been defeated, they must, like the race of silver, leave the light of day. They are hurled far from the heavens, even beyond the surface of the earth, and they too disappear (*hupo chthonos*).[45]

Thus the parallelism between the races of gold and silver is confirmed by the fact that on each of the three planes where the image of the just king appears, so does that of his double, the king of hubris. It is further confirmed by the exact correspondence between the races of gold and silver, on the one hand, and Zeus and the Titans, on the other. We find the same structure in the account of the two first ages of mankind as in Hesiod's myths concerning sovereign power.

The race of bronze involves a different sphere of action. Consider how Hesiod puts it: "a brazen race, sprung from the ash-trees; and it was in no way like the silver age, but was terrible and strong. They loved the lamentable works of Ares and deeds of violence."[46] One could not state more clearly that the excesses of the race of bronze do not bring it closer to but contrast it with the race of silver. The hubris that characterizes it is exclusively military, a matter of the warrior's behavior. We have moved from the juridical and religious plane to that of manifestations of brute force (*megalē bíē*), physical energy (*cheires aaptoi...epi stibaroisi melessi*), and the terror (*deinon, aplastoi*) that the warrior inspires. The people of bronze do nothing but make war. In their case, there is no mention of the exercise of justice (with fair or crooked sentences) or of any worship of the gods (piety or impiety), just as in the preceding cases there was no mention of any kind of military activity. Equally, the race of bronze does not participate in the activities that characterize the third group, the race of iron: the people do not eat bread, which suggests that they know nothing of work on the land and the cultivation of grain.[47] Their death is consistent with their life. They are not destroyed by Zeus but die in war, falling under the blows they deal each other, overcome "by their own arms," in other words, by the physical strength that is the expression of their essential nature. They are entitled to no honors: "terrible though they were," they pass away into the anonymity of death.

Apart from this explicit information, Hesiod supplies certain symbolic details that complete the picture. First, bronze has a no less precise a meaning than gold. The god Ares is described with the epithet *chalkeos*.[48] Bronze, by virtue of certain of its attributes, appears to be closely linked in Greek religious thought with the power possessed by the defensive arms of the warrior. The metallic sheen of the "flashing bronze" (*nōropa chalkon*), the sheen from the bronze that sets the plain alight and "goes up to the heavens," fills the enemy's soul with terror.[49] The sound of bronze against bronze, the *phōnē* that reveals its true nature as living, animated metal, wards off the witchcraft of the enemy. Defensive arms made of bronze — the breastplate, helmet, and shield — are complemented in the panoply of the mythical warrior by some kind of offensive weapon — a lance or, even better, a javelin — made of wood.[50] To be even more precise: the lance is made of wood that is both extremely supple and very hard, the wood of the ash tree. The word *melia* is used on some occasions of the javelin itself and on others of the tree from which it is made.[51] It is easy to understand why Hesiod said that the race of bronze came from the ash trees (*ek melian*).[52] The Meliai, the nymphs of the trees of war, which reach up to the sky like lances, are constantly associated in myth with the supernatural beings that represent the warrior. Along with the race of bronze, born of ash trees, there is the giant Talos, whose entire body is made of bronze. He is the guardian of Crete and, like Achilles, endowed with a qualified invulnerability, over which only Medea's magic wiles can triumph. Talos too was born of an ash tree. The Giants have a direct relationship with the *meliai*. Francis Vian has shown that the Giants represent a typical military brotherhood, and they too enjoy conditional invulnerability.[52] Hesiod's *Theogony* tells how "the great Giants in gleaming armour [made of bronze] with long spears [made of ash wood] in their hands, and the nymphs whom they call Meliai" were born together.[54] And in the group around the cradle of the infant Zeus of Crete, alongside the *kourētes* doing their war dance and clashing their arms and shields to make the bronze ring out, Kallimachos still includes the *Diktaiai Meliai*, whom he calls, significantly, *Kurbantōn hetarai*.[55]

The ash trees or the nymphs of the ash trees from whom the race of bronze was born also play a role in other accounts of early mortals. In Argos, Phoroneus, the first man, is descended from a *meliad*.[56] In Thebes, Niobe, the primeval mother, produces seven *meliads*, and as *hetairai* and as wives, they probably become the female counterparts to the first native men.[57] These accounts of indigenous origins belong, in most cases, to a body of myths about the role of the warriors that appear to correspond to ritual scenes mimed by a band of young armed warriors. Vian has emphasized these points in the case of the Giants, who form *ho gēgenēs stratos*, "the armed band born from the earth," to borrow a phrase from Sophocles.[58] This band conjures up an image of lances brandished on the plain (*logchē pedias*) and brute force (*thēreios bia*). The Arcadians described as "those famed for their lances" in the *Iliad* and as *autochthones hubristai* by the scholiast of Aeschylus's *Prometheus* claimed descent from a tribe of giants whose chief was Hoplodamos.[59]

The mythical origin of the Thebans was similar. The Spartoi, their forebearers, were also *Gēgeneis* who rose from the earth fully armed and immediately started to fight each other. The story of these Spartoi (the word means "sown") is worth examining more closely. It illuminates certain details concerning the lifestyle and destiny of the race of bronze. When Kadmos arrived at the place where he was to found Thebes, he sent some of his companions to fetch water at the fountain of Ares, which was guarded by a snake.[60] This snake, which is represented sometimes as one of the Gēgeneis and sometimes as a son of Ares, kills the band of men — whereupon the hero slays it.[61] Acting on Athena's advice, he sows its teeth across a plain or pedion. Immediately, fully grown, armed men (andres enoploi) sprout up in this field. As soon as they are born, they engage in a fight to the death among themselves and, like the race of bronze, all perish, except for five survivors, who become the ancestors of the Theban aristocracy. The same ritual pattern is to be found, in a more detailed form, in the myth about Jason at Kolkhis. The test that King Aietes imposes on the hero is a strange feat of ploughing. Jason has to go to a field not far from the town, the pedion of Ares. There he must yoke two monstrous, fire-belching oxen with brazen hooves, harness them, and plough a four-acre field. In the furrow, he must sow the teeth of the dragon, from which immediately spring a cohort of armed, fighting giants.[62] Thanks to a potion Medea has given him, which makes him temporarily invulnerable and makes his body and arms supernaturally strong, Jason emerges triumphant from this feat of ploughing, all of whose details emphasize its fundamentally military character: it takes place in an *uncultivated* field, consecrated to Ares; in this field are sown *not the fruits of Demeter but the teeth of the dragon*; Jason arrives there dressed not as a peasant but as a warrior, wearing a breastplate and carrying a shield, holding his helmet and lance; *he uses his lance as a goad* to control the oxen. When the ploughing is done, the *Gēgeneis* spring up from the earth, like the Spartoi. According to Apollonius Rhodius,

> The plot bristled with stout shields, double-pointed spears, and glittering helmets. The splendour of it flashed through the air above.... Indeed this army springing from the earth shone out like

the full congregation of the stars piercing the darkness of a murky night.[63]

Thanks to Jason's trick of throwing a huge boulder into their midst, the soldiers fall upon and massacre each other. This ploughing is a strictly military exploit; it has nothing to do with the soil's fertility and has no effect on its productivity. Thus it perhaps explains one of Hesiod's observations — one whose paradoxical nature has often been pointed out, although no satisfactory explanation for it has yet been given. The poet specifies that the race of bronze "eats no bread"; a little further on he states that "their armor was of bronze and their houses of bronze and with bronze they ploughed."[64]

There seems to be a clear contradiction here. Why would they plough the fields if they did not eat wheat? The difficulty would be removed if the ploughing of the race of bronze, like that of Jason, were considered a military ritual and not an agricultural task. Such an interpretation can be supported with one final analogy between the race of bronze and the "sown ones," the sons of the furrow. The Spartoi born of the earth belong, like the race of bronze, to the race of ash trees. They too are *ek melian*. Indeed, they can be recognized by the sign of the lance, the distinctive mark of their race, which is tattooed on their bodies and marks them as warriors.[65]

There is a difference of value as well as function between the lance, a military attribute, and the scepter, the symbol of royalty. The lance is supposed to be subordinate to the scepter. When this hierarchy is no longer respected, the lance comes to express hubris, just as the scepter expresses *dikē*. Hubris, for the warrior, consists in wishing to recognize nothing but the lance and devoting oneself entirely to it. This is the case of Kaineus, the Lapith with a lance, who — like Achilles, Talos, the Giants, and all those who have undergone initiation as warriors — enjoys a qualified invulnerability. (He can be killed only by being buried beneath a mound of stones.)[66] He plants his lance in the very center of the agora, devotes a cult to it, and forces passersby to worship it like a

39

god.[67] This is likewise the case of Parthenopaeus, who is a typical incarnation of warlike hubris: he worships nothing but his lance, revering it more than a god and swearing by it.[68]

The race of bronze is born of the lance, is devoted to Ares, and has no legal or religious function. It projects into the past an image of the warrior dedicated to hubris, in the sense that he does not wish to know about anything foreign to his own nature. But the exclusively physical violence glorified in warlike man cannot cross the threshold of the afterlife: in Hades, the race of bronze fades away like a wisp of smoke, into the anonymity of death. This same element of military hubris is also embodied in the Giants, in the myths of kingship that tell of the struggle for power among the gods. After the defeat of the Titans, the Olympians' supremacy is assured by their victory over the Giants. The Titans, who were immortal, were sent away in chains, into the depths of the earth. But the Giants suffer a different fate. The gods deny them their invulnerability, and they perish. For them, defeat means that they will have no part of the privilege of immortality, which they covet.[69] Like the race of bronze, they share the common fate of mortal beings. The hierarchy of Zeus, Titans, and Giants corresponds to the sequence of the first three races.

The race of heroes is defined in relation to the race of bronze, as its counterpart in the same sphere of action. The heroes are warriors; they wage war and die in war. Far from bringing them closer to the race of silver, the hubris of the men of bronze sets them farther apart. Conversely, the heroes' dikē, instead of separating them from the race of bronze, in fact associates them with it; the two races form a pair of opposites. The race of heroes is called dikaioteron kai areion: it is more just and more courageous in battle than the race of bronze.[70] Its dikē serves the same military function as the hubris of the race of bronze. The warrior who is dedicated by his very nature to hubris is contrasted with the warrior who is just and who, acknowledging his limitations, is willing to submit to the superior order of dikē. These two antithetical figures of the fighter confront each other dramatically in Aeschylus's *Seven against Thebes*. A warrior representing hubris, wild and frenzied, stands before each gate. Like a Giant, each aims impious sarcasms at the sovereign gods and at Zeus, and each is opposed by a "more just and more courageous" warrior who, since his ardor in battle is tempered by *sōphrosunē*, knows how to respect all things deemed sacred.

The heroes embody the just warrior and, thanks to Zeus, are transported to the Islands of the Blessed, where for all eternity they lead a life similar to that of the gods. In the kingship myths, one category of supernatural beings corresponds exactly with the race of heroes, and in the hierarchy of divine creatures, it occupies the place reserved for the warrior, the servant of order. The Olympians' reign presupposed a victory over the Giants, who represented the military function. But sovereign power could not exist without force. The scepter must depend on the lance. Zeus needs to be constantly accompanied by Kratos and Bia, who never leave his side.[71] In order to achieve their victory over the Titans, the Olympians were obliged to resort to force and call in "soldiers" to aid them. The Hundred-Handed (Hekatoncheires), who help them prevail, are warriors similar in every respect to the Giants and the race of bronze. They are insatiably bellicose and proud of their strength; their size and the immeasurable power of their arms strike terror on all sides.[72] They are the embodiment of Kratos and Bia. According to Hesiod, the struggle between the Titans and Olympians had already been going on for ten years.[73] Victory was undecided between the two royal camps. But Gaia had revealed to Zeus that success would be his if he could win the help of the Hekatoncheires, which would be decisive. Zeus managed to enlist their support. Before the final attack, he asked them to unleash their "great might" (*megalēn biēn*), and their "unconquerable strength" (*cheiras aaptous*) in battle against the Titans.[74] But he also reminded them never to forget to repay the "friendly kindness" he had shown them.[75] On his brothers' behalf, Kottos, who had been given the title *amumōn* for the occasion, paid homage in his reply to Zeus's superior wisdom and understanding (*prapides, noēma, epiphrosunē*).[76] He undertook to fight the Titans (*atenei noōi kai epiphroni boulēi*) "with fixed purpose and wise

41

determination."[77] In this episode, the Hekatoncheires are behaving in a way entirely opposed to warlike hubris. They are subject to Zeus and no longer appear to be creatures of pure pride. The military valor of these *phulakes pistoi Dios*, these "faithful guardians of Zeus," as Hesiod calls them, is henceforth matched by their *sōphrosunē*.[78] To persuade them to cooperate, and to repay them for their help, Zeus grants the Hekatoncheires a favor that in certain aspects recalls the one he conferred on the heroes when he made them "demigods," endowed with immortal life in the Islands of the Blessed. On the eve of the decisive battle, he offers the Hekatoncheires nectar and ambrosia, the food of immortality that is the exclusive privilege of the gods.[79] He thus allows them to participate in a divine status that was not previously theirs; he confers upon them a full and perfect immortality that they, like the Giants, had lacked.[80] From a political point of view, Zeus's generosity is not entirely disinterested. The function of fighting, henceforth associated with sovereign power, is now integrated with this power instead of being in opposition to it. Nothing remains to threaten the reign of order.

There is nothing particularly surprising about the picture of human life in the age of iron in *Works and Days*. Hesiod had already described it in the introduction and conclusion to the myth of Prometheus. The picture is one of disease, old age, and death; ignorance of what the morrow holds and anxiety about the future; the existence of Pandora, of woman; and the need to toil. While these elements appear rather disparate to us, for Hesiod they come together to form a unified picture. The themes of Prometheus and Pandora are like two panels depicting one and the same story: human wretchedness in the age of iron. There are the need to toil on the land to provide sustenance and man's need of woman to reproduce, be born, and die, to experience each day both anxiety and hope regarding an uncertain future. The race of iron leads an ambiguous and ambivalent existence. Zeus willed that for this race good and evil should be not simply intermingled but in fact fused, inseparable. That is why man cherishes this life of misfortune, just as he surrounds Pandora with love — Pandora,

42

the "lovable evil" that the gods, in their irony, saw fit to present to him.[81] Hesiod indicates quite clearly the origin of all the sufferings endured by the men of iron — all their trials, wretchedness, sickness, and anxiety. It is Pandora. If she had not raised the lid of the jar in which all the evils were shut up, humans would have continued to live as they had previously lived, "remote and free from ills and hard toil and heavy sicknesses which bring the Fates upon them."[82] But all these evils were spread throughout the world. Hope survives, however, for life is not all darkness, and humans still find blessings mixed in with the evils.[83] Pandora is the symbol and expression of this life of mixtures and contrasts. Hesiod calls her *kalon kakon ant' agathoio*, "a beautiful evil, the price of a blessing."[84] She is a terrible scourge introduced among humans, but she is also a marvel (*thauma*), adorned by the gods with attractions and graces. She represents an accursed race that man cannot abide but that he cannot do without. She is the opposite of man but also his companion.

In her twofold character as woman and earth, Pandora represents the function of fertility as it is experienced in the age of iron: in the production of food and the reproduction of life.[85] There is no longer the spontaneous abundance that, during the age of gold, made living creatures and their sustenance spring from the soil simply as a result of the rule of justice, without any external intervention. Henceforth, man must entrust new life to the woman's womb, just as the farmer works the land and makes the grain grow in it. All wealth that is acquired must be paid for with a corresponding effort. For the race of iron, earth and woman are both the source of fertility and the force of destruction: they exhaust the male's energy, squandering his efforts, "burning [him] up without a flame, however strong he may be," and delivering him over to old age and death by "reaping the toil of others into their own bellies."[86]

Hesiod's farmer is plunged into this ambiguous universe. He must choose between two courses, which correspond to the two sorts of *eris* mentioned at the beginning of the poem. The good strife incites man to work, urging him not to be sparing in his

43

efforts to increase his possessions. It presupposes that he has recognized and accepted the harsh law on which life in the age of iron depends: that there is no happiness or wealth that has not been paid for in advance by hard labor. In the case of a man whose function is to provide food, *dikē* consists in total submission to an order not of his creating and imposed on him from without. For the farmer, respect for *dikē* lies in dedicating his life to work. If he does this, he becomes dear to the immortals; his barn is filled with grain.[87] For him, good triumphs over evil.

The other Strife incites the farmer to seek wealth not through toil but through violence, deceit, and injustice, tearing him from the work for which he is made. This *eris*, which "fosters war and quarrels," represents the introduction into the farmer's world of the principle of hubris, which is connected with the second sphere of action, that of waging war.[88] However, a farmer who revolts against the order to which he is subjected does not on that account become a warrior. His hubris is not the frenetic zeal that spurs the Giants and the race of bronze to do battle. It is closer to the hubris of the race of silver and is characterized negatively by the absence of all the "moral and religious" sentiments that rule human lives, in accordance with the will of the gods. There is no affection for guest, friend, or brother; no gratitude toward parents; no respect for oaths, justice, or goodness. This hubris knows no fear of the gods, nor is it familiar with the fear that the coward feels when faced with a courageous man. This hubris incites the coward to attack the *areīon*, who is more courageous than him, and to defeat him, not in fair combat, but with twisted words and false oaths.[89]

This picture of the farmer misled by hubris, presented in the age of iron in its decline, is essentially that of a revolt against order, an upside-down world where every hierarchy, rule, and value is inverted. The contrast with the image of the farmer who is subject to *dikē,* from the beginning of the age of iron, is complete. A life of mixtures, where good things still compensate for bad, is opposed by a negative universe of deprivation, where all that remains is unadulterated disorder and evil.

44

In sum, a detailed analysis of the myth from every angle confirms and emphasizes the pattern that, from the start, appeared to emerge from the main structure of the text. We have here not five races in chronological succession, arranged in the order of a more or less progressive decline, but rather a threefold construction, each level being divided into two opposite and complementary aspects. The same framework that controls the cycle of ages also governs the organization of society among humans and in the world of the gods. The "past," as presented by the stratification of the races, is built on the model of a timeless hierarchy of functions and values. Thus each pair of ages is defined not only by its position in the sequence (the first two, the next two, and the last two) but also by a specific temporal quality that is closely linked to the type of activity with which it is associated. The gold and silver are ages of vitality, still in their youth. The bronze age and the heroes represent an adult life unfamiliar with both youth and age. The iron age entails an existence that declines as it becomes older and more exhausted.

Let us undertake a closer examination of these qualitative aspects of the different ages, and of their meaning in relation to other elements of the myth. Both the race of gold and the race of silver are "young," just as both are royal. But the symbolic meaning of youth is opposite in the two cases: for the former it is positive, while for the latter it becomes negative. The race of gold lives "forever young" in time, forever new, free from fatigue, sickness, age, and even death, in a time still close to that of the gods.[90] On the other hand, the race of silver represents the opposite of "youth," not the absence of senility, but plain puerility and the absence of maturity. A man of silver lives for a hundred years in the state of a *pais*, clinging to the skirts of his mother, *mega nēpios*, like a big baby.[91] As soon as he emerges from childhood and crosses the crucial point marked by the *metron hēbēs*, the threshold of adolescence, he indulges in a thousand follies and dies forthwith.[92] It can be said that his whole life amounts to nothing more than an endless childhood and that *hēbē* is, for him, the final point of existence. Thus he has no part in *sōphrosunē*, the characteristic

45

of maturity, which can be especially associated with the figure of the *gerōn*, as opposed to that of the young man.[93] Nor does he ever reach the state of those who, having passed the *metron hēbēs*, constitute the age group of the *hēbōntes*, the *kouroi*, who are subjected to military discipline.[94]

Hesiod gives no indication as to how long the lives of the race of bronze and the heroes last. All we know is that they do not have time to grow old: they all die in battle, in the prime of life. No mention is made of their childhoods. It is possible that Hesiod says nothing about their childhoods, after having spoken at length about those of the race of silver, because the members of the race of bronze do not have them. In the poem, the men appear from the start as grown, at the height of physical prowess, never having concerned themselves with anything other than the works of Ares. There is a striking analogy here with the myths of indigenous origin, in which the *Gēgeneis* spring out of the ground, not as little children who have just been born and have to grow up, but as adults, fully formed, armed, and prepared for battle, as *andres enoploi*. The activity of making war is associated with a particular age group, so the figure of the fighter is opposed to both the *pais* and the *gerōn*. Vian has written the following comment about the Giants, which, it seems to me, applies exactly to the race of bronze and the heroes: "There are neither old men nor infants among them. From their very birth they are the adults or rather the adolescents that they remain until their death. Their existence is confined within the narrow limits of one age group."[95] The entire life of the race of silver is over before *hēbē*. The life of the race of bronze and of the heroes begins at *hēbē*. Neither group ever experiences old age.

Old age, on the contrary, is a characteristic of the time of the race of iron. Life is spent in a continuous aging. Toil, labor, disease, anxiety — all the evils that constantly exhaust a human being — gradually transform him from a child into a young man, from a young man into an old man, and from an old man into a corpse. This is a doubtful, ambiguous time, with the old and the young associated, inextricably linked, the one implying the other, just as good does evil; life, death; and *dikē*, hubris. The time in which the young grow old is opposed, at the end of the age of iron, to a time totally given over to old age. If men give way to hubris, a day will come when everything that is still young, new, vital, and beautiful will have disappeared from human life: men will be born with their hair already white.[96] The time of mixture will be succeeded by the reign of pure hubris. It will be a time when old age and death take over completely.

Thus the features that give the various races their particular temporal quality fit into the same tripartite pattern that seems to provide a framework for all the elements of the myth.

This pattern's main outlines recall the tripartite classification of functions whose important influence on Indo-European religious thought has been demonstrated by Georges Dumézil (whether there is a direct link between the two or not).[97] The first stage of Hesiod's myth describes the function of kingship, according to which the king pursues his juridical and religious activities; the second, the military function, in which the warrior's brute force imposes a lawless rule; and the third, the function of fertility and vital foodstuffs that are the special responsibility of the farmer.

This tripartite structure forms the framework within which Hesiod reinterprets the myth of the races of metals, and it makes it possible for him to include the episode of the heroes with perfect coherence. Thus modified, the story becomes part of a larger body of myth, which it evokes throughout by the subtle yet strict interplay of corresponding relationships at every level. Because it reflects a classificatory system of general relevance, the story of the races carries multiple meanings. It tells of the sequence of the ages of humanity, but, at the same time, it also symbolizes a whole series of fundamental aspects of reality. If this interplay of symbolic images and connections is translated into our own conceptual language, it can be presented as a diagram that may be viewed from various angles, in which the same structure, regularly repeated, establishes analogical relationships among its different parts. The series of races, the different functional roles, the types of actions and agents, the age categories, the hierarchy of the gods in the kingship myths, the hierarchy of human society, the hierarchy of the supernatural powers other than the *theoi* — in each case, the various elements evoke and correspond to one another.

While Hesiod's account illustrates particularly neatly the system of multiple correspondences and overlaid symbolism that is characteristic of the thought processes of myth, it also contains a new feature. The material is arranged in a definite pattern of dichotomies, which dominates the tripartite structure and establishes a tension that pulls all the elements in two contrary directions. This tension between *dikē* and hubris determines the structure of the myth and the various planes on which it operates, and regulates the interplay of oppositions and affinities. It not only governs the form of the myth as a whole and gives it its general meaning but also gives, in a manner appropriate to each, a certain polarized aspect to the three functional levels. This is where Hesiod's profound originality lies, and it makes him a true religious reformer whose manner and inspiration have been compared to those of certain prophets of Judaism.

Why is Hesiod so preoccupied with *dikē*, and why does it occupy such a central position in his religious universe? Why does it assume the form of a powerful goddess, a daughter of Zeus, honored and revered by the gods of Olympos? The answer to these questions will not be found through a structural analysis of the myth but would emerge from a historical inquiry. Such an inquiry would aim to reveal the new problems that small-scale farmers in Boeotia faced as a result of changes in social life around the seventh century and that prompted Hesiod to rethink the substance of the old myths so as to give them new meaning.[98] Such an inquiry is beyond the scope of the present study. However, this analysis of the myth allows me to briefly suggest certain possible lines of research.

It is noticeable that in Hesiod the figure of the warrior, unlike that of the king or the farmer, has a purely mythical significance. In the world where Hesiod lives and that he describes, and among the figures he addresses, there does not seem to be a place either for the warrior function or for the warrior, as they are presented in the myth.[99] The aim of the story of Prometheus, of that of the races, of the entire poem in fact, is to instruct Perses, who is a small-scale farmer like his brother. Perses is to renounce hubris, settle down to work, and stop suing Hesiod and picking quarrels with him.[100] But this lesson, from one brother to another, one farmer to another, also concerns the *basileis*, in that it is their duty to settle quarrels and adjudicate lawsuits justly. Their sphere of activity is quite different from that of Perses: their role is not to labor, and Hesiod does not exhort them to do so. They must show their respect for *dikē* by pronouncing just verdicts. To be sure, the mythical picture of the good ruler, master of fertility, dispenser of all wealth, is far removed from the "bribe-devouring" kings whose displeasure Hesiod risks incurring (and that is no doubt partly why, in Hesiod's eyes, *dikē* seems already to have left the earth for heaven).[101] However, the poet remains convinced that the way the kings perform their judicial function has direct re-percussions on the world of the laborer, either favoring or impeding the abundance of the fruits of the earth.[102] There is, then, a connection, both mythical and real, between the first and third functions, between the kings and the laborers. And Hesiod focuses his interest precisely on those problems that concern both the first and the third function — those that affect them *both together*.[103] In this sense, there are two aspects to his message. It is in itself ambiguous, as is everything in the age of iron. It is addressed to the farmer Perses — grapping with the unproductive earth, with debts, hunger, and poverty — to exhort him to work hard. It is also addressed, over and beyond Perses, to the kings, who live in quite another fashion, in town, spending their time in the agora, and who do not have to work. Hesiod's world, unlike that of the age of gold, is a world of mixtures, where great and small, nobles — *esthloi* — and humble folk — *deiloi* — kings and farmers coexist side by side but are set in opposition by their functions.[104] In this dis-cordant universe, help can come only from *dikē*. If *dikē* disap-pears, everything founders in chaos. But if *dikē* is respected, both by those whose lives are dedicated to *ponos* and by those who lay down the law, there will be more blessings than evils; it will be possible to avoid the sufferings that are not inherent in the mortal condition.

What, then, is the place of the warrior's activity? In Hesiod's picture of the society of his time, the warrior no longer represents an authentic functional category corresponding to an existing human reality. Its only role is to justify, on the level of myth, the presence of a harmful and sinister principle in a world of kings and farmers: the hubris that is the source of discord and strife. It provides an answer to what one might (anachronistically) call the problem of evil. What, after all, is the difference between the justice and fertility that preside over the age of gold and their manifestations in the age of iron, in a world of discord? In the age of gold, justice and abundance are "pure." They do not have any counterparts. Justice exists for its own sake: there are no quarrels or lawsuits to settle. Similarly, fertility brings abundance "automatically," without any labor being necessary. The age of gold is unfamiliar with *eris*, in all its senses. In contrast, the way of life of the age of iron is characterized by strife, or to be more precise, two contrary forms of strife, the good and the evil. Thus *dikē*, whether it be that of the king or that of the farmer, must always operate *through* one *eris* or the other. The *dikē* of the kings consists in settling quarrels and arbitrating the disagreements provoked by the evil *eris*. The *dikē* of the farmer lies in making a virtue of *eris*, by directing struggle and competition away from war to agriculture, so that instead of sowing ruin they bring forth fertile abundance.

But where does *eris* come from? What is its origin? Strife is inevitably associated with hubris and represents the very essence of the warrior's activity. It is an expression of the innermost nature of the fighter. And this is the principle that, "by increasing wicked war," presides over the second of the three functional roles we have discussed.[105]

The myth of the races thus indicates how a mythical thought like that of Hesiod can be at once innovative and rigorously elaborated. Not only does Hesiod reinterpret the myth of the races of metal within a tripartite framework, but he also transforms this tripartite structure itself: by devaluing the warrior's activity, he makes of it — in accordance with the religious perspective specific to him — less one functional element among others than the source of evil and conflict in the universe.

CHAPTER TWO

Hesiod's Myth of the Races:

A Reassessment

In a reassessment of Hesiod's myth of the races, Jean Defradas closely criticized the interpretation that, following Georges Dumézil, I had suggested for the text of *Works and Days*.[1] His analysis led him to a total rejection of my conclusions, which, according to him, depended on a superficial reading of the myth and a systematic simplification of the evidence it provides. Defradas's objections take the following form.

First, he claims that "in substituting a structural pattern for a chronological one," I have neglected the temporal aspects of Hesiod's myth to the point of suggesting that the races do not succeed one another in time. He suggests that according to me, "the myth groups the races into pairs which do not succeed each other but are simply a transposition of the three fundamental functions of Indo-European society."[2] Defradas remarks that Hesiod took care to make it quite clear that the second race was created later than the first (*metopisthen*), that the third race did not appear until the second had disappeared and nor did the fourth until the third had disappeared, and that the fifth is introduced by the word *epeita*.[3] There can therefore be no doubt that the races appear in a diachronic sequence.

Second, it is generally held that, with the exception of the race of heroes, each race is inferior to the one that precedes it. In asserting that nothing of the kind is said of the race of bronze compared with the race of silver, and that it is presented as being "in no way similar" rather than inferior to the silver, I have substituted a "structural difference" for a "qualitative difference." In this way, I have sought to establish a thesis according to which, "in effect, the myth does not express an idea of decline in the course of time."[4] Defradas points out that there is an indisputable degeneration between the ages of gold and bronze. It is only briefly interrupted by the race of heroes — which indicates that this episode was a late insertion. Even if it is true that the text emphasizes in particular the difference between the race of bronze and the race of silver, the fact remains that in any classification referring to metals, bronze is considerably inferior to silver. Furthermore, the fate after death of the men of silver who are promoted to the rank of the Blessed of the Infernal Regions (*makares hupochthonioi*) indicates their superiority over the men of bronze, whose fate in the afterlife is to be among the anonymous dead in Hades. Defradas concludes that it would thus be excessively subtle to claim that the process of decline is suspended when the race of bronze appears.

There is still worse. Defradas suggests that, following Dumézil, I was obliged for the purpose of symmetry to discover, or invent, a sixth race to make a pair with the race of iron, which is that of Hesiod himself. Defradas points out that Hesiod never speaks of a sixth race; he simply imagines that there will be a progressive deterioration, that it will culminate in the death of the race of iron, and that this will be when men are born with their temples already white. Thus there are not three pairs of races that correspond with three Indo-European social functions. The myth must originally have consisted of four races of metal of regularly decreasing worth. Hesiod inserted a fifth race, the race of the heroes, which does not correspond with any particular metal; this is what upsets the normal succession, temporarily interrupting the progressive process of decline.

One final point: Hesiod, who lives among the men of the fifth race, the race of iron, expresses the regret that he did not die earlier, or, alternatively, was not born later. I observed that this is an incomprehensible remark in the context of a human time constantly on the decline, but that it makes perfect sense if one accepts that the sequence of the ages forms a renewable cycle, like that of the seasons. To this Defradas replies: "To read into this simple remark a conception of cyclical time is already to find in it Orphic doctrines or echoes of them such as in Plato — concerning the eternal return. There is nothing at all in Hesiod's text to warrant such an extrapolation."[5] What then, according to Defradas, does Hesiod's remark signify? As Paul Mazon has already indicated, its meaning is quite banal. It is not a precise reference to a well-defined anterior or posterior state but simply a way of indicating that Hesiod would have preferred to live at any time other than his own. Defradas adds to all this some personal reflections on what he calls Hesiod's "empiricism." He suggests that the poet had no planned system and felt no qualms about interrupting the process of decline in order to insert the epic heroes into the sequence of the ages. Nor is there, to Hesiod's mind, any reason why the future should be as gloomy as the present. He is far from envisaging the advent of a sixth race worse than the race of iron.

I have summarized as faithfully as I can the four lines of argument along which Defradas believes he has refuted an interpretation he sees as "a brilliant essay, but one without foundation."[6]

It is not through a taste for polemic or a need to justify myself that I have chosen to reply to these objections in detail. Defradas is quite right on one point: the debate is important. It involes not only the myth of the races but also general problems of method that affect the entire interpretation of a work like Hesiod's *Works and Days*. How should we approach the writings of Greece's earliest theological poet? How should we read him to decode his message? How can we hope to understand through the texts a system of religious thought whose archaic nature may prove entirely baffling to the twentieth-century mind?

When I read Defradas's criticisms, I sometimes feel that we do not speak the same language and that I have not been understood. I fear I have not been explicit enough on questions that appear to me to be self-explanatory. I will therefore take this opportunity to explain myself more fully and, by returning to an analysis that to me still seems valid, to make my position more precise on several essential points.

Did I really neglect the temporal aspects of the myth? Did I claim that the races do not succeed one another? It seems to me that Defradas's own final objection answers this point. If, as he reproaches me in the final point above, I was wrong in suggesting that the sequence of the races forms a complete temporal cycle so that they succeed one another like the seasons, it follows that I clearly recognized their sequence as having a temporal quality. Cyclical time is no less temporal than linear time, but it is so in a different way. The presence in Hesiod's text of terms such as "later" and "afterward" thus in no way compromises my interpretation.[7] A large section of *Works and Days* is devoted to a description of the calendar of agricultural tasks punctuating the cycle of the seasons. Hesiod opens his account with the sowing of seed, at the time of the autumn rains, when the crane is crying and the Pleiades disappear into the sea when they set in the morning.[8] The account closes with the same autumn sowing, with the same setting of the Pleiades, since the end of men's labors introduces a new seasonal cycle.[9] Should one then conclude that according to Hesiod there is no before or after in the sequence of agricultural labors, that they all take place at the same time?

But possibly the contradiction lies not so much with my critic as in the presentation of my study. Did I perhaps maintain in some passages that the time of the races is cyclical and in others that there is no succession in time? Let us examine the question more closely. I first presented my interpretation of the myth of the races orally, in 1959, during the *Entretiens sur les notions de genèse et de structure*. In the discussion that followed, I was asked whether I had not tended to carry the elimination of temporality too far. My reply was as follows:

> I recognize that a temporality exists for Hesiod, but I believe it to be very different from our present-day linear and irreversible notion of

time. I would venture to say that it is a time that consists not of a succession of moments but of a stratification of layers, where the different ages are superimposed upon one another.[10]

Here I was taking up a theme I had previously discussed. In an earlier study, I had written on the *Theogony* and the myth of the races:

> This genesis of the world recounted by the Muses involves a before and an after, but it does not unfold over a homogeneous period, in a single time scale. This past is punctuated not by any chronology but by genealogies.... Each generation, each race (*genos*) has its own time, its own age, the duration, flow, and even orientation of which may be different in every respect from those of all the others. The past is stratified into a sequence of races. These races make up ancient time, but they still exist, and some of them are more real than present-day life and the contemporary race of humans.[11]

Perhaps, in order to avoid misunderstandings, I should have repeated what I had already written — but one cannot go on repeating the same point indefinitely. Besides, I assumed that the work undertaken by historians of religion, anthropologists, psychologists, and sociologists on the different forms of temporality, especially the aspects of what is known as mythical time, were today familiar to all educated readers. However, it is clear that the misunderstanding between Defradas and me arises from the fact that he identifies time, quite purely and simply, with chronology, whereas I am at pains to distinguish between them. In reproaching me for substituting a structural scheme for a chronological one, he concludes that I have excluded all temporality from Hesiod's poem. Yet what I had written was this:

> The order in which the races follow one another on earth is not, strictly speaking, chronological. How could it be? Hesiod does not imagine a unique and homogeneous time within which each of the races has a fixed and definite place. Each race has its own time, its

57

own age, which expresses its particular character. This time, just as much as its way of life, its activities, its qualities, and its defects, defines its status in contrast to that of the other races.[12]

Strictly speaking, one should not talk of chronological time unless each event in the temporal sequence is defined by a date and is, so to speak, characterized by that date. This would presuppose both a concern with providing accurate dates and a means of establishing a precise and exact chronology. This is only possible where time is conceived of as a unique, homogeneous framework following a linear, continuous, indefinite, irreversible course. In these circumstances, each event occupies one and only one position in the sequence; nothing can ever be repeated. Every event, therefore, has its own date. In the works of not only Hesiod but also the Greek historians, not to mention the tragedians, time does not possess these characteristics; it acquires them only with the development of modern history. Using Jacqueline de Romilly's work defining the nature of historical time in Thucydides, Ignace Meyerson notes that "Thucydides, who readily supplies precise numerical and topographical data when these can illuminate his account, never gives a single date." He concludes: "The sequence of events is logical in Thucydides. Everything, in his history, is a construction, and indeed a rigorous one.... Time for Thucydides is not chronological: it is, if one may so call it, logical."[13]

Of course, the sequence of the races does not follow logical imperatives in Hesiod as it does in Thucydides. Hesiod was not educated in the school of the sophists. But the very idea of chronology is even more inadequate in his case, since he is not dealing with historical time or historical events. I therefore asked myself in what kind of order the story of the successive races was constructed. It seemed to me that time passed not continuously but in a succession of alternating phases and the races followed one another in antithetical pairs:

> Instead of a continuous temporal succession, there are phases that alternate according to whether they oppose or complement one

another. Time unfolds not according to a chronological sequence but according to the dialectical relationship of a system of antinomies. We must now indicate some of the correspondences between this system and certain permanent structures in human society and the world of the gods.[14]

Thus the order of temporal succession as expressed in a genea-logical account seemed to me to correspond with the hierarchi-cal order that permanently presides over the way society — both human and divine — is organized. How did I understand the rela-tionship between the genetic myth and the structural pattern? Is it true that I "substituted" the latter for the former, to the point of doing away with the genetic aspects? My thesis was exactly the opposite. In my view, what characterizes Hesiod's thought — in the *Theogony* as in the story of the races — is the fact that the genetic myth and the structural divisions are not clearly opposed, as they are to our way of thinking, but indissolubly linked.[15]

As far as Hesiod is concerned, one cannot speak of an antimony between the genetic myth and the structural arrangement. In myth-ical thought, any genealogy is also the expression of a structure, and there is no way to account for a structure other than to present it in the form of a genealogical narrative. The myth of the ages is not, in any respect, an exception to this rule.[16]

In other words, each part of Hesiod's text can be read in two ways: it can be interpreted from a diachronic point of view and from a synchronic one. For us today, who think of time as possess-ing its own structure and strictly chronological order, any tem-poral sequence modeled on a permanent structure hardly seems genuinely temporal. Therefore, some of the expressions I have used may have suggested that in my view there was no true time in Hesiod. But for Hesiod, who does not think of time as obeying purely chronological rules, there is still authentic temporality.

Apart from this question, what, really, is Defradas's position? In the last part of his article, he first contrasts with my views and then himself adopts the interpretation of Goldschmidt that my essay takes as its starting point.[17] Defradas writes: "Thus we may say that Hesiod used the myth of the races to explain the hierarchy of divine beings and to locate the human condition in the totality of beings." He concludes: "In trying to explain the existing structure of religious society — the hierarchy of the divine beings — he transposes the material into a theogonic myth, and in a sequence of different generations he rediscovers, set in a chronological order, the origins of the various divine families."[18] At the end of his critical study, then, Defradas seems to me to accept, at least on this particular point, the type of interpretation that I took up from Victor Goldschmidt — although, for my part, I had attempted to analyze precisely the psychological implications of the exact nature of time in Hesiod's thought.

When I remarked that the race of bronze was presented not as inferior but as "in no way similar" to the race of silver, which preceded it, was I attempting to prove that the myth did not convey an idea of decline in time? On the contrary, my view was that the sequence of the races made up a complete cycle of decline. Starting with the age of gold, when youth, justice, mutual friendship, and happiness reign, all in their pure state, we end with an age that is its opposite in every respect: it is entirely given over to old age, injustice, quarrelsomeness, and unhappiness: "In the age of gold, everything was order, justice, and joy: this was the reign of pure *dikē*. By the end of the cycle, in the latter part of the age of iron, everything will be abandoned to disorder, violence, and death: this will be the reign of pure hubris."[19] My claim was that this process of decline did not follow a regular or continuous course. As far as the heroes are concerned, all interpretations agree: Hesiod expressly says they are superior to the men who preceded them. It is thus perfectly clear that they interrupt the process of decline. It has been suggested that this is evidence that the episode was inserted at a later date. I agree, and I also accept the hypothesis that the myth must originally have been composed of four races of metal whose value followed a line of progressive decline. However, the primitive myth, as we can reconstruct it hypothetically, is one thing, and Hesiod's account, as he was obliged by his own preoccupations to rethink it and as it is presented in a text that mentions the heroes alongside the races of metal, is quite another. Whatever the reasons that led Hesiod to insert the heroes into the sequence of the races where he does, this insertion shows that in his eyes the myth no longer had the meaning we are tempted to give to the original version. Hesiod did not intend to describe a continuous process of decline in the human condition. There is no getting away from this dilemma: either Hesiod meant to suggest something other than a simple, continuous decline, or he openly contradicts himself.[20] Before accepting the second hypothesis, it seems only right to examine the text more closely in order to discover Hesiod's intention within the myth, how he characterizes the various races in accordance with this intention, and in what order he arranges them so that their sequence, from the beginning through the end of the cycle, illustrates the moral he draws from the story.

Works and Days opens with a surprising announcement. There is not just one Strife (*Eris*) but two contrasting ones, a good and a bad. In the *Theogony*, Hesiod classes Eris among the children of Night, that is, among the dark powers of evil.[21] Among the sinister offspring of Nyx, following immediately after Nemesis, Eris appeared in close association with Apatē (Deceit), Philotēs (Friendship), and Gēras (Old Age). Eris in her turn gave birth to a whole series of evils. Along with Ponos (Hardship), Lēthē (Oblivion), Limos (Famine), and the Algea (Sorrows), who begin the list, and Dusnomia (Lawlessness) and Atē (Ruin), who close it, in the company of Horkos (Oath), who comes last of all, she birthed two symmetrical groups of powers. The first consisted of the four murderous powers of war; the second consisted of the three powers of false words, whose nefarious effects were felt not in warlike conflicts but in legal disputes and disagreements.[22]

Works and Days adopts this theology of evil but at the same time corrects it on various essential points. Alongside the evil *eris*, which makes men fight each other in war or brings them into legal conflict in the agora, we must recognize a different *eris*, one to be praised and not condemned, for it is profitable to men.[23] It is this *eris*, in fact, that incites them to work and urges them to plough and plant in order to increase their livelihood.[24]

Hesiod then solemnly addresses his brother Perses, a farmer like himself, calling upon him to choose between these two kinds of *eris*. He should renounce the wicked *eris* (*eris kakochartos*), for, by encouraging him to go to the agora looking for quarrels and lawsuits in the hope of unjustly acquiring someone else's property, it distracts him from working on the land.[25] The good *eris*, on the other hand, encourages him to labor and will justly procure for him ease blessed by the gods.

After this come two mythical narratives. The meaning of the first is crystal clear. The myth of Pandora, which is introduced with the word *gar*, provides a theological justification for the presence of *eris* in the world of men and for the obligation to work that stems from this necessary presence. The gods have in fact hidden from men their livelihood (*bios*), that is, their food.[26] Men must toil on the land, plough it season after season, and fill it with seed in the autumn so that the grain may grow. It has not always been so. Originally men lived without working, in such abundance that they had no reason to envy each other and no need to compete at work to be rich. But Prometheus tried to deceive Zeus and give men more than they had a right to possess. Despite the Titan's great cunning, his *apatē* finally backfires.[27] Prometheus is caught in his own trap, thereby plunging all humanity into misfortune. Zeus's revenge takes an ambiguous form, just as the figure of Eris is ambiguous in the world of men: Pandora is an evil, but a desirable evil, the counterpart and the reverse of a blessing.[28] Men seduced by her beauty will surround her, a plague that has been sent to them, with love.[29] They cannot tolerate her, but they could not do without her. She is their opposite and their companion. As a match to Prometheus's deceit, Pandora herself is a trick, a snare, a *dolos*; she is deceit incarnate in woman, *apatē* in the guise of *philotēs*.[30] Aphrodite grants her irresistible *charis*, Hermes endows her with a deceitful mind and a

62

lying tongue, and she introduces into the world a kind of fundamental ambiguity.[31] She fills human life with mixture and contrast. Indeed, with Pandora not only are Night's powers — the Algea of disease, Ponos, and Gēras, evils that were unknown to humanity in its original purity — spread through the world, but, furthermore, every blessing now contains its evil counterpart, its dark aspect, a shadow that follows it everywhere.[32] From now on, abundance implies *ponos*, youth implies old age, *dikē* implies *eris*. Similarly, man presupposes that opposite him there will be his double and his contrary, the "race of women," accursed and at the same time cherished.[33] If a man shuns the *mermera erga gunaikōn*, the works and wearisome labors that women bring with them, and decides never to marry, he has bread in abundance throughout his life.[34] But misfortune awaits him in a different direction: he has no children to support him in his old age, and all his possessions pass into the hands of his relatives after his death. If, on the other hand, a man marries, even if he happens upon a good wife, his lot is no better: throughout his life, "evil comes to offset good."[35] A problem arises here. Why does the bachelor, unlike the married man, not lack for bread? Hesiod's text makes the answer clear and explains the connection, so strongly emphasized in the myth, between the creation of the first woman, the introduction of evil, and the need for unceasing rivalry in agricultural labor. In several passages, woman is presented as a famished belly swallowing up all the food that man exhausts himself in making the land produce. Even before she is married, woman is already casting an eye toward the granaries of her future husband, who allows himself to be trapped by her seductiveness (*philotēs*) and duped by her deceitful chatter (*apatē*).[36] Once she is married, the woman is a hunger (*limos*) at the heart of the house, installed there forever. She cannot tolerate poverty (*penia*) and seeks ever more in her craving to be satisfied (*koros*), so she urges her man to labor but stores up in her own belly the fruits of the toils of others.[37] Just as she is responsible for the other evils she has introduced into the world, so too she brings man the sadness of old age (*gēras*). She exhausts the male's strength, as do disease, anxiety, and toil; she "dries him up without a fire."[38] Because she is *deipnolochēs*, always ready to sit down to table, always ready to feast, however vigorous her husband may be, she delivers him over to a premature old age.[39] When we bear in mind that Hesiod in fact associated Apatē, Philotēs, Gēras, and Eris in the same group in his list of the children of Night, we can understand how the use of the myth of Pandora to explain the presence of evil, in its various forms, in the lives of men today.[40]

The first myth thus incorporates three lessons. First, it is impossible to deceive Zeus. No trick escapes him. Sooner or later, every injustice is found out and punished.[41] Second, Zeus's answer to Prometheus's trickery establishes the great law that is henceforth to be the rule among men: you cannot get something for nothing; everything must be paid for. The farmers are the first to feel the effects of this decision. Wheat no longer grows of its own accord; in order to have enough, men must pay for it personally, competing in work and wearing themselves out at the task. The farmer must accept the harsh law imposed on him by Zeus as punishment for Prometheus's mistake. If the farmer wants to obtain abundance without committing any injustice for which he would later have to atone, he must toil day after day in his field. In this way, he will become dear to the immortal gods. His *dikē* is realized through competition in work through the good *eris*. Third, misfortunes never come alone. The powers of evil are related, and they stick together. All the gifts of the earth must be paid for by the sweat of the farmer's brow. Pandora — all the gifts of the earth — is not only a goddess of the earth, the power of fertility, but also woman, who, because of her twofold nature, symbolizes a human condition in which evils exist side by side with blessings and the two are inextricably mingled together.

These opening remarks may seem rather long. But I consider them necessary. They make it clear that Hesiod's poem in no way lacks coherence. His work's systematic character is revealed not only, as scholars have shown, in his methods of composition but also in the consistency of certain themes, whose meaning operates on several levels.[42] These themes, which are restated or redevel-

oped in many passages, form a network of very close correspondences among the various parts of the work; they all complement
and enrich one another without ever becoming repetitious. Hesiod's work, therefore, shows a highly developed system of thought
that does not have the rigor of a philosophical construction but
nevertheless possesses its own coherence and logic in the organization of its themes and mythical images. Hesiod declares that
he is inspired by the Muses; because of this, he considers himself,
in a sense, the equal of kings.[43] His message does not come from
his imagination; whatever his subject may be, he pronounces the
"truth."[44] From one generation of Greeks to the next, this message
was taken seriously. In order not to misunderstand it completely,
we must read it in the same spirit, in the belief that every item,
even a tiny detail, has significance once it is included in the text.

The second myth is that of the races. It shares several features
with the first. Both explain the present state of humanity, whose
life offers a mixture of blessings and evils, and both present the
theme of *eris*, or rather of the double *eris*. In the age of gold, there
are no evils, men enjoy every blessing, and there is no place for
either *eris*. In the first place, the men of gold do not make war
(*hēsuchoi*). Second, being free from jealousy of each other (*ethelēmoi*), they are also unfamiliar with disputes and lawsuits. As
Mazon has rightly pointed out, they know nothing of *koros* (insatiable desire) or *zēlos* (jealousy), and these are what gives rise to
hubris.[45] Finally, they do not need the good *eris*, the encourage-
ment to toil, in order to eat. The earth spontaneously brings forth
all its fruits in abundance without men having to till it. [46] Hesiod,
on the contrary, foresees at the end of the cycle of the races a life
in which nothing will remain but evil: "And bitter sorrows will be
left for mortal men and there will be no help against evil."[47] This
is because men will have entirely abandoned themselves to the
wicked *eris*, against which Hesiod warned his farmer brother:
zēlos kakochartos, envy, foul-mouthed, delighting in evil, with a
scowling face, will go along with wretched men one and all."[48]
Jealous hatred will even insinuate itself between those who were
formerly united by ties of mutual and disinterested affection: the

friend will cease to be dear to his friend, the brother to his brother, the guest to his host, and parents to their children. The son will deny food to the father who fed him.[49]

Fortunately, the men among whom Hesiod and Perses live have not yet come to this. True, they will continue to suffer the fatigue and wretchedness sent to them by the gods, but at least they will find that "even these shall have some good mingled with their evils."[50] Equally, the poet's advice to his brother indicates that while the age of gold knew nothing of *eris*, good or bad, and while life at the end of the age of iron will be entirely given over to the wicked *eris*, Hesiod and Perses live in a world characterized by the combined presence of the two contrasting forms of *eris* and by the still open possibility of choosing the good over the bad.

Not only is this mythical theme repeated and enriched from one story to the next; there is also a shift in emphasis. The emphasis is no longer on the pair formed by good and evil *eris* but on a different, though still symmetrical, pair — the opposed powers of *dikē* and hubris. The lesson of the myth of the races is, in fact, formulated by Hesiod with all possible precision. This lesson is addressed most directly to the farmer Perses, and Hesiod advises him to pay attention to it.[51] The myth is followed by a kind of parenthesis, a short fable, directed this time not at Perses but at those who, quite unlike him, are endowed with a power they might be tempted to abuse: kings.[52] The moral that Perses should derive from the tale is as follows: Listen to *dikē*; do not allow hubris to grow.[53] Hubris is especially bad for humble folk, for small farmers such as Perses; on the other hand, even for the great, such as kings, it may lead to disaster.[54] Perses should therefore prefer the path that leads to *dikē*, for in the end, *dikē* always triumphs over hubris.

Having described the myth's framework, I return to the text itself, so as to establish the order of the first four races. Even the most superficial reading immediately reveals that there is a difference between the transitions from the first to the second and the third to the fourth, on the one hand, and the transition from the second to the third, on the other. The relationship between

66

the first and the second race, like that between the third and the
fourth, is expressed by a comparative: *polu cheiroteron* in the first
case and *dikaioteron* in the second.[55] What does this comparative
mean? In both cases, it expresses a difference in value, measured
in terms of justice or, on the contrary, excess. The race of silver is
"much inferior" to the race of gold, in that it is characterized by a
hubris from which the race of gold is entirely free. The race of
heroes is "more just" than that of bronze, which is pledged to
hubris. But no such comparison is made between the second and
the third race, the silver and the bronze. The difference between
them is not expressed by a comparative that would place them
higher or lower on the same scale of values. They are described
not as better or worse than each other but as "in no way similar"
to each other.[56] Of course, it is impossible to draw any definite
conclusion from this point alone. I based my argument on a comparison of this *ouden homoion* with the earlier *polu cheiroteron* and
the later *dikaioteron*. We must determine whether this difference,
which stands out even on a first reading, is indeed significant, and
whether this distinctive feature appears pertinent or not when
placed in the overall context. It seems to me that there is a clear
answer to this question. Whereas the race of gold is opposed to
the race of silver because the former has more *dikē* and the latter
more hubris, and the race of bronze is opposed to the heroes
because it has more hubris and the heroes more *dikē,* the race of
silver and the race of bronze are equally defined by their hubris
(*hubrin atasthalon* in the case of the silver and *hubries* in the case
of the bronze).[57] How can a race characterized by its hubris be
called "in no way similar" to another race also characterized by
hubris? If it were a matter of degree, it would have to be great
enough to place the two races described as "in no way similar" at
opposite ends of a scale of values. Hesiod would have expressed
this, as he has done in the other cases, in a comparative, such as
"much inferior" or "much more just." But the text says nothing of
the sort; moreover, Hesiod's picture of the follies and impiety of
the men of silver does not suggest that he intended to present
them as much less advanced in hubris than their successors. Only

one solution remains: the two races, equally committed to hubris, differ by the very nature of this hubris. In other words, while the first and second races and the third and fourth races are opposed to each other as *dikē* is to hubris, the second and third races are contrasted as two opposed forms of hubris. A close reading of the text makes such an interpretation undeniable. Indeed, having said that the race of bronze is "in no way similar" to that of silver, whose impious hubris provoked Zeus's punishment, Hesiod explains this radical difference by declaring: "They [the men of bronze] loved the lamentable works of Ares and deeds of excess of hubris."[58] One could not indicate more clearly that it is precisely the hubris of the men of bronze that is "in no way similar" to that of the men of silver. The hubris of the men of bronze is shown in Ares's works: this is the excess of warriors. The hubris of the men of silver is shown in the injustice from which they cannot refrain in their mutual relationships, and in their impiety with regard to the gods. Zeus makes this race disappear because it refuses to honor the Olympian gods with the worship that is their due. This excess is juridical and theological, in no way that of the warrior. What follows in the text supports this interpretation. The race of heroes, which succeeds the race of bronze, is described as not only more just but also *dikaioteron kai areion*: both more just and more courageous.[59] Their *dikē*, like the hubris of the men of bronze, concerns their role as warriors. That is why I wrote, "Far from bringing them closer to the race of silver, the hubris of the men of bronze sets them farther apart. Conversely, the heroes' *dikē*, instead of separating them from the race of bronze, in fact associates them with it; the two races form a pair of opposites."[60] Thus the series of the first four races is presented not in the form of a regular and progressive sequence (1–2–3–4) but as a sequence operating on two levels: first, 1–2; then, 3–4. Each pair of antithetical aspects represents two races that are mutual counterparts, contrasted as *dikē* and hubris. Thus gold followed by silver = *dikē* followed by hubris, but this *dikē* and this hubris are both located on the juridico-theological plane. Next, bronze followed by the heroes = hubris followed by *dikē*, but on a plane that is "in no way similar" to the first plane; in other words, this *dikē* and this hubris are those of war.

So what, now, of Defradas's twofold objection on this point? He argues that in all classifications of metals bronze is inferior to silver, and that the fate in the afterlife of the race of silver, which is worshipped by men, proves its superiority over the race of bronze, which disappears into the anonymity of death. It seems to me that the interpretation I have defended is unaffected by both of these criticisms. My point was that there was a distinct asymmetry between the two pairs I had distinguished:

> In the first pair, the dominant value and the starting point is *dikē*; hubris is secondary, treated as its counterpart. In the second pair, the opposite is true: the principal consideration is hubris. Thus while each of the two pairs has a just and an unjust aspect, it can be said that, taken together, they too are opposed to each other, like *dikē* and hubris. This explains the difference between the two sets of races in their fates after death. The races of gold and silver are promoted, in the strict sense of the term: from being perishable beings they become daemons. As in their existence on earth, they are linked in the afterlife by opposition. The race of gold becomes *epichthonian daemons*, the men of silver become *hupochthonian daemons*, and mortals do honor to both of them.... The posthumous fate of the race of bronze and the heroes is quite different. Neither is promoted as a race. The race of bronze's destiny cannot be called a promotion for it is thoroughly commonplace: having died in battle, the people become the anonymous dead in Hades.[61]

In other words, the sequence of the four races, grouped into two pairs, of which one extreme represents *dikē* and the other hubris, reveals a shift at the point of the change from the second to the third race, since this is not a move from *dikē* to hubris or the reverse but instead a move from one kind of hubris to another. What is the significance of this shift? The races of gold and silver are pledged to a function that, for Hesiod, is rightfully the business of kings: the exercise of justice in both its aspects — the relationships among men and the relationships between men and the gods. In carrying out this task, the first race conforms to *dikē*, while the second neglects it utterly. The race of bronze and the race of heroes are both exclusively pledged to war: they live and die fighting. The men of both these races are warriors, but the men of bronze know only war — they are unconcerned with justice. The heroes, on the other hand, recognize the superiority of *dikē* even in warfare. For Hesiod, the royal function, with its judiciary activity, on the one hand, and the warrior function, with its military activity, on the other, do not operate on the same plane. The warrior function should be subordinate to the royal function, for it is the nature of the warrior to obey his king. I explained this subordination as follows:

> There is a difference of value as well as function between the lance, a military attribute, and the scepter, the symbol of royalty. The lance is supposed to be subordinate to the scepter. When this hierarchy is no longer respected, the lance comes to express hubris, just as the scepter expresses *dikē*. Hubris, for the warrior, consists in wishing to recognize nothing but the lance and devoting oneself entirely to it.[62]

This, precisely, is the case of the men of bronze.

Although the men of bronze are inferior to the men of silver, this inferiority is different from that which separates the silver from the gold or the bronze from the heroes. It is not the inferiority that hubris confers upon one race, compared to another, more just race that is associated with it in the same functional sphere, but the inferiority in the hierarchy of functions of the activities belonging to one pair of races, compared to those of another pair.

Is all this really too subtle, as Defradas, who in any case appears not to have fully understood what I was saying, claims? The real problem is to determine whether the subtlety is actually present in Hesiod's text. Historians of religion have taught us to find a remarkable wealth and complexity of thought in myths whose archaic nature seemed to imply a primitive simplicity.

At any rate, one feature that Defradas can legitimately invoke to prove the inferiority of the men of bronze compared to the men of silver — the inferiority of their status in the afterlife — is equally the case for the heroes. Once the races of gold and silver have disappeared, they become the objects of worship. Mortals pay royal honor (*basilēion geras*) to the men of gold, who intervene directly in their lives as guardians and dispensers of wealth; they also pay a *timē* to the men of silver, even though they are inferior.[63] No such honor is due to the men of bronze, but then it is not due to the heroes either. The former, who perish in battles in which they all slay one another, have a thoroughly commonplace fate in the afterlife: they depart for Hades, leaving no name behind them — in other words, death takes them over.[64] The overwhelming majority of the heroes, who also perish "in grim war and dread battle," share this common fate: death envelops them.[65] Only a few privileged individuals are granted an exceptional destiny: these people are transported by Zeus to the ends of the earth, far from men (*dich' anthrōpōn*), and in the Islands of the Blessed they lead a carefree existence.[66] But in Hesiod's text, even this minority of the elect, unlike the two first races, is not revered or worshipped by men. Erwin Rohde is quite correct on this point; he writes:

> Hesiod says nothing of any influence upon this world exerted by the souls of the Translated in the Islands of the Blest, such as is attributed to the Daimones of the Golden race, nor of any religious worship, which would be implied by such influence if it existed, such as the underworld spirits of the Silver Age receive. All relations with this world are broken off, for any influence from this side would completely contradict the whole conception of these blessed departed.[67]

How are these features of Hesiod's account to be explained? It is important to recognize that the status in the afterlife of the heroes who are swallowed up by death, not miraculously spirited away by Zeus to the Islands of the Blessed, is considerably inferior to that of the men of silver, who, as underworld spirits, are honored with a *timē*. Yet the heroes are much more just than the men of silver, who are pledged to a terrifying hubris. It must be, then, that the inferiority indicated by their lower status in the afterlife is in no way connected with an excess of hubris or a greater degree of corruption. Indeed, subtlety here would be to claim, despite the text, that it is not necessary to distinguish between the two different kinds of inferiority: the first, which contrasts a race of hubris with a race of *dikē*, within a framework of a single function, and the second, which distinguishes between lower and higher in the hierarchy of functions.

If we accept this distinction, which the text itself insists upon, the account becomes intelligible. The men of gold, the royal ones, who are the incarnation of the justice of the ruler, obtain in the afterlife an honor described as "royal." The men of silver enjoy a lesser, or to be more precise, a "secondary" honor compared with the royal men of gold, for they are inferior by reason of their hubris. Nevertheless, they receive an honor, which can be justified not by their virtues and merits, for they have never possessed them, but by the fact that they have the same function as the men of gold: the royal function, the highest in the hierarchy.[68] This close functional link between the first two races is expressed in the complementary nature of their status after death. The just race becomes epichthonian daemons, while the unjust race becomes hypochthonian daemons. Conversely, the vast majority of the heroes, even though they were just, suffer the same fate after death as the men of bronze, who, like them, were pledged to the role of warrior, which is subordinate to that of the king. However, the inferiority of the unjust warriors compared to the just warriors is also expressed by a difference in the afterlife. All the men of bronze, without exception, are lost amid the anonymous masses of the forgotten dead in Hades, whereas a few heroes escape this anonymous death. They lead a happy existence in the Islands of the Blessed, and their names, celebrated by the poets, live on forever in the memory of men. Nevertheless, they are not revered or worshipped; that lot is reserved for those who, during their lifetimes, were royal and who, even in the afterlife, retain connections with the royal function, in that they watch over it to see that it is exercised justly.[69]

In my reply to Defradas's second objection, I have deliberately restricted myself to as precise an examination of the poem's framework and its main articulation as possible. But to decode the myth we must analyze its contents. In particular, we must draw up a list of the distinctive features Hesiod attributes to each race and determine what they mean. These features include the symbolic value of each metal; the race's type of life; what activities are practiced and what are unknown; psychological and moral characteristics; the various types of youth, maturity, or old age; the form of death assigned to the individuals of each race; how each race is destroyed or becomes extinct; and the race's fate in the afterlife. At this point, it is no longer sufficient to consider the account on its own; we must compare it with other passages from *Works and Days* and the *Theogony* and even consider some of Hesiod's mythical imagery in light of the data on Greek religious practices and well-documented legendary traditions. Much of my earlier article was devoted to a study of this kind. I shall not repeat my thesis, which I have already presented in detail. One remark must, however, be made. The conclusions drawn from the formal analysis summarized in the last few pages are so closely linked to the results that emerged from a study of the content that it would be impossible to reject the former without undermining the latter. The interpretation I propose draws its strength from the complementarity of these two categories of evidence, which fit together exactly. Toward the end of my inquiry, I was in a position to conclude, "In sum, a detailed analysis of the myth from every angle confirms and emphasizes the pattern that, from the start, appeared to emerge from the main structure of the text."[70]

Let us restrict our investigation to the sequence of the first four races. The framework revealed by formal analysis is, essentially, filled out in the following manner. The various features that characterize the races of gold and silver show them to be closely associated and at the same time opposed, like two sides of a coin

— one positive, the other negative. Neither of these two races is familiar with war or work, for the *dikē* of the one and the hubris of the other are exclusively concerned with the functions of administering justice, the prerogative of kings. The antithetical pair consisting of the races of gold and silver reappears in Hesiod's picture of life under the reign of the good king, the king of justice, and under the reign of the king of hubris, the impious king who has no interest in Zeus's *dikē*. In the *Theogony*, this same opposition separates Zeus, the ruler of order, from his rivals for sovereignty over the universe, the Titans, who are the rulers of disorder and hubris. The link between silver and gold is again revealed, as I have already remarked, by the obvious symmetry between the epichthonian daemons, who enjoy royal honor and who, in the name of Zeus, supervise the way the kings dispense justice, and the hypochthonian daemons, who also have a *timē*. There is, finally, one more feature: the man of gold lives forever young, never knowing old age; the man of silver lives for a hundred years like a big baby, clinging to his mother's skirts, and as soon as he crosses the threshold to adolescence, he commits a myriad of follies and dies forthwith.[71] Both the men of gold and the men of silver, then, are young. But for the former, youth means a lack of senility, while for the latter, it means a lack of maturity, that is, pure childishness.

The same similarity in their roles, and the same contrasts, exist between the men of bronze and the heroes. The mythical image of the good ruler is projected onto various scenarios, in each of which he contrasts with the ruler of hubris. In the past, this takes the form of the two successive races, gold and silver; in the present, it assumes the guise of the good king and the bad king; among the gods, it appeared as Zeus versus the Titans, and among the supernatural powers other than the *theoi*, as epichthonians and hypochthonians. In the same way, the unjust warrior is contrasted to the just warrior: thus the Giants fighting against Zeus are opposed by the Hekatoncheires, Zeus's faithful guards, who ensure the Olympians' victory over the Titans. Finally, the anonymous dead are contrasted with the glorious heroes.

Whereas the men of gold and of silver are young, the warriors — the men of bronze and the heroes — seem as unacquainted with the state of *pais* as they are with that of *gerōn*. Right from the start, they are portrayed as adults, mature men, already past their adolescence, that *metron hēbēs* which represented the very limit of existence for the race of silver.

It is, of course, perfectly possible to wholly reject this interpretation. Defradas is afraid that it oversimplifies a highly complex historical reality. But it seems that one might well, on the contrary, attack it as being too complex, since, to explain the sequence of races, it introduces not just a simple linear pattern but progression that follows alternate phases and that suggests, on the one hand, a coupling of the races into pairs that share the same function and on the other, the presence, at all levels of the account, of the theme of opposition between *dikē* and hubris. In any event, in order to succeed in undermining my thesis, any refutation would have to address the essentials. It would have to demonstrate that neither the first two races nor the next two are especially linked, either in the poem's formal sequences or in the picture it paints of the races' lives, deaths, and posthumous fates. In my view, this demonstration has not yet been made.

Let us go on to the third objection. According to Defradas, a need for symmetry induced me, following Dumézil, to discover a sixth race, which could act as a counterpart to the race of iron, to which Hesiod belongs. Defradas argues: "Only a superficial reading of Hesiod's text could give rise to such a misinterpretation, which would be demolished by a serious study."[72] This is quite true. Indeed, it is so patently true that no one would be tempted to adopt such an interpretation, and only a superficial reading of my text could result in its being attributed to me. I wrote: "The fifth race does seem to present a problem. It introduces a new dimension, a third category of reality, which, unlike the other two, does not seem to be divisible into two antithetical aspects but appears to be presented as a single race."[73] If I had discovered a sixth race where Hesiod states most clearly that there are five, I would not have seen this as a problem. I do not speak of a sixth race; I claim that, unlike the others, the fifth race is not indivisible and that it comprises two successive types of human existence that strictly oppose each other, the one still having a place for *dikē,* while the other knows only hubris. It is because it is double that the episode of the age of iron is able to complete the overall structure of the myth.[74] Sometimes I call this second aspect of the age of iron "the latter part of the age of iron"; sometimes I call it "the age of iron in its decline"; never do I call it "a sixth race."[75]

But this is not the most crucial point. Is it true that in the case of the age of iron there are two different types of human existence, which must be distinguished? First of all, Hesiod does not and could not speak of the race of iron in the same terms as the other races. The first four races belong to the past; they have disappeared, so when Hesiod speaks of them he is speaking in the past tense of what is over and done with. In contrast, where the age of iron is concerned, Hesiod is no longer turned toward the past. He expresses himself in the future tense, talking of what humanity can henceforth expect. To Perses, whom he addresses, he reveals a future, part of which is close at hand and, as it were, "already there" (I refer to the *nun,* the "now" of line 176). But the other part of this future is still a long way off, and most certainly neither Hesiod nor Perses will ever see it. It will come when all that is left for Zeus to do is to destroy this race, whose men will be born with their hair already white, in its turn. This moment, which can be seen in silhouette on the horizon, takes on the character of an apocalypse, an end to time. No other race is described in such terms, as capable of undergoing a change in its original conditions of existence during its own timespan; that is, none is described as having declined in the course of its own age.[76] Each past race remains unchanged from beginning to end, lacking true temporal character. This very temporal character, however, is typical of the fate of the race of iron, precisely because its destiny has not yet been accomplished but is in the process of being lived out in a present that constantly opens on to the future. Hesiod says that *now* is the age of iron. Men will not cease to be tormented by

the evils the gods send them. He adds: "But notwithstanding...
these [men] shall have some good mingled with their evils."[77]
This remark is not at all surprising, since the life that Hesiod
and Perses must experience in all its hardship is the life of mixtures and contrasts symbolized in the preceding part of the poem
by Pandora.

This *nun* where good is still mixed with evil is contrasted with
the terrifying prospect of a much more sinister future, which will
be entirely given over to the nocturnal powers of evil.[78] The conclusion of this last paragraph clearly echoes the conclusion of the
earlier passage. To "these [the men of now] shall have some good
mingled with their evils" corresponds the line "Bitter sorrows will
be left for mortal men, and there will be no help against evil."[79]

In the one case, there is a mixture of blessings and evils; in the
other, nothing but evils. Even if this were the only difference
between the existing state and the future state of the race of iron,
it would suffice to distinguish the two types of existence within
the race, for the fundamental meaning of the whole myth depends on precisely this point. Let us recall that the men of the
race of gold are *kakōn ektosthen hapantōn*, far from every evil;
every blessing is theirs: *esthla de panta toisin eēn*. The men of gold
have no evils and all the blessings. The men among whom Hesiod
and Perses live have both blessings and evils. The men of the
future will have no blessings and all the evils.

But this is not the only feature that situates the age of iron
(that is, present-day life, insofar as it must be explained and its
deeper significance must be revealed to Perses) halfway between
the race of gold, at the beginning of the cycle, and the race of iron
in its decline, at the end. Just as they know nothing of *ponos* and
oizus (two of the children of Night), the men of gold are unacquainted with old age (*gēras*). They are born young and remain
forever as they have always been (*homoioi*).[80] Hesiod lives in a
world where men are born young and die old, with youth gradually changing into old age as a result of anxieties, toil, disease, and
women. By the end of the age of iron nothing will remain except
gēras: men will be born old, with their temples already white.[81]

Since each race is characterized by its identification with one of the ages of human life, the myth can be understood by giving full weight to the opposition Hesiod sets up between the two aspects of the age of iron.

The men of gold live, in all their justice, *ethelēmoi hēsuchoi*.[82] They are peaceful and are unacquainted with violent encounters on the battlefield. They feel no jealousy and know nothing of quarrels or lawsuits — with their train of perjury, slander, and deceit — which are the weapons of the legal *eris* that operates in the *agora*. As we have seen, by the end of the age of iron, the evil *eris* will reign supreme. Neither *dikē* nor oaths nor the gods will be feared or respected. Hubris alone will be honored.[83] Human speech will take the form of lies, deceit, and perjury.[84] Jealousy (*zēlos*), just as evil-minded as the wicked *eris* (*kakochartos*), will have supreme power over all human beings. This jealousy is not the good *eris* that makes potter jealous of potter and carpenter jealous of carpenter. It does not stimulate a man to do better than his rival, to work harder in order to produce a better result. This jealousy seeks, through fraud, deceit, and perjury, to misappropriate the fruits of a rival's labor.[85]

Where does Hesiod's own world stand in relation to this point? Is there as clear a break between the existing and the future states of the race of iron as there is in the two preceding cases? I have already noted that the poet's preface to his brother, encouraging him to choose the good *eris* and renounce the bad, proves clearly enough that both are present in their peasant life. But this is not all. Hesiod warns that when jealousy has entirely filled men's hearts, there will be no more room for feelings of friendship — for the *philia* that usually binds together host and guest, friend and friend, brother and brother, child and parent. The poet adds: "*hōs to paros per* [as was the case before]."[86] This "before," which makes room for *philia* alongside *eris*, is precisely *nun*, the "now" of present life.[87] True, in Hesiod's world there are wars, evil quarrels, and fraudulent lawsuits, such as the ones Perses tries to bring against Hesiod, but ties of mutual friendship and help also exist within the family, between neighbors, and between friends. Perses himself has experienced this: when he turned to his brother in an hour of need, Hesiod did not begrudge him assistance.[88] Moreover, even if kings do sometimes pronounce unfair sentences, they can also administer justice correctly. When they do, blessings triumph over evils throughout the land; there is no war (*polemos*), no hunger (*limos*), no disaster (*atē*).[89] The people feast happily on the fruits of the fields they have worked; women present their husbands with children "who resemble their fathers," whereas by the end of the age of iron sons will no longer even "resemble their fathers."[90] Thus a careful reading of the text seems to confirm that the race of iron has two aspects, which are carefully distinguished and even contrasted by Hesiod. The race of iron means, in the first instance, contemporary life, the same life that is accounted for by the myth of Pandora and to which all the religious, moral, practical, and agricultural advice that *Works and Days* dispenses so generously applies. This age of iron has a special place in the myth, since the account is, in effect, aimed at explaining its ambiguous nature, its "mixed" state, and at justifying the choice in favor of *dikē* and work that Hesiod recommends to his brother.[91] In the second instance, the age of iron refers not to contemporary life as the poet describes it but to a life yet to come, as his inspired wisdom allows him to foresee it. This terrifying prediction of a world entirely given over to hubris is at the same time a solemn warning to Perses: if he and those like him continue to behave as they do, ignoring *dikē* and despising work, then the world will most certainly end up in such an extreme state of misfortune. Thus the poet's prophetic vision has a double purpose. It determines the length of a cycle of ages that will have an end just as it had a beginning; it completes the circle that has led humanity from *dikē* to hubris, from happiness to misfortune, from youth to old age, from *philia* to the wicked *eris*. But, furthermore, it makes an appeal to Perses and the wicked: There is still time; understand the lesson, agree to listen to *dikē* and not allow hubris to grow any more, and perhaps the nefarious powers of Night will not be able to invade the whole of existence; there could still be a place for happiness among poor human beings.

The analyses just undertaken also answer Defradas's fourth objection, at least with respect to the following point: the sequence of the races does indeed form a complete cycle of decline, which Hesiod envisages as a whole, with a beginning and an end in strict opposition to each other. But one further point must be made. The men of the race of gold live "like gods," in a state that is not yet truly separate from the blessedness of the immortals and in which the original kinship between the divine race and the human is reflected.[92] Similarly, in the *Theogony*, the dispute that sets gods and men against each other at Mecone over the apportionment of the sacrificial beast (a confrontation that Prometheus, through his trickery, will decide in favor of men) suggests that even if gods and men did not live together with complete success, at least they met frequently and had close dealings with one another.[93] In contrast, the end of the cycle of the races presents a hopeless picture of a human world entirely cut off from the world of the gods; Aidōs and Nemesis, who used to inspire men with a respect for the gods and who offered them a chance to communicate with them, abandon the earth forever, departing for Olympos. They leave behind a humanity given over to Evil and Night and go off to rejoin the shining race of the blessed.[94]

Since Hesiod's poem thus encompasses the entire destiny of the human race as one would tell the story of an individual's life cycle, from his earliest youth to the end of his old age, I was led to look more closely at the meaning of line 175. Hesiod regrets that he was not "dead earlier or born later." "Dead earlier" is easy to understand: he might have been born in the youth of the golden age. But "born later" raises a problem. At the point where he is situated in the sequence of the races, the future offers only the gloomiest of prospects. Hesiod cannot be wishing to be born into a world that, according to him, will know nothing but old age, misfortune, and injustice. He must therefore imagine that once Zeus has annihilated the race of iron in its turn, that is to say, once what has been shown to be a complete cycle is over, it will be possible for a new race of men to be born, and had the poet been more fortunate, he might have been among them. There is no way

80

to tell how Hesiod envisages the coming of this race, for he gives no other information about it. For this reason, any remarks made on this subject must perforce be hypothetical.

However, it does not seem illegitimate to suppose that, given that Hesiod conceived of the sequence of the races as a cycle, he must have imagined what followed (since something does follow) according to a cyclical model as well. Just as generations of men succeed one another within one race, and just as the races succeed one another within the total cycle of the ages, so the cycles might well succeed one another. This renewal of the cycle after the destruction that Hesiod predicts for the race of iron at the final point in the decline has, of course, nothing to do with the "eternal return" of the Orphic doctrines or their eschatology, except possibly for Defradas.[95] Quite simply, in Hesiod's conception, the course of the human races is like that of the seasons. Hesiod's calendar has a cyclical character. All the temporal landmarks he mentions are regularly repeated each year. On the other hand, he never gives any indication of a way of dating the years that would make it possible to distinguish one year from another and arrange them in a linear sequence (as, for instance, when they were later distinguished by the names of their civil or religious magistrates). It could be said, to borrow an expression from Maurice Halbwachs, that the social framework of the notion of time is still essentially cyclical in Hesiod's peasant world, as in other archaic societies.[96] Time is composed of a sequence of seasons clearly separated from one another by "breaks" marked by particular temporal points, which serve as landmarks within an annual calendar.[97] This sequence of distinct seasons forms a complete cycle, which begins again when it reaches its final point. The influence of this cyclical image of time is equally marked in Homer: when he evokes the destiny of "perishable" men, he is not expressing the nostalgia of the individual faced with the inexorable flight of time, as the lyric poets did later. He is comparing the sequence of human generations with the periodic return of the seasons: "The wind scatters the leaves, each in turn, over the ground, and the lush forest gives them birth when the season of

81

spring arrives. So it is with men: one generation is born at the instant another fades away."[98]

The hypothesis of the renewal of the cycle of ages suggested by line 175 is supported by the passage in the *Statesman* where Plato playfully evokes the old myths about days gone by and says that the human generations succeed one another in a cycle and that once this cycle has reached its conclusion it begins all over again, but in the opposite direction.[99] The allusions to Hesiod in this passage seem quite obvious. Thus the state of humanity under Kronos is described as follows: "They had fruits in plenty from the trees and other plants, which the earth furnished them of its own accord, without help from agriculture *automatēs anadidousēs tēs gēs*."[100] According to Plato, what happens at the end of the cycle, at the moment when the universe begins to move in the opposite direction? "Every mortal creature stopped growing older in appearance and then reversed its growth and became, as it were, younger and more tender; the hoary locks of the old men grew dark, and bearded cheeks grew smooth again as their possessors reverted to their earlier ages."[101] It is hard not to see the Platonic humor of this passage as a reply to Hesiod's description of the progressive aging of the human races.

True, one can, like Mazon, choose not to take line 175 literally and instead interpret it as "an expression similar to those familiar antitheses so frequent with the Greeks, which are used to convey the idea of anyone or anything."[102] However, this antithesis involving the past and the future appears in Hesiod in too precise a context for it to be immediately associated with ready-made expressions such as are to be found in Sophocles's *Antigone* — *it' it, opaones hoi t'ontes hoi t'apontes* ("Go, go, servants, those of you that are there and those that aren't") — and *Electra*.[103] To show that there is indeed a chronology in the sequence of the races, Defradas refers to the word's *metopisten*, in line 127, and *epeita*, in line 174. He might have remarked that of the seven temporal adverbs contained in the hundred or so lines of the text, four are concentrated precisely between lines 174 and 176: *epeita* in line 174, two *prosthen* and *epeita* in line 175, and *nun* at the beginning of line 176.[104] The meaning of the text is thus as follows: "Would to the gods that it were not *afterward* [that is, *after* the race of heroes] that I myself had to live amid the men of the fifth race, but that I had been either dead *earlier*, or born *later*; *now* truly it is the age of iron." It would seem that if ever there were a passage in which it was necessary to give full value to every expression of time, this is it.

At the close of his critical study, just before the conclusion, Defradas surveys the ruins that he believes he has brought down around him, and he feels a certain sadness: "It pains me to bring this disappointment to those who believed they had uncovered a coherent and solid explanation, by showing them that it rests upon a superficial reading of the texts or upon a systematization that falsifies the complexity of the real facts." And, "so as not to leave the reader on this negative note," he refers to Goldschmidt's work and adopts its conclusions.[105] This is the very study that provided the starting point for my own research. I borrowed Goldschmidt's principle of interpretation: he emphasized "the tendency toward *systematization* in Hesiod's text" and detected in it the establishment of a correspondence between, on the one hand, a myth of origins and, on the other, a structural division determining the hierarchy of the supernatural powers other than the *theoi*, that is to say, the daemons, the heroes, and the dead.[106] Goldschmidt did not undertake a complete analysis of the myth of the races. This was not the purpose of his article, in which he was only incidentally concerned with Hesiod. My purpose, therefore, was to take up the inquiry for its own sake, and along the lines indicated, in an attempt to answer the questions that Goldschmidt had not addressed and resolve the difficulties that his interpretative schema had left open. I thought that I had solved the problem, not by abandoning the schema but by developing it even further, integrating it into a more extensive and more complex interpretation that, while still respecting the systematic nature of the myth that Goldschmidt quite rightly emphasized, might make it possible to explain it fully.

Goldschmidt was not unaware of the difficulties the text presents if one sees in it a *direct* link, *without any intermediaries*, between, on the one hand, a myth of origins in which the metals have a regularly declining value and, on the other, a classification of divine beings. First, the race of heroes, whose presence is indispensable for the classification of divine beings, distorts the structure of the account; from the point of view of the sequence of races, it appears to be an episode tacked on afterward, not integrated into the whole. Second, the race of silver raises problems in every respect. If Hesiod really based his text on a traditional legend that presented the sequence of the races in an order of progressive decline, why does he describe the race of silver as he did? Given that he places it immediately after the race of gold, at the top of the scale of metals, why does he give it the negative characteristic of "inordinate hubris"? He was not obliged to do so. There are two possibilities: either he is conforming to tradition, and the tradition itself did not follow the pattern of a regular progress of decline; or, as I believe to be the case, Hesiod modified the tradition on this point and invented the features that characterize the race of silver in his account. He had reasons for doing this, so we must attempt to see what they were.

The difficulty is aggravated when we move from the genetic to the structural perspective. We may suppose that Hesiod linked these two points of view, seeking to show that the various races' status in the afterlife and their promotion to the rank of divine powers (other than *theoi*) are the reward for the kind of life they led on earth. Goldschmidt points out: "In the case of the race of silver, this is not without difficulties. They are buried under the earth by a Zeus angered by their refusal to pay homage to the Olympian gods. And yet the members of even this impious race are revered."[107] Hesiod thus had two separate reasons for depicting the race of silver in favorable terms: in the first place, because it immediately follows the race of gold, and in the second, to justify men's worship of it. It becomes necessary, then, to answer this question: Why did Hesiod do the exact reverse?

There is an even more serious problem. The classification of divine beings for which the myth of the races is supposed to provide an etiology includes (apart from the *theoi*, with whom the myth is not concerned) the following series: daemons, heroes, and the dead. We should note right away that the normal order is not respected and that the dead appear in the myth before the heroes do. This does not occur in any other text concerned with this series: the heroes are occasionally classed before the daemons, but they never come after the dead.[108] But most important is the fact that there is a sequence of four races to account for three categories of supernatural beings. After their death, the men of gold become *daimones*, described as *epichthonioi*; the men of bronze, called *nōnumnoi*, populate the damp abode of Hades (they are the ordinary dead); the heroes remain what they already are — heroes. What, then, is the position of the men of silver, who are described as *makares hupochthonioi*? Either they form a category on their own, a fourth kind of divine being, which would not fit into the framework of the traditional classification and whose nature is difficult to imagine, or they are associated with the men of gold, and, as hypochthonians, make up the category of daemons with their epichthonian counterparts. This is the solution that Goldschmidt, following Rohde and followed by Defradas, had good reason to adopt. Goldschmidt writes: "We may accept the fact that Hesiod split the class of daemons in two in order to accommodate the race of silver within the system."[109] But who can disregard the whole chain of consequences that this remark entails? For the sake of the system's coherence, that is, for both the genetic and the structural perspectives to be unified, Hesiod was obliged to link the first two races extremely closely, to conceive of them as a pair, and moreover an inseparable pair, since they complete each other to form the single category of the daemons. It is therefore understandable that he gave the men of silver the features that, in every detail of the picture he draws of their life, make them the antithesis of the men of gold. This also explains why the men of silver, whose place in the scale of metals is immediately below that of the men of gold, are only slightly inferior to the men of gold and considerably superior to the races that follow them. It is because, in fact, the men of silver are the antitheses of the men of gold. They present an inverted picture of the life of that race, a picture where inordinate hubris has taken the place of *dikē*.

These remarks apply to the next two races as they do to the first two, for the reasons already given. Each of these two races accounts for a particular category of the powers in the afterlife (the inhabitants of Hades, on the one hand, and the Islands of the Blessed, on the other) because for Hesiod these are two types of deceased, neither of which is the object of a *timē*, as are the daemons. Neither in Homer nor in Hesiod is there evidence of a cult of heroes comparable to the one that appeared in an organized form within the framework of the official state religion.[110] The heroes are simply the dead, but they are dead men who, instead of joining the anonymous crowd in Hades, have been transported far from men to the Islands of the Blessed. In fact, not all those who belong to the race of heroes go to the Islands of the Blessed. The vast majority of them join the men of bronze in Hades. On this point, it is interesting to compare lines 154–55, in which black Death takes the men of bronze (*thanatos heile melas*) to line 146, where the majority of the heroes (*tous men* as opposed to *tois de* in line 179) *thanatou telos amphekalupse* are enveloped by death, which completes everything.

Thus, if we accept Goldschmidt's principle of interpretation and agree with him that Hesiod intended to combine a genetic myth and a structural division, we must complete Goldschmidt's analysis by pointing out that in order to establish a correspondence between a series with four terms (the four races) and one with three (the three categories of supernatural powers other than the *theoi*), the myth had to be recast in a different form, elaborated on, and given a new pattern. If we bear in mind all the details of the account and consistently place them in the context of the myth as a whole, and if we situate the myth in turn in the context of Hesiod's work as a whole, then we can discern the principles by which this reorganization took place. First, the races have been regrouped into pairs, and each pair has a precise meaning in terms of function. Second, each function thus split into two antithetical aspects expresses, on its own level, the opposition between *dikē* and hubris, the central theme and lesson of the myth.[111]

Therefore, my interpretation amplifies Goldschmidt's and does not contradict it. It does not simplify it; rather, it makes it more complex, in order to account for a whole series of elements that Goldschmidt did not include in his inquiry. To oppose his thesis to mine is possible only on a very cursory reading of both.

Indeed, the problem raised by this too lengthy discussion is, in the end, one of reading. How should Hesiod be read? Should we follow Goldschmidt, who was "struck by the tendency toward *systematization*" in Hesiod's text, or Defradas, for whom, on the contrary, Hesiod "had no precise system" and felt no compunction about interrupting the process of decline in order to find a place for his heroes, and for whom Hesiod, in his "empiricism," envisaged a future less gloomy than the past?[112]

In the former case, one considers the text from its heights; one assumes that the task of the interpreter is to raise himself to the level of a work that is rich, complex, and systematic and possesses its own kind of coherence, which one must attempt to discover. All easy solutions must be refused. It is necessary to work at a patient, attentive reading, going back to it day after day, taking account of all the details and integrating them into the whole. If difficulties remain in deciphering the text, this will be attributed to a lack of understanding in the reader rather than to contradictions or carelessness on the part of the author.

In the latter case, however, one interprets Hesiod's text from below.

CHAPTER THREE

Structural Method and
the Myth of the Races

In his book *Questions platoniciennes*, Victor Goldschmidt included a study published twenty years earlier in the *Revue des études grecques* titled "Theologia." In an addendum to this study, he discusses a reading of Hesiod's myth of the human races that, inspired by him, I had proposed. The purpose of the addendum is to expand his reflections "on the details of the interpretation of the myth, and on this interpretation as a whole." There are two aspects to this "reassessment": first, after recognizing that our views often converge and at times are in "complete agreement," Goldschmidt lays out the objections or (as he calls them) the questions my thesis raises, according to him; then, with regard to his own thesis, he clarifies certain points that I had seen as problematic, and he extends his analysis, following a study by Peter Walcot that had appeared in the meantime, by introducing new elements that confirm his point of view as well as solidify its foundations. The question was very important to him. He returned to it in his last published article: evoking our "friendly debate" and "our basic agreement, up to a certain point," he refers to our "two attempts at a solution," in order to define the conditions for a valid use of the structural method in reading literary or philosophical texts.[1]

I would like to honor his memory — as I believe he would wish — by pursuing the dialogue and by attempting a reassessment of my own. I will address the problem as a whole, stressing the debt I owe my friend, emphasizing his contribution to our understanding of the myth, and clarifying my position in a debate that, beyond our personal investments, engages a question that was essential for him: What procedures of decoding should the modern inter-preter, whether a historian of philosophy or of religion, use to reconstruct the meaning of a text?

In the case of the myth of the races, the task was to render intelligible an account whose narrative sequences do not fit to-gether and make grasping its global order and signification diffi-cult. Therefore, it was also necessary to seek the key to this account in a structure that is not immediately legible but is clearly visible in other documents and lends coherence to the text as a whole, while also accounting for its apparent distortions. For Victor Goldschmidt, this structure is, roughly speaking, that of traditional Greek theology, which distinguishes, in addition to the gods properly speaking (the *theoi*), three categories of beings worshiped by man in the hierarchy of supernatural powers: dae-mons, heroes, and the dead (after their disappearance, the first four races are raised to the rank of these three religious entities). For me, this structure was that of the tripartite functional system — kingship, war, fertility — that dominated the religious thought of Indo-Europeans, as Georges Dumézil has shown. To my mind, the two solutions were not contradictory; the triple structure as I conceived of it seemed capable of including the theological struc-ture within it. Indeed, I wrote:

> Thus, if we accept Goldschmidt's principle of interpretation and agree with him that Hesiod intended to combine a genetic myth and a struc-tural division, we must complete Goldschmidt's analysis by pointing out that in order to establish a correspondence between a series with four terms (the four races) and one with three (the three categories of supernatural powers other than the *theoi*), the myth had to be recast in a different form, elaborated on, and given a new pattern. If we bear in mind all the details of the account and consistently place them in the context of the myth as a whole, and if we situate the myth in turn in the context of Hesiod's work as a whole, then we can discern the principles by which this reorganization took place. First, the races

have been regrouped into pairs, and each pair has a precise meaning in terms of function. Second, each function thus split into two antithetical aspects expresses, on its own level, the opposition between *dikē* and hubris, the central theme and lesson of the myth.[2]

What was it, then, according to Goldschmidt, that made our two readings if not incompatible then at least different enough in orientation to raise questions concerning the methodological principles he advocated? His detailed criticisms of my thesis, and mine of his, were not essential in this respect. At the heart of the debate was a division that Goldschmidt clearly presented when he explained the stakes involved:

> The functional trichotomy, if it can be objectively correlated with the text (and thereby provide a contribution to religious sociology), does not clarify its internal aim; whereas the tripartite theology allows us to grasp the meaning — indeed, the completely new meaning — that the poet confers on the ancient account of the ages of the world as he turns that account into the etiological myth of this hierarchy. In other words, it allows us to discover the author's intention. And the author's intention will, in the final instance, have to legitimate the correlations; on that basis, one can more precisely pose the problem of the structural method as it is applied to philosophical texts.[3]

These remarks raise two types of questions. The first concerns the tripartite function. Is it true that this structure can be objectively correlated with the text, and if so, what is the nature of this correlation? How can it be valid on the level of religious sociology without clarifying the internal aim of the text it is being applied to? The latter concerns the "author's intention." What exactly does this mean? And can the intention of the author of a philosophical text be considered in the same way as that of a poet who revives an ancient myth to give it a new meaning?

First, the tripartite function: We know that while this model does not have the same resonance in Greece as it does in India or Rome, where it is the keystone of the religious system, it survives nonetheless in certain parts of the legend, in the grouping of certain divine figures, and even in the philosophical thought of Plato, specifically his theory of the three social classes, described in the *Republic*. From the point of view of religious sociology, it is thus historically possible that Hesiod could have used this classificatory scheme. Of course, this possibility would be meaningless if the tripartite structure were not present in the text, explicit in the order of the narrative itself. But the four first races' succession appears intelligible only on two conditions: the races must be regrouped in pairs (gold and silver, bronze and hero), where the two associated races have in common a systematic set of features that clearly opposes them to the two others; and the paired races must contrast with each other in terms of *dikē* and hubris, where justice and excess are manifest in the domain that is specific to these two races and that distinguishes them from the other pair. Within the framework of a series of races alternating between *dikē*-hubris and hubris-*dikē*, Hesiod emphasized these relations of complementary opposition (within each couple) and these functional differences (between the two couples) with too much clarity and precision for us to assume that he was not fully aware of it. Whatever the poet's aim or intention may have been, in order to convey his message he used two types of structures that must have been familiar to his audience: the opposition *dikē*-hubris, which is at issue throughout the text, and the opposition kingship-military activity, in terms of which the first two races are contrasted to the next two. The men of gold and the men of silver are associated with the function of kingship, which assures the correct exercise of justice among men and the observance of piety toward the gods; the men of bronze and the heroes are located entirely in the field of military activity and are devoted to war and combat.

The text clearly opposes the figure of the king (who sometimes respects and sometimes neglects his obligations) to the figure of the warrior (who sometimes knows only the brutal violence proper to his nature and sometimes grants a place to the values of justice and piety that go beyond him). However, I now recognize that the third function, fertility, presents a problem.[4]

To be sure, the fifth race, the race of iron, to which Hesiod himself belongs, is condemned to hard toil and agricultural activity. It is, more than anything else, a world of peasants. But there are kings in this world as well, and at times it can be plagued by war. Above all, the picture of this race in decline — in an age when nothing is as it was before, because *hubris* has invaded every part of human existence, and there is no way to stop the evil, because there is no justice — goes far beyond the framework of the third function. The men it depicts are not merely producers; their errors and crimes are not limited to activities associated with nourishment, wealth, and fertility. Therefore, although Hesiod uses the the model of the three functions, he manifestly distorts the third one, since its corresponding race represents all of present humanity. The tripartite schema interests the poet less in terms of its own significance than as a way to articulate the four first races among themselves, that is, as a way to group them in pairs in order to relate each functional pair, and each race within the two pairs, to the fundamental categories of *dikē* and hubris. The royal function and the military function are, in general, opposed as *dikē* and hubris. Thus, because of his juridical and religious role, the king's relation to the warrior, who serves the spirit of strife (*eris*) in battle, is analogous — from the point of view of justice — to the relation of the men of gold to the men of silver, within the framework of kingship, and of the heroes to the men of bronze, in the framework of military activity. The aim of the text is not trichotomy as such but the *dikē*-hubris opposition. Dividing up the four first races according to the order of the two great traditional functions of kingship and war allows us to give this opposition — in which Hesiod's intention is expressed, since it is the lesson of the myth ("Heed *dikē*; do not let hubris grow") — its full extension and its full systematicity.

Walcot's study, used very appropriately by Goldschmidt, should be considered here. It completes these remarks and clarifies their meaning. Walcot clearly showed that the four first races form a complete cycle that circles back on itself and is thereby separated from the fifth race, which contrasts with the preceding four as a whole. The posthumous existence of the heroes — or at least of those who are transported to the Islands of the Blessed after their death — closely resembles the lives led by the race of gold. Hesiod describes both in deliberately identical terms. As Goldschmidt notes: "The story arrives at its point of departure."[5] At the end of the fourth race, the blessed heroes find in the beyond the full beatitude first enjoyed by the age of gold.

The break between the fourth race, the heroes, and the fifth, the race of iron, is sharper and more decisive than any of those between the first four races. The border is of a different nature this time. The reason is clear: the first four races have all disappeared; they belong to a distant past, a time other than our own. They have no reality other than the posthumous existence that has been given to them; they are what they became when they ceased to live in the light of day. For the men of each race, the story of their lives is thus a prelude to the description of the fate reserved for them and of their status after they are buried. That is not the case for the race of iron, to which Hesiod belongs; it constitutes his time and his world, the place from which he speaks. It is "now" and "here below." Far removed from ancient times, it foretells no posthumous destiny, nor does it open up onto anything beyond the human condition. It leads to a purely earthly future, a tomorrow that risks being even worse than today — if one misses the lesson of the story and allows hubris to grow — and that may constitute a radical reversal of that golden age inaugurated by the first race and found again by the fourth after its disappearance. In the age of gold, as on the Islands of the Blessed, all available good is accessible to everyone, and there is no evil; today, good and evil are mixed together; tomorrow, perhaps there will be nothing but evil, and no remedy for it. Any divinities who have facilitated contact between mortals and immortals will leave the earth for Olympos. By its own fault, in its contempt for *dikē*, humanity will find itself radically separated from the divine, cut off from the heavenly ones. The two aspects and phases of the fifth race — Hesiod's "now" and the "tomorrow" that he prophesies and dreads — stand in contrast to the cycle of previous races, which the heroes complete. Hesiod's picture of this cycle, while explaining present misfortune and indicating something even worse in the future if hubris is allowed to triumph, accounts for the existence of three categories of religious powers alongside the *theoi*, going back to the first human generations, which have disappeared: the daemons (epichthonian and hypochthonian), the dead in Hades, and the heroes on the Islands of the Blessed.

The myth of the races, as reshaped by Hesiod, thus unites two purposes, two internal aims. The poet's intention is at once to illustrate the original kinship of gods and men (by associating the first races of mortals with the three categories of supernatural beings recognized by popular belief, alongside the *theoi*) and to warn the men of today, asking them to learn the story's lesson and to respect *dikē*, so that their poor existence will remain connected to the divine and not be given over entirely to hubris and evil.

Goldschmidt acknowledges this twofold aim when he notes in his "Addendum" that the theological intention is not necessarily incompatible "with the no less evident intention (without which the account would not be able to provide the culmination of the Prometheus myth) to explain humanity's progressive decline in terms of the ideas of justice and excess." In examining how Hesiod managed to harmonize these two aims, Goldschmidt takes another step. He observes that by adding the heroes to the series of races of metal and by placing them after the bronze race, Hesiod

> interrupts, certainly, the movement of decline outlined in the first three terms; but by inserting the heroes at this point, whose lives in the Islands of the Blessed resemble those of the race of gold, he renders the myth's moral lesson more vivid by opposing the age of gold to the age of iron — an opposition that had already provided the framework for the Prometheus myth. In other words, after passing through the stages of decline, the myth of the races, like the myth of Prometheus, comes to an end on the contrast, *without any intermediaries*, between the age of gold and the age of iron.[6]

The myth of the races reconnects with the myth of Prometheus at its terminal point. But if that is the case, then its internal aim also takes us outside the account, which would, of course, first have to be compared with the two versions of the Promethean episode in Hesiod. But it would also, and to an equal degree, have to be compared with the set of myths in the *Theogony* that recount the births of the various gods and the gradual emergence of an organized divine world, up to the moment when Zeus's victory establishes the order that must reign forever and that nothing and no one will ever have the power to modify. Without this background on the genesis of the gods, the distribution of honors and privileges among them, and their race's status as immortals, it would be impossible to understand the transformations successively undergone by men who can perish.

But this broader perspective raises new problems for the interpreter. For Goldschmidt, the myth of the races is, "in a certain sense, a continuation of the *Theogony*."[7] This first poem establishes the great Olympian family, the gods properly speaking, the *theoi*. The matter is settled as far as they are concerned. But in the hierarchy of divine beings recognized in the cultic practices of the poet's time, there was yet another series: daemons, heroes, and the dead. The *Theogony* says nothing of these, which means they continued to pose a problem. Hesiod's intention, says Goldschmidt, was to fill this gap and to complete the overall picture of the supernatural powers. By linking the existence of the daemons, the heroes, and the dead to the earlier human races that gave birth to them, the text thus takes on a properly "theogonic" function. It provides the chapter missing from the genesis of divine beings as narrated in the *Theogony*. And it is this "internal aim" that Hesiod expresses at the very beginning as a prelude to the account, in line 108 — which was disqualified by Paul Mazon and for that reason not at first considered by Goldschmidt. If we accept the authenticity of the line, which from a paleographic point of view is not at all in doubt, it would have to be read in conjunction with the preceding line, such that Hesiod's warning to his brother Perses on the importance of the myth he is about to recount would have to be understood thus: "Keep it well in mind that gods (*theoi*) and men have the same origin." Goldschmidt points out that in this line, Hesiod provides at the outset the meaning he intends to give to the myth of the races: if the gods created the successive human races (the first two were created by "the immortals who held Olympos," the next two by Zeus; nothing is said about the origin of the fifth), these races, in return, gave birth to divine beings.[8] Gods and mortal men, therefore, have the same origin.

At this point, the aim of the text as reconstructed by the modern interpreter links up with the poet's project as the poet himself formulated it, and everything seems to be definitively accounted for by Goldschmidt's reading. But it is precisely here that an entire series of questions arises. First, about the text itself: Does line 108 indeed have the meaning attributed to it? Next, there are questions about how this line is articulated with the myth of Prometheus and Pandora, which immediately precedes it and of which it is the "culmination." Finally, to the extent that this interpretation presents the classification gods–daemons–heroes–dead as a given in the religious tradition Hesiod presumably inherited, is this interpretation compatible with what we know about the realities of religious practice between the eighth and the seventh century? Before, I essentially expressed my reservations regarding Goldschmidt's point of view in terms of these three points, especially the first and the third. What about today?

The meaning of line 108 depends on the expression: *homōthen gegāasi*. Does this mean that because they descended from a single ancestor or because of the bonds of filiation that unite them, gods and men belong to one and the same race? Or does it mean that gods and men made their appearance from a common point of departure — that they emerged from a state in which they were not clearly distinguished from one another? The account's intention could be to illustrate, in the first case, something like an identity in nature between the race of the gods and that of the mortals, or in the second case, an original proximity in their mode of life, a primary community of existence.[9] Is it possible to decide between these two interpretations? The notion that Hesiod wanted to claim that the *theoi* and the mortals belonged to the same family presents a number of difficulties. The gods created men not in the sense of engendering them but in the sense of producing or fabricating (*poiein*) them. At the same time, the divine powers to which the first four races give birth are not *theoi*, even though the men of the race of gold "live like the gods" (as Goldschmidt observes in response to my objection on this point), and even though the heroes are the "divine race" (*theion genos*) of what are called demigods (*hēmitheoi*).[10] When Hesiod evokes the *theios anēr*, the divine man who is able to urinate during the night without offending the immortals, the use of *theios* does not signify that this man, in Hesiod's eyes, is included among the divinities.[11] To be sure, it is always possible to disagree on details of this kind. But there appears to be one decisive reason for discounting the reading that claims an identity of race. Line 108 is integrally linked with the line preceding it, which it clarifies and in which Hesiod presents the myth of the races as a *hēteron lōgon*, another or a second story that will follow and complete the first, the story of Prometheus. In other words, it recapitulates this first story by expressing what is essential in it. But what does the story of Prometheus say? It shows how the two different races, men and gods, while originally sharing the same blessed existence — since in primordial times humans lived among the gods and "like the gods" — one day found themselves caught up in a process of separation. If this divorce ended up reducing the mortals to their current state of suffering and privation, this is Prometheus's fault: at the time of the division, when it was a matter of determining each race's status, the Titan, driven by Eris, the spirit of jealous strife, rebelled against Zeus, whose infallible intelligence he tried to deceive. As an alternative to the myth of Prometheus, the story of the races provides another way, one that is fitting and full of knowledge (*eu kai epistamenōs*), to illustrate the same theme: the separation of gods and men, beginning with a state in which they lived and prospered together.[12] But even though the two stories' aim is the same, their differences are significant. In the first, the separation takes place suddenly and permanently. At the end of the separation brought about by Prometheus, the human race finds itself forever fixed between the animals and the gods. Like animals, humans are henceforth subject to hunger, disease, and death, but they differ from the animals in that they recognize justice and piety. Humans are now separated from the gods by an unbridgeable distance, but they maintain contact and commerce with them through religious practices, the honors they pay them, and the sacrifices they offer. In the myth of the races, the distance is established gradually and in successive stages; even in Hesiod's time, it is not definitively set, since the poet envisages a moment during the time of the iron race when the gulf widens even further and the last remaining bonds uniting humans to gods will be severed. Aidōs and Nemesis, the two divinities that have remained on earth with the mortals, will leave for Olympos. There will then be a total separation between two races whose existence was originally similar and common.

Moreover, in the Prometheus myth, humans do not have any direct responsibility for what befalls them. They suffer the consequences of a separation they neither wanted nor caused. They are not culprits but victims. Their only wrong is Prometheus's affection for them, or perhaps the secret complicity that unites them with the rebellious nature of the Titan, his spirit of *eris*. In the second story, however, the distance between gods and men varies according to the different races. The breach becomes more or less pronounced, more or less indistinct, according to whether the mortals' conduct partakes in *dikē* or hubris. Humans thus play their part in the stages of a decline that is not necessarily linear, as the case of the heroes shows. There is a risk that in the end the fall will be total, but this acopalyptic apocalyptic end, the threat of which lingers on the horizon of the race of iron, will not occur unless humans fail to heed the poet's solemn warning. In the myth of the races, humans are no longer the passive spectators of a drama that is played out against them and beyond them.

From this point of view, the episode of the heroes, as Goldschmidt clearly saw, no longer appears misplaced but is central.

99

He stresses the story's moral and pedagogical importance. The race of heroes has a double character. First, the historic: it precedes the race of iron so closely that it remains alive in the memory of Hesiod's contemporaries, thanks to the epics.[13] But it also has an equally important mythic character, since it closes the cycle of the races of old, which have now disappeared and exist only in the supernatural beings to which each has given birth.

Just before us, then, existed a race of warrior-heroes dedicated to the exploits of battle and destined to perish in combat, like the previous race. But the heroes, better and more just than the men of bronze, set everything back on course and corrected the errant ways that had separated humans from gods since the age of gold. To be sure, the heroes did not live like the race of gold, in complete proximity with and likeness to the gods and in the happiness of peace and plenty, free from the spirit of strife and warlike confrontation. However, in the heroic age, gods and goddesses still came to mix with mortals and to engender, at the meeting point between the two races, demigods (*hēmitheoi*), whose existence proves that the separation between mortals and immortals was not as unbridgeable then as it is now. During their lives, the heroes were more just and closer to the gods; after their death, they receive from Zeus the privilege from an existence free from all cares and troubles.[14] They become the "blessed," the "fortunate ones" who have regained in the hereafter the form of divine life that reigned in the age of gold, in the time of Kronos, when gods and men had not yet separated. They regain this life, but with two restrictions. First, they do not enjoy this felicity until after death; second, while their posthumous existence recalls that of the gods, they still do not live among or in close proximity to the gods.

These demigods, these *hēmitheoi*, who occupy a pivotal position between the two races, were indeed placed by Zeus at the far ends of the world, in a location so remote that it isolates them from both gods and men. The mortals and immortals, who once intermingled, still coincide in human beings, who are the closest to Hesiod's world since they are adjacent to it in time and, in fact, the noble lines of the race of iron claim to be descended directly from a heroic ancestor, a *hēmitheos*. But they are also the farthest from it, if one considers their posthumous location and status, especially compared to the location and status of the first races, who became daemons and are still present on the earth, where their actions have direct effects on humans.

Many commentators, following Erwin Rohde, have stressed this difference in condition between gold and silver, on the one hand, and bronze and heroes, on the other.

Created by the "immortals who occupied Olympos" when Kronos reigned, the gold and the silver races represent the youth of the human beings who succeeded each other on earth. The first remains young throughout its very long life; it knows no old age. The second lives one hundred years of childhood, dying as soon as it enters adolescence; it knows nothing but childhood. Both live in every way close to the gods, who are "always young" and whose nature excludes both age and death. Surrounded by abundance, they do not know the hard necessity of work and of competition in labor, of the good *eris*; nor do they confront each other in military combat, provoked by the bad *eris*. The men of silver, during the brief moment after they have left their mother's skirts and their childish games, are unable to hold back from excess, but they do not wage war against each other and do not even seem to possess the instruments with which to do so. Having just come into their own after a century of childhood, they display two forms of immaturity and thoughtlessness: injustice in their relationships with each other and impiety with respect to the gods, whom they neglect to worship properly, either because they believe that they are able to do without the gods or because they consider themselves equal to them, perhaps by reason of their proximity. In that sense, they recall Homer's Cyclopes, for whom the earth provides everything of its own accord, without sowing or labor, but who in their ingratitude show neither fear of nor respect for the gods.[15] In his dwelling, where he rules as sole master, each Cyclops lays down justice as he pleases (*themisteuei hekastos*), with no concern for others (*oud' allēlōn alegousi*), believing his strength to be so great that he need not be concerned with the gods or with Zeus (*ou gar Kuklōpes Dios ... alegousin ou de theōn makarōn*). In the land of the Cyclopes, with its evocations of the age of gold, there are neither deliberative assemblies for determining justice in common (*out' agorai boulēphoroi oute themistes*) nor altars to the gods. Everyone is king, but only in and for his own house. Enjoying the same privileges as the men of the race of gold, the men of the race of silver are separated from their predecessors, showing no more respect for each other and the immortals than the Cyclopes for *themis*. They refuse to sacrifice to the blessed (*makares*) in accordance with the *themis* of men. Furious at seeing them disregard the *timē* of the blessed gods (*makares theoi*) and the lords of Olympos, Zeus does away with them.

When the earth has covered over the men of the race of gold, it is Zeus's will that they become "epichthonian daemons" — which means that they live not in the heavens, like the Olympian *theoi*, but on earth. There they watch over "mortal men" and "guard" them as *phulakes*. What does this guarding consist in, and in what way is it exercised? Hesiod sets up an opposition between, on the one hand, the prosperous city, the abundant nature and flourishing people of a just king who is always and in every way respectful of *dikē* (a picture that, in many of its features, evokes the life of the race of gold), and on the other, the calamities of plague and famine that strike an entire population when its rulers think of nothing but hubris and render unethical judgments.[16] Then he addresses the kings — not, as before, his brother Perses — and invites them, too, to meditate on *dikē*. Hesiod warns them that in their decisions on justice and in their royal function, they are closely watched by a myriad of divinities whom Zeus has set among them as guards (*phulakes*):

> "For the immortals are close to us, they mingle
> with men, and are aware of those who by crooked decisions
> break other men, and care nothing for what the gods think of it.
> Upon the prospering earth (*epi chthoni poluboteirē*) there are thirty
> thousand immortal spirits, who keep watch for Zeus and all that men
> do (*phulakes thnētōn anthrōpōn*]). They have an eye on (*phulassousin*)

decrees given and on harsh dealings, and invisible in their dark mist they hover on the whole earth."[17]

How could we not see these immortals who watch over the earth of mortal men (*epi chthoni ... phulakes thnētōn anthrōpōn*), the *daimones epichthonioi phulakes thnētōn anthrōpōn* who, by the will of Zeus, became the men of the race of gold? Since they have been given the task of watching over the correct exercise of the royal function in its twofold aspect — not mistreating others with crooked judgments and respecting the gods — we can better understand why their posthumous status would be granted as a "royal privilege" (*geras basilēion*) and why they would be described as *ploutodotai*, dispensers of wealth: it is indeed the direct justice of the sovereign that brings to his subjects this happy abundance, this flourishing peace, that constitutes for the race of iron the precious reflection of a long-past golden age.

The men of the race of silver follow the race of gold in the first ages of humanity, but what happens to them after they disappear? Like the bad kings addressed by Hesiod — who are guilty of two faults: mistreating one another (*allēlous tribousi*) and not fearing the gods — the men of silver, at the end of their extended childhood, show great excess in relation to one another (*hubrin ... ouk edunanto allēlōn apechein*) and disregard all their duties to the gods. Paired with the race of gold, whose *dikē* it turns into hubris, the race of silver is the only one of the four first races that provokes the wrath of the king of the gods (*choloumenos*). Zeus hides this race (*ekrupse*), just as, in his wrath against the Titan Prometheus (*cholōsamenos*), he hid (*ekrupse, krupse*) from men what had previously allowed them to live in the abundance and happiness of the age of gold. The king of the gods does away with this race as punishment for not giving the blessed immortals the honors (*timai*) due to them, for not offering them the sacrifices that *themis* requires of men. The paradox is that the fate reserved for these impious mortals after their punishment, when the earth has covered them over, nonetheless includes a *timē*. It is a restrictive one, as indicated by the adverb *empēs*, and is inferior by far to the *timē* owed to the blessed gods; it is also inferior (*deuteroi*) to the *timē* granted by Zeus to the race of gold as a royal *geras*. But it is a *timē* nonetheless, which implies that for Hesiod the men of silver, after their death, are in one way or another the object of what must be called a cult. What is the nature of this cult, and to what kind of religious power is it addressed? The answer to this question is all the more difficult in that the text lends itself to several readings. It is certain, in any case, that those belonging to the category of the deceased that is honored by men "are called *makares*, blessed." In the paragraph on the race of silver, Hesiod uses this term twice, once to designate the immortals (*athanatoi*), the gods (*theoi*) who hold Olympos, just as the word *timē* is used both for the honor owed to the *theoi* and for the honor that still accompanies the posthumous status of this second race. However, although *makares* refers in Hesiod to the immortals, the Olympian gods in almost every case, there are two exceptions to this in *Works and Days*. The first has to do with the *nēsoi makarōn*, the Islands of the Blessed, the dwelling place of the demigods, the fortunate (*olbioi*) heroes; the second, concerns the mere mortal whose fields are fertilized by a cloud "heavy with grains," which it scatters from the sky.[18] In these two examples, *makar* refers to a state of felicity, good fortune, and abundance. This state evokes, either constantly (the Islands of the Blessed) or for the year to come (the mortal whose crops will flourish), the existence of the true *makares* and renders certain mortal creatures comparable in that respect to the blessed gods, who know no fatigue, no pain, no care. But the dead of the second race are not only called *makares*. They are also *hupochthonioi*, a term that associates them with the men of gold, described as *epichthonioi*, and opposes them as those beneath the earth are opposed to those on the surface of the earth.

One might therefore be tempted, as Goldschmidt and I were (following a few others), to "divide" the posthumous destinies of the two first races and to see in each one the origin of the powers that, together, form the category of the *daimones*: first, for the race of gold, *daimones* who are characterized as *esthloi*, to mark their higher value, and as *epichthonioi*, since they dwell on the earth;

second, *daimones* who are said to be inferior (*deuteroi*) but whose daemonic quality is connoted by the term *makares* and confirmed by the parallelism *hupochthonioi-epichthonioi*. This interpretation is at least partly consonant with the emendation of line 141 — proposed by Rudolf Peppmüller and adopted by Paul Mazon and Aloisis Rzach — from *thnētoi* (in the manuscripts) to *thnētois*. The passage on the destiny of the men of silver after their race's disappearance would read thus: "And they too are called by men blessed *hupochthonioi*." But if we keep the *thnētoi* of the manuscripts, as other editors (West in particular) do, the meaning changes: they are called *hupochthonioi*, blessed mortals (*makares thnētoi*). Joined to *thnētoi*, the term *makares* no longer describes a state related to that of the *daimones*. On the contrary, it expresses the opposition between the dead of the first race and those of the second. West comments: "Just as *hupochthonioi* answers *epichthonioi*, *thnētoi* answers *daimones*. These are not gods. The word also serves to exclude the divine connotation of *makares*."[19] *Thnētoi* thus assumes a double function: it emphasizes the gap between the race of gold and the race of silver, and it makes explicit the contrast between the *makares thnētoi* and the true *makares*, the *theoi athanatoi*.

This interpretation brings up a number of difficulties. It does not take into account the close links between gold and silver that make them a complementary pair, even in their opposition (*dikē-hubris*). It does not explain how or why, after its disappearance, the race of silver — like the race preceding it — becomes the object of a *timē*, of a cult. If Hesiod's intention was to deny the race of silver any post mortem access to divine status — or, at any rate, to near-divine (that is, daemonic) status — why apply to it the qualifier *makares*, which, even if specified as *thnētoi*, cannot fail to evoke the *makares theoi* of the preceding lines? Finally, if they are not heroes, what can the *makares thnētoi* be, if not a kind of *daimones*? West recognizes that in tragedy *makaritēs* and *makarios* are associated with the status of *daimōn*, and that the expression *makares thnētoi* can refer to a condition at once mortal and divine, similar to that of the Dioscuri, who, even "underneath the earth," are given a *timē*, like the gods.[20] At the end of Euripides's *Rhesos*, the Muse, mother of the king of the Thracians, slain by the sword of Odysseus, proclaims the fate awaiting her son in the afterlife. He will not go down into the depths of Hades like an ordinary dead man. "Hidden" in the hollow of the earth, he will remain there, alive, "both man and god, *anthrōpodaimōn*."[21] Isocrates uses an analogous expression when he refers to the mortal who, through his superiority in all domains and his complete happiness, his *eudaimonia*, revealed himself at the end of his life to be *makaristotatos*, most happy: he is like a god among men and can be called *daimōn thnētos*.[22] As Gregory Nagy has pointed out, Hesiod himself mentions a mortal daemon in the *Theogony*.[23] Phaeton, a man altogether like the gods, is taken by Aphrodite after his death to be the underground guardian (*nēopolos muchios*) of her temple.[24] This means that an underground cave, a *muchos*, in the sacred dwelling of the goddess has been set aside as a tomb for this mortal, who has now become a *dios daimōn*, a divine daemon.[25]

Although *thnētoi*, instead of *thnētois*, is retained in line 141, this does not appear to undermine the hypothesis that the men of the race of silver were promoted to the rank of daemons after death. Even though their faults separate them from the immortals by leading them to disregard the proper *timē* that they owe, they are close to the gods during their lives, like their predecessors in the race of gold, and they receive their proper share in the dividing up of honors; that is, they receive the honors due to daemons of inferior rank who live and act underground. They do not intervene everywhere, out in the open, invisible in the midst of mortals, like the epichthonian daemons charged by Zeus to watch over the living to ensure that the kings' *dikai* conforms with his sovereign justice. Intermediate between gods and men, auxiliaries of Zeus, residing not in the heavens like the *theoi* but here below, mixing with this race of ephemeral creatures whom they preceded on earth, Hesiod associates the daemons with the powers venerated in connection with burial chambers such as the Mycenaean tombs that became the object of a cult in the eighth century, or like the cave in *Lebadeia* used for consultations with Trophonios.

It may be very difficult to move from Hesiod's text to actual religious practices by directly linking the *daimones epichthonioi* and the *makares hupochthonioi* to very specific contemporary cults (and it is here that Goldschmidt's thesis, if taken literally, presents difficulties). But we need not depart from the text to say that, in the case of the races of gold and silver, Hesiod clearly indicated that these first mortal humans, who still lived in proximity with the gods — although the gods had begun to depart, because of the humans' hubris — became, after death, sacred beings distinct from the gods but, like them, objects of worship and of cults.

It is a different matter for the next two races, both of which were created by Zeus. The men of bronze are not punished by the king of the gods. Despite their hubris, there is no allusion in their case to impiety or a refusal to sacrifice to the immortals. Thinking of nothing but the work of Ares, they die as they have lived, waging war. Their race disappears when the combat ceases, and for the same reason: no more combatants. They massacre each other, they perish "brought down by their own arms"; they leave the sunlight and go en masse to the damp dwelling of Hades. When the earth covers them, they vanish like a puff of smoke in the mist of the land of the dead. In this sense, their posthumous status is related to that of ordinary men. This raises a question: In evoking the destiny of the race of bronze, did Hesiod have in mind the practices of funerary cults? He was certainly not thinking of this in any direct way. He says nothing whatsoever about a *timē* paid to them, contrary to what he indicates for the previous pair of races; moreover, in calling them *nōnumnoi*, "nameless," he makes any kind of commemorative celebration for them on the part of the living impossible. The anonymity that engulfs the men of bronze, however terrifying they may have been, and their disappearance into the depths of Hades, leaving no trace or memory in this world, establish a clear opposition between them and the race that follows, with whom they are closely associated. Like their predecessors, the heroes perish by killing each other in deadly combat. But since they are more just and more courageous, their name and their glory are sung indefinitely by the poets, and they remain forever present in men's memory. Can we speak in their case of a *timē* rendered to them by men, and could Hesiod's intention be to refer precisely to the hero cults? Goldschmidt's response is affirmative. For him, as for Marie Delcourt, whom he quotes, "if Hesiod calls the heroes *demigods*, this is because they received in his time semidivine honors."[26] I argued the contrary when I wrote: "Neither in Homer nor in Hesiod is there evidence of a cult of heroes comparable to the one that appeared in an organized form within the framework of the official state religion."[27] This was a rapid and summary judgment, which was rendered more specific and nuanced in a long note, with whose terms and, especially, conclusions Goldschmidt was in "complete agreement." I will attempt to be more explicit now. I expressed reservations on two different levels, which must be clearly distinguished: that of the text, in its specific logic, and that of the hero cult, in its birth and development.

Concerning the text, we must begin by saying a word about Homer. It is clear that in the *Iliad* and the *Odyssey*, the term "hero" does not have any cultic signification: it refers to a prince or a simple fighter. However, contrary to what I believed, this does not mean that when the poems were composed no hero-type cult — that is, a cult practiced by a group of humans at the tomb of a figure who had lived in times long past — existed yet. Recent archaeological discoveries have shown that in the second half of the eighth century in many regions of mainland Greece, a rapid development occurred in which Mycenaean tombs that had been ignored came to be used again for religious purposes.[28] Considered the tombs of legendary figures made famous by the epic tradition, these monuments were the objects of a consistent funerary cult distinct from the rituals carried out for the dead by close relatives within the sphere of domestic life. Several passages in the *Iliad* that mention tombs of men from the past, even if they do not explicitly evoke a cult, can only be understood in relation to this practice.[29] This is also true for the tomb (*tumbos, sēma, stēlē*) of Ilos, the eponymous hero of Ilion. Located in the plain outside the city walls, it served as the site of rallying and counsel (*boulē*) for the Trojan leaders who had a voice in the council (*boulēpheoroi*), a function that foreshadows the tombs of heroes in the *agora* in the age of the classical *polis*. The funerary monument raised by the work of their hands "to godlike (*theîos*) Ilos" assumes this "pre-political" role, in that it covers the mortal remains of a *palaios dēmogerōn*, of an old man of the people from times long past.[30]

The difference between the heroes depicted in the Homeric epic and those worshipped by the emerging cult can be described as a change of temporal perspective. To celebrate their exploits, the epic poet places himself in the time of the heroes and transports his listeners to that time; he inserts himself into the age in which they lived, becoming the contemporary of men who gloriously fought beneath the walls of Thebes and on the shores of Troy. On the contrary, for those who honor them, the heroes of the cult are associated with a distant, ancient past; they belong to another age and represent a humanity different from that of the mortals who pay homage to them. They are "the divine race of heroes" who are now long gone and whose only vestiges still visible in this world are their tombs. This second perspective emerges, very fleetingly, in the text of the *Iliad*. The expression *hēmitheōn genos andrōn*, the race (or generation) of demigod men, used in reference to the heroes, occurs only once in the entire poem.[31] It is found in a passage whose meaning and function have been persuasively explicated by Gregory Nagy.[32] These few verses bring the poet out of the time of his story and place him at a distance from the heroic age in which the events he narrates unfolded. Opening the perspective of a future still to come, when the actions that provide the material for his song are visible in the distance, the bard projects himself for a moment into a time when Troy has been conquered and destroyed, when the wall the Greeks constructed to defend their ships has disappeared, wiped out by the waves: the fighters in both camps have long ceased being the living men among whom the Muse's knowledge places us. The plain that provided the theater of war shows no trace of the great deeds related by the song. At this point, the text somehow escapes from its own temporality, and rather than calling the

109

actors of the story "heroes," as it usually does, it speaks of them as "the race of demigod men."

What about Hesiod's text? The men of the fourth race "were taken in evil war and painful fighting," some beneath the walls of Thebes, others at Troy, beyond the sea. These are clearly the heroes of the epic tradition. There is no mention of a *timē*, no reference to any vestiges or tombs where a cult would be offered to them. There are two distinct categories of heroes. Some of them (*tous men*), Hesiod writes, were "hidden by the end of death (*thanatou telos*)," which relates them to the men of bronze, who are gripped by black death (*melas thanatos*); the others (*toīs de*) received from Zeus a life (*bioton* as contrasted with *thanatos*), and a dwelling place said to be "apart from humankind," in a separate world – that is, on the Islands of the Blessed, where they find, as it were, another age of gold.[33] But one characteristic of their condition, according to the text, is that it has no connection with the world of the mortals of the race of iron, the present humanity to which Hesiod belongs. In the posthumous destiny of the heroes, an elect group is given the privilege – through an exceptional favor bestowed by Zeus – of being transported from this world into a blessed life beyond. But this destiny, like that of the men of bronze, is nonetheless opposed to the condition enjoyed by the dead of the first two races, who are promoted to the rank of daemons and, as such, receive on this earth the honors owed to them by the mortals with whom they continue in some way to mingle. There does not, then, seem to be any direct and specific reference to a hero-cult in the text. However, it is true that when Hesiod mentions "the divine race of hero-men called demigods," he does not envisage the members of this race as the epic poems do. In a way that is much more radical than Homer's single passage cited a moment ago, Hesiod distances himself from the heroic age. He situates himself in a present that casts the entire race of its predecessors back to a time different from his own, a past that has been destroyed. To speak of the epic heroes, Hesiod adopts the temporal perspective corresponding to that of the hero cult: the heroes are presented as men of another time, when gods and mortals could still come together because they were not yet separated the way they are now.

The text's purpose and logic remain distinct from the realities of religious practice. It does not coincide exactly with these realities, even if they help define the religious framework within which the story of the races must be situated in order to clarify its intentions. Between 750 and 650 BCE, a religious practice emerged in which a human, mortal figure who had lived in distant times was venerated at a tomb from the Mycenaean age; whatever the reasons may have been for this practice and the forms it originally took, which were perhaps purely local or even familial, the practice was manifestly meant to engage the relationships between mortals and immortals, the distance between men and gods. Given that certain mortals who lived in a time other than our own were the objects of a permanent and regularly practiced cult, an entire series of questions arises: What justified their promotion? What was their role? What place did they occupy in the economy of supernatural powers? How can we situate them in relation to the immortal gods, on the one hand, and the ordinary dead, on the other? These questions were all the more acute in that the religious practices, still somewhat fluid and unfixed, seem not to have clearly responded to them. Goldschmidt refers to inscriptions such as those at Dodona, which present the series of gods, heroes, and daemons — but these inscriptions are from no earlier than the fourth century. Some later indications suggest that the division of the supernatural powers into these three categories can be attributed to the Pythagoreans and to Thales, but this would lead to a past no more distant than the sixth century. This classification is certainly not a gratuitous invention on Hesiod's part. All the terms he attributes to the various past races were already in use, but their technical sense and their cultic specificity are not well established. In Hesiod, the daemons of the races of gold and silver take on functions quite similar to those assumed in the rituals associated with heroic figures — and this is not surprising given that in the religious practice of the classical period, generally speaking, the daemons were not thought of as divinized dead men. Hesiod's systematic construction maintains a certain distance from the popular traditions of the religion of his time, while also responding quite closely to the new questions being raised by the emergence of a hero cult. This has led the well informed Gregory Nagy to argue that the dead of the first two races correspond — under the name *daimones* — to the twofold aspect of the heroes *in the cult*, while those of the next two races correspond to the twofold (and equally contrasting) aspect of the heroes *in the epic*.[34]

In the long note I referred to a moment ago, I remarked that "in Homer the term *hērōs* has no precise religious significance" and that in "Hesiod, the term appears for the first time with a religious meaning in the context of the classification of supernatural powers. But there is still no question of a *timē*, a cult, or at least a public cult extending beyond the family circle, within which rituals connected with honoring the dead normally remain." And I observed that, here too,

> Hesiod seems situated between the Homeric world and the world of the *polis*. From a theological point of view, he truly seems to be a precursor, given his terminology and his classification of divine beings into gods, daemons, the dead, and heroes. This was apparently the opinion of Plato (*Cratylus*, 397eff.) and of Plutarch (*Moralia*, 415B); for Homer neither classes the heroes in a religious category nor distinguishes clearly between the *theoi* and the *daimones*. Plutarch is therefore quite correct when he writes that Hesiod was the first to distinguish between the two kinds: *katharōs kai diōrismenōs*.[35]

Quoting these remarks, Goldschmidt writes: "Our agreement here is complete, and I am pleased to see that it is placed under the sign of the sage of Chaironeia."[36] In this agreement, my debt to my friend is great, and owing it to him adds to the joy of finding ourselves together again, at the end of our debate, under the great shadow of Plutarch.

PART TWO
Mythical Aspects of
Memory and Time

Chapter Four

Mythic Aspects of Memory

In an issue of the *Journal de Psychologie* devoted to the history of man's elaboration of various conceptions of time, Ignace Meyerson pointed out that memory, insofar as it can be distinguished from habit, was invented only with difficulty; it is the result of man's progressive conquest of his individual past, just as history represents the social group's conquest of its collective past.[1] The conditions that made this discovery possible in the protohistoric period and the forms that memory originally took are problems beyond the scope of scientific investigation. On the other hand, evidence does exist concerning the place, orientation, and role of memory in ancient societies for the psychologist who investigates the stages of its historical development. The documentary evidence that serves as the basis for this study concerns the deification of memory and the elaboration of a vast mythology concerning remembrance in archaic Greece. At issue here are religious representations. They are not at all gratuitous. I believe they are directly concerned with the history of memory. At different periods and in different cultures, there are close links between the techniques for mental recall, the inner organization of the function of memory, the place it occupies in the system of the ego, and the ways men picture memory to themselves.

The Greek pantheon includes a deity who bears the name of a psychological function: Mnēmosynē (memory). No doubt this is not the only example of such a deity. Greek gods often represent passions and feelings, such as Ērōs, Aidōs, and Phobos; mental attitudes, such as Pistis; intellectual qualities, such as Mētis; and faults or aberrations of the mind, such as Atē and Lyssa.[2] Many phenomena that we would call psychological can thus be the objects of cults. In the context of religious thought, they take the form of sacred forces that are greater than man and beyond his power, even when he experiences them within himself. However, Mnēmosynē seems to be a special case. Memory is a very complicated function related to important psychological categories, such as time and identity. It brings into play a whole collection of complex mental operations that can be mastered only with effort, training, and exercise. The power of recall is, as we have pointed out, a conquest. The sacralization of Mnēmosynē indicates its value in a civilization whose traditions were entirely oral, as was the case with Greece between the twelfth and the eighth century BCE, before the spread of writing.[3] We must define the nature of this memory that the Greeks made into a deity. In what domain, by what means, and in what form does the power of recall, presided over by Mnēmosynē, operate? Toward what events and what truth is it oriented? To what extent is it aimed at knowledge of the past and the construction of a temporal perspective? We have no evidence apart from the mythical accounts. But through their information about Mnēmosynē, the activities she patronizes, and her attributes and powers, we may hope to discern some of the features of this archaic form of memory and to understand certain aspects of the way it functions.

Mnēmosynē is a Titan goddess, the sister of Kronos and Okeanos; she is the mother of the Muses, whose chorus she leads and with whom she is sometimes confused, and presides over the poetic function.[4] It was self-evident to the Greeks that this function required some supernatural intervention. Poetry represents one of the typical forms of divine possession and madness, the state of "enthusiasm" in the etymological sense of the word. The poet, through being possessed by the Muses, is the interpreter of

Mnēmosynē, just as the prophet, through being inspired by Apollo, is the interpreter of that god.[5] Moreover, as has often been pointed out, there are affinities and even a reciprocal influence between prophecy and oral poetry as it is practiced in the archaic period among the brotherhoods of the bards, singers, and musicians.[6] The bard and the diviner share the same gift of "second sight," a privilege for which they have had to pay with their vision. They are blind in the light of day, but they can see what is invisible. The god who inspires them shows them, in a kind of revelation, the truth that eludes the sight of men. This double vision relates in particular to the parts of time that are inaccessible to mortal creatures, namely, what happened in bygone days and what is yet to come. The knowledge or wisdom, *sophia*, that Mnēmosynē dispenses to her chosen ones is an omniscience of the divinatory type.[7] The expression Homer uses to describe the art of the diviner Calchas is applied in Hesiod to Mnēmosynē: she knows — and she sings of — "all that has been, all that is, and all that is to be."[8] But unlike the diviner, who usually has to solve problems concerned with the future, the poet is almost exclusively concerned with the past. Not his own personal past, or even the past in general, as if it were an empty framework quite independent of the events that take place within it, but rather "ancient times," with all their own particular content and quality; for example, the heroic age, or, even further back, the primeval age or the time of origins.

The poet has an immediate experience of these bygone days. He knows the past because he has the power to be present in the past. To remember, to know, and to see are all interchangeable terms. A commonplace in the poetic tradition is the contrast between the knowledge of the ordinary man (knowing by hearsay, based on information provided by others and reported speech) and the knowledge of the inspired, which, like that of the gods, is a direct, personal vision.[9] Memory transports the poet into the midst of ancient events, back into their own time.[10] The organization of time in his account simply reproduces the sequence of events at which he is somehow present, in the order in which they occurred, from the beginning.[11]

All these features defining the inspiration by the Muses — direct presence in the past, immediate revelation, a gift of the gods — in no way obviate the need for the poet to undergo a difficult training, a kind of apprenticeship, for his state of second sight. Nor does the use of improvisation in the course of the song preclude his fidelity to a poetic tradition preserved from one generation to the next. On the contrary, the rules of oral composition insist that the bard have at his command not only a whole body of themes and tales but also a technique of formulaic diction that comes to him ready-made and involves the use of traditional expressions, predetermined combinations of words, and established rules of versification.[12] We do not know how the apprentice was trained to master this poetic language in the brotherhoods of bards.[13] Presumably a large part of the training involved exercises in memorization and, in particular, the recitation of extremely long passages learned by heart.[14] There is an indication of this in Homer. An invocation of the muse or Muses (apart from the instances where, as expected, it appears at the beginning of a book) may introduce one of those interminable lists of names of men, places, or peoples that are known as catalogs. Thus, in the second book of the *Iliad*, with the catalog of ships is given a veritable inventory of the Greek army, listing the names of the leaders, the divisions under their command, their places of origin, and the number of their ships. The list is two hundred sixty-five lines long. It opens with the following invocation: "Now tell me, you Muses who have dwellings on Olympos — for you are goddesses and are present and know all things, but we hear only a rumor and know nothing — who were the leaders and the lords of the Danaans."[15] The catalog of the ships is immediately followed by the catalog of the best Greek warriors and horses, which opens with a fresh invocation of the Muses and is almost immediately followed by the catalog of the Trojan army. The whole passage accounts for about half of Book Two, about four hundred lines in all, composed almost exclusively of a sequence of proper names; reciting this would require a rigorously trained memory.

Such collections of names may seem boring. But the taste for them shown by Homer, and even more by Hesiod, indicates that their role is of the first importance. Through them, the repertoire of knowledge and familiar references enabling a social group to piece its past together is established and transmitted. They constitute the archives of a society that has no writing. These archives are purely legendary: they serve no administrative needs, are not intended to glorify kings, and are not driven by historical concerns.[16] Their purpose is to set up an order in the world of the gods and heroes, and to draw up as accurate and complete as possible a record of their names. In these collections of names — the list of human and divine agents and the details of their families, their countries, their genealogies, and their hierarchy — the various traditional legends are codified and the subject matter of the mythical stories is organized and classified.

This concern for exact classification and complete enumeration gives ancient poetry a correctness like that of ritual, even when its primary intention is to entertain, as is the case with Homer. Herodotus could later justifiably maintain that it was in the poems of Homer and Hesiod that the crowd of hitherto anonymous Greek gods were distinguished, defined, and named.[17] This ordering of the religious world is closely related to the poet's attempts to determine "origins." In Homer, it is simply a question of fixing the genealogies of men and gods, of specifying the origins of peoples and royal families, and of establishing the etymologies of certain proper names and the *aition* of the epithets attached to cults.[18] In Hesiod, this inquiry into origins takes on a truly religious aspect and gives on the poet's work the character of a sacred message. When the daughters of Mnēmosynē present him with the rod of wisdom, the *skeptron* cut from a laurel tree, they teach him "the Truth."[19] They also teach him the "divine song" with which they charm Zeus and which tells of the beginning of all things. The Muses do indeed sing, starting at the beginning — *ex archēs* — of the first appearance of the world, the genesis of the gods, the birth of humanity.[20] The past thus revealed represents much more than the time prior to the present: it is its very source. By going back to this past, the process of recall seeks not to situate events within a temporal framework but to reach the very foundation of being, to discover what lies at the origin, the primeval reality from which the cosmos emerged and which makes it possible to understand the process of becoming as a whole.

This genesis of the world recounted by the Muses involves a before and an after, but it does not unfold over a homogeneous period, in a single time scale. This past is punctuated not by any chronology but by genealogies. Time is included within the relations of filiation. Each generation, each race (*genos*) has its own time, its own age, the durations, flow, and even orientation of which may be different in every respect from those of all the others.[21] The past is stratified into a sequence of races. These races make up ancient time, but they still exist, and some of them are more real than present-day life and the contemporary race of humans.[22] Primeval realities such as Gaia and Ouranos, which were contemporaneous with the time of origins, remain the unshakable foundation for the world of today. The powers of disorder, the Titans, the offspring of Ouranos, and the monsters vanquished by Zeus continue to live and move far beneath the earth, in the night of the underworld.[23] All the ancient races of men that gave their names to bygone times — from the age of gold under the reign of Kronos, through the ages of silver and bronze, to the age of the heroes — are still present to those who know how to see them. They have taken the form of spirits skimming over the surface of the earth, or subterranean daemons, or the inhabitants of the Islands of the Blessed, beyond Okeanos's rim.[24] The Olympians who succeeded Kronos and whose reign established the order of this world are also forever present and forever alive, as their title indicates.[25] Ever since their birth, they have lived in a time that knows neither aging nor death. The vitality of their race extends and will continue to extend throughout all ages, with all the energy of an undying youth.

So it cannot be said that the evocation of the "past" makes what is no longer live again, giving it, for us, the illusion of existence. Never for a moment does the journey back in time make us leave contemporary realities. In moving away from the present, we are only separating from the visible world. We step outside our own human universe and discover behind it other regions of being, other cosmic levels normally inaccessible to us. Beneath are the infernal world and all its inhabitants; above is the world of Olympian gods. The past is an integral part of the cosmos. To explore it is to discover what is hidden in the depths of being. History as sung by Mnēmosynē is a deciphering of the invisible, a geography of the supernatural.

What, then, is the function of memory? It does not reconstruct time, nor does it abolish it. By removing the barrier that separates the present from the past, it creates a bridge from the world of the living to the beyond, to which everything that leaves the light of day must return. It brings about an "evocation" of the past comparable to that effected for the dead by Homer's ritual of the *ekklēsis*.[26] This is a summons, for one brief moment, of one of the dead out of the underworld and back into the world of the living and the light of day; it is also comparable to the journey mimicked in certain oracular consultations: the descent of a living person into the underworld for the purpose of finding out — and seeing — what he wants to know. The privilege that Mnēmosynē confers on the bard is the possibility of contacting the other world, of entering and returning from it freely. The past is seen as a dimension of the beyond.

By communicating the secret of origins to Hesiod, the Muses are explaining a mystery to him. In a body of poetry whose inspiration is moral and religious, *anamnēsis*, remembering, appears to be in itself a kind of initiation. The chosen one who benefits from it is transformed by it. As the "truth" of becoming — that is, the definitive establishment of divine and cosmic order, and the progressive disorder among mortal creatures — is unveiled before his eyes, the poet's vision of the ancient times liberates him, to a certain extent, from the evils that beset contemporary humanity, the race of iron.[27] It is as if memory brings him a transmutation of his own temporal experience. Through the contact it establishes with the first ages, the divine *aiōn*, primeval time, it enables him to

121

escape from the time of the fifth race, so fraught with fatigue, wretchedness, and anxiety.[28] For Hesiod, Mnēmosynē, she who makes one remember, is also she who erases the memory of evils, the *lēsmosunē kakōn*.[29] The necessary counterpart to recollection of the past is the "forgetting" of present time.

It is therefore not surprising that at the oracle of Lebadeia, where a descent into Hades was enacted in the cavern of Trophonios, Lēthē, forgetfulness, was associated with Mnēmosynē, and the two formed a pair of complementary religious powers.[30] Before venturing into the mouth of hell, the person consulting the oracle, having already undergone rites of purification, was taken to two springs, named Lēthē and Mnēmosynē. He drank from the first, immediately forgot everything about his human life, and, like a dead man, entered the realm of Night. The water of the second spring enabled him to remember all that he had seen and heard in the other world. When he returned, he was no longer restricted to knowledge of the present moment: contact with the beyond had revealed both past and future to him.

Oblivion is thus a water of death. Without drinking it, that is to say, without losing both remembrance and consciousness, no one can enter the kingdom of the shades. In contrast, memory is a source of immortality, the *athanatos pēgē* mentioned in certain funerary inscriptions, which ensures the deceased's survival in the beyond.[31] Precisely because death is defined as the realm of oblivion, the *Lēthēs pedion*, he who retains his memory in Hades transcends the mortal condition.[32] For him there is no longer any opposition or barrier between life and death. He can move freely from one world to the other. In this respect, he resembles Aithalides, the son of Hermes, who was granted by his father "a constant memory" to make him immortal: "Even when he crossed Acheron, oblivion did not submerge his soul; and although he inhabits now the abode of the shades, and now the light of the sun, he always retains the memory of what he has seen."[33] In Aithalides's case, this privilege of nondeath takes on a particular significance, which we shall have to study in more detail in connection with the belief in metempsychosis. But in a more ancient tradition, the same privilege already belongs to all those whose memory is able to discern, far beyond the present, what is buried deep in the past and what is preparing, in secret, to come to pass in the future. Such people include diviners like Teiresias and Amphiaraos.[34] Amid the wavering shades of Hades, they remain animate and lucid and have forgotten nothing of their earthly life, just as they have succeeded here in acquiring remembrance of the invisible times that belong to the other world.

The Mnēmosynē of the Lebadeia ritual is still related in many ways to the goddess who presides over poetic inspiration in Hesiod. As the mother of the Muses, she reveals "what has been and what will be." But in her association with Lēthē, she is an infernal power, operating on the threshold of the afterlife. The beyond to which she gives the initiate access is identified with the world of the dead.[35]

In a series of documents of varying date, origin, and significance — but all equally "mystical" in orientation — the pair memory-forgetting appears once again, this time at the center of a doctrine concerning the reincarnation of souls. In the context of these eschatological myths, Mnēmosynē has undergone a transformation. She is no longer the one who sings of the primeval past and the genesis of the cosmos. Now she is the power on whom souls depend for their destiny after death, and as such she is connected with the mythical history of individuals and with the transformations that occur in their successive incarnations. By the same token, what she brings to mortal creatures is no longer the secret of origins but the means to reach the end of time and to put an end to the cycle of generations.

This change reflects a whole order of new preoccupations and needs that are absent from the poetry of Homer and Hesiod. It corresponds to a quest for salvation. And in the context of current thought pursued here, this quest goes hand in hand with an interest (investigated more or less philosophically) in the problems of time and the soul.

The transposition of Mnēmosynē from cosmology to eschatology

alters the whole balance of the myths of memory. Even if they
appear to retain the old themes and symbols, the meanings of
these themes and symbols undergo profound changes. Images that
in traditional descriptions were connected with Hades — the des-
olate region, the icy abode, the kingdom of the shades, the world
of oblivion — are now applied to earthly life, which is seen as a
place of trial and punishment.[36] The soul's exile no longer occurs
when it leaves a man deprived of life and flies away beneath the
earth, a phantom devoid of strength and consciousness. Its exile
occurs, on the contrary, when it returns to earth to join the body.
The soul is more "lucid" and less "forgetful" to the extent that it
has been able to free itself from this union.[37] The waters of Lēthē
no longer receive on the threshold of Hades those who, moving
from life to death, will soon forget the light of the sun in the
infernal world. Now they affect those who are returning to earth
for a new incarnation, erasing the memory of the celestial world
and its realities, with which the soul is more closely related. The
water of oblivion is now the symbol not of death but of a return
to life and to existence in time. The soul that has not abstained
from drinking these waters, "being satiated with oblivion and
wickedness," is once again thrust upon this earth, where the
inflexible law of becoming holds sway.[38] It believes that with birth
it is entering a life that will come to an end with death. But in the
realm of time there is no true beginning or end. The soul simply
starts the same cycle of trials all over again, indefinitely. And,
because it forgets the preceding phases every time, it can never
come to the end, the telos — a word meaning the end of a period
not only in the temporal sense but also in a religious sense, the
initiation that consecrates the entry to a new form of existence of
anyone who has "completed" a phase of his life.[39]

Swept along in the cycle of becoming, the kuklos geneseōs,
turning in the "circle of necessity," chained to the "wheel of birth
and death," the life of those whose souls alternate between the
bodies of men, plants, and animals, represent the earthly incarnation of the legendary tormented in the infernal regions: Sisyphos
forever pushing his rock up the mountain, only to watch it roll

back down every time; Oknos plaiting a rope out of reeds while a she-donkey constantly nibbles it away; the Danaides striving in vain to fill a leaking barrel with water that runs away through a sieve riddled with holes — the sieve that Plato compares to the soul of the unfortunates who, through their forgetfulness, are incapable of stopping the contents from leaking away.[40]

In the inscriptions on the gold strips the deceased carry to guide them through the winding paths of the beyond, Lēthē appears on the left side of the crossroads, as the spring that they must not approach if they desire to "escape from the sad cycle of griefs" forever, that is, to escape reincarnation and to be changed from men into gods.[41] The same themes and images appear in Plato's *Republic*: the parched souls must avoid drinking from the river of the plain of Lēthē "those waters that no receptacle can possibly retain," which, in bringing them oblivion, return them to the process of generation.[42] In Plato, this oblivion, the essential flaw in a soul, its peculiar illness, is none other than ignorance. In the waters of Lēthē, souls forget the eternal truths that they were able to contemplate before returning to earth and that *anamnēsis* will enable them to rediscover by restoring them to their true nature.

In Plato, then, the myths of memory are integrated into a general theory of knowledge. But the link between these myths and the belief in reincarnation that subsists even in his philosophy suggests that originally they must have had a more direct association with the transformations of the soul in the course of its previous existences.[43] A comparison between the various texts that reveal traces of these legends confirms this hypothesis.

In the tablets from Petelia and Eleutherna, the soul that has managed to avoid Lēthē and take the correct road, the one on the right, comes upon a spring in the lake of Mnēmosynē. The soul proclaims its purity and its heavenly origins and asks the guardians if it can quench its thirst: " Give me quickly the cold water flowing forth from the Lake of Memory. And of themselves they will give thee to drink from the holy well-spring, and thereafter among the other heroes thou shalt have lordship."[44] In the text of the tablets found at Thurium, the soul who takes the road on the right and who similarly proclaims itself to be pure and of the heavenly race is hailed as the soul who, "having suffered the punishment," "having paid the price for unjust acts," has escaped the sad cycle of griefs: "You will be a god and no longer a mortal. . . . Once a man, you have become a god."[45]

This idea that in order to rise in the scale of beings and eventually attain the condition of heroes and gods, the soul must, in the course of its life, purify itself through expiation, paying the price for its faults, is more explicit in certain texts by Pindar and Empedocles.[46] These texts speak of "ancient errors," of the evil that the soul may have committed at other times in its previous existences.[47] According to Pindar, the souls of those "who have paid the ransom for an ancient stain" give birth, in their last incarnation, to kings, victors in the games, or "sages."[48] These are three types of "divine men" who will be honored as heroes after their deaths.[49] For Empedocles, a soul that has been sullied by bloodshed or treachery "wanders from the blessed ones for three times countless years, being born throughout the time as all kinds of mortal forms."[50] When this cycle of expiation is completed, they become incarnate in men whose knowledge and function make them into daemonic figures: "In the end they have become prophets, poets, doctors, and leaders of men on earth. They are then reborn amid the ranks of the gods. . . . They share the abode of the other immortals and, free from human anxieties, they elude destiny and destruction."[51] The *magus* Empedocles is himself at once a diviner, poet, doctor, and leader of men. Thus he describes himself as a *theios anēr*, already freed from the mortal condition: "I am delivered, forever, from death, an immortal god revered by all."[52] In contrast to those he describes as "men of short destiny," because the duration of a life spanned by birth and death makes up the whole of human existence for them, the sage, once he has reached understanding of all things, knows that in truth there is neither beginning nor end for mortal creatures, only cycles of metamorphoses.[53] Empedocles himself still remembers all this past, which others forget at each rebirth: "Now a wanderer exiled from the divine abode, . . . at other times I have already been a boy and a girl, a bush and a bird, and a dumb fish in the sea."[54]

This recollection of previous lives, with all their faults and defilements, does more than simply justify the rules of the ascetic life, which, according to the doctrine of the *Purifications*, ensure the soul's salvation and its escape from the cycle of births. The very effort involved in remembering is itself a "purification," an ascetic discipline. It constitutes a truly spiritual exercise, and there is one indication in Empedocles that allows us to glimpse the form it took and the scope of its effect. This man who proclaims himself a god among mortals pays homage to the exceptional wisdom of one of his predecessors, a man whose thought, instead of confining itself to the present existence, "encompasses with ease things that are met with in ten, or twenty, lives of men."[55] This is most probably an allusion to Pythagoras, whose sequence of previous lives was legendary.[56] The story went that Pythagoras could remember having lived during the Trojan War, in the person of Euphorbos, who was killed by Menelaus. The list of his previous incarnations also included Aithalides, mentioned above, who retained an unwavering memory through life and death. It was claimed that, starting from Aithalides, the gift of *anamnēsis* had been passed on to all the members of the series, right down to Pythagoras.[57] These accounts should be set alongside the regular "memory exercises" of the Pythagorean life.[58] The requirement that all the members of the fraternity recall in the evening all the events of the day had more than the moral value of an examination of conscience. The effort of remembering, if undertaken in an attempt to follow the example of the sect's founder and encompass the soul's story throughout ten or even twenty different lives, would make it possible for the person remembering to learn who he was and to know his own *psuchē*— the daemon that has become incarnate in us.[59] According to Proclus, the *anamnēsis* of previous lives constitutes a purification of the soul: to recapture the whole web of its past lives, the soul must liberate itself from the body that fetters it to the present.[60] Empedocles describes this ascetic exercise of memory as "a tension between all the forces of the mind," and Plato, following what he calls "a longstanding tradition," describes it as a concentration of the soul, which, as it emerges from every part of the body, manages to gather itself together and concentrate itself, pure and unadulterated, totally separate from the body with which it used to be fused.[61] Empedocles's thought and that of Plato are not directly comparable. But Empedocles is the direct continuation of a tradition that Plato transposes to the level of philosophy: this is the very ancient tradition of the magi, the memory of which has come down through Pythagoreanism. Louis Gernet has pointed out that to indicate "mind," Empedocles uses the old term *prapides*, one of those words that refer to both an organ of the body and a "psychic" activity, without distinguishing very clearly between them.[62] The literal meaning of *prapides* is "diaphragm," whose "tension" regulates or even stops respiration. We are familiar with the links in archaic Greek thought between the soul and breath. Plato's descriptions of the soul collecting itself together from every part of the body recall the belief — which, according to Aristotle, was shared by the Orphics — that the soul is dispersed throughout the body during respiration, carried on the winds.[63] Tension of the *prapides*, concentration of the *psuchē*'s breath: these spiritual exercises in recollection might in ancient times have been among the techniques for controlling breathing that were supposed to allow the soul to concentrate itself in order to escape from the body and journey to the beyond. According to legend, these are precisely the powers that are attributed to the magi. Their souls depart from their bodies and reenter at will, leaving them — sometimes for many years — lying breathless and lifeless in a kind of cataleptic trance.[64] The soul returns from such travels in the other world enriched with prophetic knowledge. In a case like that of Epimenides, this power of divination is entirely "retrospective."[65] It concerns errors committed in ancient times that have remained unknown, which it reveals, washing away defilement by the appropriate rites of purification.

The similarity between Epimenides's ecstasy of recollection and the *anamnēsis* of the previous lives of Pythagoreanism seems all the more striking in that the figure of the purificatory diviner is already characterized in his private life by his ascetic discipline. The shift from the shamanist techniques cultivated by the magi to spiritual exercises of memory takes place, within a sect preoccupied with salvation, when the old idea of a reciprocal exchange between the dead and the living is redefined in the new form of a theory of palingenesis. This doctrine according to which *anamnēsis* is a matter of the individual history of souls gives the effort involved in recollection a moral and metaphysical significance that it did not previously possess. By recovering the memory of the whole series of his past existences and of the faults he may have committed in them, man can pay the full price of his injustices and thereby end the cycle of his individual destiny. His current life then becomes the last link, the one that makes it possible for the chain of incarnations to be definitively completed. Once it has atoned for everything, the soul, restored to its original purity, can at last escape from the cycle of births, leaving generation and death behind it, and gain access to the form of unchanging and permanent existence that is the prerogative of the gods.

In Pythagoreanism, *anamnēsis* represents the full development of what was only suggested in Hesiod: an initiation into a new state and a radical transformation of temporal experience. Fleeting and elusive time, made up of an indefinite succession of constantly renewed cycles, is brought at last to its conclusion, its *telos,* by the recollection of previous lives. It is replaced by a time that is totally subdued, a cycle that is entirely finished. Thus the enigmatic expression of the doctor Alcmaeon of Kroton, who is associated with the Pythagoreans, becomes clear: "Men die because they are not able to join the beginning to the end."[66] By enabling the end to join up with the beginning, the exercise of memory wins salvation, deliverance from becoming and from death. Oblivion, on the other hand, is intimately linked with human time, the time of the mortal condition, whose "never-ending" flux is synonymous with "inexorable necessity." It is said that on hearing time praised as that "in which one learns and remembers," the Pythagorean Paron asked if it were not rather the case that time created forgetfulness and declared that time was the king of ignorance.[67]

The central place given to memory in eschatological myths indicates an attitude of refusal with regard to temporal existence. Memory is exalted because it is the power that makes it possible for men to escape time and return to the divine state. One remark will make clear the link between the high value attached to *anamnēsis* and the development of a critical and negative attitude toward time. In the circle of sects where belief in metempsychosis took root, there arose, alongside the interest in memory in the sense of recollection of earlier lives, a whole body of a more or less mythical doctrine in which time was considered the principal and fundamental notion.[68] For Pherecydes, considered Pythagoras's teacher since he was said to have been the first to proclaim the immortality of the soul and formulate the theory of reincarnation, time, Chronos, is a god and has a place at the very origin of the cosmos.[69] From his seed were born the two antithetical elements of which the universe is made. Chronos, a living being and at the same time an abstract notion, thus plays at the origin of all things the role of the principle of unity transcending all contraries. Chronos is also to be found in the Orphic theogonies, where he assumes a similar function.[70] He is a polymorphous monster who engenders the cosmic egg that, when it splits in two, gives birth to the sky and the earth and brings forth Phanes, the firstborn of the gods, a hermaphrodite deity in whom the opposition between male and female disappears.[71]

It is important not to misunderstand the significance of this deification of Chronos or the new significance accorded to time in this type of theogony. The time that is sacralized is time that does not age, time immortal and imperishable, as it is celebrated in the Orphic poems under the name Chronos Agēraos. Like another mythical figure, the river Okeanos, which encircles the entire universe in its untiring course, Chronos is a snake whose body forms a circle, a cycle that, by enfolding the world and binding it together, makes the cosmos a single eternal sphere, despite the appearances of multiplicity and change.[72] Thus the deified

image of time betrays an aspiration toward the unity and ever-
lastingness of the Whole comparable to the one expressed, in
another context, in Parmenides's philosophy and his critique
of becoming. Insofar as it is a principle of unity and permanence,
the divine form of Chronos appears as the radical negation of
human time, which is, by contrast, experienced as a source of in-
stability and destruction presiding, as Paron declared, over oblivion and death.

The development of a mythology of Chronos alongside that of
Mnēmosynē seems to correspond with a period of difficulty and
anxiety regarding the representation of time. Time becomes the
subject of doctrinal preoccupations and assumes the form of a
problem when a domain of the experience of time is found to be
incompatible with the ancient conception of a cyclical becoming,
which applied to the whole of reality, regulating at once seasonal
activity, the timing of festivals, and the sequence of generations
(in other words: cosmic time, religious time, and human time).
This crisis took place in the Greek world in about the seventh
century, at a moment when a new image of mankind was finding
expression with the birth of lyric poetry.[73] The heroic ideal was
abandoned, and there emerged values directly associated with the
affective life of the individual and subject to all the vicissitudes of
human existence — pleasures, emotions, love, beauty, and youth.
The corollary to all this was an experience of time that no longer
fit a circular model of becoming. In the archaic conception of
time, emphasis was placed upon the renewal of human generations one after another, through a process of ceaseless interchange
between the dead and the living.[74] In this manner, human time
appeared to be integrated into the cyclical organization of the
cosmos. But when the individual considers his own emotional
life and, in the thrall of the present moment and all its attendant
pleasure and pain, locates the values to which he has become
attached in time as it passes, he feels swept along in a moving,
ever-changing, irreversible flux. Because it is dominated by the
fatality of death, which affects its whole course, the time in which
his existence takes place looks to him like a power of destruction

that irremediably ruins everything he finds rewarding in life. The clearer conception elaborated in lyric poetry of a human time fleeing, never to return, along an irreversible line calls into question the idea of an entirely cyclical order and of a periodic and regular renewal of the universe.[75]

The thought articulated in the philosophical-religious sects in reaction to this appears to have taken two different courses. On the one hand, we find an attitude that is violently negative toward the time of human existence and sees it as an evil from which man must be liberated. On the other, we find an effort to purify divine existence from everything that binds it to any type of temporality at all, even a cyclical one. The "always" used to define the life of the gods, expressed in the notion of the divine *aiōn*, no longer means the perpetual starting over of that which ceaselessly renews itself by returning to its beginnings, and comes instead to signify permanence in an eternally immobile identity.[76] The image of the circle, symbolizing the temporal order, now takes on an ambiguous significance and can, according to the circumstances, become charged with directly opposed affective values. In one sense, the *kuklos* remains a model of perfection, and the soul that, through the *anamnēsis* of its previous lives, has managed to "join the end to the beginning" becomes like the stars, whose circular course — a moving image of immobile eternity — forever preserves them from destruction. And yet, in completing its cycle, the soul is seeking not to begin it all over again, endlessly, like the stars, but to escape definitively from it and to leave time forever.[77] The *kuklos* in the new image of time becomes the sad cycle of necessity and suffering, the cruel wheel of births from which one longs to escape and which in descriptions of the infernal regions is a symbolic instrument of torture and punishment.[78]

These discrepancies in the representation of time, and the anxieties they arouse in certain milieux, clarify the significance and implications of the memory exercises. The effort to recollect that is so exalted and praised in myth does not point to an awakening of interest in the past or an attempt to explore human time. *Anamnēsis* is concerned with temporal sequence, as the individual

132

apprehends it in the course of his affective life and as he conceives of it in the mode of nostalgia and regret, only to the extent that it seeks to escape it. It seeks to transform the time of an individual life — time as it is lived through, incoherent and irreversible — into a cycle reconstructed as a totality. It seeks to reintegrate human time into cosmic periodicity and divine eternity.[79]

A similar development of memory is to be found in the relationship between *anamnēsis* and the concept of the individual soul. As discussed above, in Pythagoreanism the recollection of previous lives may be a means of knowing oneself — not in the somewhat banal sense given to the phrase by the oracle of Delphi, that is, not claiming to be equal to the gods, but in a new sense: knowing our soul, apprehending and recognizing its unity and continuity through all its multiple incarnations.[80] Meanwhile, the *psuchē*, whose transformations make up the web of each man's individual destiny, is represented as a *daimōn*, a supernatural being that lives an independent existence within us. Even if from now on the *psuchē* is opposed to the life of the body, and if it is all the more pure the more separated it is, this does not mean that it becomes the vehicle for man's individual psychic life. Empedocles makes a clear distinction between, on the one hand, sensation, thought, and reason itself — all the forms of human knowledge — and, on the other, the *daimōn* that lives within us.[81] The fact that this *daimōn* is individualized, assigned to a particular human being who discovers his own destiny within it, does not alter its character as a mysterious power; it is foreign to man, a reality present in the very heart of the whole of nature, in wind, animals, and plants, just as much as in man.

The memory of the incarnations that the *daimōn* of a man's soul has previously been through bridges the gap between his existence as a man and the rest of the universe. The ancient image of a world full of souls and breaths, all interrelated and ceaselessly circulating among all nature's creatures, thus acquires the value of an experience that the individual is capable of living at his own level. This explains in what sense and within what limits one should see memory exercises as an attempt made by the individual to know himself through his *psuchē*. It is not a matter of the individual's apprehending himself in his personal past and finding himself again within the continuity of an inner life that differentiates him from all other creatures. He must place himself within the framework of a general order and reestablish, on every level, the continuity between himself and the world, systematically connecting his present life with the entirety of time, human existence with all of nature, the destiny of the individual with the totality of being, the part with the whole.

What is striking about all this evidence for the deification of memory is that the high value placed on this function and the importance of the role attributed to it did not lead to any attempt to explore the past or to the construction of an architecture of time. Wherever memory is revered, it is exalted either as the source of knowledge in general, of omniscience, or as the instrument of escape from time. Nowhere does it appear to be linked with any development of a properly temporal perspective. Nor does it have anything to do with the category of the ego. The Mnēmosynē that presides over poetic inspiration is an impersonal memory; it is not concerned with the individual's past. As for the Mnēmosynē that answers to the new need for individual salvation within the sects, this is directed not toward self-knowledge as we understand it but toward an exercise of purification that transfigures the individual and promotes him to the rank of the gods.

Both these features of mythical memory — escape from time and union with the gods — are found in Plato's theory of *anamnēsis*. For Plato, recollection no longer focuses on the primeval past or previous lives. Its object is the truths that together constitute reality. Mnēmosynē, a supernatural power, has been internalized and becomes the very faculty of knowing in man. The attempt at recollection, once the instrument of a mystical ascesis, becomes identified with the search for truth.[82] There is another side to this identification: for Plato, to know is the same thing as to remember or, in other words, to escape from the time of the present life, to flee far from this earthly world and return to the soul's divine

134

homeland, to come again to a "world of ideas" opposed to the earthly world, like the beyond with which Mnēmosynē enabled us to communicate.

In Plato's theories, mythical thought lives on even as it is being transformed. Anamnēsis here does not have the function of reconstructing the past and setting it in order, and it is not concerned with a chronology of events; rather, it reveals eternal and unchangeable Being.[83] Memory is not the "thought of time" but an escape from it. Its aim is not to trace the history of an individual in which the uniqueness of personality would be revealed but to unite the soul with the divine.

The persistence in Platonism of a mythical perspective with regard to memory is all the more striking in that Plato profoundly altered the concept of the human *psuchē* and developed it in the direction of the idea of an "inner man."[84] The soul is seen no longer as a spiritual being that is within us but foreign to us, but as our own spiritual being. The soul of Socrates is Socrates himself; it is the individual Socrates whose portrait Plato draws in all its singularity.[85] And yet the *psuchē* remains something that is other. In the first place, it is not entirely fused with our inner being, since it can equally well be incarnate in another man or in the body of an animal. And second, it is only truly itself after we die, when we no longer exist, or in those short moments — which give a foretaste of death — when it breaks its bonds with our organic and sensory functions and becomes pure thought. To borrow Maurice Halbwachs's striking phrase, in Plato the *psuchē* does not mean psychic life and functions: it is their copy, just as in Homer it was the copy of the body.[86] This spiritual double, which is separated from the inner man after his death and survives him, remains for Plato, just as it was for the Pythagoreans and Empedocles, a *daimōn*, a divine principle whose function it is to tie our individual destiny directly to the cosmic order.[87] In effect, each immortal soul is linked with a star to which the demiurge has allotted it and to which it returns once it has been purified through remembering.[88]

For each individual, the soul defines what he really is. But at the same time, the number of souls, which is equal to the number of stars, always remains the same, never increasing or decreasing, despite the never-ending renewal of the human generations.[89] In a passage in the *Phaedo*, Plato justifies this constancy in the number of souls with an argument that explains the balance in his system between soul, time, and memory.[90] If each individual at birth brought with it a new soul instead of allowing the soul of a dead man to be reborn for a new cycle, men would have no other time than linear time, which flows in one direction, from birth to death, and which, for Plato, is the expression of pure disorder and leads to chaos.[91] By contrast, a fixed number of souls — like a fixed number of stars in nature or a fixed number of homes in the city — implies that human life follows a circular course, which makes it possible to integrate it within the order of cyclical time encompassing nature, society, and the existence of the individual.[92]

Memory in Plato has lost its mythical aspects: *anamnēsis* no longer brings the memory of previous lives back from the beyond. But in its relationships with the category of time and the notion of the soul, it retains a function analogous to the one that was exalted in myth. It does not seek to make the past as such an object of knowledge. It does not seek to organize temporal experience; it seeks to pass beyond it. Memory becomes an instrument in the struggle against human time revealed as pure flux, like the realm of *panta rheei* in Heraclitus. Against this human time it sets the conquest, through *anamnēsis*, of a knowledge capable of transforming human existence by connecting it to the cosmic order and to divine immutability. At the moment when individual salvation becomes a preoccupation, man seeks to achieve it by integrating himself with the whole. What he asks of memory is not knowledge of his own past but the means to escape time and be reunited with the divine.

One conclusion emerges from this analysis of the myths of memory and the remaining traces of them in early Greek philosophy: there is not necessarily a link between the development of memory and progress toward a consciousness of the past. Memory appears to predate any consciousness of the past and any interest in the past as such. At the dawn of Greek civilization, a sort of intoxication before the power of memory is perceptible, but the memory in question has quite a different orientation from our own, and it serves different ends.

The image of memory that is reflected in myths and the function these myths assign to memory are in no way gratuitous. They are, as we have seen, linked with very particular techniques of memorization, practiced within esoteric groups for specific purposes. In the brotherhoods of the bards, these techniques are a part of the apprenticeship in poetic inspiration and the "second sight" this inspiration procures. In the milieu of the magi, they are a preparation for the achievement of divinatory ecstasy. In the religious or philosophical sects, they are spiritual exercises of purification and salvation. Taken out of the institutional framework and the mental context in which they belong, these techniques of memorization lose their meaning and become pointless. They no longer have a place in our own organization of memory, which is directed toward acquiring knowledge of man's individual past.

The distance between these archaic forms of memory and memory today is very great. It was not enough that ancient techniques of memorization should disappear for today's memory to emerge. It was necessary to forge mental tools that would allow for a precise knowledge of the past, an accurate chronology, and a rigorous ordering of time. Because Greek civilization did not forge these new tools, once it had stripped memory of its mythical powers, it could only grant memory a subordinate position. As memory's relation to time and the past became more defined, it lost the prestigious aura that had originally surrounded it.[93] Aristotle, for example, distinguishes between memory (*mnēmē*) and recollection (*anamnēsis*), the former being simply the ability to preserve the past, the latter its effective and voluntary recall.[94] But both are necessarily linked with the past. Both are conditioned by a lapse of time. They imply the existence of distance in time, distinction between "earlier" and "later."[95] According to Aristotle, then, we remember and perceive time through one and the same organ.[96] Memory is therefore only "incidentally" connected with the faculty of thinking; it is really attached to the faculty of sense-perception. This explains why many other animals apart from man possess *mnēmē*.[97]

Once the object of memory is no longer being but rather the determination of time, it is demoted from the place it formerly occupied at the top of the hierarchy of faculties. It is now no more than a *pathos* of the soul, which, because of its union with the body, is plunged into temporal flux. There is a radical incompatibility between intellection — *noēsis* — and the apperception of time, and this cuts memory off from the intellectual part of the soul and brings it down to the level of the sensory part.

In Aristotle there is no longer anything that recalls the mythical Mnēmosynē or of the exercises in memorization whose function was to liberate the soul from time and open up a path to immortality. Memory is now included within time, but it is a time that, even for Aristotle, resists intelligibility. Memory as a function of time can no longer claim to reveal being and the truth. But it cannot ensure true knowledge of the past either. It is not so much the source within us of authentic knowledge as a sign of our incompleteness. It reflects the insufficiencies of the human condition, our inability to be pure intelligence.

CHAPTER FIVE

The River Amelēs and the
Meletē Thanatou

The *Republic* closes with a description of a landscape in the underworld. At the end of his journey through the beyond, Er the Pamphylian comes upon the plain where souls wait, in suffocating heat, at the last stage before being sent back to earth for a new incarnation. The picture is in keeping with an entire tradition that inspired this passage of Plato's. The desiccated plain of oblivion, Lēthē, the parched souls, the cool water flowing from a spring with supernatural powers: none of these was invented by him. However, Amelēs, the name Plato gives to the underground river where the souls come to drink and where they lose their memories, is not, as far as we know, found in any description of the world of the dead before the *Republic*. What is the exact meaning of the term? How can we explain its presence in Plato's account? What is the connection between the river Amelēs in the *Republic* and the fountain of oblivion that appears in mystical literature?[1] (This is the fountain from which the soul must be able to turn aside, in order to draw from the lake of memory, whose water liberates it from the wheel of rebirths and mercifully brings it blessed immortality in the company of the heroes and the gods.)

When Léon Robin translates Amelēs as "carefree," he appears to see what amounts to only a tenuous link between *ameleia* and *lēthē*: if oblivion submerges souls that have drunk immoderately from the river Amelēs, this is because all anxiety within them has

139

disappeared.[2] Henceforth content with their earthly lives, at ease in the prison into which they have been cast — the body — they desire nothing further and are satisfied with an ignorance of which they are no longer even conscious. Within the framework of Platonic thought, *ameleia* should be seen as the opposite of the mental anxiety, the unease of the soul, that philosophers such as Socrates aim to arouse.

However, it is not certain that this is really what the term means. One may well wonder whether the connection between the plain of Lēthē and the river Amelēs is not closer, and whether, on this point too, Plato has not so much introduced an innovation as picked up and modified a tradition in which the themes of *meletē* and *ameleia* were very closely associated with the myths of memory and oblivion.[3]

Pausanias tells us what the Muses of Helikon were called, according to the most ancient tradition, when there were still only three of them. Their names were Meletē, Mnēmē, and Aoidē — Practice, Memory, and Song.[4] Mnēmosynē, the mother of the Muses, presided over the poetic function; moreover, the brotherhoods of bards valued memory exercises, which prepared the way for the "inspired vision" that the form of composition of oral poetry, combining recitation and improvisation, required.[5] It is therefore not surprising to find memory and *meletē* alongside song in the list of the Muses, for *meletē* is the practice of a mental exercise, a training in memory necessary for an apprenticeship in poetic technique. It appears again, still associated with the cult of the Muses, in brotherhoods like those of the Pythagorean sect, which were engaged in philosophical thought.[6] In this new milieu it acquired a wider significance. It no longer was restricted to the acquisition of a particular kind of knowledge but trained men for *aretē*, or human excellence in general. It operated on two levels: in the context of the individual, it was an *askēsis*, bringing salvation through the purification of the soul, while in the context of the city it was a *paideia*, educating the youth in virtue and preparing those who were most worthy for the exercise of sovereignty

in accordance with justice. This double character brings philosophical "discipline" close, on the one hand, to the religious way
of life dear to the mystic sects, who were only concerned with the
salvation of the individual and paid no attention to the political
domain, and on the other, to the collective training founded
essentially upon military tests and exercises, *hai tōn polemikōn
meletai*.[7] In the warrior societies of Greece, these tests represented an early educational system aimed at selecting the young
according to their aptitude for exercising power.[8] However, the
philosophical *meletē* is distinguished by its replacement of ritual
observances and military exercises with a properly intellectual
education, a mental schooling that, like the poetic *meletē*, emphasizes memory training above all. The philosophical *meletē* is a
virile virtue, and like the warrior *meletē*, it involves tense concentration, constant attention, *epimeleia*, and hard work, *ponos*.[9] In a
traditional version of the *aretē* reflected in the myth of Herakles
at the crossroads of vice and virtue, meletē is set in opposition to
relaxation and lack of training (*ameleia* and *ameletēsia*), laziness
(*argia*), softness (*malachia*), and pleasure (*hēdonē*).[10] But in the
case of the philosophical *meletē*, the exercises and training concern the soul and the intelligence, not the body. To be more
specific, and to borrow the words Iamblichus used when defining the Pythagorean *askēsis*, it is a matter of a *gumnasia kai epimeleia mnēmēs*, an exercise and training for the memory.[11] On two
occasions, Iamblichus emphasizes the great value placed by the
Pythagoreans upon the effort of recollection for the purpose of
gaining wisdom. On the first occasion, he suggests that the *anamnēsis* of previous lives with which Pythagoras was traditionally
credited was the source and principle of his teaching.[12] Later, he
notes that the Pythagoreans were under an obligation to commit
everything to memory, never losing their hold on anything learned,
seen, or heard, and he interprets the daily examination of conscience, which was a rule for the sect, as a mnemonic exercise.[13]

The *Golden Verses* give some interesting details about this
examination of conscience. It was forbidden to give oneself up to
the sweetness of sleep before reviewing all the actions of the day,

starting with the first and considering each one in turn, right through to the end.[14] This was a difficult task, and the disciple was encouraged to undertake it with the following words: "*Tauta ponei, taut' ekmeleta* [it is necessary for you to make this effort and accomplish this exercise]." The text goes on: "You must love to do it, and it will set you on the track of divine virtue.... You will no longer hope for what is beyond hope, and nothing shall be hidden from you (*mēte ti lēthein*)."[15]

Hierocles notes in his commentary that the poet exhorts his readers to examine all the actions of the day, even the most insignificant, in order from first to last, without overlooking any in between. The reason for doing this, he says, is that this *anamnēsis* of the events of our daily lives can call to mind our previous lives; it is a *meletē tōn probebiōmenōn anapoleseōs*. Continuing his comment, Hierocles suggests that the Pythagoreans' *askēsis tēs aretēs* depends on three powers, *dunameis*, of the soul: *ponos*, *ērōs*, and *meletē*, defined as a training imposed on the rational part of the soul and meant to *noein*. In *The Education of Children*, Plutarch also emphasizes the importance of *meletē*, in association with *ponos*, in the *paideia*.[16] The passage has a polemical purpose. Plutarch is attacking those who in matters of *aretē* emphasize nature over study and exercise. They imagine that a bad temperament cannot be corrected by a *meletē orthē pros aretēn*. But in this they are totally mistaken: *ameleia* ruins the best of souls, just as it does the best land and the healthiest body, but *epimeleia* and *ponos* are both fertile and productive. Thanks to them, what was contrary to nature ultimately defeats what was according to nature: "Even easy things elude those who do not practice, while difficult things are obtained through painstaking care."[17] The very banality of Plutarch's text makes it interesting. He is defending a commonplace of the often-discussed theme of the respective advantages of nature and study. A boundary separating the position of the philosophers from traditional poetry on this matter must have become apparent very early. The poets — not just Pindar, but even as early as Homer — emphasized personal talents and inspiration over apprenticeship and study. In contrast, Epicharmus, whose

links with Pythagorean thought are well known, upholds the opposite point of view in a pronouncement to which Plutarch's text
appears to be a commentary: "*ha de meleta phusios agathas pleona
dōreitai, philoi* [practice brings forth more than natural talent
does]."[18] In Epicharmus's work, this praise of *meletē* and its fruits
goes hand in hand with the exaltation of *ponos* and a warning
against the dangers of softness (*malachia*) and pleasure.[19]

In Plutarch's text, the dialogue continues with a paragraph
that has an exact equivalent in Pythagoras's speech to youth as it is
reported by Iamblichus. There is, therefore, all the more reason to
evoke Pythagorean themes at this point. Plutarch writes that, for
men, all goods are unstable and inconstant; only *paideia* represents a definitive gain that remains "immortal and divine," for
only the mind grows stronger as it grows older, and time, which
destroys and disperses all things, adds knowledge to old age.[20]
The same opposition between enduring and fleeting good is found
in Iamblichus. According to him, when Pythagoras praised *paideia*
to the *neoi*, he equated corporeal good and the *epimeleia* of the
body with faithless friends who desert us at the first opportunity;
the fruits of *paideia*, on the other hand, last until death and for
some people even bring an eternal glory beyond death. While
other goods must first be relinquished by whoever possesses them
if they are to be transmitted, *paideia* can never be exhausted by
being exchanged. Of all human things, it is the only one that can
be acquired and preserved forever: *ktēsasthai*.[21]

Plutarch closes this part of his essay by describing memory as
the storehouse (*tamieion*) of *paideia* and remarking that Mnēmosynē has been called the mother of the Muses because nothing
but her can *gennan kai trephein*, make things grow and nourish
them.[22] So we see clearly here that the theme of a good that can be
stored up and withstand the destructive flow of time is linked with
the doctrine that makes the effort of memorization the basis for
intellectual discipline. We thus have an image of memory as the
inexhaustible granary of wisdom, which defies the onslaught of
time and in which the soul may find the food of immortality. We
might imagine this to be the fruit of Plutarch's own imagination if

it did not also appear in Empedocles in a context that directly evokes the Platonic themes of *anamnēsis*, *lēthē*, and *ameleia*. Empedocles proclaims: "Blessed is he who has acquired *ektēsato*, the wealth of divine *prapides*."[23] *Olbios*, *ploutos*, and *ektēsato*: these terms associated with the idea of the divine could not fail to evoke for any Greek the figure of Zeus, who bears the threefold epithet of Ktēsios, Plousios, and Olbios, and who is indeed enshrined in the storehouse in the shape of a vessel (*aggeion*), a little barrel (*kadiskos*), which is always filled with ambrosia, the drink of immortality.[24] The little barrel of Zeus Ktēsios, a symbol of constant health and abundance, watches over domestic goods and keeps all the riches of the house intact. According to Empedocles, one divine man possessed this vast "treasure" of *prapides*, and the ancients took him to be Pythagoras, who had the power of preserving intact in his memory all the events of his previous lives. Empedocles tells us: "When this man stretched his *prapides* he could easily discern each one of the things that belonged to ten or even twenty human lives."[25]

Following Louis Gernet, I have emphasized the indications of ancient beliefs and practices in Empedocles's text that use the ancient term *prapides*, which originally meant diaphragm, to refer to intelligence.[26] In a phrase like "stretching the diaphragm" I thought it possible to discern an echo of a discipline like yoga, based on a technique for controlling breathing. This would account for the strange privilege described in legends of the magi, who were said to be able to liberate their *psuchē* at will, make it leave the body, which would lie breathless and lifeless in a cataleptic trance, journey in the beyond, and bring back knowledge of the past, as Epimenides's soul did. Under the influence of the new interests and ideas that emerged among the philosophical brotherhoods, this ecstatic discipline must have been transformed into a training for the mind, a *meletē* in which three features were closely associated. These were the attempt at recollection projected as far as possible into previous lives, the purification of the soul and its separation from the body, and escape from the flow of time by gaining access to a perfectly stable truth. Is this not the kind of training that Plato describes before expounding his theory of *anamnēsis* in the *Phaedo*, where, in agreement with what he calls a very ancient tradition, he defines philosophy as a *meletē thanatou*, a training or practice for death, consisting in purifying the soul by concentrating it and drawing it together from every part of the body in such a way that, thus collected together and isolated, it is able to release itself from and escape the body.[27] Purification, concentration, and separation of the soul: all these terms, for Plato, suggest recollection, *anamnēsis*. This *meletē thanatou* still has something of the character of a *meletē mnēmēs*, as is shown by the *Phaedrus* when Plato deplores the invention of writing. He suggests that by substituting the specific effort of recollection with a trust in marks that exist outside the mind, writing allows forgetfulness to infiltrate the soul through *ameletēsia mnēmēs*, that is, through the absence of a practice of memory.[28] Furthermore, this is how, in his commentary, Proclus interprets *ameleia*: "The soul that has drunk immoderately from the river Amelēs forgets all its previous lives; for having become enamored of becoming, it ceases to recall the unchangeable principles and forgets them (*di' ameletēsian kai argian*)." He adds: "Indeed, we need an exercise which can constantly renew the memory of what we have known, *dei gar tēs meletēs ananeousēs hēmin aei tēn mnēmēn hōn egnōmen*."[29] Of course, this practicing for death is, in fact, training for immortality: by liberating itself from the body, which Plato describes with the same images of flux and flowing that he uses for becoming, the soul emerges from the river of time and wins an unchanging and permanent existence as close to the divine as man is permitted to be.[30] In this respect, the old mythical theme of Mnēmosynē, the source of inexhaustible life, the fountain of immortality, is transmitted to the Platonic *anamnēsis* via the Pythagorean memory exercises. And when Plato describes, in the plain of Lēthē, the river Amelēs, "whose water cannot be retained by any receptacle (*aggeion ouden to hudōr stegei*)," he remains faithful to the interpretation of the myths of memory and oblivion dominant in the philosophical circles of "Magna Graecia."

The reason why nothing can retain this water is that, since it is made to flow forever, it escapes (*pheugei*); it runs out of any receptacle into which it is poured, just as, according to Pythagoras, the corporeal deserts human beings, and just as the *epimeleia* of the body — which is the *ameleia* of the soul — runs through them. Pythagoras opposes this *ameleia* to the definitive acquisition obtained through the *meletē mnēmēs* on which his *paideia* is based. True, for Plato, the river *Amelēs* has taken on a truly metaphysical meaning. As well as representing the relaxation of a soul abandoning itself to pleasure instead of subjecting itself to the severe discipline of memory, for Plato — as Proclus notes — the river symbolizes the endless flux and reflux of becoming, whose terrible flow (*tēn deinēn ekroēn*) cannot be contained by any receptacle or any existing thing.[31] In the meantime, the Pythagorean Paron had, according to Aristotle, already associated *lēthē* closely with time, and, censuring those who saw Chronos as a wise divinity, had proclaimed him, on the contrary, the source of all ignorance.[37]

But perhaps we can pinpoint the origins of the mythical image of the river Amelēs more precisely. This water that cannot be contained by any receptacle recalls the *amuētoi* in the *Gorgias*, where, in a similar fashion, leaking vessels are unable to retain water, which flows out of them as soon as it is drawn.[33] Socrates says that these receptacles, as full of holes as a sieve, are the souls of unfortunates who, through forgetfulness and lack of faith (*pistis*), can retain nothing. And he adds that, according to the myth — which is Italian or Sicilian — the *pithoi* refer to the part of the soul where the desires reside, because that part is docile and credulous, *pithanon* and *peistikon*. To Socrates's way of thinking, this fable should convince Callicles of his error in proclaiming that the ceaseless flow and abundant flux of pleasures make life worthwhile. Socrates's reply is that this sort of life is terrible and monstrous (*deinon*), and should rather be called death. To illustrate this theme of the two kinds of life, the two *bioi* of which man must know how to choose the trustworthy one, Socrates recalls another comparison, which he says springs from the same *gumnasion* as the preceding one: the wise man is like a man who possesses barrels that are in a good state of repair and full of things that are necessary to life, and some of which are filled with rare and precious liquids that are difficult to come by, however hard one tries.[34] Once these barrels are full, they remain so always. But the fool, the profligate, whom the author of the myth calls *amuē-tos*, has only rotten and leaky barrels to hold these liquids, and he has constantly to refill them to avoid terrible suffering.

The reference to life that is perhaps death and the play on the words *sōma-sēma* point in a direction confirmed by Plato's geographical references to Italy and Sicily. One might imagine that this was a Pythagorean text on the two *bioi*, on the theme of transitory and permanent goods. However, several details in Plato's text suggest that the reference is more precisely to Empedocles.

First, there is the contrast between *peithō* and *pistis*, which are connected with two different parts of the soul. *Peithō*, in fact, belongs to the part of the soul where the desires are located, which the author of the myth represents as a *pithos*. *Pistis* belongs to a different part of the soul, symbolized by a sieve (*koskinon*) whose holes allow everything to escape through faulty memory and forgetfulness, *lēthē*, and through an absence of faith. We should therefore recognize that *peithō*, which is condemned, and *pistis*, which is recommended, are evaluated differently and situated at different levels. *Peithō*, associated with *hēdonē* and *pothos,* is an ambiguous power that can be used for good or, just as easily, for evil, and it symbolizes the allure of pleasure, especially physical pleasure.[35] *Pistis* represents a different type of trust: faith placed in a superior divinity whose revelations man must accept and whose teachings he must follow. The ambiguous phrases Plato uses are, moreover, associated with terms drawn from the mysteries. A word such as *amuētoi* means both what is not closed and those who have not been initiated, who are incapable of holding or "retaining" (*stegein*) the secret.

The same opposition between *peithō* and *pistis* is also found in the work of Empedocles. In his treatise *On Nature*, he presents his teaching in the form of a revelation to his disciple Pausanias of a secret similar to those of the mysteries; it will enable him to command the winds and bring the soul of a dead man back from the kingdom of the shades. The poem starts off with the theme of *pistis*: the understanding and destiny of men are extremely limited, and their lives are nothing but ignorance and misfortune; in what should they place their trust? Men allow themselves to be "persuaded" (*peisthentes*), in accordance with their desires and are tossed about in all directions.[36] Pausanias should not bestow his *pistis* lightly.[37] Does that mean that he should not bestow it at all? Not in the least, but he should look higher, aiming at what is superior to men, at that which has power and authority, *kratos*, over him. For to withhold one's trust (*apistein*) from something higher than oneself — in other words, from divine inspiration and teaching — is exactly what the wicked (*kakoi*) do.[38] Pausanias should therefore listen to the *pistōmata*, the trustworthy proofs, of the muse of Empedocles.[39] Finally, he should keep secret the teaching thus revealed: he should "retain" it (*stegein*) in the depths of his speechless heart.[40]

Another fragment from the end of the poem throws some light on the significance of these similarities, which are too numerous and too precise to be coincidental. Here Empedocles places Pausanias at the crossroads of two *bioi*, between which he must choose. If he pursues the thousands of inferior things in which men usually place their trust, then very soon, with the unfolding of time, these things will abandon him, for they desire (*poetheonta*) to rejoin their own kind.[41] If, on the contrary, with his *prapides* firm, he concentrates steadfastly on the teaching he has received, if he allows himself to be initiated (*epopteusēis*) by holy exercises (*katharēsioi meletēisin*) then all these blessings will be forever his, and, possessing them, he will be able to acquire many others, for they increase of their own accord, each according to its nature.[42]

The firm *prapides* and the holy exercises clearly recall the *Purifications*, particularly the firm *prapides* of Pythagoras and the exercises that made it possible for him to recall all the details of his previous lives. It seems that in the background of the *Purifications* one can discern, as a symbol of the treasure of constant wisdom, the image of Zeus Ktēsios in the form of the receptacle, the little barrel containing the precious liquor of immortality. Thus, for Empedocles, the fortunate man who has been successful in gaining the virtue of an initiate, comparable to incorruptible ambrosia, is contrasted with men who care only for corporeal goods, which move through them without becoming established within them, and which leave them forthwith, rushing away to reunite with similar elements: water to water, fire to fire, and air to air. On the one hand, the wise man who "retains" in the depths of his heart a teaching that is the source of life eternal evokes the image of the barrel of Zeus Ktēsios; on the other hand, the men who cultivate (*epimeleia*) the body and who are attached to goods that always flow through them like a river suggest the image of the leaking *pithos*. This is all the more so because an object already charged with religious significance is involved; in the funerary cults, it is the symbol of an existence cut short by death before it has reached fulfilment, while in the context of the mystery religions it symbolizes the unfortunates who have never been initiated.[43]

Had Empedocles already developed this myth in the form in which we find it in Plato? Did he explicitly compare the souls of the profligate with leaking barrels and associate this image with that of a river of the underworld whose water, which no receptacle can retain, cause those who drink it to forget their former nature, to fall into the *kuklos geneseōs*, and to be reincarnated in a body? This problem obviously cannot be resolved. However, we must point out one final, very striking similarity.[44] In Empedocles, the fall of the *daimones* precipitates them into a dark cave in the meadow of Atē, which contrasts with their place of origin, the meadow of Alētheia — just as in Plato the plain of Lēthē is opposed to the plain of Alētheia.[45] Atē and Lēthē can easily overlap in the mythical imagination. They have the same origin, both being descended from Night, Nyx, and they are both related to Darkness, Skotos: each is an image of the darkness that suddenly enshrouds the human spirit, enfolding it in shadows, hiding from it the straight way of truth and justice, and dragging it to its doom.[46] As well as being oblivion and the spirit of error, they are criminal error (*hamartēma*) and the defilement, punishment, and death that result from it.[47] In the *Purifications*, the soul, wandering in exile in the plain of Atē, is a *daimōn* that has become horribly defiled through criminal error (*hamartēsas*): it has shed blood or sworn a false oath.[48] In both cases, the outcome of the error is the same: discord (*neikos*) has arisen in the world of the gods, where there should be nothing but pure friendship. Those who have given way to *neikos*, being momentarily devoted to hatred, are precipitated into the meadow of Atē, where all the elements hate one another.[49] Empedocles himself is forced to wander far from the gods because he has allowed himself to fall under the spell of frenzied Discord.[50]

The meaning of this text becomes clearer if we compare it with Hesiod's *Theogony*.[51] Among Nyx's descendants are not only Lēthē and Atē but also other children of Eris Stugerē. They are, on the one hand, Murders and Disputes, the Neikea, and, on the other, Horkos, Oath, who is the greatest scourge of the human race. At the end of the *Theogony*, Horkos appears as the water of the river of the underworld, the Styx, the *stugerē theos,* the deity hated by the immortals.[52] This water that falls from a steep rock and flows away through the black night is "the great oath of the gods" to which, despite the great horror that it inspires in them, they resort each time some strife or discord (*eris kai neikos*) arises among them. On these occasions, they seek out the water of the Styx so it can settle their quarrel, and he who perjures himself at the moment when, following the rites, he sprinkles the water on the ground is immediately struck down breathless and lies there on the ground for a whole year. The foods of immortality, ambrosia and nectar, no longer pass his lips; he lies breathless and voiceless, and a cruel torpor envelops him.[53] Once this trial is over, another, even harder one awaits him: for nine long years he dwells apart from the society of the gods, and only at the end of this period can he resume his place among the immortals. Thus the wandering in the meadow of Atē of the *daimones* who have perjured themselves following some quarrel appears in Empedocles as the transposition of a mythical theme that centered on the water of the Styx, which brought torpor and exile to gods who were guilty of swearing a false oath.

It seems legitimate to assume that Plato, for his part, also had the water of the Styx in mind when he wrote of the river Amelēs, for in the *Republic*, as soon as the souls drink from the river, they fall into a coma like the one that envelops the erring gods of the *Theogony*, in darkness.[54] And despite thunder and earthquakes, the souls do not awake throughout the journey that carries them like shooting stars toward their births. There is more: following Herodotus, Pausanias describes a river he has come across in the wild mountains of Arcadia, which the Greeks call the Styx.[55] It flows from the top of a huge, precipitous rock between Pheneos and Nonacris, and thence joins the river Krathis. It is a water of death: no living creature, man or beast, can drink from it with impunity. Its destructive power is such that it shatters and punctures any receptacle made by the hand of man — whether it is made of glass, crystal, stone, or terra cotta — and it erodes and dissolves those made of metal. It even attacks gold, even though gold is as incorruptible as the gods. Only the bone from a horse's hoof can withstand this power of destruction and retain the water poured into it — no doubt because the hoof of a horse is itself related to the sinister realm of the impure.[56]

Not far from the Styx is a grotto where, legend has it, the daughters of Proitos went into hiding when they were possessed by the frenzied delirium of mania. It was here that Melampos came and found them, to cleanse their defilement with secret purifying rites, which he administered in a place called Lousoi, the baths, in the sanctuary of Artemis Hēmerasia, she who soothes. And there is another spring of fresh water just a little farther on, next to which grows a plane tree; Pausanias explicitly connects this spring with the first one, contrasting them as good to evil, or remedy to suffering.[57] Anyone who has become enraged because of a mad dog — and, more generally, anyone who is a prey to the delirium of *lyssa,* in other words, to an attack of uncontrollable madness — is cured by drinking this water. For this reason the spring is known as *Alyssos*, the spring that dispels madness.

Thus Arcadia (at the time of Pausanias a veritable museum of antiquities) reveals, if not the origin of the myth about the two fountains of life and death, at least one of its least reconstructed versions, and one that is still very close to actual religious practices. We have seen that the Styx, the river of the underworld, which possesses the power to defile and brings destruction to everything in this world, became the river Amelēs, which symbolizes the soul's being forced into the body and into the temporal flux. But for this process of transposition to happen, it was necessary for the myth to undergo a long elaboration by the religious brotherhoods and the philosophical sects, culminating in Plato's texts.

Of course, the theme of the Styx lent itself to such a mythical reinterpretation. As a river of the underworld, it already had a place in the eschatological accounts of the soul's peregrinations after death. As the river of impurity, contrasted with a fountain with cathartic properties, it corresponded to the major preoccupations of the religious sects, especially their obsession with defilement and their thirst for purification. However, within the framework of mystical thought, the legendary theme of two springs had to be fundamentally re-elaborated before it could be used to represent the search for salvation, which, within the sects, had become the very aim of religious life. Henceforth earthly existence is seen as a defilement, as if it were the death of the soul after the blessed life that it originally shared with the gods. And conversely, as a purification against evil, the water of Life no longer offers health and strength on this earth but opens up a way for the soul to reach the true life beyond death. With this reversal in attitude, life becomes charged with the mythical values attached to death, and death acquires those that were hitherto associated with life. At the same time, the two opposed fountains, memory and oblivion, take over the place in the mystical texts that, according to Pausanias, the river Styx and the spring of Alussos occupied in Arcadia. In the myths of reincarnation, the defilement that is brought about by the water of death becomes, with the fall into a new corporeal existence, oblivion of all previous lives and ignorance of the soul's destiny. The purification bestowed by the water of life comes to mean the initiate's infallible memory concerning things in the beyond, the wisdom that will make possible his definitive escape from the cycle of becoming. It was thus that the path soon taken by philosophical reflection was opened up — by myth. If the meaning of Lēthē is a return to generation, if the impure life is that of becoming, this is because temporal flux is itself a force of destruction, comparable to the Arcadian Styx — the fatal power that annihilates all things on this earth, the terrible flow that nothing can contain.[58] In these circumstances, *meletē mnēmēs* practice of remembering, takes on within the philosophical brotherhoods the double significance of an intellectual investigation aimed at acquiring the most complete knowledge and a training for salvation that will bring victory over time and death.[59]

In the closing lines of the *Republic*, Plato rejoices that the *muthos* of Er the Pamphylian has not perished. Those who continue to believe in it will also have a chance of salvation: they will be able to cross the river Amelēs without "defiling" their souls. With this remark, Plato, half-serious and half-joking, acknowledges his own debt to the legendary themes that he has modified and that retain an incomparable power of suggestion thanks to their deep roots in the religious past of the Greeks. Certainly, for him, philosophy has dethroned myth and taken its place, but one reason why philosophy is valid is that it has been able to preserve the "truth" that was expressed, in its way, by myth.

PART THREE

The Organization of Space

CHAPTER SIX

Hestia-Hermes: The Religious Expression of Space and Movement in Ancient Greece

On the base of the great statue of Zeus at Olympia, Pheidias carved the twelve gods. Between the Sun (Helios) and the Moon (Selene), the twelve deities were arranged in orderly pairs, a god and goddess in each couple, and in the center of the frieze appeared Aphrodite and Ērōs — the two deities (female and male) who preside over unions.[1] In this series of eight divine couples, there is one pair that poses a problem: Hermes and Hestia. Why are they together? Neither their genealogies nor their legends can explain this association. They are not husband and wife, like Zeus and Hera, Poseidon and Amphitrite, and Hephaistos and Charis; they are not brother and sister, like Apollo and Artemis and Helios and Selene; they are not mother and son, like Aphrodite and Ērōs; they are not even protector and protégé, like Athena and Herakles.

What link, in Pheidias's mind, unites a god and goddess who appear to be without connection? The pairing can hardly be ascribed to the sculptor's personal fancy. The artist of classical times was bound to conform to certain models when creating any sacred work of art: his creativity could be expressed only within the forms laid down by tradition. Hestia — the name of a goddess but also the noun meaning *hearth* — was less suited to anthropomorphic representation than the other Greek gods and goddesses. She is seldom depicted, and when she is, she is often, as in this case, Hermes's partner.[2] In the plastic arts, then, the Hermes-Hestia association is invested with real religious significance. It is meant to express a definite structure in the Greek pantheon.

Meagerly represented in the arts, Hestia is even more poorly served in mythical tales: remarks concerning her birth by Hesiod and Pindar, an allusion to her virginal status in the *Hymn to Aphrodite*. We would know practically nothing about her that could explain her relations with Hermes were it not for a few lines in the *Homeric Hymn to Hestia*. In this text, the two deities are associated in the closest possible way. The hymn opens with six lines invoking Hestia, followed immediately by six lines of invocation to Hermes, whose protection is sought "in agreement with the worshipful goddess who is dear (*philē*) to him," and it closes with two lines addressed to the god and goddess jointly. On two occasions, the poet stresses the feeling of friendship that Hermes and Hestia nurture for each other. This mutual *philia* explains why Pheidias places them with the other couples under the patronage of Aphrodite and Ērōs. Nevertheless, this reciprocal affection is based neither on blood ties nor on ties of marriage nor on personal interdependence. It is the result of an affinity of function, for the two powers are present in the same places and carry out their complementary activities side by side. Neither relations nor spouses nor lovers nor vassals — one could say that Hermes and Hestia are "neighbors". Each is related to the terrestrial sphere, the habitat of a settled people. The hymn sings that the two gods "in friendship together dwell in the glorious houses of men who live on the earth's surface (*epichthonioi*)."[3]

That Hestia should reside in the house goes without saying: in the middle of the quadrangular *megaron*, the rounded Mycenaean hearth marks the center of the human dwelling. According to the *Hymn to Aphrodite*, "Zeus the Father gave her [Hestia] a high honor instead of marriage, and she has her place in the midst of the house (*mesōi oikōi*)."[4] But Hestia does not only represent the center of the domestic sphere. Fixed in the ground, the circular hearth is the navel that ties the house to the earth. It is the symbol and pledge of fixity, immutability, and permanence. In the

Phaedrus, Plato evokes the cosmic procession of the twelve gods.[5] Ten deities follow in Zeus's wake as he leads them across the heavens. Only Hestia remains at home and never leaves her abode. For the poets and philosophers, Hestia, the node and starting point of the orientation and arrangement of human space, could be identified with the earth, immobile at the center of the cosmos. According to Euripides, "the Sages call the Earth-Mother Hestia because she remains motionless at the center of the Ether."[6]

Hermes is also associated, though in a different way, with man's habitat and, more generally, with the terrestrial sphere. In contrast to the distant gods who dwell in the beyond, Hermes is a familiar god who frequents this world. Living among mortals on terms of intimacy, he introduces the divine presence into the very heart of the world of mankind. As Zeus says to him in the *Iliad*: "Hermes, you love above all else to serve as a mortal's companion (*hetairissai*)."[7] And Aristophanes salutes him as the most "friendly to man" of all the gods.[8] When Hermes manifests himself on earth — when, with Hestia, he inhabits the dwellings of mortals — he does so in the form of the messenger (he is specifically invoked by the name Hermes Angelos in the *Hymn to Hestia*), as a traveler who comes from afar and is already preparing to depart. Nothing about him is settled, stable, permanent, restricted, or definite. He represents, in space and in the human world, movement and flow, mutation and transition, contact among foreign elements. In the house, his place is at the door, protecting the threshold, repelling thieves because he is himself the thief (Hermes Lēistēr, the robber, Pulēdokos, the watcher at the gates, Nuktos Opōpētēr, the watcher by night), for whom no lock, no barricade, no frontier exists.[9] He is the wall piercer who is depicted in the *Hymn to Hermes* as "gliding edgewise through the keyhole of the hall like the autumn breeze, even as mist."[10] Present at the front doors of houses (Hermes Pulaios, Thuraios, Strophaios), he also stands at the gateways of towns, on state boundaries, at crossroads (Hermes Trikephalos, Tetrakephalos), as a landmark along paths and tracks (Hermes Hodios, Enodios), and on tombs — the gateways to the underworld (Hermes Chthonios, Nuchios).[11] In all the places where men gather outside their private dwellings and enter into contact for the purpose of exchange (whether for the exchange of ideas or for trade), as in the agora, or for competition, as in the stadium, Hermes is present (Hermes Agoraios, Hermes Agōnios). He is the witness to agreements, truces, and oaths between opponents; he is the herald, messenger, and ambassador abroad (Hermes Angelos, Diaktoros, Kērukeios). A wandering god, the patron of the roads both on and leading to the earth, he is the traveler's guide in this life, and escorts souls to Hades — and sometimes brings them back in the other (Hermes Pompaios, Kataibatēs, Psuchopompos). He leads the dance of the Charites, introduces the seasons, brings about the change from waking to sleep and sleep to waking, from life to death, from one world to another. He is the link, the mediator between mortals and the gods, both those of the world above and those of the underworld. The bust of him at the Villa Albani bears the inscription *coeli terraeque meator*, and Electra addresses him in these words: "Herald (*kērux*) supreme between the world above and the world below, oh nether Hermes, come to my aid and summon me the spirits beneath the earth to attend my prayers."[12] In mingling with humanity, Hermes remains at once elusive and ubiquitous. He makes an abrupt appearance where least expected, only to disappear again immediately. When there was a sudden pause in the conversation and silence reigned, the Greeks used to say: "Hermes is passing."[13] He wears the helmet of Hades, which grants the wearer invisibility, and winged sandals that do away with distance. He carries a magic wand that transforms all he touches. He is the unpredictable, the uncontrollable. He is also chance, good or bad luck, the unexpected meeting. In Greek a godsend is *to hermaion*.

Through this profusion of epithets, this variety of attributes, Hermes emerges as an extraordinarily complex figure. He has been so baffling that it has been suggested that in the beginning there must have been several different Hermes gods, which later merged into one.[14] The various characteristics that are combined in the god's general makeup seem, however, to fall into order more easily if he is considered in light of his relations with Hestia.

If the two deities form a couple in the religious beliefs of the Greeks, it is because they belong to the same plane, their action applies to the same field of reality, and their functions are interrelated. Now, Hestia's significance is obvious; her role is strictly defined. Because her fate is to reign, forever immobile, at the center of the domestic sphere, Hestia implies, as her complement and her contrast, the swift-footed god who rules the realms of the traveler. To Hestia belongs the world of the interior, the enclosed, the stable, the retreat of the human group within itself; to Hermes, the outside world, opportunity, movement, interchange with others. It could be said that, by virtue of their polarity, the Hermes-Hestia couple represents the marked tension in the archaic conception of space: space requires a center, a nodal point, with a special value, from which all directions, all qualitatively different, may be channeled and defined; yet, at the same time, space is the medium of movement, implying the possibility of transition and passage from any point to another.

Obviously, by interpreting the relationship between Hermes and Hestia in terms of these concepts, we distort it. The Greeks who worshipped these deities never saw them as symbols of space and movement. The organization of a pantheon was ruled by a logic that does not follow our criteria. Religious thought obeys its own rules of classification. It defines and orders phenomena by distinguishing different types of agents, by comparing and contrasting various kinds of activities. In this system, space and movement are not yet interpreted in the form of abstract ideas. They remain implicit in that they are incorporated into more material and more dynamic aspects of reality. Hestia appears capable of "centering" space while Hermes can "mobilize" it because, as divine powers, they are the patrons of a series of activities dealing with the organization of earth and space and even constituting, in terms of praxis, the framework within which, for the ancient Greeks, the experience of spatiality took place — but which nevertheless covers a much wider field than that implied by talk of space and movement.

The relationship of the Greek Hestia to the Roman Vesta has given rise to more than a few disagreements.[15] There was no persona or function in Greece that compared to the Vestal Virgins. It is, however, difficult not to believe that the care of the Mycenaean hearth, in particular the royal hearth, was at first a sacred office performed by women and that this duty fell to the daughter of the house prior to her marriage.[16] Louis Deroy has even argued that the word *parthenos* (virgin) is a functional designation meaning "she who tends the fire."[17] Be that as it may, if fire (the sacrificial fire as much as that of the forge or the cooking fire) is related to Hephaistos, a male god, the round altar of the domestic hearth is, on the contrary, associated with a virginal female deity. The usual explanation in terms of the purity of fire is not satisfactory. For one thing, Hestia is not fire but the altar-hearth; for another, Hephaistos, who is precisely the incarnation of this power of fire, is anything but pure.[18] In order to interpret these facts, therefore, it would be better to go back to the short passage in the *Homeric Hymn to Aphrodite* concerning Hestia, which is sufficiently explicit.[19] The hymn exalts Aphrodite's supremacy: nothing can withstand her, neither beasts nor men nor gods. But the goddess's prerogative is not the brutal domination and physical coercion appropriate to the warrior deities. Her weapons, even more successful, are tenderness and charm. No creature in the heavens, on earth, or in the sea can escape the magic powers of the forces she mobilizes: Peithō (persuasion), Apatē (alluring charm), Philotēs (the bonds of love). In all the universe, there are only three goddesses able to withstand her magic arts: Athena, Artemis, and Hestia. Unshakeable in their determination to remain virgins, they oppose Cytherea with such staunch hearts and such resolute will that neither the wiles of Peithō nor the fascinations of Apatē succeed in changing their sentiments or altering their status. The hymn particularly emphasizes this fixity of purpose, this obstinacy in refusing to change, with regard to Hestia. Wooed by Poseidon and Apollo, who both desire her, Hestia firmly (*stereōs*) rejects their suit, and to make this refusal irrevocable she takes the grand oath of the gods — "that which can never be retracted" — and vows to remain an eternal virgin. There can be no doubt that Hestia's function as goddess of the hearth is related to the permanence of her virginal status: the text specifies that Zeus gives her the right to take up residence at the center of the house in compensation for the nuptials (*anti gamoio*) she has renounced forever. For Hestia, the wedded state would have been the negation of the values she represents at the heart of the house (*oikos*, signifying both the dwelling place and the human group inhabiting it): values of fixity, permanence, seclusion. Does not marriage, after all, imply the twofold transformation of the young girl — of herself as a person and of her social status? On the one hand, it is a form of initiation by which she accedes to a new status, to a different world of human and religious realities; on the other, it uproots her from the domestic milieu to which she once belonged.[20] When she is established at her husband's hearth, she becomes part of another house.[21] Speaking more generally, the union of the sexes is a contract and, of all contracts, the one that involves the two greatest natural opposites — male and female. In this connection, one of the essential aspects of Greek *charis* should be emphasized: *charis* is the divine power manifest in all aspects of gift giving and reciprocity (the round of generous liberality, the cordial exchange of gifts), which, in spite of all divisions, spins a web of reciprocal obligations, and one of the oldest of all the functions of *charis* is a woman's giving herself to a man.[22] Thus it is not surprising that Hermes, who is closely linked with the Charites (Hermes *charidotēs*), also plays a part in the union of the sexes and appears side by side with Aphrodite as the true master of Peithō, of the persuasion capable of shaking the most fixed resolves, of changing the most confirmed opinions.[23]

But this analysis can be taken further. In Greek, the domestic sphere, the enclosed space that is roofed over (protected), has a feminine connotation; the exterior, the open air, has a masculine one. The woman's domain is the house. That is her place, and, as a rule, she should not leave it.[24] In contrast, in the *oikos*, the man represents the centrifugal element. It is for him to leave the reassuring enclosure of the home, to confront the fatigues and dangers of the outside world, to brave the unknown, to establish contact with the outside, to enter into negotiations with strangers. Whether he is engaged in work, war, trade, social contacts, or public life, whether he is in the country or the *agora*, on sea or on land, man's activities are oriented toward the outside. Xenophon is merely expressing a common belief when, after contrasting mankind with beasts as needing a roof over its head instead of living in the open — *en hupaithrōi* — he adds that the gods have endowed men and women with opposite characters. Body and soul, man is made for the *erga hupaithria, ta exō erga*, the open-air life and outside activities, and woman, for the indoor life, *ta endon*. Therefore, "to the woman it is more honorable to stay indoors than to go out into the fields, but to the man it is unseemly to stay indoors rather than to attend to the work outside."[25]

Nevertheless, there is one instance when the man's orientation toward the exterior and the woman's toward the interior is reversed. In marriage, in contrast to all other social activities, the woman is the mobile social element whose movement creates the link between different family groups, whereas the man remains tied to his own hearth and home. The ambiguity of the female's status lies in the fact that the daughter of the house (who is, by virtue of her femininity, more closely linked to the domestic sphere than the son) can not fulfill herself as a woman in marriage without renouncing the hearth of which she is in charge. The contradiction is reconciled in the sphere of religious representation by the image of a deity who personifies the permanent aspects of feminine nature, while remaining, through her virginal status, a stranger to mobility. This permanence of Hestia's is not only spatial. As she bestows on the house the center that anchors it in space, so Hestia ensures the domestic group's continued existence in time. It is through Hestia that the family line is perpetuated and remains constant, as though in each new generation the legitimate offspring of the household were born directly "of the hearth." Through the goddess of the hearth, fertility, dissociated from sexual relations (which, in an exogamous system, postulate relations between different families), can appear as an indefinite prolongation of the paternal line through the daughter, without the need for a "foreign" woman for procreation.

This dream of a purely paternal heredity never ceased to haunt the Greek imagination. It is openly expressed in the *Eumenides* when Apollo proclaims that maternal blood can never run in the veins of the son, seeing that "the mother of what is called her child is not its begetter; the begetter is the man, he who plants the seed, whereas she doth but preserve the sprout as a stranger would tend a stranger (*xenō xenē*)."[26] Doctors and philosophers disguise this dream as scientific theory when they maintain, as Aristotle did for instance, that in procreation the female emits no seed, that her role is entirely passive, that the active regenerating function is exclusively male.[27] The same dream is discernible in the royal myths in which the newborn child is compared to an ember from the paternal hearth. The stories of Meleagros and of Demophoon recall the Latin legends — most likely Greek in origin — in which the king's son is born from a brand or spark leaping from the fire into the lap of the virgin tending the hearth.[28] The ritual appellation "Hearth-Child" (which, in the historic age, designated the city's representative to the deities of Eleusis) has very much the meaning and import that Gernet gives it when he specifically emphasizes the close relationship between the hearth and the child in Greece: *Pais aph' hestias* literally represents the child "issued from the hearth."[29] And, as we shall see, the ritual of the Amphidromia, whereby a seven-day-old child is attached to its father's hearth, should be understood in this context.

Hestia thus expresses — by pushing it to its limits — the *oikos's* tendency toward self-isolation and withdrawal, as though the ideal for the family should be complete self-sufficiency, which means total economic self-sufficiency and strict endogamy in marriage.[30] This ideal does not conform with Greek reality. But it is nevertheless present in family institutions and the forms they take to ensure their continued existence, and it is one of the axes around which the domestic life of ancient Greece was organized.

There is an example in Sophocles's *Electra* that allows us to judge the magnitude and the limits of the a *oikos's* tendency toward introversion. This is the dream that reveals to Clytaemnestra the imminent return of Orestes, the son she attempted to dispose of after murdering her husband, Agamemnon, with the help of her lover, Aegisthus. Once the lawful king is dead, Aegisthus shares the throne with his wife, the queen.[31] Clytaemnestra gives Aegisthus the scepter Agamemnon inherited from his forefathers, and the libations that the new king pours out for Hestia in the palace hall are in fact to honor an alien hearth.[32] In relation to the royal hearth of Mycenae, therefore, Aegisthus is in the same position as the woman normally is in her husband's *oikos*. In the tragedy, this inversion of the social status of the spouses corresponds to a similar inversion of their relations and their psychological characteristics. In the couple, Clytaemnestra is the man and Aegisthus is the woman.[33] All the great tragic writers agree in depicting Aegisthus as effeminate, cowardly, a voluptuary, and a womanizer, who succeeds through women and whose prowess is confined solely to the domain of arms and battle ruled by Aphrodite.[34] To Clytaemnestra, on the other hand, belong the qualities and dangers of an entirely masculine nature.[35] Deliberate, authoritative, bold, born to command, she disdainfully rejects all the frailties of her sex. It is made very clear that she reverts to womanhood only in bed. In her decision to murder Agamemnon, the legitimate grievances she could invoke against her husband weigh less than her refusal to accept masculine domination, her determination to take the man's place in the home.[36] This is her dream: "She beheld Agamemnon in bodily presence standing by her side, revisiting the light of day. He took the scepter of Aegisthus, once his own, and at the household altar planted it, and from it sprang and spread a fruitful bough till it overshadowed all Mycenae's land."[37]

The sexual symbolism (Agamemnon planting the seed of the young shoot in Hestia's bosom, where it will sprout) is inseparable in this instance from the social symbolism. The *skēptron* is a kind of mobile representation of sovereignty. Zeus transmitted it through Hermes to the House of Atreus. The king entrusts it to his herald and his ambassadors. In the assembly of the elders, the scepter passes from hand to hand, conferring on each orator in turn the authority and respect he requires in order to speak. The scepter's royal quality could not remain intact throughout all these delegations and transfers if it were not firmly rooted in the hearth. Corresponding to the staff (the *rhabdos*, the *kērukeion* that Hermes brandishes or waves is the symbol that in all representations is placed in Hestia's hand as her ritual attribute, the *skēptron* in its proper meaning.[38] But Aegisthus did not receive the scepter *aph' Hestias*. It was transmitted to him obliquely through a woman, herself a stranger to the House of Atreus, and moreover in a feminine way — in and by way of the bed. By reestablishing it in the hearth, Agamemnon wrenches it from the usurpers and returns it to his own descendants, who alone are truly implanted in Mycenaean soil. Analogous to the burning brand of the Latin legends, the staff set in the hearth symbolizes the royal seed (*sperma*) placed earlier by Agamemnon in Clytaemnestra's womb, where it grows: Orestes, the child become man, hated and feared by his mother because in him the father finds his avenger and his perpetuation.[39] The dream could not say more clearly that Agamemnon in fact begot Orestes beyond the person of Clytaemnestra, in his own hearth, which roots the royal house to the soil of Mycenae. Just as in her wifely role she should always have effaced herself before her husband, as a mother Clytaemnestra should efface herself before Hestia, her own role being confined to cherishing, as a stranger would, the human seedling entrusted to her safekeeping by her husband.[40] But instead, by asserting her masculine determination, she aspires to displace the male in all spheres. She lays claim to the active function in the government of the state, in marriage, in procreation, in all her relationships, just as she assumes it, sword in hand, in carrying out a crime in which she leaves to her confederate the feminine part: instigation, complicity, and cunning.[41] Clytaemnestra mounts the throne in Agamemnon's place.[42] She takes over the scepter and the power. She summons to the House of Atreus, which henceforth she proclaims her own, the bedfellow she has decided to make a husband.[43] She asserts that in begetting the woman's role prevails over that of the man.[44] She denies the children she has had by

167

Agamemnon, who belong to the paternal line. As for those she has by Aegisthus, that *oikouros*, that "domesticated man" who preferred to stay with the women at home rather than set off with the men to war, Clytaemnestra wants them; she makes them so completely hers that they take their name from their mother instead of from their father.[45] In Euripides's tragedy, Electra, confronting Aegisthus's corpse, denounces the "inverted" relationship of Agamemnon's murderers: "And through all Argos the people called the man by the woman's name, and not the wife by her husband's name. Yet shame is this when foremost in the home is wife, not husband. I hold in horror the sons whom the city calls not by their father's name, but by their mother's."[46]

It is Hestia who expresses herself through Electra. Agamemnon's daughter represents the paternal household, from which she, like her brother, has been cast out and which she wishes to restore with him by expelling the intruders who have established themselves there. But, in her relationship with Orestes, Electra is not only the sister so closely linked to the brother that their two lives merge in a single soul; she is also the mother — in truth the only mother of Orestes.[47] As a child, she cherished, protected, and safeguarded him: "For never were you your mother's love as much as mine. It was I, your sister, who fed you, and it was always me you called for."[48] As he grows up, she urges him to take vengeance, she supports and guides him in carrying out the double murder that makes them the "saviors of the father's hearth."[49] At her young brother's side, taking the place of the mother whose dominating and vigorous character she has inherited, Electra is a double to Clytaemnestra and at the same time stands in opposition to her.[50] As a virgin (*Elektra* can be associated with *alektra*, without wedlock,[51] and Euripides's Electra remains chaste even in marriage), she wishes to be all the more pure in contrast to the sensuality and licentiousness she imagines in her mother.[52] She loves her father as forcefully as Clytaemnestra hates him.[53] Of these two equally masculine women, one has embraced the saying of Athena, a goddess who, like Hestia, is dedicated to virginity: "With all my soul I am for the male, in all things, save wedlock."[54]

In contrast, the other, the "polyandrous woman," the "female killer of men," is against man in all his aspects; she wants him only as a bedfellow.[55] For inverse reasons, both are outside the domain of marriage: one does not enter its orbit, the other goes beyond it. Electra unreservedly takes the part of the father because, being attached to the home, she refuses the conjugal relationship and recognizes no progeniture of her own; her brother perpetuates the paternal line and, for her, simultaneously takes the place of son, father, and husband. Clytaemnestra declares herself unreservedly on the side of the mother insofar as she rejects the status of wife. She disowns the children who remind her of the husband's home and of the wife's subjection to him. Like the Erīnyes, who defend her cause at the level of the divine powers, she scorns marital ties.[56] Of the blood ties that she upholds against them and that she prefers to them, she wishes to retain only the ones that connect the child with the womb that bore it, the breast that nourished it. For her, the husband is restricted to the role of sexual partner. He no longer leads his wife to his domestic altar, nor is he the progenitor of her children. He enacts for his wife the role normally assumed by a concubine in relation to a man — that of bedfellow.[57]

It has become a platitude that in Greek theater, the story of Orestes expresses through tragedy the conflicts that tear apart the institution of the family, particularly those which set man and woman against each other within the home: the conflicts between man and wife, son and mother, paternal and maternal lines. But in insisting so strongly on the antagonism between Electra and Clytaemnestra, who are alike in so many ways, the tragedies also emphasize the contradictions that divide a woman against herself and the oppositions within her social and psychological status. Being deities, Hestia, Aphrodite, and Hera can personify a single facet of feminine reality to the exclusion of all others. But this "purity" is impossible for human beings. Every mortal woman has to take on the totality of the female state, with all its tensions, ambiguities, and conflicts. In wishing to be fully associated with

Hestia or completely against her, Electra and Clytaemnestra present a split picture of woman, deformed and contradictory. They destroy their femininity and emerge, both of them, as equally manly. By associating herself with the home in which she was born, Electra identifies herself with the men of her paternal lineage. By seizing her husband's home to found her own maternal line, Clytaemnestra makes herself a man. She is right in — unlike Electra — accepting the sexual union (woman and man being complementary), forsaking her father's house, and adopting that of her husband (the woman's function of mobility). On the other hand, Electra is right in focusing the whole life of the couple around the husband's hearth (the "patrilocal" nature of marriage, the submission of the wife to the husband, the domestic vocation of the woman). Electra is not wrong when she associates the child with the paternal line (the precedence of the masculine line), but Clytaemnestra is telling the truth when she proclaims that the child is of the blood of the mother (the rules prohibiting incest are stricter on the maternal side).[58] They both make the mistake of disavowing one aspect of consanguinity (affiliation among the Greeks is bilateral).

In a masculine society such as Greece, the woman is seen from the man's point of view, and from this standpoint, she fulfills through marriage two major social functions that diverge, if they are not polar opposites. In its oldest form (and among the nobility described in epic poetry), marriage is a formalized transaction between family groups and the woman is one element of the exchange. Her role is to seal the alliance between opposing groups. Like a ransom, she may be the means of bringing a vendetta to an end.[59] One of the normal wedding gifts that seal the new agreement is explicitly given in exchange for the woman and is, in fact, the price paid for her. This is the *hedna*, a valuable commodity of a very definite type: prize animals from the flocks and herds, especially bulls of great prestige value, which are often represented as infinite. Through this practice of purchase, woman becomes an exchange commodity. Mobile like other commodities, she is similarly the medium for gifts, exchanges, and abduction.[60]

In contrast, the man who welcomes his wife to his house (this is *sunoikein*, cohabiting with the husband, which defines the state of marriage for the wife) represents the landed property of the *oikos*, the *patrōia*, generally inalienable, which through the rise and fall of succeeding generations maintains the bond between the family line and its native soil. This idea of symbiosis or, even better, communion between a plot of earth and the human group that cultivates it exists not only in religious thought (witness the myths of autochthony: men asserting that they are the "sons of the soil" they inhabit) and in the rites of sacred ploughing (discussed below) but also, and with remarkable persistence, in city institutions. Since the term *oikos* has both a family and a territorial meaning, it is easy to understand the undercurrents that hamper purchases and sales in the case of family landed property (*klēros*) in a fully mercantile economy. Equally comprehensible is the refusal to grant strangers the right to own "the city's" land: this is the privilege and right of the authochthonous citizen.

Marriage, however, does not solely consist in this form of commerce between families. It also allows men of a particular lineage to found a family and thus to ensure the continued survival of their house. The Greeks compared marriage to ploughing the soil (*arotos*), the woman symbolizing the furrow (*aroura*) and the man, the ploughman (*arotēr*). This imagery, almost obligatory for the tragic poets but also employed by the prose writers, is much more than a mere literary device.[61] It is in line with the plighting of troth in the stereotypical declaration made familiar by the comedies. The father or the *kurios* authorized to arrange the daughter's marriage pronounces the pledge of betrothal (*egguē*): "I bestow this girl in order that ploughing shall bring forth legitimate children."[62] Plutarch, referring to the existence in Athens of three ceremonies of sacred ploughing (*hieroi arotoi*), remarks, "But most sacred of all sowings is the marital sowing and ploughing (*gamēlios arotos*) for the procreation of children."[63]

The woman, at one moment as an element of commerce, equivalent to a flock by virtue of being movable property, is now, in her procreative function, identified with a field. Paradoxically, however, she embodies not her native land but that of her husband. And it must be the husband's land, for otherwise the sons issuing from the ploughed furrow would not have the religious qualifications to take over their father's property and work the land productively. Through Clytaemnestra, but also in opposition to her, as a "foreigner," the land of Mycenae fosters the germination and growth of the tree that casts its shadow over all the land of the House of Atreus, marking its boundaries in the process. This shadow (*skia*), projected by the royal scion born of the hearth and rooted at the center of the domain, possesses beneficent properties. It protects the land of Mycenae. It transforms it into a domestic enclosure, a place of security, where everyone feels at home, protected from want, in a climate of family friendship.[64] Handed down from father to son, the *sacra*, the privilege of royal houses or of certain noble *genē*, ensures simultaneously the defense of the land against dangers from outside, internal peace with justice, and the fertility of the soil and flocks. Should a prince be unworthy or illegitimate, the land, the flocks, and the women will be barren, and war and dissension will be rife. But if the rightful king acts according to the rules and upholds justice, then his people will flourish in boundless prosperity: "For them Earth bears plentiful food and on the mountain the oak carries acorns and bees at its centre; The fleecy sheep are laden down with wool; the womenfolk bear children that resemble their parents."[65] It seems legitimate to believe that the practice of sacred ploughing, which was still the custom right up to historical times and which in the city was carried out by such priestly families as the Bouzygai, was an extension of ancient royal rites designed not only to introduce and regulate the agricultural calendar but also to promote, through the act of tilling, the king's marriage to his land, as in earlier times Jason was joined to Demeter on thrice-ploughed fallow land.[66]

The need for the husband to summon a strange wife to his home, there to personify the family land where his children will grow, seems less paradoxical if a further aspect of Hestia is considered. In the words of the Homeric hymn: "For without you

[Hestia], mortals hold no banquet — where one does not duly pour sweet wine in offering to Hestia both first and last."[67] It is therefore Hestia's prerogative (*timē*) to preside over repasts that, by beginning and closing with an invocation of the goddess, form a cycle enclosed within time as the *oikos* forms an enclosed circle in space. Having been cooked on the altar of the domestic hearth, the food engenders a religious fellowship among those at table. It creates a kind of common identity among them. From Aristotle we know the epithet Epimenides of Crete used for members of the *oikos*: homokapoi, those who eat at the same table or, according to another reading, those who inhale the same smoke (homokapnoi).[68] By virtue of the hearth, the table companions become "brothers," as if of the same blood. Thus the expression "to sacrifice to Hestia" has the same meaning as our proverb that charity begins at home. When the ancients sacrificed to Hestia, no portion of the offering was given to anyone. The household shared its collective repast in privacy, and no stranger was allowed to participate.[69] Under the sign of the goddess the family circle shuts itself in; the domestic group strengthens its ties and asserts its unity in consuming food forbidden to the stranger.

But there is a counterpart to this. The verb hestian — in both its generally accepted meanings: receiving in the home and accepting at the table — is usually applied to a guest being celebrated in the house. The hearth, the meal, and the food also have the property of opening the domestic circle to those who are not members of the family, of enrolling them in the family community. The suppliant, hounded from his home and wandering abroad, crouches at the hearth when he seeks to enter a new group in order to recover the social and religious roots he has lost.[70] And the stranger must be led to the hearth, received, and fed there, for there can be neither contact nor exchange with those who have not first been integrated within the domestic space. Pindar wrote that at the always ready tables of sanctuaries where Hestia was the patron goddess, the justice of Zeus Xenios was respected.[71] Relations with a stranger (*xenos*), are thus Hestia's province as much when receiving a guest in the home as when returning to one's own house after a journey or a mission abroad. In both cases, contact with the hearth assumes the value of deconsecration and reintegration into family space.[72] The center symbolized by Hestia, therefore, not only defines a closed and isolated world but also presupposes, as a corollary, other, analogous centers. Through the exchange of goods and the movement of people — women, heralds, ambassadors, guests, and table companions — a network of "alliances" is built up among domestic groups. Without being part of the family line of descent, an outside element can become joined to and integrated within a household other than its own, more or less permanently. The "foreign" wife thus enters her husband's *oikos* through the ritual of the *katachusmata* and becomes part of his home. As long as she dwells in her husband's house, she can by virtue of her procreative powers assume the attributes of permanence, continuity, and rootedness in the soil that Hestia represents.[73]

Each stage of this analysis has shown the polarity between the static and the mobile, the open and the enclosed, the interior and the exterior: a polarity that is not only evident in the interplay of domestic institutions (division of labor, marriage, consanguinity, meals) but also inscribed even in the nature of man and woman. It is also present among the heavenly powers in the structure of the pantheon, for neither Hermes nor Hestia can, in fact, be viewed in isolation. They fulfill their functions as a couple: the existence of the one implies that of the other. Each is a necessary counterpart to the other. Furthermore, their very complementarity implies a contradiction or internal tension in each of them that gives their characters as gods a fundamental ambiguity.

Hestia, in her chastity, remains outside the sexual relations that belong to the wife or concubine in the household. But, in order to fulfill her function of permanence in time, the virgin goddess must also be seen as a mother. It will be remembered, in this connection, that in associating Gaia and Hestia, Euripides uses the expression Gaia-Mētēr, Earth-Mother.[74] Hestia is thus represented in the paternal line of descent as woman both as virgin daughter and as procreator, as the reservoir of life. Porphyry stresses this polarity, pointing to the existence of not one but two images of Hestia: on the one hand, the model virgin (*parthenikon*), but on the other, since Hestia is the power of fertility (*gonimos*), the matron with protuberant breasts (*gunaikos promastou*).[75] These two aspects, normally separated in human practice, find themselves in harmony only in the *epiklēros*. At first, Greek family system's custom of *epiklēros* seems to be a complete anomaly. It is, in fact, an extreme case and a particularly valuable one in that it momentarily upsets the usual balance and reveals one of the trends of domestic organization — the very one that can be detected in the figure of the goddess of the hearth — in its purest state.

The best way to define the institution of the *epiklēros* is by reference to the definition in *The Laws of Manu* concerning the equivalent Indian practice.[76]

> He who is without a son may instruct his daughter to provide him with one by marrying her in such a way and according to a convention such that the child she gives birth to will become his own and perform the funeral ceremony for him. The day the girl married in this way gives birth to a son, the maternal grandfather becomes the father of the child.[77]

In Greece, as in India, it means in practice that the daughter of a man without male descendants gives her father the son he lacks, who alone has the right qualifications to inherit the paternal *klēros*. The daughter is termed *epiklēros* in that she belongs to her father's *klēros* and is joined to him (in Sparta and Crete she is called *patrouchos*). On her father's death, and in accordance with a carefully regulated preferential order of marriage, the *epiklēros* must be married to the male member of her family who, being closest in kinship to the deceased father, is designated to represent him: first, the father's brothers (the girl's paternal uncles), then their sons (the girl's first cousins), then the brothers of the girl's paternal grandfather (her paternal great-uncles), or one of their children (her first cousins once removed); failing these, the sons of the father's sisters, or, in the last resort, the sons of the paternal grandfather's sisters.[78] The successional aspect of the practice, very strongly marked in the classical period, should not deceive us. The custom of *epikleros* establishes clearly, in the absence of any direct male heir, which kinsman should inherit the daughter and the estate associated with her. But it is far less a matter of transmitting property to a relative than one of preserving through the daughter the continuing existence of a hearth. From this point of view, a blood relative's marriage to the *epikleros* is not a right to an inheritance but a family obligation that imposes on the person concerned a real renunciation, for the son born of the marriage will perpetuate not his father's but his maternal grandfather's line. The term used to describe this child is *thugatridous*: "son of the daughter" or "grandson." Immediately upon reaching majority, the *thugatridous* has the right to take full possession of his maternal grandfather's *kleros*. Neither his father nor even his mother was really its owner. They were simply intermediaries whose duty was to ensure that it was handed down from the grandfather to the grandson.

Brief though they are, these remarks should suffice to situate the place and role of the various players in the institution of the *epikleros*. Contrary to the usual rules, the daughter remains attached to the paternal hearth after marriage. It could even be said that she is identified with it. It is literally in her that her father's line is continued by a new male. The man chosen to beget a child in this home is the one most closely related to the father and becomes, in performing his marital duties, the father's substitute. The child born of a marriage that joins him directly to his maternal grandfather becomes as much the brother as the son of she who gave him birth.[79] In the institution of the *epikleros*, the whole system of matrimonial relations is inverted. Now the woman represents stability; the man, mobility. The wife is no longer a stranger brought into the husband's home, eclipsing herself for the benefit of the domestic Hestia and assuming Hestia's attributes, to give birth to sons who truly "resemble the father," without disturbing the continuity of the line. In this instance, the wife, as the daughter of the house, *is* the paternal home. And so, this time, the husband must integrate himself within the *oikos* of his wife. It is for him to stand aside in favor of the father he represents, and in this way, the daughter can beget a child resembling its real father — that is, its maternal grandfather. Instead of the line of descent continuing (as it usually does) from father to son, *per viros*, via a stranger who by her cohabitation, her *sunoikēsis*, is attached to the home, the line is perpetuated *per feminas*, from mother to son, via the closest male relative whose blood affinity, his *suggenis*, joins him to the father.

The *epiklēros* is not, therefore, an aberration. It does not exist on the fringe of the matrimonial system. On the contrary, it is coupled with ordinary marriage and forms with it a whole that contains two opposite and symmetrical solutions to the same problem. The point is always to ensure the continuity of a line of descent, the survival of a home that must, through the ages, remain true to itself. And this is achieved in a marriage that by joining a man and a woman also unites one household with another, while at the same time preserving their two separate hearths. In the case of the *epiklēros*, the daughter of the house personifies, even in marriage, the paternal hearth, thus uniting the two aspects of Hestia that are normally dissociated among mortals: the virgin daughter of the father, and the woman as a lineage's reservoir of life. But it should be noted at once that the *epiklēros* is the outcome of quite exceptional circumstances that justify the reversal of the ordinary rules of marriage. It requires that both father and son, who usually constitute the continuity of the family line, be absent. It is due to the *lack of males* — the links in the chain of descent — that the daughter acquires the procreative capacity to give birth to a child capable of carrying on the paternal line. And even then, in order for her to be able to continue her father's line, a kinsman of the father must be joined to her in a marriage that effects, in a form that is lawful because it is only symbolic, the forbidden union of father and daughter, which seems the best way to safeguard the purity of the domestic hearth from generation to generation. But the price paid for the gain in consistency, from the point of view of Hestia's relations with the young woman, her representative, is a further and fundamental contradiction. In order to give a son to a man who does not have one — that is, to conform to the principle of descent *per viras* — the inverse principle of female consanguinity has to be exceptionally invoked, and the son of the *epiklēros*, the *thugatridous*, is attached not to his father but to his mother.

Therefore, in Greek social thought, confronting the image of the male as the sole agent in the act of procreation, the no less powerful image of the woman takes shape as the true source of life nourishing the fruitfulness of the house. Depending on the circumstances, the hearth goddess is able to justify either of these two contradictory images. It would seem that Hestia's particular function is to set the seal on the "incommunicability" of different hearths. Rooted as they are in specific locations, they can never mix; instead they remain "pure," even in the union of the sexes and in family alliances. In ordinary marriages, the purity of the hearth is ensured by the wife's integration into her husband's household. (Hestia being a virgin, the woman personifies her own hearth only while she remains a virgin as well. In marriage and procreation she no longer represents it. One might say she is "neutralized." She plays no definite part and is purely passive. The man alone is active.) In the *epiklēros*, in contrast, the purity of the hearth as symbolized by the daughter seems even better protected, in that the husband is less concerned in the act of procreation. If this view were taken to extremes, the daughter could be considered the only true generating force and the child treated as though it belonged solely to the mother.[80]

Hestia's "maternal" aspect strengthens the analogy between the circular hearth and the *omphalos*, that other circular, centrally situated symbolic object. In some cases, Hestia is pictured sitting not on a domestic hearth but on an *omphalos* and we know that the *omphalos* of Delphi was considered Hestia's seat.[81] In historic times, the altar of the communal hearth of Hestia

Koinē in the center of the town was called the *omphalos* of the city.[82]

The *omphalos*, a protuberance in the ground or an ovoid stone associated with the earth and occasionally referred to as Gē, represents at once a central point, a tomb, and a reservoir of souls and of life. Marie Delcourt has particularly studied the latter aspect.[83] She notes that the word "umbilicus" and the protuberant form of the *omphalos* evoke the two cases in which the navel protrudes instead of being hollow: the umbilicus of a woman in the later stages of her pregnancy and that of the newborn child, which recedes only after several days. Furthermore, the *omphalos* denotes, besides the navel, the umbilical cord, which joins a child to its mother as a stem connects a plant to the earth that has nourished it. It is easy to see why Greek physicians saw the *omphalos* as a root, the root of the abdomen, and why Philolaos, the fifth-century Pythagorean, made it the basis of his theory of the rootedness (*rhizōsis*) of man: each generation rooted in the previous one, but also the human descendants rooted in the soil of the paternal house.[84] As Artemidorus writes in his *Interpretations of Dreams*: "*The omphalos* symbolizes the parents for as long as they live, or the mother country in which each was born as he was born of the umbilicus. To dream of a mishap to the navel means one will be deprived of one's parents or country, and for he who is on foreign soil, *epi xenēs*, that he will never return home."[85]

As a corollary, the circular altar of the hearth, the symbol of the enclosed space of the house, can evoke the female abdomen, the source of life and children. Artemidorus writes: "The hearth signifies the life and the wife of the one who sees it," and later: "To light a fire which burns brightly in the hearth or in the oven signifies the begetting of children, for the hearth and oven are like a woman ... and fire in them foretells that the woman will become pregnant."[86] The religious significance of certain geometric forms should be noted here. Like the *omphalos,* and in contrast to the quadrangular Hermes (Hermes *tetragōnos*), Hestia's hearth is round.[87] There is every reason to believe that in Greece the circle was characteristic of chthonic and feminine powers associated with the image of the Earth-Mother containing within her bosom the dead, the successive generations of mankind, and plant life.[88] During the period of the city and the establishment of the communal hearth in the *prytaneum*, Hestia was associated with a rotunda, the *tholos*, the sole example of the circular form in Greek religious architecture, recalling the *aedes vestae* and the *mundus* of the Romans.[89] For a long time it was believed that the communal hearth was situated in the *tholos*, but it is now known that this was not always so. The *prytaneum* and the *tholos* could be distinct from each other, but, as Gernet points out, this negation should not be exaggerated.[90] At Delphi the communal hearth was indeed situated within the *tholos* of Marmaria. At Mantinea, according to Pausanias, the Hestia Koinē was found in a rotunda that also contained the tomb of a heroine.[91] At Olympia, at Sikyon, the *prytaneum* was composed of several buildings, and those sheltering Hestia may well have been circular. Furthermore, it would seem that the very name of the *tholos* at Athens, as at Sparta, emphasizes the affinity between this type of circular edifice and Hestia's religious symbolism. In both cities, the *tholos* is called the *skias*, a term that sometimes evokes the *skiades* (huts built with branches and leaves in the form of a tent, erected by the Spartans on the occasion of the Karneia), and at other times suggests the *skiron*, the large parasol (*skiadeion*) the Athenians carried at the feast of the Skirophoria. In any case, the epithet *skias* binds the tholos to the sphere of shadow and obscurity that, in contrast to outside space, characterizes the various forms of the protected enclosure, the interior: the underground world, the domestic space, the female abdomen.

We have already seen how the child that Agamemnon implanted in his hearth at the center of the kingdom "shaded," as he grew, all the land of Mycenae, or, in other words, extended to the farthest limits of the territory the protective shade that makes the house a covered shelter, an intimate realm where women can feel at home.[92] In contrast to the open air, dazzling with sun and light during the day and filled with dread in the dark of night, the hearth space, shaded and feminine, in the semidarkness of the fireplace, implies security, tranquility, and even a certain easy

softness incompatible with virility. Xenophon would later say that
artisans were moral cowards and physically soft because their
trade obliged them to remain indoors and live in the shade (*skia-*
trapheisthai) next to the fire, like women.[93] In the *Phaedrus*, Plato
contrasts the strong and vigorous boys brought up *en hēliō katharō*,
out in the sunlight in the stadium and *palaestra* (connected with
Hermes), with weak, tender shoots whose flesh is as white as that
of women because they have been nourished (*hupo summigei skiai*)
in the shelter of the twilight shadows.[94]

The *Homeric Hymn to Demeter* is more precise on this point.[95]
Demeter, wandering in the countryside after fleeing her Olympian dwelling place, has stopped not far from a well. Seated in the
shade (*en skiē*) under a dense olive tree, she resembles an old
woman such as a king's nurse or even a housekeeper (*tamiai*) in
the depths of her home. The daughters of Keleos, ruler of Eleusis,
see her. They are surprised to find her there, out of doors, and
they question her: "Why have you left the city instead of drawing
near to the houses? For there, in the *shady halls* are women of
just such an age as you and others younger."[96] The *megara skioenta*
evoke the expression used by Apollo in *Eumenides* to define the
family status of Athena: he declares that this goddess never had a
mother; she was not nursed on a shaded lap (*en skotoisi nēduos*).[97]
Does this comparison allow us to imagine that in the interplay of
mythical themes there is an association between the image of the
shadowy house symbolized by Hestia and that of the shelter of a
woman's lap? A study of the semantic values of a word like *thala-*
mos, itself related to *tholos*, would seem to indicate that there is
such an association. The word denotes the quarters reserved for
the women in the farthest, most secret depths of the house.[98]
Strictly forbidden to the stranger (an interior space) and closed
by a bolted door so that even the male slaves cannot have access
(a female space), the heart of the human dwelling place, often
described as *muchos*, has a chthonic aspect: the *thalamos* occasionally expresses the specific idea of an underground hiding
place; Danaē's prison, Trophonios's cavern, a tomb, could all be
called *thalamos*.[99] But, at the same time, the *thalamos* is related to

marriage. It denotes sometimes the young girl's room before her wedding and sometimes the nuptial chamber or, more explicitly, the nuptial couch, and the meaning of the verb *thalameuō* is to lead to the bridal bed, to marry.[100] Finally, a further meaning of the word *thalamos* is that of the hiding place in the most secret parts of the dwelling, where a woman stows her reserve stores, the domestic riches over which she, as mistress of the house, rules.[101] Sometimes the wife and sometimes the daughter is described as the keeper of the keys to this secret "treasure."[102] Because the woman is dedicated to the interior, her role is to store the goods that the man, who is oriented toward the exterior, brings home. From the point of view of economic activity, the woman personifies the act of storing and the man that of acquiring. The woman arranges, stores, and distributes within the *oikos* the riches the man has earned through his labors outside. This polarity between the functions of the two sexes is so strong that it is expressed by both adulators and detractors of women, always in the same type of comparison. Xenophon compares the model wife to the queen bee, who dwells in the hive watching over the honey collected outside and seeing that it accumulates in abundance in the cells of the honeycombs (those circular alveoli also bear the name *thalamos* or *thalamē*).[103] For Hesiod, in contrast to the man laboriously toiling outside to increase the earth's riches and make the necessities of life flow into the house, the woman is in the heart of the hive, like a drone, storing the riches acquired by the bee-husband not in the *thalamos* of their mutual dwelling place but directly in the depths of her own belly: "She remains indoors, within the shelter of the covered hives, and stores in her own belly the fruits of the toil of others."[104]

If, as in Plato's words, the woman "imitates" the earth by receiving the seed that the male implants in her, the house, like earth and woman, receives and keeps in its heart the wealth the man has brought to it. The enclosure of the dwelling place is intended not only to shelter the family group but also to gather, store, and preserve domestic goods. It is thus not surprising to see the goddess who symbolizes the interior, the center, and fixity, directly associated with this function of the dwelling place, which inflects the life of the *oikos* in two directions. First, in contrast to the circulation of riches under Hermes's patronage (exchange, profits, and expenditure), there is a trend toward accumulation (which in ancient times took the form of collecting food supplies in jars in the storeroom and accumulating precious objects such as *agalmata* locked up in the coffers of the *thalamos*; when a monetary economy was established, this became capitalization). Second, in contrast with the communal forms of social life, there is the tendency toward appropriation. Within the framework of a distributive economy, each house appears to be bound up with a plot of ground.[105] Each household is separate and differentiated and wants to have full control of the *klēros* on which it subsists and which distinguishes it from other domestic groups.

Under the title of Hestia Tamia, the hearth goddess assumes this joint role of the concentration of wealth and the delimitation of the family patrimonies. In the palaces of the Homeric kings, the *tamia* was the thrifty housekeeper who organized the household work and watched over the provisions.[106] In the age of the city, the word *tamias* was used to describe the treasurer administering state funds or sacred treasures, the property of the gods. There are two later confirmations of Hestia as the patron of the gathering in of riches. The first is Artemidorus's statement that when a citizen dreams about Hestia, this symbolizes "public revenue funds."[107] The second, connected with a ritual of Kos alluded to in a third-century inscription, includes a significant detail. It concerns a sacrifice to Zeus Polieus, with whom Hestia is closely associated in the feast. The animal to be sacrificed is selected from among the cattle presented by the groups of different tribes after a long procedure, probably similar to that employed in Athens at the *dipolies*. Once chosen, the victim is led to the agora. The herald (*kērux*) publicly declares its price. Its owner then declares that his fellow citizens should pay this amount not to him but to Hestia. As Gernet remarks, the value of the bull in a monetary economy is "capitalized" by Hestia, who is guardian and guarantor of the city's wealth.[108]

On the other hand, it is important to stress Hestia's relationship with what Gernet calls a discretionary economy, dominated by the *suum cuique*. At Tegea, the communal hearth of the Arcadians was associated with Zeus Kleros, the apportioner (*klēros*: portion, patrimony) — an epithet that recalls the first allocation of Arcadian land divided among the three sons of Arcas by drawing lots.[109] In Athens, when the archon (the magistrate who, according to Aristotle, derives his office from the communal hearth, and who, from the earliest days, always resided in the *prytaneum*) is installed, his first act is to have the herald proclaim that "all men shall hold, until the end of his office, those possessions and powers that they held before his entry into office."[110]

Such testimony is concerned with the communal hearth, the *hestia* of the city, once it became the center of the state and symbol of the unity of the citizens. In order to evaluate it properly, we should put it in historical perspective and relate it to what can be ascertained of a more ancient past, before the city-state, when Hestia was not yet the communal hearth but the family altar, and symbolized most specifically the superior virtues of the royal house.[111]

There are two aspects to the wealth of the king — one could even say two opposite poles. First, there are the goods that can be collected and stored in the palace: food supplies, of course, but also various types of *agalmata* — cloth; precious metals; sacra invested with power, used as signs of authority; coats of arms; instruments of investiture. Thus Penelope, in Odysseus's palace, goes with her women into the depths of the *thalamos* where the master has locked up his treasures: cloth in coffers, bronze, gold, wrought iron, and the bow that Odysseus alone can bend and that appears later in the poem as the instrument of his vengeance, the symbol and restorer of legitimate sovereignty.[112] The word *keimēlia* is applied to all these objects, emphasizing that they are immobilized, intended to stay in place (the verb *keimai* means to be laid down, immobile).[113] The other aspect of royal wealth is represented by flocks and herds.[114] On the level of economic value, the treasure is contrasted with these animals as the exterior is to the interior, the mobile to the static, the open space of the *agros* to the domestic enclosure. Unlike the world of town, house, and even cultivated fields, what the Greeks call *agros* is actually the pastoral sphere, land for pasturage, open country to which animals are led or where wild animals are hunted — wild and distant country filled with herds.[115] Xenophon contrasts men with beasts precisely because men need a roof over their heads, while herds live *en hupaithrōi*.[116] Moreover, the word for grazing stock, *probaton*, is quite revealing; it literally means that which moves, that which goes forward. The phrase *keimēlion kai probasis* (which, through the antinomy of *keimai*, to be lying down, and *probainō*, to go forward, expresses the twofold aspect of wealth as a whole), emphasizes the contrast between riches that "lie" in the house and those that "roam" the country.[117] Across the sweep of the *agros*, the herdsman Hermes (Hermes Agrotēr, Hermes Nomios) drives the flocks, controlling them with his magic staff.[118] As god of the shepherds, he has power over them, just as Hestia, the domestic goddess, is patron of the goods within the house.[119] In the closing words of the *Homeric Hymn to Hermes*, Zeus commands "that Hermes should be lord (*anassein*) over the cows in the fields, the horses and mules, the lions, the boars and the dogs, and over the sheep that the wide earth nourishes and over every animal that moves about on four legs (*pasi d'epi probatoisi*)."[120]

But it is not only in their wanderings that the herds exemplify the aspect of movement in wealth. They also constitute the first form of riches, which, instead of remaining constant, has the capacity to increase or diminish. This is because — with the complicity of Hermes, the cattle thief — neighbors' lands can be raided and the booty added to one's own herds, and because — with the favor of Hermes Epimēlios, Hermes Polumēlos (of abundant herds) — stock will multiply and riches will beget riches.[121] Ownership and the preservation of goods are the domain of Hestia. But the increase and decrease of wealth, acquisition and loss, like exchange, depend on the god who, like Hekate, knows (as Hesiod says) how to "increase (*aexein*) the livestock in their sheds — the herds of cattle, the flocks of goats, the long columns of sheep

185

heavy with wool: he makes the few the many and the many the few."[122] Later on, in a fully mercantile economy, the Greeks had no difficulty recognizing the ancient god of the shepherds beneath the features of their god of trade. In the movement of money, which increases itself through interest, they could still discern the increase of livestock multiplying at regular intervals. They used the same word, *tokos*, for interest on capital and for the new born animals brought forth at the turn of the year.[123]

The opposition between the space of the hearth, enclosed and stable, and the space of the countryside, open and variable, gives us a better understanding and a greater appreciation of a family feast such as the Amphidromia. This ceremony was celebrated on the fifth, seventh, or tenth day after birth and sometimes coincided with the naming of the infant.[124] Its specific function was to consecrate the official recognition of the newborn child by its father. The ritual is obviously aimed at enrolling the child in the space of the *oikos*, attaching it to the hearth of which it is the issue. According to the existing evidence, the ritual consisted of two parts between which a distinction should be made: on the one hand, the ring run around the hearth by one or more naked people holding the baby in their arms; on the other, the laying of the child at a given moment (probably before the running) directly on the ground.[125] The two elements reinforce each other. The motion of the child in a closed circle around the fixed hearth begins, and direct contact with the floor of the house completes, the baby's integration into the domestic space. Nevertheless, in certain legends in which these two rituals are closely associated, there is a marked opposition between them, despite their various similarities. The tales concerning immortalization stress the difference between two procedures followed for the newborn child: holding the infant over the hearth amid the flames, and putting it on the ground next to the hearth. The first procedure recalls the rite of immortalization in the flames of the hearth, while the second demonstrates the failure of the attempt at immortalization and a return to normal practice. If the child could have been completely purified by the fire, it would have become immortal, but when placed on the ground and included in the household space, it shares the ordinary condition of mankind. Thus, in the palace of Keleos, Demeter "hides" (*kruptein*) Demophoon in the blazing fire as though he too were the spark (*dalos*) that is identified in some myths with the royal scion. The goddess would thus have made Demophoon immortal, had not his mother, witnessing the scene, uttered a cry of terror and reproached the stranger concealing her son in the flames. Incensed, Demeter snatches the child from the fire and puts him on the ground. "I would have made your son deathless and unaging all his days," she says to Metaneira, "but now he can in no way escape death and the fates."[126] The same antithetical structure is found in the story told by Apollonius Rhodius about Thetis's attempt to immortalize her son Achilles.[127] During the night, the goddess puts the child into the heart of the fire to consume his mortal body. When Peleus sees Achilles in the flames, he cannot prevent himself from crying out. Angry, Thetis abruptly sets the infant down on the ground, and Achilles's fate is sealed. Child of man that he is, he is doomed to die. But one common feature brings the two opposing procedures closer together, sometimes even makes them coincide: they are both *ordeals* imposed on the baby. No doubt the ordeal by fire appears infinitely greater and therefore more important than simply being put down on the ground. But let there be no mistake: direct contact with the earth and the powers that dwell there, especially the chthonic deities associated with the realms of the dead, is not without great peril. Legend has it that placing the child upon the ground sometimes causes its death and sometimes ensures its immortality. It should also be remembered that the rite of immortality by fire in which the child is "hidden" has an analogy in Medea's "hiding" her children in the earth to make them immortal (*katakrupteia*).[128] It is obvious that the two rites of immortality correspond to and contrast with each other as the two forms of funeral rites practiced by the Greeks do. The dead are sometimes "hidden in fire" (incineration), sometimes "hidden in the ground" (interment). In both cases, their disappearance from the visible world is the condition and sign of their return to the otherworld.[129]

Two symmetrical legends illustrate the dangers and the virtues of contact with the ground. The first is the story of Hypsipylē, the nurse of the royal infant Opheltes. She makes the mistake of laying him on the ground for a moment. A snake, the incarnation of the chthonic powers, bites him, and he dies instantly. Had not an oracle advised that he never be placed on the ground before he was able to walk?[130] The other story goes in the opposite direction. The Eleans are defending their territory against the Arcadians, who have invaded it. Before the battle, a woman with a baby at her breast suddenly appears. Claiming to be inspired by a dream, she offers her child to the Eleans, to fight with them. The military leaders accept the child from her, carry it out in front of the army, and lay it naked on the ground. At once the newborn child turns into a snake. At the sight of the serpent, the enemy camp is thrown into confusion and routed. At the exact spot where the child disappeared into the ground, the Eleans erect a sanctuary dedicated to the child-god Sosipolis, the native daemon (*daimōn epichōrios*) that their land, in the name of the goddess-mother Eileithyia, made appear in men's midst in order to help them.[131]

Naturally the significance of being put on the ground differs according to whether the newborn child is placed in contact with the humanized ground within the house or the untamed ground of a far outdoors. In the context of the Amphidromia, placing the infant on the ground close to the hearth, within the circle traced by the ritual ring run around Hestia, has the value of a trial of legitimation.[132] When the ceremony is over, the newborn baby, joined to the domestic hearth, is accepted, recognized, by his father. This rite of integration within the family space and the paternal line of descent has its counterpart in the practices connected with the rejection of a child and its exclusion from the enclosed space of the *oikos*. This is the point of the rites of exposure in Greece. In exposure, as in the Amphidromia, the infant is *laid down* on the ground (this act of laying down is expressed by

188

the verb *tithēmi*). But the locality chosen is seen as a wild and distant space, in contrast to the household enclosure and nearby farmland.[133] It can be the sea or a river, in that these can be symbols of the otherworld, but above all it is the uncultivated land where the flocks and herds live, far from houses, gardens, and fields — the alien and hostile space of the *agros*. In the heroic myths, everything combines to depict the setting of a pastoral landscape around the exposed child. The parents, who expel their offspring from the world of the living, entrust the infant to a shepherd, who carries it away and abandons it on the heaths or in the hills, on the wastelands where he leads his flocks to pasture. Another shepherd discovers the child and gives it a home. It grows up among the herds and flocks. Sometimes wild animals give it sustenance.

The antinomy in the feast of the Amphidromia and the rites of exposure, with their alternative implications, is stressed in the famous *Theaetetus* passage in which Socrates compares himself, in his role in the birth of minds, to his mother, who was a midwife.[134] Just as the *maia* helps women in labor deliver their babies, Socrates helps young men bring forth the truths they contain within themselves and are unable to express. But his art goes further than that of the ordinary midwife. It is also his duty to put the child that is born to the test (*basanizein*) in order to detect whether it is a sham (*eidōlon kai pseudos*) or a product of genuine and sound stock (*gonimon te kai alēthes*).[135]

What is this test? And what is the outcome if the child appears incapable of passing it? Socrates explains these two points with great clarity. When young Theaetetus has succeeded, at the cost of violent effort and with the help of the philosopher, in giving birth to the product of his mind, Socrates says to him:

Well, we have at last managed to bring this forth, whatever it turns out to be; and now that it is born, we must in very truth perform the rite (*amphidromia*) of running around with it in a circle — the circle of our argument — and see whether it may not turn out to be, after all, not worth rearing, but only a wind-egg, an imposture. But perhaps you think that any offspring of yours ought to be cared for and not sent away to be exposed (*trephein kai mē apotithenai*)? or will you bear to see it examined and not get angry if it is taken away from you, though it is your first-born?[136]

This text of Plato's should be compared with the information given by Plutarch on related Lacedaemonian customs. The community spirit that characterizes the city of Sparta leaves no room for the Amphidromia in their traditional form. As it is a question not of uniting the newborn child to either his father's hearth or the family (*klēros*) but of including it in the civic community of the *equals*, the progenitor is deprived of his authority in deciding the fate of his offspring. But the dilemma has still to be resolved: should the child be nurtured (*trephein*), that is, integrated into the group space, or should it be exposed (*apotithenai*), that is, ejected from the mortal world?

> Offspring was not reared at the will of the father, but was taken and carried by him to a place called the *leschē*, where the elders of the tribes officially examined the infant, and if it was well-built and sturdy, they ordered the father to rear it, and assigned it one of the nine thousand lots of land as a *klēros*; but if it was ill-born or deformed they sent it to the so-called "deposits" (*apothetai*).[137]

In his comment following this passage, Plutarch — like Plato — emphasizes the aspect of ordeal, pointing out that, for reasons he has already stated, the women of Sparta bathe newborn children not with water but with wine, "thus making a sort of test (*basanon*) of their constitutions."

The feast of the Amphidromia focused on the hearth implies in terms of the space with which it is concerned the same polarity that is expressed for the Greeks by the Hermes-Hestia pairing in the structure of their pantheon. It is therefore necessary to investigate other rituals concerning the hearth goddess and determine what form of spatial representation they involve.

Two examples seem particularly illuminating in this respect. Knowledge of the first comes from a text by Plutarch, who is a first-hand witness, since this example concerns a ritual in Chaironeia, his birthplace.[138] The rite of expulsion of hunger (*boulimou exelasis*) from the Boeotian city took place on two levels: each individual conducted the rites for his own family within the home, and, at the same time, the archon followed the ritual on behalf of the group, at the city's communal hearth. The ceremony was identical in the two cases. A slave was beaten with a willow rod (*rhabdos*), and pushed over the threshold, with the exclamation "Hunger without, riches and health within."[139] The ritual is based on the opposition between an enclosed and fixed interior, where the wealth is kept (Hestia), and the exterior to which the injurious forces of hunger are expelled, with the very staff of Hermes.

In Athens, this same opposition characterizes the organization of the space where the Prutaneion, the seat of Hestia Koinē, is situated. In its immediate vicinity was a piece of land dedicated to Boulimos, Hunger.[140] This was a field that was always left to lie fallow and that, lying in the heart of the humanized space of the city, represented the wild land that man must not touch, since to do so would be a sacrilege, punishable by famine.[141] In relation to the Prutaneion, therefore, the terrain of Boulimos is the counterpart of the Bouzugion, the field at the very foot of the Acropolis, which was annually subjected to a ritual ploughing by the Bouzygai in the name of the city.[142] One further point should be made: while conducting the ploughing ceremony, which periodically renewed the union between the original Athenian peoples and their native soil and deconsecrated the Attic earth for them to use and cultivate freely, the Bouzygai uttered curses that fell on the newly turned soil and ensured its productivity. The priest anathematized, on the one hand, "those who refuse to share water and fire" (referring to the space of hospitality — Hestia) and, on the other, "those who do not point the way for wanderers (*planō-menois*)" (referring to the space of the traveller — Hermes).[143]

The second example is from the Achaean city of Pharai, near Patras.[144] It concerns a rather special divinitory ritual that associates

Hestia and Hermes very closely. A stone statue of Hermes, bearded and quadrangular, stands in the middle of a vast agora surrounded by a *peribolōs*. The god, who is called *agoraios*, pronounces oracles. Facing this statue of Hermes is a hearth (Hestia). It includes an altar and a number of bronze lamps bound with lead. The procedure for the delivery of oracles is as follows. At dusk, the person consulting the oracle enters the agora. First he goes to the hearth, where he burns incense, fills the lamps with oil, and lights them. Then he puts on the altar of Hestia a coin of the country, no doubt sacred, called a "bronze." Only then does he turn to Hermes and whisper in the god's ear the question he wants answered. Having done this, he puts his hands over his ears and walks away, leaving the agora. As soon as he exites the *peribolōs* and goes outside (*es to ektos*), he removes his hands from his ears, and the first voice he hears as he goes on his way will provide him with the god's answer.

In this instance, the agora is a circumscribed and centered space, under the twofold patronage of Hermes Agoraios and Hestia. It is in front of Hestia, in the center, that the person coming from outside to consult the oracle first stops. By contact with the hearth in the actions of burning incense and lighting lamps all around the goddess, the stranger is infused with the religious qualities necessary for consulting the local oracle. And he pays his consultation fee to Hestia because in the divine couple she represents the force of permanency and storage. In contrast, the way the oracle is consulted emphasizes Hermes's mobility. The god's answer is revealed, first, through the very movement of the questioner, who must start walking before he can learn it; second, at the moment when he leaves the enclosed space of the *agora* and enters exterior space; third, in catching the sound of a voice — a moving, faint, elusive *phōnē*, the voice of the first one who happens to cross his path; last, in the distance established by the oracle between the question, asked in the center of the agora (just as the consultation fee is paid in the center, to remain there forever), and the answer, which the god provides outside, in a space other than that where his statue is erected.

192

This essay took as its point of departure the presence in the Greek pantheon of a particular and often seen structure — the couple Hestia-Hermes. An analysis of texts that stress the bonds uniting the god and goddess has clarified each deity's relationship to certain definite and contrary aspects of space. This has led away from the domain of purely religious representation and the Greeks' ideas regarding their gods, and toward the social systems of which these ideas seem to be an integral part. An examination of the various institutions whose very function refers explicitly to the hearth and the religious values it represents has shown that this set of institutional practices, gravitating around the hearth established as a fixed center, expresses one aspect of the archaic experience of space in ancient Greece. To the extent that these practices constitute a well-regulated and orderly system of conduct, they imply a mental organization of space.

Whether in a discussion of marriage, family relationships, lines of descent, the heritage of the family *klēros*, the domestic status of husbands and wives, the social and psychological contrasts between men and women, their activities in and out of the house, or the double aspect of wealth and of land improvement — the aim has always been to throw light on the structures of thought pertaining to space, as shown in the interplay of symbolic representations and structures of behavior. It seems that the spatial values associated with a center, immobile and withdrawn, had their regular counterpart in the opposite values of an open space, unstable, a place of distance, contacts, and change.

Nevertheless, the analysis has been one-sided. It has consistently been approached from the point of view of Hestia and the center, so Hermes has been seen only as Hestia's complement, the god as the antithesis of the goddess. In order to complete the study of these two deities' relationship, the approach should be changed and the investigation carried out from the converse point of view, from the standpoint of Hermes, through an examination of the groups of images evoked by the god in Greek consciousness and the activities and institutions of which he is the patron. But before abandoning the subject of Hestia, I should point out that the polarity that is so marked a characteristic of all the goddess's relations with Hermes is such a basic feature of archaic thought that it is an integral attribute of the hearth goddess, as though part of Hestia already belonged to Hermes.

In order to fulfill her function as the power giving domestic space its center, its permanence, and its boundaries, Hestia must root the human dwelling place in the ground. This is the significance of the Mycenaean hearth, that *fixed* altar-hearth. This in fact gives a chthonic aspect to the epichthonian goddess dwelling on the earth's surface. Through her, the house and the household enter into contact with the underworld. In a fragment of the *Phaethon*, Euripides identifies Hestia with Demeter's daughter, Kore, who, sometimes reigning at Hades's side and sometimes living in the world of men, is responsible for establishing communication and passage between two worlds separated by an insurmountable barrier.[145]

Furthermore, in the Mycenaean *megaron*, the circular hearth welded to the ground is in the center of a rectangular space bounded by four columns. These reach to the roof of the house, where they enclose an open lantern through which the smoke escapes. When incense is burned, when meat is cooked on the hearth, or when, during a meal, the portion of food dedicated to the gods is consumed by the flames of the fire on her domestic altar, Hestia sends the family offerings up to the dwelling place of the Olympian gods. Contact between earth and the heavens is established through her, just as she acts as a passageway to the infernal regions.

The center of which Hestia is the patron represents for the domestic group the spot of earth that enables terrestrial space to be stabilized, demarcated, and fixed. But it also represents the passageway *par excellence*, the channel of communication between separate and isolated cosmic levels. For the members of the *oikos*, the hearth, the center of the house, also marks the path of exchange with the gods below and the gods above, the axis through which all parts of the universe are joined together. The hearth also evokes the image of a ship's mast, firmly rooted in the deck and raised straight toward the sky.

Should we believe, like Louis Deroy, that there is an early link between the hearth and the mast or colonnade, postulated by the lexicographical analogy, which, even in Homer's language, changed the old word *hestiē*, (hearth) into *histiē* (colonnade), the confusion of the two terms being explained by the fact that the Mycenaean hearth was surrounded by wooden pillars (*histoi*) supporting the roof-lantern (*melathron*)?[146] Hesychius comments that *histia* means both the altar of the hearth (*eschara*) and the mast of a ship, and that *histia* means the woman who weaves, because *histos* also denotes, apart from column and mast, a loom (always upright among the Greeks), which is firmly fixed in the ground while reaching upward.[147]

It should be noted, in any case, that Plato, who is so faithful to the teachings of the sacred writings and the suggestions of the ancient myths, merges the figure of Hestia, alone of all the gods to remain immobile at home, with the great goddess Anagkē, the Spinner, enthroned at the center of the universe.[148] On her knees Anagkē holds the spindle whose movement controls the rotation of all the celestial spheres. It is fixed to the great shaft of light in the center of which Anagkē is seated, which is as straight as a mast or a column and stretches from top to bottom through the sky and the earth, uniting the entire cosmos as the various parts of a boat are linked from bow to stern.

Immobile, but mistress of the movements around her, as central as a main shaft traversing a machine throughout and holding its component parts together: this is the image of Hestia that Plato appears to have inherited from the oldest of the Greek religious traditions. That is why, when he claims in the linguistic game of the *Cratylus* to reveal the secrets of the divine names, the philosopher of the Academy suggests a double etymology for the word Hestia.[149] Of his two contrary explanations, Plato certainly prefers one to the other. But it is very significant that he should present them, in spite of their antinomy, as two equally possible interpretations of the same divine name. For some, Hestia corresponds with *ousia*, which is sometimes also called *essia*, that is, the immutable and permanent essence. But for others, essence is

195

termed *ōsia*, because, like Heraclitus, they think that all that exists is mobile and nothing remains static. According to these people, everything is caused by and based on the impetus of movement (*to ōthoun*), which they call *ōsia*.

Hestia as the principle of permanence, Hestia as the principle of impetus and movement — in this twofold and contradictory interpretation of the name of the hearth goddess can be seen the very foundations of the relationship that opposes and unites in a single contrasted couple joined in inseparable "friendship" the goddess who immobilizes space around a fixed center and the god who renders it unendingly mobile in all its parts.

CHAPTER SEVEN

Geometry and Spherical Astronomy
in Early Greek Cosmology

The problem that I would like to address concerns less the history of scientific thought as such than the relationship between certain fundamental scientific ideas — a particular image of the world — and certain facts of social history. At the beginning of the sixth century BCE, astronomical thought in Greece was not yet founded on a continuous series of observations and experiments. It was not based on any established scientific tradition. If I had to describe how a discovery was made in the nineteenth or twentieth century, I would have to refer for the essential facts to the development of science itself, the state of theories and techniques, and, in short, the internal dynamic of research in any particular scientific discipline. But in archaic Greece, science was not yet established. The meager astronomical knowledge that the Ionians would soon put to use was not the result of their own discoveries. They borrowed them from their Near Eastern neighbors, in particular the Babylonians. We are thus faced with the following paradox. The Greeks were to lay the foundations for cosmology and astronomy; they were to give these disciplines the orientation they would follow throughout the history of Western thought. Right from the start they were to give them a direction that, to some extent, they still have today. And yet it was not they but the Babylonians who over centuries had undertaken detailed observations of the stars and recorded on tablets the ephemerides that indicated the various phases of the moon and the rising and setting of the stars in the sky. The Greeks, then, put to use observations, techniques, and instruments that had been developed by others. Nevertheless, they integrated the knowledge that had been transmitted to them into an entirely new system. They founded a new astronomy. How are we to explain this innovation? Why did the Greeks organize the knowledge they had borrowed from other peoples into a new and original framework?

Babylonian astronomy, which was highly developed, has, broadly speaking, three characteristics.

First, it was always an integral part of astral religion. The Babylonian astronomers observed the planet we call Venus so carefully because to them it was a deity known as Ishtar, and they believed that the direction men's destinies took depended on its position. To their eyes, the heavenly world was a collection of divine powers. By observing the heavens men could understand the intentions of the gods.

Second, those whose role it was to observe the stars belonged to the category of scribes. The function of the scribes in Babylonian society was to write down every detail of economic life and to preserve these records in archives. They drew up accounts of what was happening in the heavens just as they did of what was happening in human society. In both cases, the scribes acted in the service of the figure that dominated all of Babylonian society and whose function was as much religious as political: the king. It was essential for the king to know what was happening in the heavens; both his personal destiny and the fate of the kingdom depended on it. As the intermediary between the heavenly and earthly worlds, he had to know at exactly what moment he should perform the religious rites that were his responsibility. Astronomy was therefore connected with the religious calendar, which it was the privilege of a class of scribes, working in the service of the king, to regulate.

Third, this astronomy was strictly arithmetic. The Babylonians, who had accurate knowledge of certain celestial phenomena and could forecast an eclipse empirically, had no geometric model to represent the movements of the stars in the sky. All they did was note down the positions of the stars, one after another, on their tablets, and keep an accurate record of them. In this way, they produced arithmetical formulas that made it possible for them to predict whether a certain star would appear at a particular moment in the year. But their astronomy was not projected onto a spatial schema.

On all three points, Greek astronomy was, from the start, radically different. In the first place, it seems to have been quite unconnected with any astral religion. The Ionian "physicists" — Thales, Anaximander, and Anaximenes — propose in their cosmological writings to present a *theōria*, a view or general conception that can provide an explanation for the world without any religious preoccupations, without the least reference to deities or ritual practices. On the contrary, the "physicists" are conscious of holding, on many points, views that were opposed to traditional religious beliefs.

It was, then, a type of knowledge that from the very beginning aimed at intelligibility. In this respect, the Ionians showed an extraordinary audacity. They wanted every man to be able to understand how the world originally came into being with the help of a few simple examples, often borrowed from everyday life and familiar practices. For example, they would explain the formation of the world with the image of a sieve being shaken, or with that of muddy water being swirled around in a bowl, with the heavier particles remaining in the middle while the lighter ones are dispersed outward, toward the edges. They attempted to give a purely positive and rational account of the way the universe is organized.

In this sense, the image of the world presented by the first Ionian physicists is radically different from that which existed before — in the work of Homer and Hesiod, for example. The ancient concept, the archaic picture of the world can be fruitfully compared with the schema that was already clearly developed by Anaximander. It is noticeable that there is a change in the very way space is represented. To take an example that is more familiar because it is more recent: for centuries, throughout the Middle Ages as in Antiquity, men believed the world was motionless, at rest in the center of the universe. It is well known what an intellectual revolution was brought about by the abandonment of this view in favor of a heliocentric theory: the world was no longer motionless, it was no longer at the center of the cosmos, so the world had not been created for a man made in the image of God. This new conception of space brought about a very real transformation in man's idea of himself and his relationship to the universe.

The intellectual revolution under discussion here is no less radical. According to Homer and Hesiod, the world is a more or less flat disk surrounded by a circular river, Okeanos, which has no beginning and no end and flows into itself.[1] This theme is already found among the Babylonians, in the great fluvial plains where cultivated land had been reclaimed from the waters with great difficulty by means of a system of dikes and drainage ditches. The genesis of the world and its organization were therefore conceived of as a drying out of the earth, which gradually emerged from the waters all around it. The bronze sky rises above the earth like an inverted basin resting on the outside rim of the ocean. It is described as bronze in order to express its unchangeable solidity. The sky is the realm of the gods and is indestructible. What is beneath the earth? For a Greek of archaic times, the earth was first and foremost what one could safely walk upon, a "solid and sure base" that was in no danger of collapsing. So they imagined roots beneath it, safeguarding its stability. But where did the roots go? Nobody really knew. Xenophanes was later to say that they grew downward forever.[2] In any case, where they went was not important; what mattered was that one could be sure that the earth would not move. An alternative to the roots growing downward forever was Hesiod's belief in a huge jar that ended in a narrow mouth, from which grew the roots of the world.[3] Within the jar, whirlwinds blew in all directions: this was the world of disorder, of space not yet organized. The cosmogonies relate, in fact, that when Zeus became the king of the universe, he closed the neck of the jar forever, so that the subterranean world of disorder

— the world where every spatial dimension is muddled in an inextricable chaos, where up is confused with down and right with left — would never again emerge into the light of day. Why a jar, in this mythical view of the cosmos? Because the Greeks' ancestors used to bury in the earthen floor of their storerooms huge jars containing the fruits of the earth, as well as the remains of the household's dead. The subterranean world that the jar symbolizes is the world from which plants grow, where seeds germinate, and where the dead dwell.

The main characteristic of this mythical view is that it represents a universe with different levels. The space above is completely different from the space in the middle and the space below. The first is for Zeus and the immortal gods, the second is for men, and the third is for the dead and the subterranean gods. One cannot pass from one level to another except under special conditions. On earth, similarly, directions in space have different properties: right is auspicious and left is bad, and east and west have different religious meanings.

Compare this ancient mythical view with Anaximander's.[4] For Anaximander, the earth is like a truncated column in the middle of the cosmos, able to remain immobile because, being at an equal distance from all the points on the celestial circumference, it has no reason to go right rather than left or up rather than down. Anaximander, then, already conceived of the universe as spherical. He introduced a new kind of space — no longer the space of myth, with its roots and its jar, but a geometrical space. This space is essentially defined by relationships of distance and position, where it is possible to explain the stability of the earth by the geometric definition of the center in relation to the circumference. Another text ascribed to Anaximander by the doxographers shows clearly that he was conscious of the reversible character of all spatial relationships. He proposes not a mythical space, where up and down and right and left have opposing religious meanings, but a homogeneous space constituted by symmetrical and reversible relationships. In this text, Anaximander accepts the existence of the antipodes.[5] And to judge from certain documents from the Hippocratic corpus, for Anaximander what appears to be up to us is down to the inhabitants of the antipodes, while what is right to us is left to them.[6] In other words, absolute value is no longer attached to the directions of space. The structure of space, at the center of which is the earth, is truly mathematical.

How are we to explain this development in astronomical thought, this intellectual revolution? It could be said that the Greeks were "born geometers," but this explanation seems rather inadequate. I would like to propose another one. Between the period of Hesiod and that of Anaximander, a whole series of social and economic transformations took place. Their importance has often, quite rightly, been emphasized. In my view, this change is essentially a political matter, that is, it concerns the birth of the Greek *polis*. What must be explained is a certain astronomical conception of the universe — thought, therefore, that is the result of conscious, considered reflection. This thought is expressed in a precise vocabulary and organized around certain fundamental concepts. It is presented as a coherent, structured conceptual system. This vocabulary, these basic concepts, and this conceptual system are quite new in comparison with what had gone before. In order to understand how they came into being, we must try to find out in what form the transformations that took place in social life were transposed on a conceptual level. In other words, we must ascertain what sector of social life acted as an intermediary among the conceptual constructions of thought and among the institutions being transformed. To discover this mediating link between the social practices of the Greeks and their new intellectual universe, we must find out how, confronted with the crisis provoked by the extension of sea trade and the beginnings of a monetary economy, the Greek of the seventh century BCE came to rethink his social life in an attempt to remodel it in keeping with certain egalitarian aspirations. Since we want to know how he turned it into a subject for reflection and how he conceptualized it, we shall draw comparisons between things that can indeed be compared, since they are homogeneous. We will put two mental systems side by side, to underline their possible correspondences and the similarity in their structure. Each system has its own vocabulary, fundamental concepts, and intellectual framework. One of these systems was developed in the practice of social life, while the other was applied to the understanding of nature.

From this point of view, Greece represents a remarkable phenomenon, indeed an extraordinary one. For the very first time in human history, social life became the object of conscious, deliberate research and reflection. The institutions of the city imply that there was not only a political domain but also a political thought. The expression used to refer to the political domain, *ta koina*, means "that which is common to all," in other words, public affairs. In effect, Greek life took place on two clearly separated levels. One was the private domain, the family, domestic life (what the Greeks called *oikonomia*), while the other was the public domain, which included all decisions affecting the common interest, all that turned the collection of citizens into a united, coherent group, a *polis* in the strict sense. Within the framework of the institutions of the city (which appears precisely during the period between Hesiod and Anaximander), what belongs to the public domain can no longer be settled by a single individual, even the king. All things held in common must be the subject of free debate among those who constitute the political body. This debate must take place publicly, in the open, in the agora, and must take the form of speeches that make arguments. Thus the establishment of the *polis* involves a process of desacralizing and rationalizing social life. No longer does the priest-king, following a religious calendar, do everything that needs to be done in the group for its members. Now the men themselves take their shared destiny into their own hands and make decisions, after due discussion. (When I say "men" I am, of course, referring only to citizens, for, as is well known, this political system presupposed that there were other men who were devoted to the essentials of productive work.) As far as the citizens were concerned, the city's affairs could be decided only following a public debate in which each man was free to participate in order to make his own arguments.

The *logos*, the instrument for these public debates, thus takes on a double meaning. On the one hand, it is the word, the speech pronounced by an orator at the assembly. But it is also reason, the faculty of argumentation that defines man as not just an animal but a "political animal," a reasonable being.

The new importance attached to the word, which from this time on was the instrument *par excellence* of political life, is accompanied by a change in the social significance of writing. In the Near Eastern kingdoms, writing was the privilege and specialty of the scribes. It allowed the royal administration to keep account of and thus to control the economic and social life of the state. It was used to set up archives, which were always kept more or less secret inside the palace. Writing of this kind existed in the Mycenaean world between 1450 and 1200 BCE. It disappeared when the Mycenaean civilization was ruined, and during the period under discussion here, the moment of the birth of the city, it was replaced with a form of writing whose purpose was the exact opposite. Instead of being the privilege of one caste, the secret of a class of scribes working for the king, writing became the common property of all the citizens, an instrument for making things public. It made it possible to introduce into the public domain everything that goes beyond the realm of private life and is of interest to the community. Laws had to be written down. In this way they became truly the property of everyone. This transformation of the social status of writing was to have a fundamental effect on intellectual history. Writing made it possible to make public and reveal to everybody things that had always remained more or less secret in the Eastern civilizations, with the result that the rules of the political game — free debate, public discussion, and contentious argument — also became the rules of the intellectual game. As with political affairs, each philosopher's knowledge, discoveries, and theories concerning nature were to be made public; they were to become common property: *koina*. There exists a letter, apocryphal of course, but nonetheless indicative of a certain collective psychology, that Diogenes Laertius believed had been written by Thales to Pherecydes, a contemporary of Anaximander's and, according to some, the author of the first work to be published in prose.[7] Thales rejoices in Pherecydes's wise decision not to keep his knowledge to himself but to make it available *en koinōi*, to the community, thus the subject of public discussion. To put it another way: When a philosopher such as Pherecydes wrote a book, what was he doing? He was transforming private knowledge into a subject for a public debate similar to that which was becoming established for political matters. And, indeed, Anaximander discussed the ideas of Thales, and Anaximenes those of Anaximander, and through these discussions and arguments philosophy itself became established.

In my opinion, it was possible for Greek cosmology to free itself from religion and for knowledge of nature to become desacralized because at the same time social life itself was rationalized and the administration of the city became, in the main, a secular activity. But we must go further. Quite apart from the rational and positivist form of astronomy, we must consider its content and seek out its origins. How did the Greeks come to form their new image of the world? As said above, the main feature of Anaximander's universe was its circular or spherical character. The circle's special value for the Greeks is well known. They considered it the most beautiful and perfect shape. The task of astronomy was to explain appearances or, to use the traditional phrase, "to save the phenomena" by constructing geometrical schemata in which the movements of all the heavenly bodies followed circular courses. The political domain also appears to have been attached to a representation of space that deliberately emphasized the circle and its center. The emergence of the city-state was characterized in the first place by a transformation affecting the space of the city, in other words, the way towns were planned. It was in the Greek world, probably first in the colonies, that a new plan of the city appears in which all the urban buildings are concentrated around an open space, known as the agora. The Phoenicians were traders who traveled all over the Mediterranean several centuries before the Greeks. The Babylonians were also traders who developed much more elaborate commercial and banking techniques than did the Greeks. However, the agora is found in neither civilization. The existence of an agora depends on a system of social life that implies public debate on all communal affairs. This is why open public space appears only in the Ionian and Greek cities. The existence of an agora marks the emergence of the political institutions of the city-state.

What are the historical origins of the agora? It does of course have a past. It is connected with certain characteristic customs of the Indo-European Greeks, among whom the warrior class was separate from the farmers and herdsmen. Homer uses the expression *laon ageirein*, meaning to assemble the army. The warriors assembled in military formation, that is, in a circle. This circle formed a definite space used for public debate, involving what the Greeks called *isēgoria*, the right to free speech. Thus, at the beginning of Book Two of the *Odyssey*, Telemachos convenes the agora in this way, assembling the military aristocracy of Ithaca. Once the circle is formed, Telemachos enters it and stands *en mesōi*, at the center. He takes the scepter in his hand and speaks freely. When he finishes, he steps out of the circle and another takes his place and replies to his speech. The assembly of equals constituted by the meeting of the warriors marks out a circular space around a center in which each man can freely say whatever suits him. Following a series of economic and social transformations, this military assembly became the agora of the city, where all the citizens (first a minority of aristocrats and later the whole *dēmos*) were able to argue about and decide in common the affairs that concerned them collectively. This, then, is a space made for discussion, a public space as opposed to private houses, a political space within which one can discuss and argue freely. It is significant that the expression *en koinōi*, whose political meaning, "to make public, place in common," has been mentioned, has a synonym with a clearly spatial meaning. Instead of saying that a question is put *en koinōi*, that it is debated publicly, it can be said that it is placed *en mesōi*, put in the center, set down in the middle. The human group sees itself as follows: in addition to private, individual

206

houses, there is a center where public matters are debated, and this center represents all that is common, the collectivity as such. In this center, every man is his fellow's equal, and no man is subject to another. In the free debate that takes place in the center of the agora, all citizens are defined as *isoi* (equals), *homoioi* (peers, in the sense of likenesses). This is the birth of a society in which one man's relationship with another is conceived of in terms of identity, symmetry, reversibility. Human society no longer forms, as it did within mythical space, a world on different levels, with the king at the top and beneath him a whole social hierarchy in which status is defined in terms of domination and submission. Now the universe of the city-state is one of egalitarian and reversible relationships, according to which all citizens are defined in relation to one another, as politically identical. Insofar as they have access to the circular space centered on the agora, citizens enter a political system governed by equilibrium, symmetry, and reciprocity.

In order to understand the relationships among the city's political institutions, the new urban framework, and the appearance of a new view of the world, it is important to look at figures such as Hippodamos of Miletos. He lived a century later than Anaximander but belongs to the same current of thought. What form do his activities take? It was he who undertook to rebuild Miletos after the town had been destroyed. He reconstructed it according to an overall plan that reveals a desire to rationalize urban space. Instead of a city of the archaic type, similar to European medieval cities, with a maze of streets tumbling untidily down the slopes of a hill, he chose a fine open space, made a grid of straight streets intersecting at right angles, and created a town resembling a checkerboard, entirely centered around the open space of the agora. We call Hippodamos an architect, the first great town planner of the Greek world. But he was primarily a political theorist who considered the organization of urban space one element among others in the rationalization of political relations. He was also an astronomer who was interested in "meteorology," which is to say that he studied the stars. He provides a living example illustrating the connections between one man's astronomical preoccupation with the celestial sphere, his search for the best political institutions, and his attempt to build a town according to a rational, geometric model. Aristophanes's comedies provide another example. In *Birds*, he introduces an astronomer, Meton, for the purpose of ridiculing him. Meton had been successful in computing the relationship between the lunar months and the solar year. Aristophanes introduces him striding round the town declaring, "I shall make my measurements with a ruler which I shall use so that the circle shall be squared and the agora shall be found at the middle; perfectly straight roads shall lead to it, converging towards the very center, and as from a star which is itself round, there will be straight rays leading off in every direction."[8] This announcement evokes an admiring chorus from the onlookers: "This man is a very Thales!" Meton tries to resolve the problem of squaring the circle. He claims he can design a plan of a circular town whose streets intersect at right angles while at the same time converging toward the center. The streets must intersect at right angles because this is simple and rational, but all the streets must also converge toward the center because no city should be without its public space at the center and because every human group constitutes a kind of circle. He also makes reference to astronomical considerations — the rays of the sun — which is very understandable in an architect who is also an astronomer.

These two examples give reason to believe that there may have been very close ties between the reorganization of social space within the framework of the city and the reorganization of physical space in the new cosmological concepts.

To return to Anaximander, it is important to understand his vocabulary, his fundamental concepts, and his general organization more precisely. According to him, the earth remains immobile in the center of the celestial circumference because of its *homoiotēs*, its similitude (we would say its equal distance from all points on the circumference), and because of its *isorropia*, its equilibrium or symmetry. He adds that since the earth is situated at the center, *mesē*, *epi tou mesou*, *peri to tou kosmou meson*, the earth is *hupo mēdenos kratoumenē*, it is dominated by nothing, nothing holds power over it. What is this idea of domination doing in an astronomical context — domination being an idea from politics, not physics?[9] In the mythical view of the universe, the earth, in order to remain stable, had to be supported by something other than itself, on which it consequently depended. The fact that the earth needed something to rest on implied that it was not entirely independent, that it was in the power of something stronger than itself. In contrast, for Anaximander, the earth's central position is an indication of its autonomy. A text from the historian Herodotus — a political text — uses exactly the same terminology, fundamental concepts, and conceptual nexus of ideas involving center, similarity, and nondomination.[10] Herodotus says that when Polycrates, the tyrant of Samos, died, his successor-designate, Maiandrios, who had been won over by the ideal of democracy, refused to assume power. He therefore called together the assembly. In this privileged circle, this center of the human community, he gathered all the citizens of the town to announce that he did not approve of Polycrates's reigning as a tyrant over men who were his *homoioi*, his peers; he had therefore decided to place the *kratos*, the power, *en mesōi*, at the center (in other words, to return that which had been usurped by one individual to the community, composed of all the citizens) and to proclaim *isonomia*. This remarkable parallelism in terminology, concepts, and structure of thought seems to confirm the hypothesis that the new spherical image of the world was made possible by the elaboration of a new image of human society within the framework of the institutions of the *polis*.

I would like to pursue my analysis a little further and submit my thesis to a sort of experimental verification, insofar as this is possible within the limits of historical research. Take, at one end of the chain, the significance and values of the center in the mythical image of the universe. At the other end, consider the geometric conception of the center in Anaximander's cosmology. How, on this particular point, did the transformation come about?

There are two terms meaning *center* in Greek religion. One is *omphalos*, meaning navel, and the other is *hestia,* the hearth. Why is *hestia* a center? The house forms a clearly defined and enclosed space, different from that of other houses. It properly belongs to a family group, conferring upon that group a particular religious quality. Thus, whenever a stranger enters the house, he must first be led to the hearth. Once he touches the hearth, he is integrated into the space enclosed by the house in which he is a guest. In Greece the hearth established at the center of the domestic space is implanted in the earth. It represents, as it were, the *omphalos* of the house; it is the navel by which the human dwelling is rooted in the depths of the earth. At the same time, it is, in a sense, a point of contact between the sky and the surface of the earth on which the mortals live. Around the circular hearth, in the large room the Greeks called the *megaron,* four small columns supported an opening in the roof, a skylight through which smoke could escape. When the fire in the hearth was lit, the rising flames established communication between the earthly house and the world of the gods. Thus the center of the hearth is the point on the ground where the three cosmic levels of the universe come into contact. Such is the mythical view of the center represented by the *hestia.* And each domestic center, each hearth of each house, is different from every other. There is a kind of incompatibility between one house and the next. Different hearths cannot be "mixed."

What happens during the age of the city? When the agora is introduced, this space, which is no longer domestic but forms a space common to all, a public, not private, space, becomes the true center in the eyes of the group. In order to mark out its role as a center, the city sets up a hearth that does not belong to an individual family but stands for the political community as a whole. This is the hearth of the city, the common hearth, the *hestia koinē*. This common *hestia* is not so much a religious symbol as a political one. Henceforth all men assemble around this center to do business and to discuss their affairs in a rational way. As a political symbol, *hestia* must represent every hearth without being identified with any one in particular. It could be said that all the hearths of the various different houses are, in a sense, at the same distance from the public hearth, which represents them all equally but is not identified with any one rather than with any other. Thus *hestia*'s function is no longer to differentiate between the different houses or to establish contact between different cosmic levels. Now it is the expression of symmetry in the relationships that unite equal citizens within the city. As a political symbol, *hestia* defines the center of a space in which relationships are reversible. Thus the center, in its political sense, was able to act as an intermediary between the ancient, mythical view of the center and the new, rational idea of the center, equidistant from all parts of the circumference in a mathematical space in which relationships were reciprocal.

Is this really the way things happened? One observation seems to provide experimental verification. The name given by philosophers to the earth, immobile and fixed in the center of the cosmos, is in fact Hestia. When the astronomers and authors of cosmologies wished to indicate the central position occupied in the celestial sphere by the earth, they said that the earth constituted the hearth of the universe. In this way, they projected onto the world of nature the very same image of human society that had resulted from the foundation of the *polis*. The transformations in the symbolic meanings of *hestia* show how the change from a mythical view to a political and geometric concept came about. They show how the advent of the city, public discussion, and the social model of a human community made up of equals made it possible for rational thought to develop and for a new conception of space to be formed, a conception of space that found expression in a number of different contexts — in political life, in the organization of urban space, and in cosmology and astronomy.

CHAPTER EIGHT

Geometric Structure and Political Ideas in the Cosmology of Anaximander

Following Gregory Vlastos and Charles H. Kahn, I have pursued elsewhere the study of Anaximander's cosmology, focusing on its relationship to political thought. I have emphasized the connection between the geometric view of the universe, which appears for the first time in the work of this philosopher, and the organization of space in the city-state, where the common hearth set up on the agora forms the central point.[1] The distinguishing feature of space in the city-state is precisely that it appears to be organized around a central point. Because of the political significance attributed to it, this center is exceptionally important. First, as the center, it is contrasted with all the rest of the civic space; second, it imposes an order on this space, for each individual position is defined by it and in relation to it. As a legal inscription at Tenos puts it, in the center is the collectivity (*mesō pantes*); on the outside are the individuals (*chōris hekastos*).[2] The expressions *es meson* and *en mesōi* are exactly synonymous with *es koinon, en koinōi*. The *meson*, or middle, defines the common or public domain (the *xunon*), as opposed to what is private, individual. However different the citizens, or rather the households that compose a city, may be in terms of their dwelling place, family, and wealth, they form a political *koinōnia* or *xunōniē* by virtue of their common participation in this single center. Furthermore, despite their differences and even oppositions, they are defined in their relation to this center as *isoi* (equals), *homoioi* (peers). In the Eastern kingdoms, political space took the form of a pyramid, dominated by a king, with a hierarchy of powers, prerogatives, and functions stretching from top to bottom. In the city-state, in contrast, political space is symmetrically organized around a central point, as a geometrical schema of reversible relationships governed by equilibrium and reciprocity among equals. *Es meson tithenai tēn archēn* or *to kratos*, to place the power at the center, is to take away the privilege of supremacy from every particular individual, so that no one man dominates any other. Once fixed at the center, the *kratos* cannot be taken over and becomes the common property of all the members of the group. Each man commands and obeys himself and everyone else at the same time. For the citizens of a city to place the *kratos* at the center amounts to their proclaiming themselves free from all domination.

Herodotus writes that in Samos around 510 BCE, Maiandrios, *eiche to kratos*, held power, having received it from Polycrates. However, when Polycrates died, Maiandrios raised an altar to Zeus Eleutherios, Zeus the Liberator, and called all the citizens to an assembly to make the following statement:

> As you know, it is I who have been entrusted with *skēptron kai dunamis pasa Polukrateos*, the scepter and all the power of Polycrates.... But Polycrates did not have my approval when he ruled as master over men who were his peers, *despozōn andrōn homoiōn heōtō*.... I therefore place the power in the middle and proclaim *isonomia* for you, *es meson tēn archēn titheis isonomiēn humin proagoreuō*.[3]

Here, then, the close connections in Greek political thought among the concepts of the center (*meson*), similarity or equality (*homoiotēs, isotēs*), and nondomination (*ou kratoumenos, autokratēs*) are visible. The same connections among the same concepts, within the framework of a similar overall conception of space symmetrically organized around a central point, can also be found in the doxographers' testimonies concerning Anaximander's view of a spherical cosmos with the earth occupying the center.

214

Kahn has grouped and discussed these testimonies in a most pertinent fashion. He has also demonstrated how the geometric character of Anaximander's cosmology is radically new compared not only with the archaic representations of the universe found in the work of Homer and Hesiod but also with the theories of Thales and Anaximenes. According to Anaximander, the sole reason for the earth's remaining immobile is the position it occupies in the cosmos. Since it is situated at the center of the universe, at an equal distance from all the points that form the extremities of the world, there is no reason for it to move in one direction rather than another. The earth's stability is explained purely in terms of the geometric properties of space. The earth no longer has any need of roots, as it does in Hesiod. Nor does it have to rest upon any other element, such as Thales's water or Anaximenes's air. It remains in position without any outside intervention because there are no longer any absolute directions in this universe, every part of which is organized symmetrically, in relation to the center. Up and down, right and left exist not in themselves but only in relation to the center. And from the point of view of the center, up and down are not only symmetrical but also completely reversible.[4] There is no difference between them, any more than there is between right and left. Thus all points on the celestial sphere are exactly the same, *homoioi*, in relation to the center. Aristotle explains that according to Anaximander this *homoiotēs*, linked with the central location of the earth (*to epi tou mesou hidrumenon kai homoiōs ta eschata echon*), is what causes the earth to remain necessarily immobile, *ex anagkēs menein*.[5] In Book One of his *Refutation of All Heresies*, Hippolytus sums up Anaximander's doctrine in these terms: "*Tēn de gēn einai meteōron hupo mēdenos kratoumenēn, menousan de dia tēn homoian pantōn apostasin*."[6] Kahn translates this passage, correctly I believe, as follows: "The earth is aloft, not dominated by anything; it remains in place because of the similar distance from all points [of the celestial circumference]."[7]

Not only are the terms "centrality," "similarity," and "absence of domination" found in Anaximander's cosmology, but they are also clearly linked together there in the same way as they were in political thought. The geometric character of the new conception of the world thus seems to have been modeled on the image that the city-state presented of itself. It was expressed in a political vocabulary that conveyed what the Greeks believed to be original in their civic institutions, compared with states that were subject to a king's authority.

There is one difficulty, however. Is it correct to attribute the expression "*hupo mēdenos kratoumenēn*" to Anaximander? Should it not rather be attributed to Hippolytus? Kahn rejects this objection. In his opinion, the phrase's authenticity is demonstrated by the exceptional importance of the ideas of *kratos* and *kratein* in the earliest cosmological thought.[8] This answer has been judged inadequate, for the objection has been raised again, and in more rigorous terms.[9] It has been pointed out that by the beginning of the Christian period the usual meaning of the verb *kratein* was "to retain," "to uphold." Thus, as used by Hippolytus, *hupo mēdenos kratoumenēn* explains *meteōron* in the usual way, without implying the slightest reference to the idea of *kratos* in the sense of power of domination. The argument seems strong enough to warrant a fresh examination of the whole case. First, however, a few preliminary remarks may prove useful.

The fundamental meaning of *kratein* is "to be strong, to dominate, to overcome." However, even before the Hellenistic period, it had various nuances in different contexts. In legal terminology, in particular, it meant both "to be master of, to have rights over" and "to keep in one's grasp, to retain."[10] In medical terminology, it often has the sense of "to assimilate, to digest," as does *epikratein*. Thus in *On Ancient Medicine* that which is harmful is defined as being that which human nature cannot *krateein*, assimilate. *On Ancient Medicine* remarks that the reason why food was boiled and roasted by the first men was so that they could *epikrateein*, digest, it. It also considers what a man should eat and drink in order to be able to assimilate it most easily: *ho ti esthiōn te kai pinōn epikratēsei te autou malista.*[11] But in law as in medicine, whether the sense is "to retain" or "to assimilate," the reference to *kratos*, the power of domination, linked with an idea of strength (*ischus*) and power (*dunamis*), is always perfectly explicit. In legal terminology, *kratein* means to have the upper hand over somebody or something and thus to have legal rights over, or simply to dominate in practice, that person or thing. In medical terminology, *kratein* has the sense of assimilating or digesting, because the elements' various qualities (dry, wet, hot, cold, sweet, bitter) are conceived as *dunameis*, powers of varying strengths. In order to assimilate them, the body must be stronger and more powerful than these qualities; in other words, it must dominate them, in the true sense of the term. *On Ancient Medicine* shows that what the doctors considered harmful was "the strength of each quality, that which, being too powerful for human nature, could not be assimilated by it (*to ischuron hekastou kai to kresson tēs phusios tēs anthrōpeiēs, hou mē ēdunato krateein*)."[12] Thus, to help their digestion, one gives to the sick or the infirm food that has been made weaker (*asthenesteroi*) by reducing its strength (*to ischuron*) by cooking it or watering it down.[13] The doctor's relationship to diseases is like that of the body to the elements: the skilled practitioner is effective against the evil insofar as he possesses some instrument or means of greater power and strength:

> In cases where we are able to dominate, *epikratein*, through means either natural or artificial, we can act as craftsmen, otherwise it is not possible. So when a man suffers from an illness which is too strong for the instruments of medicine one cannot hope for it to be dominated by medicine (*hotan oun ti pathēi hōnthrōpos kakon ho kresson esti tōn en iētrikēi organōn, oude prodokasthai touto pou dei hupo iētrikēs krathēnai an*).[14]

What is true for the art of medicine also goes for other human techniques. It is always a matter of opposing force to force, power to power, in order to conquer or dominate. Similarly, Aristotle describes both the skills of the sophists and the tools of the engineers as weapons making it possible for the smaller and weaker to dominate (*kratein*) what is larger and stronger.[15] The dynamic sense of *kratos* — that is, a superior force — is present even in the technological vocabulary of Philo of Byzantium, for example, for whom the verb *kratein* has acquired the meaning of exerting pressure on a tool in order to move it, and *krateisthai*, in the case of one part of an instrument, has the meaning of being activated by another part, or "driven" by it, as we would say.

This dynamic conception of a universe in which physical phenomena are conceived of as powers and their mutual relationships as confrontations of strength no doubt explains why, even as early as Homer, the expression *krataipedon* refers to ground that is solid and resistant, in other words, capable of upholding things and beings without their sinking into it.[16] A falling body is a force in action. Thus Homer writes that each time Sisyphos was on the point of reaching the summit with his stone, "*tot' apostepsaske krataiis*, at that moment a force made it fall back again."[17] To arrest the fall and support the weight, an equal or superior force is needed. This is precisely the power of support that Gaia possesses. True, she is the Nourisher, but she is also the goddess *ēuthemethlos* with solid foundations, the cosmic power who is the *pantōn hedos asphales aiei* (the unshakable foundation for all the gods.)[18] As such, she is opposed at the beginning of the world to Chaos, the yawning chasm, the bottomless void without direction, the space in which a drop has no end, where there is never anything to stop the flight of a falling body.[19]

What is the source of Gaia's ability to uphold things, her power of stability? Why is she the support on which men may walk without fear, even when the ground sometimes shakes beneath their feet? Myth provides many answers to this, although the question is never explicitly formulated. Since these answers involve the entire mythical view of the progressive organization of the world, they are beyond the scope of this study — but a few points are worth mentioning. Gaia is stability, just as she is the universal mother who gave birth to all things, from the heavens, the waves, and the mountains to the gods and men. When Gaia makes her appearance (*geneto*) immediately after Chaos, a kind of basis, a foundation, is established in the unorganized world.[20] Space acquires the beginnings of an orientation. However, Gaia was preceded by Chaos, a force quite foreign to her, the only power with which Gaia will never be in any way united. This means that even after the generations of hostilities between the gods end and order is established, Chaos still constitutes a threat lurking in the background. Indeed, Chaos would submerge all that is stable and organized in the cosmos if Zeus, by virtue of his superior *kratos*, had not definitively fixed the place, privileges, and scope of each power.[21] When the monster Typhon stirs, he shakes the ground, confuses every direction in space with the whirlwinds of his squalls, and confounds the sky and the earth with the darkness of his storms. Nevertheless, he is controlled by Zeus's strength and is relegated to Tartarus, buried forever beneath the mass of Etna.[22] Similarly, the roots of the earth emerge from an opening that gives onto this same Tartarus, the realm of Night, the immense abyss that resembles primeval Chaos and that, like it, contains within its breast the origins (*pēgai*) and limits (*peirata*) of all that exists.[23] But by the order of Zeus this opening has now been closed. Poseidon has sealed its bronze doors on the conquered Titans.[24] No force of dissolution and disorder can henceforth reemerge into the light and threaten the stability of the world. All images, on the contrary, emphasize the unshakable character of the foundations on which Gaia rests. The doors stand on an indestructible bronze bed, born of itself. This threshold in turn rests on roots that stretch indefinitely and boundlessly into the distance.[25]

This imagery anticipates some of the problems that philosophy was to formulate in conceptual terms (the relation of nonbeing to being, of the limitless to the limit, of the undifferentiated to the defined).[26] However, it did not satisfy the positivist minds of the Milesian physicists. For them, the powers that make up the universe and whose interplay must explain its current organization are no longer primeval beings or the traditional gods. Order cannot be the result of sexual unions and sacred childbirth, nor can it arise as the result of the gods' struggles for sovereign power, which lasted until Zeus was installed on the throne of the world, flanked by Kratos and Bia.[27]

Thus the Milesians, as "physicists," had to explain the power of stability that the earth appeared to possess. Thales's answer to the problem was that the earth does not, in fact, possess any such power. Its stability comes from the primeval element out of which every-thing originates and to which everything returns, the source of movement and life in the universe. The earth floats on water, which "bears" it as it bears and animates all things. Hippolytus writes,

> Everything is supported by the water whence come the tremors of the earth, the gusts of wind, the movements of the stars; and every-thing that exists is carried and flows in accordance with the nature of the first cause of their generation (*Epipheresthai te autōi ta panta, aph' hou kai seismous kai pneumatōn strophas kai astrōn kinēseis: kai ta panta pheresthai te kai rhein tēi tou prōtou archēgou tēs geneseōs autōn phusei sumpheromena*).[28]

Since it is both the origin and the end of all that comes into exis-tence, water is, in the proper sense of the term, divine (*theion*) and as such is present in each part of the great living thing that is the universe, regulating all changes, undergoing none itself, without ever ceasing to be or to be what it is. Since it produces, governs, and envelops the whole of being, water concentrates within itself the two kinds of power that had been distinguished in myth. There, the power to engender beings in all their variety was con-ferred on primeval entities (*hoi prōtoi*) such as Gaia, Nyx, and Okeanos, while the *kratos* and *basileia* were reserved for the late-arriving Zeus.[29] For the physicists, though, the order of the world could not have arisen — as if by decree — from the decision of a single god, even if he was sovereign. The great law that rules the universe is immanent in *phusis* and had to be present at the very beginning in the primeval element from which the world gradu-ally emerged through differentiation. The physicists thus abolished the opposition established by myth between that which comes first from a temporal point of view (*ex archēs, prōtiston*) and that which comes first from the point of view of *kratos*, between the principle that is chronologically at the origin of the world and the prince who presides over the existing order.[30] As divine elements, Thales's water and Anaximenes's air play the roles Homer ascribes to Okeanos and Zeus, respectively. Like Okeanos, they are *genesis pantessi*, the origin of everything, and like him they envelop the universe and at the same time constitute its limits (*peirata*) without themselves being either enveloped or limited by anything.[31] But like Zeus they are also *kratistoi*, the most powerful.[32] Through this *kratos* they govern the cosmos, imposing upon its process of becoming a law whose necessity (*anagkē*) is immanent in their nature. *Periechein* (to envelop, with all the spatial significance that the term implies) and *kubernan* (to govern, with its political overtones) are the two aspects of the power of *kratein* that are henceforth united.[33] According to Xenophanes, *kratein* defines the divine as such: *touto gar theon kai theou dunamin einai, kratein, alla mē krateisthai, kai pantōn kratiston einai.*[34] This expression may be compared to one that Aristotle attributes to a tradition from earliest Antiquity: *periechei to theion tēn holēn phusin.*[35]

Just as, according to Aëtius, Anaximenes believed that the air *periechei* the cosmos as our *psuchē*, being air as well, *sugkratei hēmas*, so, according to Aristotle, Anaximander attributed to the *apeiron*, which he conceived of as *to theion*, the power of *periechein hapanta kai panta kubernan.*[36] From this point of view, the expression that Diogenes Laertius ascribes to Thales, "*ischurotaton anagkē: kratei gar pantōn*," becomes comprehensible when compared with the Pythagorean doctrine reported by Aëtius according to which, *Anagkē perikeisthai tōi kosmōi*, and with the fragment of Parmenides that says, "*kraterē gar Anagkē peiratos en desmoisi echei*, powerful Necessity holds it within the bonds of a limit."[37]

In the Milesians' doctrine, the old primeval or personal deities have been replaced by elements conceived of as powers. They are imperishable, as the gods were, and their strength and fields of action vary in degree and scope. These powers are not abstractions that can be conceived of independent of the "places" they occupy and their zones of activity. Each power acts within a clearly defined domain, just as for Homer each of the various gods has an allotted share, a *moira*, a portion of the universe to reign over.[38] These spatial boundaries mark out the limits within which each type of power is contained, so a *dunamis* appears to be "dominated" by what extends beyond it, what surrounds and envelops it, or, in other words, what fixes its limits, its *peirata*. That which dominates everything cannot be limited by anything but must, on the contrary, envelop all the rest. On the subject of Anaximander, Aristotle writes: "*tou de apeirou ouk estin archē: eiē gar an autou peras*, there is no *archē* to the *apeiron*, for that would be its limit.... That is why it has no *archē*, but is the *arche* of other things; it envelops and governs everything."[39] Melissos of Samos later reasons in precisely the same way when he defines nature or being as follows: "It would be impossible for Being to have either *archē* or *telos*: *archēn te kai telos echon ouden oute aidion oute apeiron estin*, nothing that has a beginning or an end is eternal or without limit."[40] Being can only be one: "If it were not one, it would have its limit in something else, *ei mē hen eiē, peranei pros allo*."[41] Being is the strongest thing to exist: "Nothing is stronger than the true Being, *tou gar eontos alēthinou kreisson ouden*."[42]

But it is perhaps Anaxagoras who demonstrates most clearly the way of thinking in which an element's *kratos* is never separate from the space it occupies. In effect, the *nous* of Anaxagoras is defined by two features: it has no limit, and it is not dominated by anything; it is *apeiron* and *autokrates*. In the universal mixture that constitutes the world, it is the only thing that is pure, *katharos*. It never mingles with anything else and remains itself alone, by itself: *nous de estin apeiron kai autokrates kai memeiktai oudeni chrēmati, alla monos autos ep' eōutou estin*.[43] Simplicius adds that anything mixed with the *nous* (that is, anything that would limit it from within if it were not pure, just as anything that enveloped it could limit it from without if it were not *apeiron*) would prevent it from dominating everything as it does, being alone itself by itself, *kai an ekōluen auton ta summemeigmena, hōste mēdenos chrēmatos kratein homoiōs hōs kai monon eonta eph' heautou*. Simplicius goes on to say: "For it is the most subtle, *leptotaton* (and therefore can penetrate everywhere and limit everything from within), and the most pure, *katharōtaton* (and therefore nothing can penetrate it to limit it from within); it comprehends everything, *kai ischuei megiston* [...] *pantōn nous kratei."*

Hippolytus's statement about Anaximander must be interpreted in relation to this type of thinking. It is not necessary to choose between two incompatible interpretations according to whether one translates the phrase as the earth "supported" by nothing or as the earth "dominated" by nothing. On the contrary, the question is whether in the eyes of the Milesians the idea of "support," like that of "envelopment," suggests a reference to the idea of a superior power or force, and whether, conversely, a *dunamis* with the power to *kratein* another *dunamis* is thereby conceived of as enveloping it or at least supporting it. In fact, a text of Aristotle's on the subject of why the *apeiron* is at rest in Anaxagoras suggests that the concepts "to envelop" and "to support" are closely linked, so a power that supports another thereby dominates and governs it as if it were enveloping it. The text runs as follows: "Anaxagoras says that the *apeiron* supports itself, and this is because it is within itself, there being nothing else that envelops it, *stērizein gar auto hauto phēsi to apeiron: touto de, hoti en autōi: allo gar ouden periechei."*[44] That which is not limited and exists in and by itself is not enveloped by anything. It therefore supports itself and is *autokratēs.*

In the light of these preliminary remarks, it seems very likely that Kahn's proposed interpretation of *hupo mēdenos kratoumenēn* is correct, since it refers to the idea of *kratos*, the power of domination. But can this not be demonstrated more clearly by showing that the use of *kratos* and *kratein* in Hippolytus and the meaning of the expression in other comparative evidence on the same problem combine to make this interpretation all but certain?

In the first book of his *Refutation of All Heresies*, Hippolytus uses the verb *kratein* on only two occasions. The first is in the fragment discussed above (at l.6); the second is as follows: "According to Anaxagoras the sun and the moon perform their turnings because they are pushed back by the air, *apōthoumenous hupo tou aeros.* But the moon turns very often because it cannot dominate the cold, *dia to mē dunasthai kratein tou psuchrou*."[45] The use of *kratein* here is entirely in keeping with its usage in cosmological and medical literature. Diels and Kranz correct Hippolytus's text, introducing *ton d' aera kratein tou pantos*, basing this addition upon the corresponding version of Diogenes Laertius, where *kratein* does indeed have the sense of "to dominate."[46] We shall have occasion to return to this passage, which directly affects the interpretation of *tēn de gēn einai meteōron hupo mēdenos kratoumenēn*, even if one does not accept the correction of Diels and Kranz. In the following book, Hippolytus again uses the term *kratos* in an astronomical context. According to the astronomers, "*kratos edōken ho dēmiourgēsas tēi tautou kai homoiou periphorai*, the creator gave domination to the revolution of the same and the similar." Hippolytus goes on,

> They say that this power of domination, *kratos* has been given to the revolution of the same, not only because it includes that of the other, that is to say of the planets, but also because it possesses such a *kratos*, that is to say, such a *dunamis*, that it also makes what is opposed to it turn with it, by its strength, *tēi oikeiai ischui*, making the planets move from west to east, as it does also from east to west.[47]

It must be concluded, then, that in the two existing books that present a historical description of the philosophers' doctrines by way of introduction to *The Refutation of All Heresies* itself, Hippolytus gives *kratein* and *kratos* the meanings that those terms had in the cosmological and astronomical writings to which he is referring.

The controversial passage can now be put it in context. As said above, Hippolytus presented the doctrines of Thales as follows: everything is produced by water, as it comes together and divides, and everything is "supported" by water, which accounts in particular for earthquakes. Aristotle expressed the same idea more precisely when he said that according to Thales *eph' hudatos keisthai* [*tēn gēn*], or *dia to plōtēn einai, menousan hōsper xulon*; Simplicius *eph' hudatos ocheisthai tēn gēn hōsper xulon*.[48]

The view of Anaximenes, for whom the limitless and all-embracing air has taken the place of water as the primary element, is reported by Hippolytus as follows:

> *tēn de gēn plateian einai ep' aeros ochoumenēn, homoiōs de kai hēlion kai selēnēn kai ta alla astra: panta gar purina onta epocheisthai tōi aeri dia platos,* the earth is flat, supported by the air; the same applies to the sun, the moon and the other stars; for all these fiery beings are supported by the air on account of their breadth.[49]

Thus the air supports and carries everything that exists and is born from it, in particular the earth, just as for Thales the primeval water from which the earth emerged had to continue to hold this earth up, giving it the support without which it would fall. But this support is at the same time a limit (*peras*), which the earth needs because it is not without limit (*apeiron*). Being thus limited by something other than itself that both supports and envelops it (in space and in time), the earth cannot be said to be *autokratēs* like the *nous* of Anaxagoras.

Another of Hippolytus's texts, which must be mentioned in connection with the preceding one, gives a clear indication of the sense of the expression Hippolytus uses about Anaximander. On the subject of Anaxagoras, Hippolytus writes, "*Tēn de gēn tōi schēmati plateian einai kai menein meteōron dia to megethos kai dia to mē einai kenon kai dia to ton aera ischurotaton onta pherein epochoumenēn tēn gēn.*"[50]

For Anaxagoras, as for Anaximenes, the earth is flat; it remains motionless, supported by the air. But Anaxagoras's explanation is more detailed. As well as flatness, Hippolytus on this occasion also mentions the size of the earth, the absence of the void (in other words, the presence everywhere of air), and, above all, the fact that the air, by reason of its very great strength, is able to carry the earth, which rests upon it.

There is no less striking similarity in the expressions used in the disputed passage concerning Anaximander. In both cases, Hippolytus uses similar phrases: *Tēn gēn einai meteōron* [...], *menousan de dia...; tēn gēn plateian einai kai menein meteōron dia.*

What is the source of this immobility, on the one hand (*menousan, menein*), and this position "in the air," on the other (*meteōron*)? With regard to the earth itself, Anaxagoras refers to its flatness and its size. But these are secondary explanations. The basic cause is the air, which, *through its superior strength*, has the power to carry the earth. The earth's flatness and size simply ensure that the air has a better hold. In contrast, for Anaximander, neither the shape nor the size of the earth has anything to do with it. There is a single and sufficient reason for the earth to be at rest: its central position at an equal distance from everything. This single explanation henceforth makes it unnecessary to refer to a support that, by reason of its superior strength, holds up the earth *meteōron*, that is to say, fixes and suspends it in place by virtue of a *kratos*, a power somehow imposed upon the earth from the outside. This concept of a *kratos*, a superior power (compare *ischurotaton*), justifies the use of *kratoumenē* even though in this *kratos* the aspect that is emphasized is force that can be *pherein epochoumenēn tēn gēn*.

But let us now leave Hippolytus in order to see how the Presocratics and other fifth-century authors deal with the problem of the relationship of the earth to the surrounding air. According to Diogenes Laertius, Archelaus believed that the water was melted by heat and formed the earth through the condensation of its lower portions under the influence of fire, and that by flowing out around the entire periphery, it gave birth to the air. Hence the earth *hupo tou aeros krateitai*, and, for its part, the air *hupo tēs tou puros periphoras krateitai*; the earth is dominated by the air and the air by the encircling fire.[51] The verb *kratein* here takes on the nuance of "containing" as well as "supporting," but the essential idea is still "holding," "dominating." The expression *hupo tēs tou puros periphoras krateitai* can be compared with the Hippolytus text where the *kratos* in the universe is entrusted precisely to the *periphora* of the Same.

At the end of the fifth century, Diogenes of Apollonia took up Anaximenes's view that air was the first element, being without limit and producing the universe through condensation (associated with the cold, immobility) and rarefaction (associated with heat, mobility). He wrote that "everything is governed by the air and it dominates everything, *hupo toutou pantas kai kubernasthai kai pantōn kratein*"; he went on: "for this is what I consider a god, it extends everywhere, orders everything and is present in everything."[52] This divine air, "great, strong, eternal, immortal and possessing immense knowledge," imposes its own measure on all things, *pantōn metra echei*, in particular the earth.[53] According to Diogenes Laertius, Diogenes of Apollonia maintained that the spherical earth is at rest and stable (*ēreismenēn*) at the center, having been positioned there (*tēn sustasin eilēphuian*) by the circular motion of the heat and the freezing caused by the cold (that is to say, in fact, by the air).[54] Other evidence shows that for Diogenes of Apollonia the earth was, indeed, "carried" by the air, *hupo aeros pheresthai tēn gēn*.[55]

These doctrines are reflected in literary texts that, precisely because they are not technical, provide clearer information about the implications that the vocabulary of the philosophers may have had for the general public. In *Clouds*, Aristophanes pokes fun at theories like those of Diogenes and, before him, Anaximenes: "*ō despot' anax, ametrēt' Aēr, hos echeis tēn gēn meteōron*, O, Sovereign Master, infinite air, you who hold the earth suspended in the air."[56] The verb *echein* is here the equivalent of *kratein*, in the sense that a deity is said to "possess" a territory; for example, Zeus *echei* Olympos. "*Echein tēn gēn meteōron*" does indeed mean "hold the earth suspended," but in a way possible only for a power invoked as *despot' anax*.

In *The Trojan Women*, Hecuba addresses to the gods a prayer whose unusual character puzzles Menelaus, unversed as he is in philosophical debate: "*ō gēs ochēma kapi gēs exōn hedran,/ hostis pot' ei su, dustopastos eidenai,/ Zeus, eit' Anagkē phuseos eite nous brotōn,/ prosēuxamēn se*."[57]

What is the nature of this mysterious deity that can be addressed equally well as Zeus, Anagkē, or Nous? It is mistress of the universe, the power of the air itself, which both supports to Gē and is enthroned above her, in other words, supports Gē but also envelops her on all sides and dominates her.

Such remarks apply to the medical writings as well as to the plays discussed here. Diogenes of Appollonia's *On Nature* says that the earth is a seat for the air and air is the support for the earth: *alla mēn chai hē gē toutou [aeros] bathron, houtos te gēs ochēma*. And where is this remark, which is identical to that of Euripides? In a passage that aims to show that air is the origin of everything, commands everything, and is the greatest and most powerful of all beings, even though it is invisible, *houtos de megistos en toisi pasi tōn pantōn dunastēs estin.*[58]

But not all the philosophers agreed that air supported and enveloped the earth and thus held it in its power. So, by way of contrast, let us examine how the opposite point of view was expressed. According to Hippolytus, Xenophanes maintained that "*tēn de gēn apeiron einai kai mētehup' aeros mēte hupo tou ouranou periechesthai*, the earth is not limited and is not enveloped, neither by the air nor by the sky."[59] Another fragment clarifies the meaning of Hippolytus's expression: "*gaiēs men tode peiras anō para possin horatai ēeri prosplazon, to katō d' es apeiron hikneitai*; we see the upper limit of the earth lying at our feet in contact with the air; but its lower part extends to infinity."[60] If the earth is indeed in contact with the air, which thus forms its limit, this only applies to the upper part; underneath, it extends into infinity, and this is what remains invisible and explains its stability. So it is not really limited by the air, which neither surrounds nor envelops it. Since it is *apeiron* through its roots, the earth owes its stability to itself alone. It does not depend on the *kratos* or the strength of the air. Thus Xenophanes's position directly opposes that of Archelaus, which Diogenes Laertius reports as follows: "*hē men [gē] hupo tou aeros, ho de hupo tēs tou puros periphoras krateitai.*"[61]

This comparison of texts reveals even more clearly the originality of Anaximander's point of view. In contrast to Xenophanes, he rejects the ancient belief that Hesiod reports according to which the earth possesses stability because its roots extend beneath it *es apeiron*, while the air circulates only above the earth's surface as far as the sky, in the direction of what is upward, in an absolute

sense. He also rejects the idea of an earth floating on the boundless waters from which it was supposed to have emerged. Like
Anaximenes, he believes that the earth is fixed at the center of the
cosmos. It must therefore be surrounded on every side and
enveloped by something other than itself. So, should not Anaximander have concluded that the earth is also "dominated" by this
other element that envelops it? The features peculiar to the doctrines of this philosopher now become important. In Anaximander's view, what envelops and dominates everything in the world
is not one of the elements of which the earth is composed: it is
neither fire nor water nor air.[62] All the evidence agrees that Anaximander does not recognize any element as *apeiron* and that for
him the *apeiron* is something other than the elements. This is not
an easy position to uphold, and it must have seemed sufficiently
paradoxical to Anaximander's contemporaries for Anaximenes
not to feel able to follow his predecessor on this point. What,
indeed, could this *apeiron* be that was not a definite limitless
thing, neither earth nor air nor the limitless water, but was, so to
speak, the boundless in itself? Yet Anaximander had his reasons,
reported by Aristotle, for maintaining a point of view that implied
an entirely new concept of the universe. According to Anaximander, if any one of the elements possessed the limitlessness that is
the property of the *apeiron*, all the other elements would finally
have been overcome and destroyed by it. The elements are, in
fact, defined by their reciprocal opposition; they are forces in conflict with one another. It is therefore necessary that they always
stand in a relationship of equality toward one another, as equal
powers, *isotēs tēs dunameōs*.[63] As Aristotle puts it:

> The contraries should always be equal to each other and none of
> them should be limitless, *isazein aei tanantia, kai mē einai hen autōn
> apeiron*; for if the power of one body is exceeded in any degree by
> that of another, for example, if fire is finite in amount while air is
> infinite, however much fire exceeds in power the same amount of
> air, provided that the ratio is numerically definite, the infinite body
> will obviously, despite everything, prevail over and destroy the finite

body.... This is why some thinkers (among them Anaximander) propose an *apeiron* which is neither water nor air, so that the other elements should not be destroyed by that among their number that is *apeiron*. In fact, oppositions do exist among them, for example, air is cold, water is wet, fire is hot; but if a single one of these is *apeiron* all the rest must be destroyed; what these thinkers say is that there is something else from which all these things come.[64]

So the *apeiron* must be "something else" that possesses the *archē* and envelops and governs everything because no individual element should be able to monopolize the *kratos* and dominate the world. The primacy that Anaximander grants to the *apeiron* aims to guarantee the permanence of an egalitarian order in which opposing powers are balanced against one another, so that if one of them is dominant for a moment, it is then dominated in turn; if any of them advances and extends itself beyond its limits, it then recedes as much as it had advanced, yielding to its opposite. The *apeiron* does not represent a particular reality, an *idion*, the other elements do; it is the common source of everything else, the *koinon*, that which is just as much air as fire or earth or water, without being any single one of these, for it comprehends them all and unites them without being identified with any one of them. Thus, when Aristotle and Simplicius have to define the exact relationship between the *apeiron* and the various elements, they do so by saying that it is not only other than the elements, *heteron toutōn ti allo para tauta*, but also the mediator, the intermediary between the elements, *to metaxu toutōn, to metaxu dia to eualloiōton*.[65] The mediator that unites the elements with one another is introduced within a framework of thought that usually opposes the category of *koinon* to that of *idion* and identifies *koinon* with *meson*, as being the "middle" of the elements, their center, *to meson autōn*.[66] Aristotle remarks: "It is not from a single one among themselves that the elements proceed but nor is it from another body distinct from them which would be as it were *meson ti* between air and water or air and fire, thicker than air and fire but more rarefied than water and air."[67] Aristotle rejects the hypothesis of an element acting as a "middle" in terms that indicate quite clearly that such a concept goes back to Anaximander: the middle would, in fact, become air or fire when a pair of opposites was added to it, and Aristotle points out that "one of these opposites is a privation from which it results that the intermediate can never exist on its own as some have claimed for that which is limitless and all-enveloping, *hōsper phasi tines to apeiron kai to periechon.*"

Thus, according to Anaximander, the limitless, which envelops, governs, and dominates all things, has, through its mediating function, the role of a *meson.* To return to the term used in the inscription of Tenos, it represents *pantes,* the collectivity, the cosmos in its entirety, and not *hekastos,* the individuality of each element as it exists with its own clearly defined mode of existence, its own private being. Therefore, to confer the *kratos* upon the *apeiron* is indeed to make this *kratos* a *xunon,* to set it down at the center.

So the rule of the *apeiron* is not comparable with a *monarchia* like that exerted by Zeus according to Hesiod, or by air and water according to the philosophers who give these elements the power to *kratein* the whole universe. The *apeiron* is sovereign in the manner of a common law that imposes the same *dikē* on each individual, that keeps each power within the limits of its own domain, and that, in the face of any show of force or abuse of power, imposes respect for what Alcmaeon was later to call the *isonomia tōn dunameōn.* In this sense, to withdraw the *kratos* from the elements that make up the universe and entrust it instead to the *apeiron* was to bring about a revolution in cosmological thought comparable to the revolution Maiandrios introduced when, rejecting the idea that one individual can dominate men who are his *homoioi,* he made the decision to pool the *kratos* or, to use Greek political terminology, to set it down at the center by proclaiming *isonomia.*

The role Anaximander gave the *apeiron* made possible a universe founded on the balance of forces and interchangeability of position. This led to the cosmos' being represented in accordance with a circular conception of space, in which the center, rather than the top or bottom, constituted the point of reference. Under the reign of the *apeiron*, all the elements had to be related to the same central point and all the *dunameis* had to gravitate around it. Because of its position, this central point represents the egalitarian order that presides over the whole of the cosmic system. It expresses the kind of balance that the *apeiron* imposes and itself embodies. The center is defined by its *isorropia*, its *homoiotēs*, its *isotēs*, just as the *apeiron* was defined by its role as mediator among the different elements. It can thus be said of the center as of the *apeiron* that it represents not so much a particular point in cosmic space, an *idion*, as the common mediator, among all the points in space, a *koinon*, to which they all refer equally and which give them all their common measure. As earth, Gaia is of course an element like any other. But with regard to her location in space, she occupies a privileged position, which sets her apart from the other elements. Apart from the *apeiron*, which remains immovable and eternal, everything in the cosmos is movement, change, transformation. Everything moves, advances, or recedes. In contrast, the earth remains immobile in its place. Why? Because under the domination of the *apeiron*, the world now appears to have a center, and it is precisely this place that the earth occupies. There is, therefore, no point in introducing a *kratos* powerful enough to "govern" the earth and fix it in its position of *meteōron*. As Plato later put it:

> If the earth is at the center of the world it has no need of air nor of any similar constraint in order to avoid falling, *mēden autēi dein mēte aeros pros to mē pesein mēte allēs anagkēs mēdemias toiautēs.* But what is enough to restrain it, *autēn ischein*, is the equality (*homoiotēs*) among all the directions of the world and the state of equilibrium (*isorropia*) of the earth itself. Since, for a thing that is placed in equilibrium at the center of a homogeneous space, *isorropon gar pragma, homoiou tinos en mesōi tethen*, there will be no cause at all for it to incline more or less in one direction than in another.[68]

To say that the earth is *hupo mēdenos kratoumenēn* is thus to declare that, being central and consequently balanced at an equal distance

from all things, it has no need of air or any constraint at all in
order to stay where it is. No *kratos* need be exerted upon it to fix
it in its place, since this very place, by virtue of its status as center,
confers upon it both the privilege of being the only thing to
remain immobile in a world where everything else is in motion
and of not being dominated by anything. Another Hippolytus
text seems to confirm that he was perfectly aware of the center's
exceptional character, which contrasts it to all other points in
space. The latter are always individual and, as such, subject to
kratos, while the center stands for what is held in common and,
linked as it is with the *apeiron*, symbolizes that which is not dominated, the *autokratēs*. Indeed, when Hippolytus describes the
views of Archelaus, he writes: "*Tēn men oun gēn* [...] *keisthai d' en
mesōi ouden meros ousa hōs eipein, tou pantos*."[69] Being situated at
the center, the earth is not a part of the whole that is the world.
Each point, each element in the universe, whatever its position or
its power, is necessarily limited and individual. Only the *apeiron*,
which is neither limited nor dominated by anything, is not in any
way particularized. However, the earth is not a part like any other.
Because it is central (*mesē, en mesōi*), it is not particular but common (*koinē, xunē*), and in this sense it is like the whole itself. On
the political plane, the same applies to the public hearth, which is
likewise not a "private" hearth like the others, since its function is
precisely to represent every hearth without being identified with
any particular one. The common hearth is set up at the center of
the city, in the *meson* where the *kratos* has been set down so that
no one man can take it for himself, and it is called the *hestia koinē*
because it symbolizes the entirety of a political community,
where, under the reign of *isonomia*, each individual element is
henceforth *homoios* to all the others.

CHAPTER NINE

Space and Political Organization

in Ancient Greece

By studying the figure of Cleisthenes the Athenian, after whom their book is named, Pierre Lévêque and Pierre Vidal-Naquet have endeavored to define the significance of a transformation that took place in the social life of the Greeks.[1] Their *Cleisthène l'Athénien* is not a biography, which would have been impossible to write, given the lack of information, nor is it simply a critical discussion of the reforms attributed to Cleisthenes and their chronology. In order to understand the revolution introduced by Cleisthenes, the authors have extended the framework of their inquiry, placing the existing evidence in a historical context, in all its scope and complexity. Their study becomes that of the Greek *polis* during the last years of the sixth century, and of the transformations that took place at various levels within it. At the same time, Lévêque and Vidal-Naquet were able to control this extensive material by indicating, the essential problems right from the start and by describing the research methods with which they hoped to resolve these problems. They seek to identify and then examine the sectors of social life in which the changes associated with Cleisthenes are shown most clearly and which offer the historian the best chance of a precise assessment of their impact.

Cleisthenes's reforms concern the political institutions of the city. They set up the framework within which the political life of classical Athens took place. Indeed, one should speak not of a transformation but of an inauguration of politics, the emergence of a true political dimension in the social existence of the Greeks. Between the time of Solon and that of Cleisthenes, there was a change in the terms in which the conflicts dividing the city were expressed. It is not just that the conflicts themselves were different. The center of gravity in the disagreements had shifted: the clash of opposing forces took place in a very different context. In the most significant shift of emphasis, economic preoccupations were superseded by a concern with civic institutions. In Solon's day, debts and land tenure were in the forefront, but now this issue gives way to a new problem: how to create an institutional system that makes it possible to unify groups of human beings of different social, family, territorial, and religious status; how to detach individuals from their former loyalties and traditional ties in order to weld them into a homogeneous city composed of similar and equal citizens sharing the same rights of participation in the direction of public affairs.

This is a turning point in the history of ancient societies. Through the constitution introduced by Cleisthenes, the city became a democracy. It did so to some extent self-consciously. The concept of *isonomia*, which dates to a period when the democrats and the oligarchs, who formed an alliance against the tyrants, were not yet clearly distinguished from each other, now takes on a new meaning, a clearly defined political significance. One feature emphasizes the new importance of the political, now conceived of as what regulates the communal exercise of sovereignty. At the time of Solon, cities faced with a crisis would appeal to some figure who was endowed with certain exceptional gifts: an arbitrator, a foreign legislator designated in many cases by an oracle, or a tyrant. In contrast, the ideal of *isonomia* implies that the city resolves its problems, thanks to the normal functioning of its institutions, through respect for its own *nomos*.

With a single-mindedness whose audacity has often been remarked on, Cleisthenes designed the political framework within which the Greeks of the classical period exercised their social activities. By making man essentially a citizen who devoted the best part of himself to public life, this framework imprinted certain features on human behavior, values, and psychology, just as it determined the group's specific way of life.

Such a transformation affecting the framework of life in society and orienting the human activities that are judged to be most important clearly affects the whole man. Lévêque and Vidal-Naquet are obviously well aware of this, for they concentrate mainly on the mental aspects of a reform they interpret as both political and intellectual. The subtitle of their book is "An Essay on the Representation of Space and Time in Greek Political Thought from the End of the Sixth Century to the Death of Plato."

Gustave Glotz has already drawn attention to the sense of geometry permeating the reforms of Cleisthenes.[2] And I myself have contrasted the geometric nature of Greek cosmology and science with the arithmetic character of Eastern scientific thought, and attempted to relate the former to the way space in the city-state was organized as a homogeneous entity in which the center alone had a privileged position, precisely because, in relation to it, all the various points occupied by the citizens appear symmetrical and reversible.[3] Lévêque and Vidal-Naquet take up their inquiry with all the rigor of historians careful to assert links among the facts of a civilization only when there is evidence that makes it possible to discern their point of contact in the chain of historical events. Far from limiting the inquiry, this insistence on the facts in reality extends it. For while the reforms of Cleisthenes may reflect first and foremost a profound transformation of civic space, they also affect other categories of thought, namely, the organization of time and numerical systems. The changes affect space, time, and number all at once, and they follow clearly parallel courses. In contrast to earlier representations of space, time, and number that were loaded with religious significance, the new ways of ordering experience are in tune with the organizational needs of the world of the city-state — that specifically human world in which the citizens themselves deliberate upon and decide their own communal affairs.

237

The most striking feature of Cleisthenes's reforms is the decisive role played by principles based on the land rather than the clan in the organization of the *polis*. The city is projected in terms of a spatial scheme. Tribes, *trittyes*, and demes are marked out on the ground as real divisions that can be drawn on a map. This space has a center, the town, which constitutes the "heart" of Attica, and in which each tribe is represented. At the center of the town, the agora, now reorganized and remodeled, forms a public space, clearly circumscribed and henceforth marked out by boundary posts. In the agora the Bouleuterion is built. This is the seat of the Council of the Five Hundred, composed of representatives from each tribe, who occupy the hall each in turn, that is, who preside over the sessions of the *ekklesia*, with the privilege of lodging at the common hearth during this period. The transformation in the significance of the center is striking as it changes from a religious symbol (Hestia, the goddess of the hearth) into a political one (the common hearth of the city, *hestia koinē*).[4] Here at the center of the city, the *hestia koinē* still evokes the memory of the family hearth. This domestic altar, since it was fixed to the ground, rooted the human house in the earth at one specific point, making each *oikos* different from every other and giving it its own individual religious character. It made the family a closed group and kept it pure and free from all contact with the outside.[5] The hearth became common; it was built on the public open space of the agora rather than inside private dwellings, and it sheltered the prytanes and hence the *boulē*, which embodied the city as a whole. It stood thereafter for the center, as the common denominator of all the houses that made up the *polis*. True, the center was established in a space, composed of different parts, but all these parts were clearly similar, symmetrical, and fundamentally equivalent in their common relationship with the single center represented by the *hestia koinē*. The center expressed in spatial terms no longer the notions of differentiation and hierarchy but rather those of homogeneity and equality. It should be added that, now that it is its function to express political realities, the symbol of the center loses its previous associations with religious

238

representations. Lévêque and Vidal-Naquet describe this aspect of the change as a secularization, as I had thought of doing. There has, however, been some disagreement over the expression.[6] And, indeed, it is perhaps somewhat anachronistic. So, having remarked that the reforms of Cleisthenes are deeply secular, the authors of *Cleisthène l'Athénien* are quite right to add "insofar as there could be any such thing in the sixth century."[7] Nevertheless, even if our terminology is somewhat unsuitable and our contemporary categories do scant justice to the relationships between politics and religion among the Greeks, the concept of the center, as it appears in the political symbolism of the common hearth, nonetheless takes on a markedly positivist and abstract character. The hearth has shed its chthonic associations and its cosmic implications; mystery is excluded. Louis Gernet writes, "Men set it up as they see fit; it is a mathematical arrangement of a territory which could quite well be anywhere; the center is arbitrary, even theoretical; a hearth can be moved at will."[8] Even if the common hearth remains associated with a religious context, this is a new form of religion, a religion that is itself political, and between the two terms, the political aspect carries more weight, for it has the "rational and almost planned-out character" that the Greeks at an early stage conferred upon anything to do with politics.[9] It has been remarked — quite rightly — that every magistracy retains a religious character. But there is a converse to this truth. After Cleisthenes, certain priesthoods, whose importance continued to increase throughout the fifth and fourth centuries BCE, were genuine magistracies. One significant fact, rightly pointed out by Lévêque and Vidal-Naquet, is that Cleisthenes appears to have invented the institution of the tribal priesthoods. These were annual priesthoods elected by lot from the entire civic body according to the same election procedure as that used for magistracies with a purely political function, which we would today call profane. These civic priesthoods present a contrast with the ancient clan priesthoods, which were the privilege of certain *genē* possessing religious secrets and associated with local cults. If, when considering Greek religion, one does not take these divisions — not to say oppositions — into account, it is impossible to understand either the development in the fifth century of the almost aggressively realistic political thought of the sophists, or the lucid rationalism shown by the historian Thucydides.

The development of an abstract space linked with the political system is accompanied by the creation of civic time, which answers the same needs. It is legitimate to connect Cleisthenes with the prytane calendar, which, throughout Athenian history, contrasted with the religious calendar. Whether this calendar established a year of three hundred sixty days (ten prytanes of thirty-six days each) or one of three hundred sixty-six days (six prytanes of thirty-seven days each and four prytanes of thirty-six), it is based on the assumption that each of the ten territorial tribes takes a turn administering the city-state. As Lévêque and Vidal-Naquet point out: "Temporal organization was copied upon [se calque sur] spatial organization: to have the prytany was, for a tribe, both to occupy such a position in the course of the political year and to delegate fifty of its own members to the public hearth at the heart of the polis."[10] Again, like space, civic time is characterized by its uniformity, in contrast to religious time, which is punctuated by festivals that divide the cycle of the year into qualitatively different and sometimes even clearly opposed portions. From a political point of view, all the periods of civic time are equivalent and interchangeable. A prytany is defined not by its peculiar temporal quality but by being like all the other prytanies. This marks a change from one temporal system to another that is, in many respects, its opposite.

The organization of the political system, civic space, and the prytane calendar are all ordered and measured by numbers. The number three is important, as it expresses the whole, but the numbers five and ten, which have a privileged role in Cleisthenes's reforms, are even more so. How should these preferences be interpreted? Should we, as Glotz suggests, detect here the influence of the politico-mystical speculations of the Pythagoreans? Lévêque and Vidal-Naquet conclude that we should not. Their conclusion is all the more acceptable in that they suggest a very convincing explanation of their own. The choice of ten is of particular interest in this connection, for, according to Aristotle, by fixing the number of tribes at ten Cleisthenes was deliberately rejecting the number twelve, which had previously been the number of the *trittyes* among which the entire citizen body had been divided. Yet the adoption of a decimal as opposed to a duodecimal system went against all the political traditions of the Ionians. It must also have conflicted with certain traditional ways of thought rooted in religion (the twelve months of the religious calendar, the twelve great gods of the Pantheon). On the other hand, possibly from as early as the beginning of the sixth century, there existed a system of acrophonic numbering — generally known as Herodian — which was clearly based on five and ten. This numerical system was probably to a large extent adopted in response to the increasing use of currency and the need to keep written accounts. It is important to remember the role played by writing in the early years of the city: once a text had been written down, it was available to all and no longer belonged to the private sector alone; it became common, public property. It was now the direct concern of the group as a whole. It became, in a sense, part of political life. So there is a perfectly natural explanation for Cleisthenes's preference for five and ten. He adopted the numerical system that the medium of writing had already introduced into the public domain and that was opposed to the duodecimal system by virtue of its profane character and its everyday use.

Thus the coherence of the reforms introduced by Cleisthenes that historians have often noted in connection with political institutions appears to be just as striking with respect to mental structures. The political transformation was the sign of a change in the intellectual domain. This raises two types of problems. First, what social factors played a determining role in these transformations? And second, to what extent can one establish a link between the new political idea of *isonomia*, which implies a geometric view of the city, and other expressions of the Greek genius from different aspects of their culture?

The answer to the first problem involves the entire economic and social history of archaic Athens. Needless to say, Lévêque and Vidal-Naquet could not deal with or even begin to address so vast a question. Instead, they focus on better defining the special place and role of the Alcmaeonid family in sixth-century Athens, where political life was dominated by rivalry between the great noble *genē*. The Alcmaeonids were a truly aristocratic family, but in a certain sense a marginal one, and they almost always stood in opposition to the other noble houses. A religious curse had weighed on them since the murder of Cylon in the second half of the seventh century, and from time to time their enemies would see to it that this was clearly remembered. Through this they acquired what Lévêque and Vidal-Naquet call a "heretical function" within the developing city. The special status of this great heretical family, its exiled members, the connections it established with Delphi, its policies based on foreign alliances and prestige abroad — all this sheds light on the twofold nature of the reforms introduced by Cleisthenes. While these reforms laid the foundations for democracy in a novel way, they also, through loyalty to family traditions, preserved certain ancient institutions of an aristocratic nature, such as the Areopagus and the census class system. The authors attempt to carry their analysis even further. When Herodotus says of Cleisthenes that "he binds the people (*dēmos*) to his *hetairia*," his terminology emphasizes the extent to which Cleisthenes's policies remained within the framework of the traditional rivalry between the aristocratic *genē*.[11] However, the *dēmos* that Cleisthenes is so anxious to bind to his own cause is no longer the same as it was in the time of Peisistratus, who depended on it for his power. In those days, it was composed of the inhabitants of the rural demes, rather than the citizens of the *astu*. Between the time of Peisistratus and that of Cleisthenes, an urban *dēmos* developed, which itself became a "political class." It was this urban *dēmos* that Cleisthenes wished to rally and that he integrated into the state by means of reforms that gave more political power to the town as such. The commanding position that the town, the center of the new civic space, thereafter enjoyed was nevertheless not of a kind to ruin the power of all the ancient families. For instance, the *eupatrids* were defined as those who lived in the town, as opposed to those who lived in the country. And in the fifth and fourth centuries, noble families still lived in the urban demes. So it was above all the rural "lords" who were adversely affected by the new political organization, and it was their individual power that was broken. The eupatrids within the town were not excluded from the state; they were, in fact, integrated into the democracy.

There is certainly evidence to support these remarks concerning the appearance of the urban *dēmos* composed of artisans and merchants alongside the urban nobility. However — to put the matter in perspective — Cleisthenes's constitution aimed precisely at bypassing the opposition between country and town and setting up a state that deliberately ignored distinctions between town and rural dwellers in the organization of tribunals, assemblies, and magistracies. This is really the meaning of the "mixture" that Cleisthenes wished to achieve, involving all the elements that had hitherto composed the city. The town was already inhabited by artisans and merchants who formed an urban *dēmos,* and it implied a particular way of life, with its own forms of activity. Nevertheless, what essentially defined the town was not a special way of living or a particular category of citizens, but the fact that it concentrated all the civil and religious buildings linked with the communal life of the group — everything that was public as opposed to private — at the center of the land, and as it were, in a single point. Within the framework of Cleisthenes's constitution, neither the city dweller nor the rural inhabitant was represented as such in the *politeia.*

In a study that is especially concerned with defining the intellectual aspects of a political reform, the relationship between Cleisthenes's revolution and other changes in thought is particularly important. Lévêque and Vidal-Naquet approach the problem from various angles and clearly indicate the difficulties a historian must face in resolving it.

In *The Origins of Greek Thought*, I emphasized the striking similarity between the following two models: the cosmological model for the order of the physical universe adopted by the first Ionian philosophers and seen particularly clearly in Anaximander, and the political model for the organization of the city that is most fully expressed in the *politeia* of Cleisthenes. In both there is a similar geometric emphasis and a comparable spatial schema that privileged the central point and the circle in that they formed the basis of symmetrical, reversible, and egalitarian relationships among the various conflicting elements in the natural or human cosmos. This similarity in structure was supported by the use of the same terminology and conceptual tools in both physical and political thought. The analysis I proposed was structural; it involved a comparison of models, which were examined in their most fully elaborated form. These models were, however, taken from different periods (the first half and the end of the sixth century) and different areas of the Greek world (Miletos and Athens). But I did not think these two disparities would invalidate the comparison I wanted to make. For one thing, a Herodotus text reporting a proposal made by Thales to the pan-Ionian assembly shows that the geometric character of Milesian physics had direct political implications.[12] Furthermore, the political concept of *isonomia* in Alcmaeon was an expression of the same balance between opposing physical forces on which, according to Anaximander, the order of the universe depended. Finally, although I was comparing the widely separated cosmology of Anaximander and constitution of Cleisthenes, I pointed out that there were intermediary links between them. For instance, the political text on the subject of *isonomia* whose terminology, fundamental concepts, and general point of view I compared with those of Anaximander's cosmological fragments does not come from the Athens of Cleisthenes's day. Herodotus reports that it comes from Maiandrios as he addresses his fellow citizens of Samos around 510 BCE.[13]

While such points are applicable, I would argue, in the context of a socio-psychological analysis, they could never satisfy historians concerned with tracing the effective course of the influences at work in the complex of historical data. Lévêque and Vidal-Naquet put it thus: "The problem is therefore whether Cleisthenean isonomy and the representation of the cosmos as it appeared in the Milesians are two parallel phenomena, perhaps, but without any point of connection between them, or whether, on the contrary, the mental universe that is that of Anaximander was liable to be understood by the founder of the new city."[14] In this way, they reopen the inquiry and pursue it on several levels. First they try to identify Cleisthenes's models. He appears to have been inspired less by his own ancestor and namesake, the tyrant of Sikyon, than by certain aspects of Lycurgus's Rhetra, with its local divisions and its *obai* that provided the framework for the army of Equals. However, two incidents seem to Lévêque and Vidal-Naquet to be characteristic of the intellectual and political climate in which Cleisthenes's generation must be situated. The first incident was precisely the one from Herodotus that I mentioned, concerning Thales's proposal to the assembly of the pan-Ionians in about 547. Thales proposed creating a single *bouleuterion* on the island of Teos because it was "at the center of Ionia (*meson Iōniēs*)."[15] Herodotus's text suggests a comparison with Cleisthenes, since, to describe the new status of the various cities in relation to this new single center for the Ionians, he uses the term "demes" in the sense it had acquired after the reforms made by the Alcmaeonids. The second incident the authors discuss is also taken from Herodotus. Around 550, the Kyreneans, on the advice of the oracle of Delphi, asked Demonax to give them a constitution. Demonax stripped the monarch of all but his religious powers and placed all the other attributes "in the middle for the people (*es meson tōi demōi*)."[16] This reform is just one example of the experiments that were tried out in sixth-century colonial cities, which were, so to speak, political laboratories. The most radical form of these experiments is, without doubt, the communist regime set up at the beginning of the century in the Lipari islands by the survivors of the expedition led by Pentathlos. The parallel between Cleisthenes's reforms and a colonial undertaking of this kind is all the more striking in that Cleisthenes, who was supported by

Delphi, gives a place of special importance in the civic religion he set up to the ten founding heroes. These were the Archēgetai, whom the Pythian oracle selected from among the hundred names of heroes put forward to be the eponymous heroes of the ten tribes. The Archēgetēs (who is at times distinguished from and at others confused with the founder) plays a role of the greatest importance in the foundation of the colonies and in their civic religion. It is therefore safe to assume that when the archaic form of Greek colonization was dying out, Cleisthenes transposed some of its traditions and adapted them to Athens. Lévêque and Vidal-Naquet's argument carries all the more weight because, according to Elean, Anaximander himself had directed the founding of a Milesian colony in Apollonia, on the Black Sea.[17]

A second line of inquiry reaches similar results by a different route. One of the most characteristic products of the geometric rationalism of the Milesians was the making of the first maps of the inhabited world. On the surface of the earth, which is bounded by the circular course of the river Okeanos, the *oikoumenē* is depicted within a regular grid system. Despite their apparent lack of order, land, seas, and rivers are grouped and arranged following strict relations of correspondence and symmetry. These maps, which presented the public with a carefully rationalized image of the *oikoumene*, may well have had a political function. Around 500 BCE, Aristagoras of Miletos, who was seeking allies against the great king, took a map of this type, engraved on bronze, to Sparta and showed it to Kleomenes, to win his support. He was unsuccessful, but he went on to Athens, where he pleaded his cause once more, this time not to a king but before the assembly of the people. Here, as in Sparta, he must have produced his map to show the positions of the various territories of the Persian empire, stretching from the Ionian coast down to Susa. Unlike Sparta, Athens decided to send ten ships. There were clearly political and circumstantial reasons to account for the contrasting behavior of the two cities, but the political differences also correspond to two different mentalities.

Clisthène l'Athénien has another facet. The innovations of the work of Antenor, whose role in relation to Cleisthenes is comparable to that of Pheidias to Pericles, bears witness to a change in mentality that calls to mind the geometric rationalism of the Milesians. Archaeologists have emphasized the precision of Antenor's spatial composition, his concern with balancing the whole work around the central theme he is illustrating, and his attention to "fitting out the center of the tympanal space in a rational way and . . . retaining for the intermediate characters a scale that relates to the interchangeable characters."[18]

Antenor has been reproached for this "excess of logic and discipline."[19] The civic space and time that Cleisthenes created "become, quite naturally, the reflection of sidereal realities, and they become so in such a way as to make the microcosm of the city participate in the macrocosm of the universe."[20]

At the end of their analysis, Lévêque and Vidal-Naquet conclude that Anaximander's type of geometric view of the world coincided with the political model of a city governed by *isonomia* such as the one Cleisthenes attempted to bring into being in Athens. A cohesive intellectual atmosphere, a correspondence between physical and civic space, and a continuity between philosophy and public life are all features of the sixth century BCE. In the fifth century, culture loses its internal cohesiveness, and the various domains of social practice and theoretical reflection lose their mutual integration. The world of the geometers and astronomers becomes separate from that of the city. With Parmenides, philosophy acquires its independence. Each type of discipline, grappling with its own problems, has to develop its own terminology and ways of thinking and elaborate its own logic. Thus a rift developed between space as conceived of by the mathematicians, on the one hand, and the space of the political community, on the other, and Lévêque and Vidal-Naquet believe this rift to have been profound. After Hippasos discovered the incommensurables in the middle of the fifth century and Hippocrates of Chios composed the first elements of his geometry, it was no longer possible for geometric space, now entirely undifferentiated, to accommodate a privileged central point. In contrast, through a kind of reversal, the city became more and more markedly differentiated in its political structure and its architectural layout. Both in the theories of the political reformers and in the undertakings of the town planners, the city was now composed of many parts, each with a different function. Here the work of Hippodamos is particularly revealing, since this Milesian appears to have been both the first town planner and the first true political theorist. His ideas on civic space include both aspects of the *polis* at once, that is, the city's political organization and its architectural design. He distinguished between different specialized functional classes within the same social group (according to Aristotle, he even invented the city's division into classes, a practice that had a remarkable history in later political theory). At the same time, in his town plans he began by distinguishing different main areas corresponding to various types of activity — political and administrative, religious, and economic. Cleisthenes's centralized civic space was aimed at integrating all the citizens in the *polis*, without differentiation. For Hippodamos, political space and urban space have a fundamental feature in common: a high level of differentiation.

However, the very progress made in mathematics was to make it possible in the fourth century for geometry and politics to come together once again. It was probably in the Pythagorean groups that came to power in Tarentum under Archytas that the first attempts were made to apply mathematical concepts to social problems arising from the crisis in the city. The simple concept of equality expressed in the ideal of *isonomia* was replaced by more sophisticated ideas. Distinctions were drawn; arithmetic was opposed to geometric or harmonic equality. In fact, proportion became the fundamental concept. This justified a hierarchical conception of the city and, at the same time, made it possible to see in the institutions of the *polis* the "analogical" image of a cosmic or divine order that was superior to man. So we should not be misled by this new convergence of geometry and the political. This is not a return to the past. The entire equilibrium among the ideas has changed. In the sixth century BCE, it was essential to define and promote a properly human order. One could say that when the sixth-century philosophers thought about the order of the world, they had the city in mind. In the fourth century, the philosophers' attention was directed toward the divine. They contemplated the heavens and the regular movements of the stars. The heavens provided the basis of their conception of the organization of the city, even though history had already undermined its traditional structures.

For Cleisthenes, the problem was to recast the institutions of Athens; for Plato, it was to lay the foundations for the city. When one moves from attempting to organize the real city to the theory of the ideal city or utopia, the relationship between mathematics and politics is reversed. The city no longer plays the role of a model. Politics no longer represents the privileged area where man believes himself able to resolve his problems by deliberate acts decided on after due discussion with his peers. Now mathematics serves as the model, because, in the minds of those exceptional men, the philosophers, it reflects divine thought. This is why, having analyzed Plato's city as presented in concrete terms in the *Timaeus*, the *Critias*, and the *Laws*, Lévêque and Vidal-Naquet point out that, despite all the features that Plato borrows from the states of his own day, his theoretical city, far from being a true representation of the city of the classical period, is in many respects its opposite. In Plato's city, it is no longer men so much as the gods who are in control, and Plato's efforts are directed less toward finding institutions through which the citizens might govern themselves than toward setting up a city that, as much as possible, will rest in the hands of the gods. The civic space and time that Cleisthenes created "become, quite naturally, the reflection of sidereal realities, and they become so in such a way as to make the microcosm of the city participate in the macrocosm of the universe."[20]

The interest of a book does not only lie in the results and new ideas presented but can also be measured by the number of problems the book raises and the thoughts or even objections it provokes. Lévêque and Vidal-Naquet express their thesis on the "reversal" in the concept of civic space during the fifth century in a deliberately radical manner. Thus they invite a whole series of questions concerning certain essential features of the city and of political thought during the archaic and classical periods. I have already expressed my agreement with Lévêque and Vidal-Naquet's conclusions on the subject of Cleisthenes's reforms, their intellectual impact, and the organization of space that they imply. But should one speak of a rupture, a reversal in attitudes toward social space, where the fifth century is concerned? Is it not rather simply a matter of a shift in emphasis, still within the framework of a similar type of political thought?

First, the example of Hippodamos cited by the authors is not particularly favorable to the hypothesis that during the fifth century a rift appeared between the astronomers' idea of space and the space of the city. True, Hippodamos appears to have been both a political theorist and a town planner, but the ancients considered him first and foremost "an adept in the knowledge of nature," a "meteorologist."[21] From this point of view, he fits into the Ionian tradition, following very directly on men such as Thales and Anaximander. Hippodamos was a philosopher seeking to explain nature, but he did not, for all that, turn aside from civic life; he appears well integrated in the world of the city. Physical space, political space, and urban space are not separate in his thought; they form part of a single complex of ideas.

But the fundamental problem remains: for Hippodamos, space is differentiated rather than homogeneous in character. Before considering the significance of this feature and attempting to determine how much it reverses Cleisthenes's perspective, we must assess a few of its implications. Hippodamos conceives of the physical universe and the human world as entities whose constituent elements, being not entirely homologous, are not organized according to equivalence but determine one another according to proportion, in such a way that their very divergence produces the unity of a *harmonia*. So it follows that, even as early as the fifth century, political thought must have developed a hierarchical model of the city and sought to justify it in terms of astronomy and mathematics. The first attempts to apply concepts of number, proportion, and harmony to the organization of the city may therefore predate Archytas — although he gave them a more precise form. They may, in fact, go back to early Pythagoreanism. The lack of contemporary evidence means that, like every other conclusion concerning the earliest Pythagoreans, this must be purely hypothetical. However, it does appear fairly probable given two well-established facts. The first is that a hierarchical model of the city certainly existed. It existed, for example, for Solon (who attempted to bring *eunomia* into being by assigning each man his exact share within the *polis* according to his worth, his *aretē*). And it is also reflected in the institutions themselves, in the system of the census classes. Second, the ancients agree in attributing to Pythagoras the theory that everything in the universe is ruled by numbers, or is number. Lévêque and Vidal-Naquet themselves correctly point out, in the pages they devote to the activities of the Pythagorean group at Kroton that for the members of the sect there was no difference in kind between public preaching aimed at political change, and geometric and astronomical thought. True, they are right that it would be anachronistic to label Pythagorean politics either aristocratic or democratic. At that stage, the problem cannot be posed in those terms. Nevertheless, on the whole, the Pythagoreans favored a hierarchical concept of the city seen as a *harmonia*. Just as Solon distinguished in the civic body between those he called the "nobles" and those he called the "villains" (using these terms in both their moral and social senses), Pythagoras, in the extant lists of pairs of opposites, did not attach the same value to the term of each pair but distinguished a positive and a negative pole, the second necessarily remaining inferior to the first in the mixture that they form.

Was Hippodamos influenced by Pythagoreanism? In any case, his theories show that the current of thought to which Pythagorean politics belongs persisted throughout the fifth century and eventually found expression through men such as Archytas and Plato. For the whole of this tradition, order, in both nature and society, implies differentiation and hierarchy. Should we not then conclude, with Lévêque and Vidal-Naquet, that civic space for

Hippodamos, and even more for Plato, is in total opposition to Cleisthenes's model?

And yet I would argue that this claim needs to be modified. In the course of comparing Cleisthenes and Pythagoras, Lévêque and Vidal-Naquet emphasize what they call the ambiguities of Pythagorean politics. The question is whether, in the Greeks' very conception of *politeia*, there was an ambiguity sufficiently fundamental to mark, to varying degrees, their political thought as a whole.[22] The Greeks did not, as we do, make a clear distinction between state and society, between the political and the social spheres. For them, the important opposition was between the private and the public. Whatever did not belong to the private domain was connected with the public, common domain, which is to say ultimately with the political sphere. (In contrast, most of the activities that bring us into contact with others fall neither within the purely private nor within the purely political sphere.) In the ancient world, every human society was considered composed of many parts, differentiated by their functions. But at the same time, in order for this society to form a *polis,* it needed to appear, on a certain level, unified and homogeneous. Since the term *politeia* refers both to the social group as a whole (society) and to the state in the strictest sense, it is difficult to construct a fully coherent theory about it, for, depending on one's point of view, the *politeia* is sometimes multiple and heterogeneous (with all its diversity of social functions) and sometimes a unified entity (with its equal and common political prerogatives defining the citizen as such). Aristotle's embarrassment when dealing with this point is significant. Aiming his remarks at Plato, whom he criticizes for wishing to bring about a complete unity in the state by means of his proposals for a communal way of life, Aristotle writes that by dint of unification the city would cease to be a city, since the *polis* (inasmuch as it is a human group) is by nature a plurality (*plēthos*) and cannot grow from individuals who are all similar (*ex homoiōn*).[23] But this does not stop him from declaring a few lines later that since the *polis* (as a state) depends on equality and reciprocity, power must be equally divided among all the citizens, who should each implement it in turn and should be considered, apart from their individual responsibilities, similar to each other (*hōs homoious*).[24] Nor does Aristotle's conclusion resolve this antinomy. When he writes, "The *polis,* which is a plurality, must, through education, be made communal and one," he does no more than formulate the problem that political thought has always attempted to solve and that arises from the double meaning of *politeia,* in the strict sense of the term.[25] The *politeia* is not totally identified with the life of the group: some activities can be called social (since they are indispensable to the life of the group and establish contacts among men) but remain outside the province of the *politeia.* Yet if it is taken to mean that which is common to all as opposed to that which is private, *politeia* expresses the very essence of all social life. Whoever is excluded from the *politeia* is, in a sense, also excluded from society. Legislators, statesmen, and philosophers all suggest different solutions to the problem, but they always formulate it in the same terms, and this gives a common orientation to all Greek political thought above and beyond the controversies and contradictions within it. Whether the *politeia* was extended to include a city's entire body of free men or whether it was limited to a more restricted group, and whether there were distinctions between the various members of the city regarding their right to the common exercise of power, it was always a matter of forming the citizens into a truly united collectivity despite all the differences between the various individuals who composed it.

Cleisthenes's solution may indeed be called exemplary. It represents one of the extreme poles of political thought. His reforms were aimed at creating a homogeneous civic space within which all Athenians, whatever their family, profession, or dwelling place, would be equals insofar as they were all citizens of the same state. Thus the *polis* tended to take the form of a world without stratification or differentiation. Admittedly, by retaining the census classes, Cleisthenes also kept an element of hierarchy in his system. But, in my opinion, this is not a decisive objection, since in defining the spirit of Cleisthenes's revolution one must consider not what it retained from the past but what innovations it introduced, taken as a whole. One must then agree that when Cleisthenes remodeled the state he was pursuing the ideal of an egalitarian city in which all the citizens would be on the same level and would occupy symmetrical and reversible positions in relation to one common central point. On the other hand, he stressed the values of equality and nondifferentiation all the more in that he was attempting precisely to remedy an existing situation characterized by separation and division. Cleisthenes's task was to unify a city torn apart by factions, clientships, and local rivalries. The establishment of a unified political framework was essential if the various separate elements of the civic body were to be welded into a single whole.

Although set in a historical context that has already undergone considerable changes, Hippodamos's preoccupations appear quite similar. Cleisthenes's type of *isonomia* did not succeed in eliminating social conflicts. Plenty of cities in the fifth century and even more in the fourth were torn by internal strife in which what we would call economic interests were much more important than they had been in Cleisthenes's period. These conflicts became increasingly serious, and it was in this light that Plato came to criticize the struggle between rich and poor, drawn up into enemy camps, that was taking place behind the democratic state's facade of unity. The division of the classes according to function appears to have been an echo of the Indo-European tradition of dividing society into three classes. In the eyes of those who supported a division of this kind, its purpose in institutionalizing the differentiation between social classes was simply to better ensure the complete unity and homogeneity of the state. Apart from this, Hippodamos's solution is still fairly close to that of Cleisthenes. Hippodamos distinguishes three classes in the social body, each of which has its own particular function — the warrior class, the artisans, and the farmers. He divides the territory into three sectors — one sacred, reserved for the gods, one public, reserved for warriors, and one private, which falls to the farmers. But all the classes are united and equal in the strictly political sphere.

Together they compose a single unified *dēmos*, which elects its own magistrates. Even if Hippodamos's system implies a differentiated view of human society, it does not introduce any hierarchy into the political sphere as such. He distinguishes and classifies the various types of activity that appear to be necessary to the life of the group but remain outside the political sphere, if this is taken to mean the common exercise of sovereign power. The one new feature of his system — and this is its key component — is that the military function becomes a specialized activity entrusted to a class of professional warriors. In contrast to the activity of the artisans or that of the farmers, the warrior's activity was believed by the Greeks to belong to the public domain; it was the concern of the community as a whole and was integrated into political life. To this extent, there is, after all, a certain disparity in the status of the three social classes. Why do the warriors enjoy this special position in the *polis*? In isolating the military function, which by nature was closely tied to the political sphere, Hippodamos aimed to purify it of all contact with economic life, with the sphere of private interests that at this point helps promote division and conflict among the citizens. Soldiers have no private property. As in Sparta, they live on common land and are kept at the state's expense. Because the special responsibility of soldiers, as a functional class, is a sector of activity belonging to the common or public domain, they can have no private possessions; their social activity must not be characterized by anything private.

The same idea is found a century later in Plato, where it takes a radical and systematic form. In the Platonic city, the differentiation among the classes gives rise to a positive segregation based on the inherent difference among the members of the various functional classes, which may not intermingle on any level. This is illustrated in particular by the myth of the metals. Each class is associated with a metal. For the best classes, as for the most precious metals, any mixture can only lead to an inferior alloy, to impurity. In this respect, Plato is the opposite of Cleisthenes, since Cleisthenes's intention was to bring about a "mixture" of all Athenians in the political sphere, regardless of their diverse professions. Yet Plato's final goal remains the same as that of Cleisthenes: to set up a truly unified and homogeneous state. But for the philosopher the ideal implies one overriding condition: those who make up the state can be similar (*semblables*), politically speaking, only if they are also similar in their social life as a whole. If rulers and guardians are to accomplish their duties and watch over the general good, everything between them must be held equally and in common. This can be possible only if they renounce all professional and economic activity and devote themselves entirely and exclusively to their political function. In other words, for Cleisthenes's model of a homogeneous *politeia* to be possible, the political sphere must be purified by the expulsion of all those who are engaged, in any capacity at all, in professional life. In a city where the specialization of functions and professions has divided the social group against itself, the unity and homogeneity of the state can be restored only by turning political activity into a separate specialization, a profession opposed to all others in the sense that, unlike the others, it concerns the public rather than the private interest.

Thus, even when Plato takes up a position in opposition to Cleisthenes's constitution, he remains in certain respects faithful to the political ideal that inspired it. So it is not surprising to find that he makes the most determined attempt to set out the territorial framework of the city according to the requirements of a homogeneous social space. In the *Laws*, Plato first considers ideal legislation, providing for the complete community of women, children, and possessions, and then goes on to what he calls the second or third city, that is to say, constitutions that are close to reality since they take the shortcomings in human nature into account. Thus, the state described in the *Laws* allows for the dividing up of land and houses, rather than a communal exploitation of the earth: each citizen enjoys his own benefits from a particular allotment. However, so that the city will still be relatively unified, each allotment must appear not to be private property but rather to belong to the city as a whole. It is also necessary that the original distribution never change. Thus Plato describes the local conditions that would be most favorable to the implementation of his plan and specifies how to organize the space of the city-state to conform with his laws.[26] He does not disguise the fact that his plan is a theoretical ideal; in practice it would no doubt be impossible for all the necessary conditions to be fulfilled. We are therefore dealing with a model — and Plato says so explicitly. The model is both geometric and political. It represents the organization of the city in the form of a spatial pattern; he traces the city out on the ground. How does Plato's civic space differ from Cleisthenes's model, and in what respects is it similar?

Plato writes that the founder of the city of the *Laws* establishes at the center (*en mesō*) of the country a circular enclosure known as the Acropolis. Starting from this point, he organizes the territory into a regular circle with the Acropolis as its center. The total area is divided into twelve parts — corresponding to the twelve tribes — so that the yield from each part is equivalent to the yield from every other part. Then, still in accordance with the same principle of equality, the 5,040 parcels of land are distributed to the 5,040 households that make up the *polis*. However, each household's allotted part is divided into two parts, one close to the town and the other in the outlying districts, out toward the state border. As it is not possible to distribute all the half-allotments in a single circle, the founder proceeds in the following fashion: whoever has half of his allotment directly adjoining the town has his other half adjoining the border; starting from the town, whoever has half his land situated on the second innermost circle has his other half situated on the second outermost circle; and so on, so that the inner half-parts that are situated farthest from the town, being midway in the territory, are adjacent to their complementary outer halves. In this way, each household will be attached to two half-portions of land whose mean distance from the center is exactly the same as that of all the others. Finally, the actual urban area is, in turn, divided into twelve sectors in the same way as the rest of the territory. Each citizen has two dwelling places: one in the urban area near the center and the other in the rural area on the outskirts of the territory.

Although Plato's political space resembles that of Cleisthenes in that it is circular and centered, it is nevertheless different in several essential respects. The central position is occupied no longer by the agora but by the Acropolis, which is consecrated to Zeus and Athena, the patron deities of the city. Thus, in contrast to practical custom in all Greek cities, Hestia has her seat not on the agora but on the Acropolis. This shift in the center is significant. The Acropolis opposes the agora as the religious domain (the *hiera*) does the profane or legal domain (the *hosia*) and as the divine does the human. As Lévêque and Vidal-Naquet point out, Plato's city is constructed around a fixed point, which, being sacred, anchors the human group to the divine. It is organized in a circular pattern that reflects the heavenly order. It was therefore to be expected that Plato, who was following the path taken by Cleisthenes, but in the reverse direction, should return to a duodecimal system whose religious significance here is unequivocal: each tribe is assigned as part of its lot to one of the twelve gods of the Pantheon. The gods, who thus possess space, are also the masters of time: each of the twelve months is devoted to a particular god. The divisions of space and time correspond to each other for the simple reason that they are both modeled on the divine order of the cosmos.

Plato thus reintegrates the political sphere that Cleisthenes had isolated into the overall structure of the universe. But, at the same time, even though the space of the city is invested with religious significance, Plato makes it perfectly homogeneous and undifferentiated in an even more systematic way than Cleisthenes did. By means of an ingenious layout, Plato's legislator seeks to make every part of the territory that he divided up exactly equivalent and completely symmetrical in relation to the common center. It is not only on the political level, as citizens, that the members of the city are equal and similar. The division of the land makes them identical and interchangeable in terms of their land holdings, their dwellings, and the locations of their residences. The city's space is organized so that all distinctions between urban and rural dwellers disappear. Every citizen is just as much a man of the town as a man of the country. At the very moment when, in real life, the opposition between the city and the country was becoming accentuated, Plato, the philosopher, was drawing up a theoretical plan for a city that completely succeeded in producing the mixture that Cleisthenes so desired. Lévêque and Vidal-Naquet show that Plato's *polis* is in many respects the opposite of the classical city. In this sense, however, it is also its truest reflection. It is doubtless in the *Laws* that the model of a political space treated geometrically that characterizes Greek civilization is found most clearly delineated in its specific features.

PART FOUR

Work and Technological Thought

CHAPTER TEN

Prometheus and the
Technological Function

Louis Séchan draws attention to a number of problems raised by the figure of Prometheus and the myths about him.[1] What is the relationship between Prometheus and the technology and crafts associated with fire, such as metallurgy and pottery, and what is his relationship to technological activity in general? What is the significance of his conflict with Zeus? Is there any connection between his quarrels with the master of the gods and the fact that he works with fire?

With the exception of a very late text by Diodorus, Greek mythology does not present Prometheus as the inventor of the technique of making fire. In the *Homeric Hymn*, Hermes is described as the first to discover how to kindle a flame. And although Georg Curtius and Adalbert Kuhn proposed that the name Prometheus derived from the Vedic Sanskrit *pramantha*, meaning the turning stick used to produce a flame by friction, this etymology is nowadays much criticized.[2] The name Prometheus, derived from the Indo-European root *man-*, has the meaning of "prudent, circumspect," which was a quality that the Greeks ascribed to him, as opposed to his brother Epimetheus, the clumsy, thoughtless one. It should be noted, however, that there is comparatively little trace of the invention of fire in the Greek myths, no doubt on account of its very great antiquity.[3] On the other hand, more recent techniques, such as agriculture, livestock raising, felling trees, building, the cultivation of vines and fruit trees, weaving, and so on, occupy an important place in the legends of the gods and the heroes.

Yet there appear to have been well-established links, in the classical period at least, between the crafts connected with fire and three deities: Athena, Hephaistos, and Prometheus. To judge by the evidence from religion, myth, and pictorial representations, in Athens this grouping of gods tends to symbolize a general type of activity, what we would call technology, and a social category, the artisans, probably because the technologies that employ fire are strongly represented in the ceramic quarter, over which these deities preside. [4] But there may be more to it than this. The crafts using fire were from the start practiced in closed corporations and developed outside the domestic context. They represent the first specialized trades.

But nothing in Prometheus's character as thus described suggests that he was predestined to enter into conflict with Zeus. Séchan appears to accept Ulrich von Wilamowitz-Moellendorf's theory that there must originally have been two different Prometheuses: the Ionian-Attic Promethos, the god of the fire industries, the potter and metal worker honored in the festival of the Prometheia; and the Boeotian-Locrian Prometheus, the Titan whose revolt and punishment is part of the great theme of conflict between different generations of the gods. The suggestion, then, is that there was a double origin and that two separate themes became fused: as soon as the god of the technologies dependent on fire is assimilated with the Titan victim of Zeus's wrath, he is seen as the fire thief who is punished as such. This would also account for a psychological and moral opposition already discernible in Hesiod: Prometheus is both "the upright son of Iapetus," the benefactor of humanity, and the creature "with cunning thoughts" who is at the source of mankind's misfortunes. [5]

The problem of origins is insoluble. But for Hesiod, the most ancient text, the myth about the theft of fire, appears in an extremely coherent form and already raises a problem concerning technology. Work is described as the consequence of the conflict between Zeus and Prometheus. The myth certainly has several different meanings. Georges Dumézil detected in it elements belonging to the Indo-European cycle of tales concerning the theft of ambrosia, the food of immortality.[6] But other meanings can be found as well. In one sense, the myth gives an account of the creation of man, presenting it as a separation of men from gods, the two having hitherto not been distinguished from each other. The apportionment of different kinds of food, which gives Prometheus the opportunity to cheat the gods in favor of mankind, marks a separation that implies a new status for the human race. The theft of fire is an expression of, among other things, the new human condition, in both its positive and its negative aspects. Fire is precious. Dumézil has shown that in Hesiod it had a culinary significance and that, far from being, as in Aeschylus, "the fire that civilizes," it was as yet no more than "the fire that cooks." However, cooking makes it possible for man to feed himself: without it, he would starve to death. For Hesiod, Zeus's action of depriving men of fire is equivalent to his hiding their food, their life, (bios), from them. In the two cases, the consequences are the same. Once wheat is hidden from him, man has to labor on the land, which had hitherto provided him with a natural harvest. Similarly, Zeus now keeps natural fire for himself, refusing ever again to send his thunderbolt to earth to the mortals' benefit. This is why it is essential for Prometheus, who wishes to save the human race, to procure artificial fire, hiding it in the hollow of a reed (en koilōi narthēki), that is, in the stem of a narthex, following a technique used for transporting fire at that time.[7] Human life is thus preserved by an action that involves artifice in two senses: it is the substitution of a technique for making fire in the place of natural fire, and it is a trick played on Zeus that catches him unawares.

The theft of fire must be paid for. Henceforth there will be no wealth without labor. It is the end of the age of gold, in which, according to the myths, the opposition between fertility and work is stressed, since in that age all riches sprang spontaneously from the earth. What is true for the products of the soil also applies to mankind. Pandora, the first woman, is another part of Zeus's answer to Prometheus's theft. Henceforth men will no longer be born directly from the earth; now, through women, they will undergo birth by procreation, and consequently old age, suffering, and death as well.

The connection between fertility and work is expressed in yet another way in the myth of Pandora. The meaning of Pandora is "she who gives everything"; in one ancient illustration, she is called Anesidora, "she who makes presents emerge from the depths," in other words, the goddess of the earth, who presides over fertility.[8] But, at the same time, myth presents her as an artifact: she is the work of a craftsman who fashions her out of earth and who is identified sometimes as Hephaistos, sometimes as Prometheus, and sometimes even as Epimetheus. Some painted vases depict her as emerging from the earth, which has been beaten by mallets, one of which is brandished by Epimetheus. According to Hesiod, Pandora is the work of Hephaistos, who also forges her a crown of gold showing lifelike depictions of the animals that dwell on land and in the sea. Athena makes her a dress and a veil and teaches her the art of weaving.

In this context, fertility and work appear to be both opposed and complementary. Precisely this duality and ambivalence characterize the human condition. Every advantage has its corresponding disadvantage; every blessing, its evil. Wealth implies work; birth, death. Prometheus, the father of men, is double: he does both good and evil. His sinister side is embodied in the figure of his brother and opposite, Epimetheus. Pandora is also double in many respects. She is an evil, but a lovable evil. She represents fertility, detests poverty, and demands abundance. But, like the drone among the bees, she is at the same time the symbol of idleness and dissipation. After all, when Hesiod describes Strife, Eris, in the opening lines of *Works and Days*, he says that she is not single, as one might suppose, but double: there are the good Eris and the bad.[9] For Hesiod, in this world of duplicity, only one thing does not lie — because it implies acceptance of the human condition and submission to the divine order — and that is work.

Work introduces a new relationship between gods and men. Men renounce hubris, while, to those who work, the gods promise riches in the form of "flocks and gold." Thus work acquires a religious value: "Those who work become a thousand times more dear to the immortals."[10]

For a Boeotian small-scale farmer in the seventh century, work was essentially limited to agriculture. There was as yet no clear conception of technological activity, nor had the figure of Prometheus clearly emerged as father of all the crafts. But Hesiod's originality lies in having used the conflict between Zeus and Prometheus to show the place of work in this complex religious thought.

Hesiod's Prometheus presents certain psychological characteristics worth emphasizing. His moral ambivalence gives him a certain resemblance to a figure such as Loki, who also appears both as a blacksmith god and as a demon who steals the food of immortality.[11] Also like Loki, he is an intelligent god, but even in the form his intelligence takes he is opposed to Zeus. For Hesiod, Zeus represents not only power and force, symbolized by the presence of Kratos and Bia at his side, but also order and justice, through his marriages with Mētis and Themis. In contrast, Prometheus's intelligence seems to consist in calculation and trickery, or "sly thoughts." His foresight often paves the way for deception. Moreover, his cunning provokes catastrophes that eventually rebound against him to such a degree that he often appears imprudent and thoughtless.[12] These psychological contradictions can perhaps be explained not by Prometheus's dual origin but by the mixed feelings of fear and scorn that appear to have been aroused by the corporations of metal workers, whose status, practices, and secrets gave them a marginal position in society.

Another characteristic of Hesiod's Prometheus reappears in the versions by Aeschylus and Plato. Prometheus seems to have had the special responsibility of distributing to each individual his particular lot. For Hesiod, as arbiter in the quarrel between men and gods, Prometheus must determine each individual's share. For Aeschylus, when Zeus divides the various privileges among the various gods and sets their rank in his empire, Prometheus is the only one to think of the human race and to oppose Zeus's plans.[13] In Plato, the gods entrust him and his brother with the mission of distributing "suitable qualities" to all the beings of creation.[14] Plato provides enough detail in his version of the story to illuminate the meaning that must be given to this role of distributor. The myth in the form that Protagoras is believed to have told it to Socrates is well known. Epimetheus squanders all the available attributes on the animals, without leaving any for mankind. To rectify this mistake, Prometheus steals fire — that is, the creative genius of all crafts — from the workshop of Hephaistos and Athena. In this way, men come to acquire every kind of technical skill. But they know nothing of the art of politics or the military, which is part of it. Zeus alone has charge of these, the gods of the crafts can have no share in them, and Prometheus cannot get near the citadel of the ruler of the gods, as it is protected by guards. Eventually Zeus has to send Hermes to bring the art of ruling cities, together with a sense of honor and justice, to mankind. However, the messenger asks for more precise instructions as to how to perform his mission. Is he to proceed like Prometheus in distributing the skills, giving a different one to each individual? The answer is no: all men must have a share in the art of politics. Plato is probably not being serious. To Protagoras's mind, the myth serves to justify the practice of Athenian democracy — praised in former days by Pericles but criticized by Plato — whereby men who worked in the trades took part in the government of the state. Protagoras sums up by declaring: "That is why your fellow citizens are right to welcome the opinions of smiths and cobblers on public affairs."[15] It is well known that Plato was among those who most strongly emphasized the incompatibility between engaging in the crafts and engaging in politics: practicing a trade disqualifies a man from exercising power. One point, however, remains valid to Plato's way of thinking, and he indulges his irony by stressing the opposition within the Prometheus myth itself between the political and military arts and the utilitarian skills. Zeus the sovereign is protected by his guards (*phulakes*) and is contrasted with deities whose place is lower in the hierarchy and who are the patrons of the arts and crafts and of work. Here, expressed in religious terms, is the pattern of the three social classes, each with its own activity, that pervades an entire current of Greek political thought. To Plato's mind, the virtues that qualify the members of the first two classes for their functions as directors and guardians also provide the foundation for a social system where property is held in common. But the psychology of men who practice trades calls instead for an economy based on private ownership. This idea is not held by Plato alone. Hesiod demonstrates what appears to be a similar way of thinking in the opposition he indicates between two different aspects of fertility: royal justice guarantees collective prosperity for the whole group, while the wealth brought to each man by his own work is, in contrast, a divine favor bestowed on the individual.[16]

The myth of Prometheus as it appears in Plato expresses a highly developed conception of the technical sphere's social function. This is not surprising. We know that during this period technical skill had an important role to play in every field. The division of labor in Athens was already quite advanced, and men practicing trades had contributed to the prosperity of the town and its political life to a degree that Plato, for one, deplored. At the same time, conscious reflection about the *technai* had become common, especially among the sophists. But for Plato, this interest in technology is revealed throughout his dialogues, in the frequent references to examples drawn from this sphere. The division of labor is closely analyzed, and its advantages are used as arguments to justify limiting political power to specialists.

It is remarkable, however, that the importance Plato attached to technology did not affect his conception of man, or rather it affected it only, so to speak, negatively. None of the psychological aspects of technology appears to him valuable in human terms: neither the concentration demanded by work as a special type of human effort, nor technical artifice as a form of intelligent inventiveness, nor technological thought in its formative role in human reasoning. On the contrary, Plato takes pains to separate and

contrast technical intelligence and intelligence proper, the craftsman and his ideal of man, just as, in his city, he separates and
contrasts technology and the two other functions. This uncompromising attitude explains the inept twist Plato gives to his theory
of the three social classes in the fourth book of the *Republic*. It is
revealed in the clumsiness of the exposition: having expounded
his idea of the three social classes, with their three separate functions and the three types of men that belong to them, he considers three virtues in turn to explain what justice in the state
consists in.[17] The first, wisdom (*sophia* or *epistēmē*), belongs to the
members of the first class, the rulers: precisely this virtue enables
them to perform their function at the head of the city. The same is
true of the second virtue, courage (*andreia*), and the members of
the second class, the warriors. It might be expected that the third
virtue would be peculiar to the members of the third class, the
artisans and farmers, and that it would also be linked with their
particular role. This virtue might be the virtue of work itself, the
source of prosperity for the state. Not at all. The third virtue,
sōphrosunē, is not in the least specialized. It pervades all the social
classes without belonging to any particular one. This astonishing
lack of symmetry can be accounted for only by Plato's refusal to
grant a positive virtue to those whose social function is to work.[18]
It can be said that Plato denies that there is any human virtue in
work and that certain aspects of it even appear to him to be the
antithesis of what is essential in man.

This assessment of the technical sphere and this restriction of
its place in man's life are part of a whole system in which philosophy, ethics, and politics are intimately linked. The discrepancy
between Plato's picture and what men were really like in this
civilization is sometimes considerable. Whereas it is common for
there to be some shift in emphasis between the psychological
facts and their literary or philosophical expression, in Plato's case
this may well be magnified by the effect of social and political
considerations. In order to understand this more clearly, it may be
useful to refer, among other evidence, to Aeschylus's version of
the myth of Prometheus.[19]

Aeschylus, like Plato, has technological activity in general in mind: his Prometheus is not specifically a metalworker or a potter. There is not even any mention of either pottery or metallurgy in the long list of techniques that he boasts of having given to men. The fire he stole is the master of all the crafts, *didaskalos technēs pasēs*, and he is the father of all technical knowledge. He declares, "Say the word, and you will know everything. All the skills come to mortal men from Prometheus."[20] However, in *Prometheus Bound*, Aeschylus shows no sign of having any reservations about technological skill. He draws no opposition between pure science and the useful arts. When Prometheus lists the blessings he has provided, he does not differentiate between the science of numbers, the art of training horses, and the exploitation of mines. Indeed, Aeschylus expands the role of technology in human life. In their specifically human aspects, intelligence and reasoning belong to the technical sphere. What marks the stages of their development is the progressive discovery of the different arts and crafts: "In the beginning, [men] saw without seeing, listened without hearing and, like images in a dream, they lived through their long existences in disorder and confusion. They knew nothing of sunny brick-built houses, nothing of woodwork, they lived beneath the ground like agile ants, down in caves shut off from the sun."[21]

It is significant that Prometheus, the deity of technology and the father of all the arts and crafts, becomes the symbol of man himself. Even more important, Aeschylus stresses certain features, namely, man's original weakness — both intellectual and material — and his painstaking attempts to transform himself from the child he was in the beginning into a creature endowed with thought and capable of organizing and directing his life by work.

In contrast with Prometheus is Zeus, who only manifests himself through the catastrophes he unleashes and the threats his ambassadors deliver, and who acts through his two acolytes, Kratos and Bia, the symbols of a power so absolute that it lies beyond justice and understanding. In *Prometheus Bound*, Zeus represents the ancient sovereign deity of past ages and, at the same time, the tyranny of a political power that is not ruled by law. He also represents everything inhuman in the world, everything that crushes man or thwarts his laborious efforts and his works.

But the *Desmōtēs* was only one part of the complete tragedy.[22] Séchan, following others, convincingly demonstrates that in the course of the trilogy there is a transformation in the character of Zeus, who becomes amenable to reason and justice, while Prometheus mends his ways and renounces his excessive taste for revenge. In the end, the two gods reconcile.

The theme of the quarrel and reconciliation between Zeus and Prometheus has many meanings in this tragedy. It is significant on every level of human experience. In it a new religious concept and a new morality take shape. For Aeschylus, it is a further declaration of faith in the city, in democracy, in the new political equilibrium between conflicting social groups. In addition, a new aspect of human nature is starting to emerge. Through the character of Prometheus, the tragedy expresses the growing importance of technology for man. It emphasizes in a literary form the inner aspects of man's technological activities, indicating the psychology behind them.

I have noted the various aspects and stages of technological activity as portrayed in three versions of the same myth. In the context of Hesiod's religious thought, work is portrayed as an enforced activity; the emphasis is placed on human effort's guaranteeing divine blessings, prosperity, and fertility to the individual. In Plato, the idea of human skill becomes fully distinct, and the place of technology as a social function is clearly defined. But in the context of this philosophical thought, which betrays a refusal to accept certain social and human changes, art is compared unfavorably with nature, and the psychological aspects of technological activity are unkown or deliberately avoided. Aeschylus seems to have a different moral and social attitude, and with it, the possibility of integrating work into the concept of man more successfully, for certain features in his picture of man stress the importance that technology has now acquired.

Nevertheless, on the whole the idea of technological activity is still ill defined and not well systematized. Even Aeschylus indicates no interest in the motivation for work — no doubt because such motivation remains purely external. The repercussions that technology and work have on human life, the opportunities they provide for creativity, and the part they play in bringing men into contact with one another are not expressed. The boundary between technical knowledge and work is indistinct. The idea of work as a major social function, as a specific type of human activity, does not emerge. There is no clear idea of what defines the domain of technology as such.

Many authors have noted the disparity between the level of technology and the attitude toward work in ancient Greece. Despite the place technological skills had already acquired in men's lives and the considerable changes in mental attitudes they appear to have introduced, technological activity and work are very seldom believed to have any moral value. However, it should be added that the psychology associated with them was not yet clearly distinguished either, and they had not acquired the character of highly organized human behavior that they have today.

CHAPTER ELEVEN

Work and Nature in Ancient Greece

The analysis of work in ancient Greece has usually been approached from two related points of view: the depreciation of work and the limitations of technological thought.[1] The present study has a different aim. Considering work as a major form of behavior that today is highly organized and unified, I ask what form it took in the ancient world and what its role in men's lives and in society was.[2] How was it defined in relation to other human activities? What activities were considered, more or less, work, and what were their features and their psychological associations?

A remark concerning vocabulary is in order. Greek has no term that corresponds to "work." A word such as *ponos* is applied to any activity involving laborious effort, not simply to productive tasks that are socially useful. In the myth of Herakles, the hero has to choose between a soft life of pleasure and a life devoted to *ponos*. And Herakles is no worker. The verb *ergazesthai* seems to apply especially to two sectors of economic life: farming or laboring in the fields (*ta erga*) and (in complete contrast) financial activity (*ergasia chrēmatōn*), earning interest from capital. But the term can also be applied with a specific nuance to activity considered in its most general form: the *ergon* of each thing or being is the product of its own particular excellence, its *aretē*. The words derived from the Indo-European root *tek-* go in a different direction. They refer to something produced — by an artisan, for instance — or to an operation that is a kind of *poiein* —

that is, to technological manufacture. This is opposed to *prattein*, the natural activity whose end is not to make an external object separate from the act of production but to perform an action for its own sake.[3] Thus, despite the two uses mentioned above, the word *ergon* can be used to mark the contrast between the "accomplishment" of *praxis* and the product of the creative (or "poietic") work of the artisan. A text in Plato's *Charmides* illustrates this point.[4] Critias, no doubt following the sophist Prodicus, is explaining the difference between doing and making, *prattein* and *poiein*.[5] The type of action referred to by the term *ergazesthai* is connected with the domain of *prattein*; it is opposed to *poiein*, just as *ergon* is contrasted with *poiēma*. And the fact that the artisans are called craftsmen (*dēmiourgoi*) does not conflict with these remarks, since for Homer and Hesiod this term did not originally refer to the artisan as a "worker" or "producer" but defined all activities pursued outside the framework of the *oikos*, for the benefit of a public, *dēmos*. It referred to artisans — carpenters and blacksmiths — and bards, but also to diviners or heralds, who did not "produce" anything at all.[6]

Such linguistic evidence suggests that among the activities constituting the single complex of working behavior there were different levels, multiple aspects, and even oppositions. Of course, the absence of a term that is both specific and general does not necessarily prove that no true concept of work existed. On the other hand, it does underline the existence of a problem that justifies this psychological inquiry.

Hesiod's *Works and Days*, written in the seventh century and sometimes considered the first poem in praise of work, provides evidence about the psychology of farming. That is, I use the term "farming," but even this is too broad. Henri Jeanmaire, noting the distinction Xenophon makes between land for sowing and land for planting, has drawn attention to the opposition in Greece between the cultivation of fruit trees, on the one hand, and grains, such as wheat and barley, combined with a little stock raising and the exploitation of a small area of woodland, on the

276

other.[7] The latter is, properly speaking, the kind of agriculture relevant to Hesiod. The opposition is not simply technological and economic. These two types of farming reveal two very different kinds of experience in man's relationship with the soil. The cultivation of trees continues the tradition of an economy based on gathering: produce appears in the form of gifts of nature, blessings that are attributed to the gods, who dispense riches — or, as the Greeks would say, *polugētheis*, those who dispense an abundance of joy: the Horai, the Charites, and the Oinotropes. Their function is to make the branches grow and the fruit swell, following the rhythm of the seasons. Man shares in this rhythm not so much by his labor as by means of the recurring cycle of festivals and feast days that effect a communion between him and the gods. However, as Jeanmaire also points out, Hesiod mentions the Charites and the Horai on only one occasion, and not to praise them. It is they who have adorned Pandora with their graces — Pandora, the trap laid for men by the gods in revenge for the theft of fire. The inclusion at this point of the story of Prometheus is by no means irrelevant to a poem about agricultural work. It not only accounts for man's need to sweat in order to make the earth bring forth its yield but also locates far in the mythical past of the age of gold the image of the earth's spontaneous generosity as embodied by the gods of vegetation. The earth's gifts must now be earned. And Pandora — representing all the gifts of the earth — becomes, for men, the image of an evil that lurks hidden beneath dangerous attractions.[8] Hesiod compares her to the drone among the bees, symbolizing idleness and the waste of hard-won goods.[9]

Hesiod's earth is one that must be ploughed. In Greek, the same word, *erga*, means both "field" and "work." Demeter is the deity of this kind of cultivated land, as opposed to uncultivated or simply fertile land. In representations of this divine power, there is always one aspect that refers to human activity and effort.[10] One speaks of the works of Demeter. And in the ritual expression *Dēmēteros aktē*, the wheat of Demeter evokes sometimes the ears of grain that must be winnowed and threshed on the sacred threshing floor of the goddess and sometimes the grain to be ground under the millstone.[11] In contrast to the gods of vegetation, Demeter functions not so much to distribute her gifts as to guarantee a regular order in her dealings with men. When Hesiod's farmer contributes through hard work to the growing of wheat, he does not feel that he is applying a cultivation technique to the soil or that he is practicing a trade. He confidently submits to the harsh law that rules his dealings with the gods. For him, work is a form of moral life that is affirmed in opposition to the ideal of the warrior. It is also a very strict form of religious experience that is deeply concerned with justice and does not manifest itself in the excitement of festivals but imbues the farmer's whole life with the strict necessity of accomplishing all his daily tasks. In this law of the fields, *pediōn nomos*, presented in *Works and Days*, it is impossible to separate the theological from the moral elements or either of these from the treatise on agriculture. These different aspects are all combined in the same punctilious ritualism. Each thing must be accomplished at the appointed time and in the right way. The sowing must be done when the crane is calling: it is then that the farmer, his hand upon his ploughshare, prays to Zeus Chthonios and Demeter so that the grain shall become heavy as it ripens. But the day ought not to be the thirteenth day of the month, which is the day for planting, just as the eighth is the day for castrating pigs and bulls, and the seventh from the middle of the month is the day for casting the sacred grain of the goddess on the threshing floor.[12] Whoever, knowing this, has not been sparing in his efforts and has spent himself "without offending the Immortals, paying attention to the heavenly signs and avoiding every error" can place his trust in divine justice.[13] His barn will be full of grain. Such is the psychological aspect of work on the land in Hesiod's text. It is not a particular type of behavior aimed at producing something of use and value to the group through technological means. Rather, it is a new form of religious experience and behavior. As far as the cultivation of grains is concerned, it is through strictly regulated efforts and hard work that man may enter into contact with the divine powers. Through work, men become a thousand times more dear to the immortals.[14]

The peasant life that Hesiod describes is that of a small property that the farmer living off his land exploits directly. The only allusion the poet makes to urban life is a warning against the temptation afforded on wintry days by the blacksmith's forge, where one can waste time gossiping in the warmth of the workshop.[15] This is archaic Greece at a stage before the establishment of the city-state. However, even during the classical period the Greek economy remained essentially agricultural, and, except in the Dorian cities dominated by the warrior class, small peasant holdings remained the general rule. At the time of the fall of the Thirty at Athens, only five thousand of the twenty thousand citizens did not possess a country property. In certain parts of Greece, possibly even in Attica, the *oikos*, the family property, remained inalienable until the end of the fifth century.[16] Land, with all its religious connotations and the special links binding it to its owner, was quite a different type of possession from money.[17] It was only with great difficulty that it eventually became integrated into the economic system based on currency. It is, therefore, not surprising that for a long time psychological attitudes toward agricultural work remained very similar to Hesiod's.[18]

In the *Oeconomicus*, Xenophon is concerned with ways of increasing the value of a patrimony by selling at a high price land that has been bought cheaply and improved. But even for him, farming on the whole is not a professional type of activity. Hesiod used to say that the gods have established that sweat must precede merit, *aretē*. For Xenophon, too, agriculture is first and foremost what makes it possible to exercise a type of *aretē*. Ability and gifts are not enough; they must be put to work: *ergazesthai*. There is no virtue that is not practical.[19] Thus, in contrast to a soft and carefree life of idleness, there is an active virtue compounded of energy, initiative, and industry: *epimeleia*. But in order to understand the psychological attitude toward this "enthusiasm for work," we must note that it appears in opposition to the activities of the artisans, which force the working man to live confined indoors, seated in the shadows of the workshop or spending the entire day working by the fire, and thus debilitate the body and

279

weaken the spirit.[20] Seen as the antithesis of the artisans' work, farming now becomes associated with military activity in the sphere of virile occupations — work (*erga*), in which neither fatigue nor effort (*ponos*) is feared.[21] Cyrus declared to Lysander: "I never yet sat down to dinner when in sound health, without first working hard at some task of war or agriculture, or exerting myself somehow."[22] Moreover, if in time of war the farmers and artisans are divided into two groups and asked what they want to do, those who cultivate the land will decide to do battle to defend it, while "the artisans decide not to fight but, as their upbringing has accustomed them, to stay quietly at home without toil or danger: *mēte ponountas mēte kinduneuontas*."[23]

Agriculture is not considered a trade any more than waging war is. Can it even be called a *technē*? *Technē* implies specialized knowledge, apprenticeship, and secret ways to ensure success. There is nothing of the kind in agricultural work. The only knowledge necessary is that which any man can acquire on his own, by looking and thinking.[24] No special apprenticeship is needed.[25] Whereas "those who practice the other arts more or less hide the essential secrets of their art," the land "has no special tricks but simply and without disguise or deceit reveals what she is capable of doing and what she is not."[26] The land generously reveals all her secrets to us.[27] Xenophon's descriptions of sowing, weeding, harvesting, threshing, winnowing, and the cultivation of fruit trees are all aimed at showing not human skills but "nature" at work in these operations. For instance, where does viticulture come from if not the vine itself? By climbing trees, the vine teaches us to give it a support; by spreading its leafy shoots when the grapes are still young, it teaches us to shade the exposed parts; by shedding its leaves, it teaches us to pick them off so that the fruit can ripen when the sun becomes mild.[28] So how is it that not everyone is equally successful at farming? It is a matter not of "knowledge or ignorance," of "discovering some ingenious method of working the land," but, as in war, of effort and vigilance: *epimeleia*.[29] Since every kind of technical skill is irrelevant, a man's farming reflects his own worth: "Just because she conceals nothing from our knowledge and understanding, the land is the surest tester of good and bad men. For the slothful cannot plead ignorance, as in the other arts."[30]

In contrast to the *technē* of the artisans, whose power is all-important within the narrow limits within which it operates, agriculture and war share a common feature: man is conscious of his dependence on the divine powers, whose cooperation is necessary if he is to succeed. The power of the gods is "as absolute where work in the fields is concerned as it is for war."[31] It would be unthinkable to undertake any military enterprise without first consulting the gods through sacrifices and oracles. Similarly, no man would undertake any agricultural task without having conciliated them: "Wise men offer a cult [*therapeuousi*] to the gods so that they will watch over their fruits and grains."[32] This worship is not something added to farming from the outside: cultivating the land is in itself a form of worship in that it establishes the most just of dealings with the gods. "The earth, being divine, teaches justice to those who are capable of learning. It is to those who best cultivate her (or offer a cult, [*therapeuousi*]) that she grants the greatest riches in exchange."[33]

What is the significance of the opposition between agricultural work and the artisans' trades that Xenophon stresses so strongly? The point is that they belong to two different fields of experience, which are to a large extent mutually exclusive. The artisan's activities belong to a sphere in which there is already a certain amount of positivist thinking in Greece. Agriculture, on the other hand, is still integrated within a complex of religious representations.[34] The technological and instrumental side of work does not figure into it, for the gap between human effort and its results is too great, whether temporally or technically. The essential part of the achievement depends on what Eugène Dupréel has called "the collaboration of the interval," which brings religious behavior into play.[35] Therefore, work on the land does not take the form of an implementation of effective procedures and rules ensuring success. It is not seen as acting on nature in order to transform it or adapt it to human ends. Even if such a transformation were possible, it would be impious.[36] Work on the land is participation in an order both natural and divine that is superior to man. The human effort expended in farming takes on a special significance because of this religious context. Undertaking the set task and working hard and tenaciously at it is valuable and prestigious insofar as it establishes a relationship, a kind of reciprocal bond, with the gods. Work can therefore correspond both to divine necessity and to divine justice, as merit in its most general sense. This theme counterbalances the assertion of the superiority of pure thought over action in Greek moral speculation.[37]

In this type of agriculture, there is as little evidence of the economic aspect of work as there is of its instrumental and technological sides. Since the *oikos* is supposed to provide for all the needs of the family, self-sufficiency remains the ideal for peasant life.[38] The fruits of the earth that are to be consumed on the spot are set in opposition to the economic values of commerce and "circulation." In this respect, too, agricultural work establishes personal contact between the farmer, on the one hand, and nature and the gods, on the other, rather than commerce among men.[39]

Nevertheless, the very insistence with which Xenophon emphasizes these differences suggests that they were challenged in other circles. In any rational system of political thought, agriculture is considered on the same level as other occupations, as far as the division of labor is concerned. Once stripped of its religious privileges, work on the land immediately loses its special dignity. The human effort involved is no longer felt to be an *aretē*. It falls into the category of servile occupations demanding nothing more than an outlay of physical energy.[40] These two opposed ways of thinking about the subject of farming are perhaps most noticeable in the Greek concept of the political community. At times farmers and artisans form two distinct, or even opposed, classes; at other times they form a single class contrasted with the warriors and magistrates. In Peripatetic circles, this ambivalence eventually leads to a contradiction. Agriculture is sometimes described as the type of activity "that is in tune with nature," in which man may express his active excellence in accordance with justice. On other occasions, it is seen as an activity altogether contrary to a free man's nature, a "servile" occupation, just like the trades of the artisans.[41]

There is one very curious figure in Greek legend. We catch a glimpse of him in one of the Homeric poems and in one brief reference in Plato. He is Margites, the man who knows all the trades but practices none correctly. It would be interesting to know more about him. His existence hints that in certain spheres of activity skill demands strict specialization.[42] Georges Dumézil has picked out the legendary themes that concern such manufacturing activities.[43] Here artisans intervene decisively in the organization of the world. By producing the works of their particular trades, they divide among the gods the spheres of activity and the privileges that correspond to each one's particular functions. In Greece, the Cyclopes have this role.[44] These figures bring to mind groups such as the Telchines and the Daktyloi.[45] These were metalworkers whose activities were more magical than technological and who, on occasion, acted as warriors. But the point is that these legendary figures belong to a bygone age. They are peripheral beings, wanderers, roaming the mountains and forests.[46] Artisans, on the other hand, are orderly folk, sedentary town dwellers.[47] They can only be imagined plying their trades within the framework of the city. It was because of the division of labor that took place in the city that two different but positive ideas about the *technē* developed. First, it was a specialized activity contributing — along with others — toward a balanced social order; second, it provided a set of rules for success in each of the various spheres of activity. In this respect, the figure of Margites is significant. Nobody expects him to set the world in order, as long as he sticks to one trade so he can perform it correctly. Whereas there is a marked continuity persisting since archaic times in psychological attitudes toward agriculture, where the work of the artisans is concerned, the city makes just as marked a break with its legendary past.

These comments can be illustrated with a point from social

history. During the classical period, there is no kind of religious organization corresponding to the professions. There is no intermediary between the artisan and the city, no corporations, no brotherhoods. This helped to ensure that trades were viewed in a purely rational light, that is, as economic and political functions.

For the ancient Greeks, the city was no abstract entity. They spoke not of Athens but of *hoi Athēnaioi*.[48] To them a city was a number of citizens linked by personal ties of friendship who pursued their activities through this *koinōnia*. In such a framework, what place did trades have? There were no doubt quite striking disparities in the perceived value of the various social categories. But these differences appear to relate rather to the moral value of the various artisan occupations and to how compatible they were with political functions. It does seem possible to make some fairly general observations about the place of the trades in the system of human activities in the *polis*.

In a way, what we call the division of labor appears to be the basis of the *politieia*. Men band together because they need one another and for the sake of a mutual complementarity. The city is based on conscious opposition to the ideal of individual or family self-sufficiency.[49] Protagoras gives a very clear expression of this theory, explaining how the various species of animals were endowed by Epimetheus with different *dunameis*, some with strength, others with speed, others with fertility, and so on, so that they all had an equal chance of survival.[50] The situation of the human race, which was left out of this distribution, was critical. It appeared doomed to extinction. Prometheus therefore decided to steal the technological *dunameis* from the gods and present them to the human race. He distributed them as his brother Epimetheus had distributed attributes to the animals, giving a different ability to each individual. So it is that men are unique in possessing the technological intelligence that enables them to make clothes, shoes, houses, and the like, and they are also unique in that they are unable to survive unless they exchange their products and services among themselves. Is this not Protagoras's way of declaring that work is the most essential social link and that men are citizens by reason of the network of complementary professional activities that unites them? It is tempting to think so, especially since Protagoras's declared intention is to justify the "democracy of artisans" — the worst kind from Plato's and Aristotle's points of view — which constitutes the assembly of cobblers, fullers, black-smiths, and potters.[51] However, neither Plato nor Aristotle seems to disagree with Protagoras about the role of the division of labor. In the *Republic*, Plato is perhaps even more explicit than Protagoras: "Society is born from the fact that each of us, far from being self-sufficient, has on the contrary need of a great many people."[52] And since each person is by nature different from his fellows, he must also specialize in a different task. Thus, "men will share with their fellows what each of them has worked at."[53] The aim of their political association will be achieved. The city is founded on this division of tasks. But does this mean that men's relationships at work constitute the links between citizens? For Protagoras, as for Plato and Aristotle, quite the contrary is true. While each man's profession defines what differentiates him from his fellows, the unity of the *polis* must be founded on something that has nothing to do with the professional activities. The specialization in tasks and the differentiation of trades are opposed to the political community of citizens who are defined as equal (*isoi*), similar (*homoioi*), one might almost say "interchangeable."[54] Protagoras expresses this in the figurative language of myth. Although men possess all the technical skills, they cannot yet establish a political society. They lack the essential factor that can unite them in the bonds of *philia*, and neither Prometheus nor Hephaistos nor Athena can give it to them because Zeus alone possesses it: *aidōs* and *dikē*, virtues that are both moral and political.[55] Hermes is ordered to bring them to mankind, but in distributing them he must proceed in a manner quite contrary to that of Prometheus. He must give not a different ability to each individual but the same to all, equally and indiscriminately. Aristotle expands on the same theme in a rigorous form. The unity of the state implies total reciprocity among equals. He adds: "As if cobblers and carpenters exchanged their work instead of the same persons always performing the same tasks."[56] But this example is only chosen because its absurdity demonstrates the incongruity, or rather the opposition, between economic activities and those that constitute the city properly speaking. Neither cobbling nor carpentry can establish the "reversible" relationships that characterize the political bond. Having made a distinction between the decision-making and the military elements of the *polis*, Aristotle immediately points out that the same citizens move back and forth between roles, just as they alternately command and obey. In contrast, farmers and artisans have to remain within the limits of their own specializations so as not to negate the inferior type of role that is theirs by virtue of their trades.[57] Aristotle concludes: "For instance, if one man were a carpenter, another a farmer, another a shoemaker... and the whole population numbered ten thousand, but nevertheless they had no mutual dealings in anything else except such things as exchange of commodities and military alliance, even then this would not be a state."[58] In saying this, he is in agreement both with those who, like Protagoras, support government by the *dēmos*, and with the exponents of rule by the "best" men. In both cases, activities connected with the trades, which are limited to the economic sphere, lie outside political society. But for the advocates of the *dēmos*, artisans can have access to this superior role outside their profession, whereas for their opponents the contrast is so profound that participation on one level automatically disqualifies them from participation on another.[59] These positivist ideas about the organization of professional activities in the city give rise not to the concept of work as the single, great social function, but to that of a plurality of professions that differentiate those who pursue them from one another.

Thus, the expression "division of labor" should not be applied to the ancient world except with certain reservations. It is psychologically anachronistic, in that it implies that a trade is conceived of in relationship to "productivity" in general. The ancient Greeks did not see a trade from this point of view. For them, it had two sides. It implied a particular *dunamis* on the part of the person who practiced it, and a *chreia*, a need, on the part of who-

ever used the product. The division of tasks arose from the contradiction between these two aspects of a trade. Each man has
many needs but limited capabilities. So the division of tasks was
not seen as an institution whose purpose was to maximize the
productive efficiency of work in general. It was a necessity resulting directly from the nature of man, who can do one task all
the better if he concentrates on it alone. Not one of the texts
commending the division of tasks conceives of it as a method of
organizing production so as to obtain more from the same amount
of work. Its advantage, rather, is that it allows the various individual talents to be exercised in the appropriate activities and thereby to create products that are as good as they can possibly be.[60] In
the *Odyssey*, Odysseus proclaims: "To each man the activity that
suits him" — a statement that is echoed not only in the practical
remarks of Xenophon but also in the analyses of Plato and Aristotle.[61] In The *Education of Cyrus*, Xenophon's comments go beyond
the differentiation of the trades to that of tasks within a single
workshop:

> In small towns the same workman makes wooden beds, doors,
> ploughshares, tables; sometimes he even builds houses as well.…
> But in large cities where each man finds many buyers, a man needs
> only one trade to support himself. Sometimes one does not even
> need a complete trade: one man makes shoes for men while another
> makes them for women. One man cuts while the other simply sews
> the shoe. One man only cuts out clothes while another sews the var-
> ious parts together.[62]

Here, as in Plato, thought seems to have an increasingly technological orientation.[63] The distinction between the different types
of operations in the making of a single product seems to imply a
grasp of the social and technical significance of the division of
labor. But, in fact, it is not so. Xenophon never manages to grasp
the idea of the division of labor as a way of distributing tasks for
the sake of productivity. He sees it only from the point of view of
improving the product by perfecting the artisan's abilities.

287

The technical abilities that the division of tasks aims to perfect are presented as natural qualities. When Protagoras places human beings' technical knowledge on the same level as animals' *dunameis*, when he compares the order of the trades with the balance of the species in the cosmos, it is not a mere figure of speech. Is not one of the most important methods of dividing tasks based on the biological opposition between men and women? Xenophon offers a theory on the matter: "Right from the start the deity adapted the nature of woman to the work and tasks of indoors and man's nature to those of outdoors."[64] Aristotle theorizes about another, equally fundamental and no less "natural" opposition: the occupations of free men demand prudence and reflection, *phronēsis*; the tasks of slaves call for the passive qualities of obedience.[65] The same principles underlie the differentiation of the artisans' trades. For Plato, the task of each man with a trade is "that to which his individual nature predestined him."[66] In the potter's workshop, one man models the clay, while another paints: the two different *dunameis* are associated to satisfy a single need on the part of the user.[67]

Thus the artisans' professional qualities are simply an extension of their natural qualities. If a distinction is made between the two, it is only for the purpose of linking them with needs that are also natural. Since the phenomenon of the division of tasks is affected by two hierarchies, one involving abilities and the other involving demands, it cannot be defined simply in its own terms. In the organization of activities within the city, there is at no point any suggestion that human effort might be considered a function that creates a social value, that is, in terms of productivity. Because the artisan's ability takes second place to the user's demands, a trade becomes a service; it is not considered work.

However, the object the artisan produces through his *poiēsis* is not natural, any more than the manufacturing processes that define the rules of each specialist's *technē* are natural. Antiphon emphasizes the contrast between the product of the artisan and that of nature: "If one buried a bed in the ground and if from its decay an offshoot were able to sprout, it is not a bed but wood that would be produced."[68] But this opposition is only relevant to a limited aspect of manufacturing: human products result from an intelligent final cause, whereas natural processes come about by chance and without design. But in other respects, the operation performed by the artisan remains contained within the framework of nature: it is not seen as an artificial means to "transform nature" and establish a human order.

The *technē* aims, in effect, to produce an *eidos*, such as health or a house, in a certain matter. Such a production presupposes the exercise of a *dunamis* for which the *technē*, in a sense, provides the method of use. For Descartes, the artisan knew his trade if he understood how his machine worked. But a *technē* consists in knowing how, and when, to use a *dunamis* — where there is no distinction between a natural force and the use of a manufactured tool.[69] In this connection, the terms used to define the exercise of a *technē* are revealing: the instrument must be stronger than the elements to which it is applied, and it must make it possible to be in control (*epikratein*).[70] A *technē* is defined by its limits as much as its power. For this kind of technological thought, there is no conception of indefinite progress. Each skill is restricted from the start to a fixed system of essences and powers. It is circumscribed within the limitations established by the number and powers of the instruments that naturally belong to it and by the article that it is its function to produce.[71] The true *technai* are limited in number, as they are in scope. Only a multiplication of men's needs could allow them to increase. But there is not an infinite number of needs, and once these are provided for, technical skills aim not to satisfy needs but to procure pleasures. Since the effect that they now produce is not their natural aim and limit, however, they produce nothing real, only illusions, imitations.[72] Thus, art is powerful and effective only within a restricted framework, and within this framework, it is in fact "natural." Contrary to Alfred Espinas, an artisan's work does not fall within the order of "human manufacture," in which man, becoming aware of his opposition to nature, attempts to humanize it through artificial devices that he can continue to work on infinitely.[73] Instead, in his work, the artisan sees his own activity becoming "natural."[74] The "artificial" sphere is a different matter: it includes activities that produce only appearances, like the professions of illusionists such as sophists or bankers. The work of artisans was opposed to agriculture, which was felt to be more natural. Now it too is integrated into the order of nature and contrasted with money making as *phusis* is to *nomos*.[75] However, between *phusis* and *nomos* there is no place for the production of a work that while being entirely real could be considered purely human. Man is not yet sufficiently distinguished from nature for human activity to be dissociated from what is natural without thereby being placed in the category of what is merely conventional.

There is a very close connection between this natural aspect of the product and the fact that the artisan's activities are considered a service rather than work. When considering a product, the ancient Greeks were less concerned with the process of manufacture, the *poiēsis*, than with the use to which the article was to be put, the *chrēsis*. For each piece of work, this *chrēsis* defines the *eidos* that the worker embodies in matter. In effect, the manufactured object is determined by a finality analogous to that of a living creature: its perfection lies in its adaptation to the need for which it has been produced.[76] Thus, for each manufactured object, there is a sort of model, which the artisan must consider a norm. This *eidos* is not a human invention the worker could create, or even alter, as he fancied. On the contrary, the artisan must conform to this necessary model as much as possible, either working with it always in mind or relying for this on the user, who is better placed than he to know the object's true *eidos*, since the user alone has the *chrēsis* of the thing. Aristotle says that as a judge of his own work the *poiēsas* is inferior to the user, for the worker's act of manufacture relates to the means, while the question of the end is beyond him.[77] Thus, when a flute is made, the flute player gives orders and the manufacturer obeys him.[78] Plato gives a more detailed explanation.[79] There are three kinds of art in relation to every object — using it, making it, and imitating it. They belong, respectively, to the user, the artisan, and the painter.

As with all other imitators, the painter knows only the article's external appearance, which he manipulates through "artifice" to create an illusion of reality. The artisan makes the article, but he does not fully understand its *eidos*, that is, its end purpose. Only the user does.

If the *eidē* of manufactured articles are somehow "natural," separate, and above the workmen, the artisans become nothing but intermediaries — they are the instruments through which an object acquires a use value. For the user, they are merely tools that serve his various needs. *Poiēsis* is thus seen as an instrumental type of operation. When Aristotle uses the terms *poiētika organa*, he is referring to that which is capable of "producing" something: this includes tools and, on almost the same level, artisans.[80]

In this sense, *poiēsis* is defined by contrast with *praxis*. In acting, a man acts for himself; he does not produce anything but his own activity. The domain of *praxis* excludes all technical operations performed by men with trades. The *ponos* of the artisan in his work cannot acquire the value of an active virtue, as it does in the case of the farmer; on the contrary, this *ponos* is seen as submission to an order foreign to human nature, that is, as pure constraint and servitude.[81]

In Greece, there is not one single type of behavior referred to as "work" in all spheres from agriculture to commerce, but different forms of activity that appear to be organized in quasi-dialectical relations. Even within agriculture, an opposition is drawn between the effects of the earth's natural fertility and the human efforts of the laborer. But agricultural activities as a whole are contrasted with the artisan's activities, as natural production is to technical manufacture. And in turn, the works of the artisans are classed with the products of the soil in the natural economy that conforms with the immutable order of men's needs. When contrasted with making money, which has no more than a conventional value, the work of the artisan, too, is seen as a part of nature.

Thus, in the activities of the farmers and artisans, the human aspect of work is apparent without ever quite being identified as such. On the whole, man feels that he is not transforming nature but conforming to it. In this respect, commerce represents a sort of scandal, both for thought and for morality.

Nor, whatever their profession may be, do men feel they are creating a social value by the effort they put into their tasks. Different human qualities correspond to the various professions, and these qualities situate each man in the hierarchy of the city. In terms of his social role, the artisan is not a producer. Through his trade, he is linked with the user in a relationship of natural dependence, of service. But the word "nature" no longer has the same meaning for the two terms of this relationship, the worker and the user. Only *chreia* belongs to the order of *praxis*, in that it is a free activity that conforms to the nature of man as a reasonable and political being. *Poiēsis* places the artisan on a different level, that of physical forces and material instruments. Just as trades lie outside the political life of the city, the artisan's manufacturing activities represent a level and type of behavior completely external to *praxis*.

CHAPTER TWELVE

Some Psychological Aspects of Work

in Ancient Greece

Work is a human phenomenon with multiple dimensions. To analyze it fully, studies must be carried out on various levels. The history of work may be technological, economic, social, and psychological. My remarks here are chiefly concerned with this last aspect of work in ancient Greece. I will consider it as a particular form of human activity and will inquire into its place within man's inner experience, its meaning, and its psychological content. But the perspective here will necessarily be historical. Just as it would not be right to apply the economic categories of modern capitalism to the ancient Greek world, we cannot ascribe the psychological functions of work today to the man of the ancient city.

For us, professional tasks, no matter how different they may be in concrete terms, belong to a single type of behavior: in all of them we see the same type of activity, set in a framework of rules and constraints, whose effects directly concern others and whose object is to produce something with value and utility for the group.[1] This unification of the psychological function of work goes hand in hand with the emergence of what Karl Marx calls abstract labor.[2] So that the various working activities may be integrated into a single psychological function, man must be able to conceive of his own particular activity — whatever form each individual task may take — as work understood in a general sense.

293

This is possible only in the context of a fully commercial economy in which every form of work aims to create products with a view to selling them. Under these conditions, a particular article is no longer made to satisfy the needs of a particular user. Every job, whether agricultural or industrial, produces a commodity intended not for any individual but for a market where things are bought and sold. Through the medium of the market, all the jobs done throughout the society are related to one another, brought into contact with one another, and thus made comparable. This has two consequences: in the first place, the activity of working no longer brings the producer and the user into more or less direct contact. When its products are put into general circulation, work takes on the aspect of a general exchange within the social body as a whole. It becomes the link par excellence among various social agents and the basis for social relationships. Second, when the products of work are brought together in a market economy, this not only changes the products themselves — which all have quite different uses — into commodities of comparable value, but also transforms all the varied and particular forms of human work into a single activity, work in the abstract, conceived of generally. In contrast, in the context of the technology and economy of the ancient world, work is still seen only in its concrete aspect. Each job is defined in terms of the product it aims to manufacture: cobbling in terms of shoes, pottery in terms of pots. Work is not considered from the point of view of the producer, as the expression of a single kind of human effort that creates social value. So, in ancient Greece the idea is not one great human function, work, encompassing all the trades, but rather a plurality of different functions, each constituting a particular type of action with its own particular product. Furthermore, whereas agricultural activities as a whole are an integral part of working behavior, for the ancient Greeks they remained outside the sphere of the trades. For Xenophon, farming has more in common with military activity than with the occupations of the artisans. Work on the land constitutes neither a trade nor a form of technological expertise nor a social exchange with others. And the psychology of the farmer toiling in his fields is the antithesis of the psychology of the artisan at his workbench.[3]

Work is thus strictly limited to the domain of the artisan trades. This type of activity is characterized first and foremost by its strict specialization and its divisions. Each category of artisans is destined for a single type of product. But as Marx noted, in the ancient world the division of labor is seen exclusively from the point of view of the product's use value.[4] Its purpose is to make each product as perfect as possible, for the artisan makes a particular article all the better when he concentrates on it alone. There is no sign of the idea of a total productive process divided up so as to obtain a greater mass of products from human labor in general. On the contrary, each trade comprises a separate system within which everything without exception is subordinated to perfecting the product to be manufactured. This applies to the instruments, the technical operations, and even aspects of the nature of the artisan himself, that is, certain specific qualities that belong to him alone. A trade is thus seen as something that differentiates citizens and sets them apart from one another. If they feel united in a single city, this is not as a result of their professional work but despite it and apart from it.[5] Social links are forged outside one's trade, in the only sphere in which citizens can feel mutual friendship, because there they all behave in the same way and do not feel different from one another: the sphere of the nonprofessional and nonspecialized activities that make up the political and religious life of the city. Because it is not conceived of as an abstract unity, work in the form of trades does not yet form a system of exchange in the sphere of social activities, as the fundamental social function.

It appears, rather, to establish between the producer and the user of a product a personal bond of dependence or a relationship of service. Within the trade, the artisan's capabilities are strictly subordinated to his product, and his product is strictly subordinated to the user's needs. The artisan and his skill exist for the sake of the product, the product for the sake of the need. It could not be otherwise, as long as the product of work was considered only from the point of view of its use value, not its exchange value.[6] As for its use value, the product is defined by its service to the person who uses it. Only when considered from the point of view of its exchange value can it be conceived independent of its concrete utility, in terms of the work put into it.[7] From the point of view of use value, the product is not seen in terms of the human work that created it, as work made concrete; on the contrary, work is seen in terms of the product and its capacity to satisfy a particular need on the part of the user.[8] Thus, thanks to the role of the product, work establishes between the artisan and the user an economic relationship of servitude and an irreversible relationship of means to ends.

To move from economic practice to philosophical theory: this system of relationships among the artisan, his activity, the product, and the user is expressed in a general theory about the craftsman's activity. In every case of production by a craftsman, the artisan is the efficient cause. He operates on a material (the material cause), giving it a form (the formal cause), that of the completed article. This form is also the goal (the final cause) of the entire operation. This is what controls the whole of the craftsman's activity. The true causality at work in this process lies not in the artisan but outside him, in the manufactured product. The essence of the manufactured product is independent of the artisan, his manufacturing methods, his skill, and his technical inventiveness. This model is changeless and uncreated, and its purpose is defined in relation to the need of the user that it must satisfy. The essence of a chair is the perfect adaptation of all its parts to the use made of it. Artificial production is the same as natural production from the point of view of the principles governing its dynamic. The principle and source of every operation are always the end of the process, the "form" actualized in the created product. The efficient cause is not really responsible for the production; its role is that of a means by which a preexisting "form" is actualized in matter.[9] Just as a man comes from a man through the intermediary of semen, a house comes from a house through the intermediary of the mason.[10]

296

Let us now consider work from a more properly psychological point of view. The operations of an artisan constitute what the Greeks call *poiēsis* (production), as opposed to *praxis* (action, properly speaking).[11] For there to be action in the strict sense, the activity must have an end in itself, so the agent accomplishing his action benefits directly from what he is doing. For example, in moral activities, the agent, by embodying the moral quality, produces something of value, which he at the same time uses. But this is not the case with *poiēsis*. This creates a piece of work external to the artisan and foreign to the activity that produced it. The work of the artisan and the essence of the work as defined by its use have nothing in common. They belong to different spheres, one of which is subject to the other, just as the means is subject to the end and is in no way part of it.[12] Manufacturing an article is one thing; using it is quite another, radically different. Thus no artisan, insofar as he works, commands the use of the article he makes.[13] Because it is alienated within the concrete form of the product and its use value, the artisan's work is considered service to others, in fact, slavery.[14] In the hands of the user, the artisan plays the role of an instrument designed to satisfy the user's various needs. So when Aristotle defines the *poiētika organa*, the instruments that "produce" an article, he places tools and artisans alongside each another.[15]

The result of this split between the productive operation and the product is that the artisan as such is not believed to have the best understanding of the "form" that he must embody in matter. His activity is concerned with manufacturing processes and technical rules, in other words, with means of working on matter. The "form" is beyond him. Knowledge of the essence of the product, that is, of the "form" or end, is the exclusive province of the man who understands what the object is for and how to use it: the user.[16] In the most extreme case, the work of the artisan is seen as pure routine, as the application of certain empirical formulas for the purpose of making some material conform to a model, the nature of which is communicated from without via the user's indications or instructions.

Being thus subject to others and directed toward an end that is beyond it, how could the *poiēsis* of the artisan possibly be considered a true type of action? In order to distinguish it from genuine activity, *praxis*], Aristotle calls it a mere movement: *kinēsis*. This movement implies imperfection: pursuing an end that is beyond it, it does not possess *energeia* (actuality) in itself. Actuality is seen in the realized "form," in the product itself, not in the effort of work, the human energy spent on it or the process of production. Aristotle writes that when human activity creates nothing outside itself, it is *praxis*, and the actuality is located within the agent himself. He adds that every time something is produced apart from the activity itself, the actuality is in the object made; thus the actuality of building, for instance, lies in what is built; the actuality of weaving lies in what is woven.[17]

It is clear that, in a social and mental context such as this, a man acts when he uses things, not when he makes them. The ideal of a free man, an active man, is to be always a user, never a producer. And the true problem raised by action, at least where man's relationship with nature is concerned, is that of using things correctly, not of transforming them by work.

Thus the same priorities seem to exist on various levels in Greek society and culture. In the economic sphere, an object's use value is more important than its market value; the product is considered in terms of the service it renders, not the work put into it. In the philosophical sphere, the final cause, that for the sake of which each object is made, is more important than the efficient cause by which it is manufactured. In the psychological sphere, the created product, completed and ready to be used, is more important from the point of view of actuality, of *energeia*, than the work effort of producer. *Praxis*, which makes an agent's action directly useful to himself alone, is judged superior, as a type and level of activity, to *poiēsis*, the manufacturing operation that brings the producer, through the intermediary of the article produced, into a relationship of dependence on and personal service to the user.

CHAPTER THIRTEEN

Some Remarks on the Forms and Limitations of Technological Thought among the Greeks

Between the seventh and the fifth century BCE in Greece, the sphere of technology became more sharply defined, and technological activity came to be recognized as having certain particular characteristics. In Homer, the term *technē* refers to the "know-how" of *dēmiourgoi* such as metalworkers and carpenters, and to certain women's tasks demanding experience and dexterity, such as weaving.[1] But it is also used to refer to the magic of Hephaesteus and the spells of Proteus.[2] There is as yet no clear distinction between technological achievement and feats of magic. The secrets of a trade and the dexterity of a specialist belong to the same type of activity and involve the same type of intelligence, the same *mētis*, as the art of the diviner, the wiles of the sorcerer, and the witch's knowledge of potions and enchantments.[3] Moreover, the social category of the *dēmiourgoi* includes the brotherhoods of diviners, of heralds, of healers, and of bards, as well as professional workers in metal and wood.

By the classical period, however, technical skills have become secularized. The artisan no longer depends on religious forces; instead, he operates on the level of nature, of *phusis*. His *technē* is essentially defined by being contrasted with chance, luck, *tuchē*, and the divine gift, *theia moira*.[4] For the artisan, success depends on the effectiveness of certain positive methods. Its sole source lies in practical knowledge acquired through apprenticeship, which lays down the rules of the trade for every specialized activity.

When *technē* was freed from magic and religion, a more precise idea was formed about the role of artisans in the city. Alongside the farmers, the warriors, and the civil and religious magistrates, the artisans now made up a separate social category with a strictly defined place and function. The artisans' activities were quite foreign to both the political and the religious spheres, and they answered a purely economic need. The artisan was at the service of others. Since he worked for money and with the purpose of selling the product that he had made, his position in the state was defined simply in terms of economic exchange.[5]

A rational view of the *technē* had emerged, the trades had become secularized, and the function of the artisan had been more precisely defined: thus the conditions for the development of true technological thought appeared to exist. Indeed, Alfred Espinas attempts to situate near the beginning of the fifth century the turning point that marked the development of technology, in the true sense of the term, from un-self-conscious technical skill.[6] He detected in the sophistic movement the first attempts to define and establish technological thought as such; he saw evidence for this, first, in the production of a series of manuals dealing with individual *technai*, and second, in the elaboration of a kind of philosophy of technology, a general theory about human *technē*, its achievements, and its capacities. Most of the sophists conceived of knowledge as the mastery of formulas that could be codified and taught to others. For them, the problem of action was not a matter of ends to be recognized or values to be defined but was expressed purely as a problem of means. What were the rules and procedures for success in the various spheres of life? All branches of knowledge, all practical behavior, morality, politics, and religion were to be considered from this "instrumentalist" point of view, as techniques of action useful to individuals or cities.

The new ideals of utility and effectiveness, which supplanted more ancient values for human behavior, were promoted during a period and in a society that nevertheless remained closed to technological progress. It is paradoxical that even while technology was emerging and was apparently highly valued by the sophists, there was what Pierre-Maxime Schuhl has called a veritable block in Greek technological thought.[7]

In fact, the Greeks, who invented philosophy, science, ethics, politics, and certain forms of art, were not technological innovators. Their tools and technical knowledge were borrowed from the East at a very early date and were not fundamentally modified by new discoveries. Such innovations or improvements as they introduced in certain fields did not go beyond the framework of the technology that seems to have already been established by the classical period. This consisted in the application of human or animal force using a variety of instruments, not in the use of the forces of nature with the help of machines supplying motive power.[8] In general, the material civilization of the Greeks did not progress beyond the stage that is described, depending on the writer, as the technology of the *organon*, as "eteotechnology," or as technology concerned with the simple adaptation of men to things.[9]

At this level of technological thought, there is no longer the archaic conception of animated instruments and living works of art, echoes of which are found in passages of Homer.[10] However, the tool, when directly manipulated by man, is still an extension of his own organs.[11] The *organon* transmits and amplifies man's force, rather than acting by virtue of its own internal structure and producing an effect through a mechanism of a type different from human exertion. When used, the tool adapts itself to the body's own rhythms. It operates within a human time scale. Unlike an instrument, it does not have its own time scale.[12] When it does, this is not as an artificial tool but as a natural instrument, such as fire, whose power, *dunamis*, manifests itself over a period of time that is foreign and incomprehensible to man. One contemplates fire cooking things in the oven as the farmer contemplates his wheat growing. It is impossible to understand either the duration of the operation or what makes it work, for both are connected with the object's own power and not with human ingenuity.

The stagnation of technology and the persistence of a premechanical mentality at a time when technical thought appears to be starting to develop are all the more surprising given that the

301

Greeks appear to have possessed the intellectual equipment that should have made it possible for them to make decisive progress in this field as they did in others.

Evidence shows, in fact, that they were able to address certain technical problems on a theoretical level quite early on, using the scientific knowledge available at the time. As early as the sixth century, the construction of an underground canal at Samos by the *architektōn* Eupalinos of Megara presupposes the use of procedures as sophisticated as triangulation.[13] There is every reason to believe that this was not an isolated case. The term *architektōn* as used by Plato and Aristotle refers to the professional who directs the work from above, as opposed to the laborer or artisan who actually sets his hand to the task. The activity of this *architektōn* is intellectual, that is, essentially mathematical.[14] Since he possesses the elements of a theoretical knowledge, he is in a position to transmit it through rational teaching, a very different matter from practical apprenticeship. In medicine, the true *iatros* is distinguished from the ordinary practitioner by his knowledge of the nature and general causes of illnesses; similarly, in his own field, namely architecture and town planning, shipbuilding, and the construction of war machines, theatrical machinery, and scenery, the *architektōn* relies on a *technē* that takes the form of a more or less theoretical system.

Furthermore, some nonprofessionals' mathematical investigations led them to write about mechanical questions and to become interested in them for their own sake. One such figure was Archytas, in the fourth century, to whom are ascribed, among other things, the inventions of the pulley and the screw and the construction of a flying automaton.[15] Archimedes, from the third century, was another example. Tradition has it that he was a military engineer by necessity and applied himself to practical matters against his inclination. Nevertheless, while he was finding endless applications for the screw and perfecting winches and pulleys for lifting heavy weights, he also wrote about the geometric properties of the spiral, established a theory of the balance of forces in the lever and scales, and defined mechanics as the science by which a given weight can be moved by a given force. The inquiries pursued in the Peripatetic school also included technological questions. *Mechanics*, attributed to Aristotle, aims to provide a rational explanation for the effects produced by the "simple machines" that are the basis for all complex mechanical devices and whose properties are, according to the author, derived from the circle, which is their common principle. These attempts at theoretical elucidation of the problems encountered in certain sectors of technological activity finally led to the work of Ctesibius and Philo and later that of Hero in the Alexandrian school. These men were known as *mēchanopoioi*, the constructors of machines. They were engineers and inventors. They produced theories about various types of machines, how to make them, the way they worked, the rules for their use. Their purpose was twofold: to provide a rational and demonstrative systematization of the subject matter based on the relevant principles, and to give details regarding the construction of these machines that were clear and precise enough to be of practical use to the craftsmen concerned.[16]

Apart from the five simple machines, the lever, the pulley, the windlass, the screw, and the wedge, the theories of which the engineers developed following Aristotle, the technology of their machines incorporated a complex use of valves, cylinders, and pistons, the cogwheel, the gearwheel, and the siphon. Since Archimedes, men knew how to calculate the distribution of weight over supports and how to achieve a state of balance using a given force by means of a certain number of pulleys, windlasses, and gearwheels. Apart from these factors, the new devices employed the torsion of cables, the elasticity of sheets of metal, the compression of air and liquids, the rise and fall of currents of air and water when they were heated and cooled, the effects of communicating vessels and of a vacuum, and the power of steam.

A series of remarkable inventions were produced by this technological ingenuity combined with research into general principles and mathematical rules, which, on occasion, enabled calculations to be made concerning the construction and use of machines.[17] Yet this ingenuity did not transform the technology of the ancient world. It did not break down the barriers imposed by the framework of premechanical thought. Two observations should be made at this point. Wherever the machines described by the engineers have a utilitarian purpose, they are used and conceived of as instruments for multiplying human strength, on which — despite their complexity — they depend for their only motive principle. When they call upon other sources of energy and, instead of amplifying a force given at the outset, act as automata producing their own movement, they turn out to be constructions that follow a whole tradition concerned with objects to be marveled at, and, as such, are only marginally relevant to technology in the strict sense.[18] They are *thaumata* made to astonish people. The very strangeness of their effects, which are brought about by some hidden device, severely limits the scope of their application. Their value and interest lie not so much in their usefulness as in the admiration and pleasure they arouse in the spectator. Not for a moment is there any hint of the idea that by means of such machines man could command the forces of nature and transform, master, and control it.

In attempting to account for the limitations that this technological thought never overcame, despite its rich inventiveness, attention has quite rightly been drawn to the ways its development was hampered by the economic and social structures of Greece, in particular the existence of an abundant slave labor force and the lack of an internal outlet for commercial production.[19] Schuhl has also commented on certain ideological features of this slave society that may well have frustrated any tendency to develop technological thought. In the Greek value system, contemplation, the liberal life of leisure, and nature were prized over their opposites, the disparaged categories of the practical, the useful, servile labor, and the artificial. But apart from these obstacles, which are to some extent external, I believe it is possible to detect certain internal reasons that account for the limitations of the particular form that technological thought took in Greece. There was in the ancient world no fixed body of technological thought that had the features that we find in technology today and that,

like ours, was oriented toward progress by a spontaneous dynamism. Each branch of technology had its own system of
thought. Intellectually, the use of a tool and the application of a
technique belonged to a particular structure of thought, as well as
to a particular social context. They not only depended on the
type and general level of existing technological knowledge but
also implied a whole set of attitudes about what a tool was, how it
worked and the nature of this action, its relationship to the object
produced and the agent producing it, and its place in the natural
and human world. We tend to ascribe to the technology of the
past the features that characterize that of our contemporary
industrial civilization. We imagine that as soon as it is disentan-
gled from magic and religion, technology must necessarily depend on science, becoming its practical implementation. Since it
is concerned with natural phenomena rather than with the supernatural, does it not have the same subject matter as science? To
the extent that it implies some type of knowledge, this knowledge
must therefore be scientific. Thus we imagine that technological
knowledge must be applied science. Similarly, we assume that
because it is in close contact with reality, dealing with concrete
things and concerned with its own effectiveness, technological
knowledge should be open to critical observation, trial and error,
prediction, verification, and modification — that is, it should
essentially be a form of experimental thought. Because it operates
on and in space and affects material objects, we imagine that it
must be most suited to mechanical schemata, and that it must
involve the sense for adjusting the various parts to a whole and
making them all work together that is typical of the handyman's
work. In sum, we assume that it is consciously seeking to transform nature, to impose upon it a human world of artificial devices
that can be improved indefinitely. A technology that is inventive,
mechanical, experimental, bound up with science, would through
its own internal logic be pledged to innovation and progress.
Stagnation in such circumstances could be explained only by
external obstacles. But the truth is that the technology of the
ancient world does not appear to have been like this, neither as it

was put into practice in the crafts nor even when it was expressed in a rational and theoretical systematization.

It was not, and could not be, applied science as we understand it. As Alexandre Koyré has shown, it operated upon the shifting realities of the earthly world, which in the eyes of the Greeks constituted the domain of the "more or less" or the "approximate" (*l'à-peu-près*), to which neither exact measurements nor precise calculations were applicable.[20] So it had a different subject matter and operated on a different plane from science. Greek science was concerned with immutable essences and the regular movements of the heavens. It obeyed a logical ideal of deductive demonstration starting from self-evident principles. Because there was no exact way of measuring time, it did not grasp the process of becoming in quantitative terms or establish any connections between mathematics and physics. How could technology apply physical laws that did not exist?

True, certain limited sectors of technological activity made some use of mathematics, and therefore it was possible to approach some problems theoretically and find rational and demonstrative solutions to them. But the reasoning remained rigorous only as long as it did not venture beyond the realm of pure theory. A concern for effectiveness and for taking purely technical details into account belongs to a different type of thought, operating on a different level — that is, no longer the level of demonstration, but what the Greeks called *empeiria* (experience), which is not the same as experimentation or experimental thought but is practical knowledge obtained in the course of more or less blind gropings. As one gets closer to physical reality, theory loses its rigor and indeed ceases to be theory. It is not applied to but rather becomes debased in concrete facts.

Hero, the engineer, is a good example: when he reasons on a theoretical level, he is very little concerned with adjusting his mechanical models to conform with technical realities. His solutions may well be quite impracticable. In *Baroulkos*, he poses the problem of how to move a weight of one thousand talents with a force of five. The calculations for the various systems of gearwheels he proposes do not take resistance or friction into account at all; since these are not measurable, they remain outside the field of theory. Hence, the results, which are quite valid as schemata of theoretical calculations, are in practice unrealizable. The gearwheels as described would not work. If an engineer actually had to construct a machine capable of lifting a thousand talents with only five, he would be obliged to make the necessary adjustments to the theory. In other passages, Hero does put himself in the position of the practitioner and uses his experience to take into account the practical difficulties of his craft. Both levels of thought can be observed in Hero's account of constructing machines; what is lacking is the link between them.

In contrast, in Aristotle's *Mechanics*, which had a profound influence on the whole school of Alexandrian engineers and by which Hero was directly inspired, the point of view is one-sided, being purely theoretical. And the theory of *Mechanics*, is certainly not applied science. In Aristotle's work, mechanical problems are considered less in themselves and for their own sake than in relation to the difficulties of logic to which they give rise. Aristotle is interested in mechanical constructions because he sees them as "paradoxical" phenomena that the philosopher must explain. The nature of his thought is not technological. Even if certain passages of his demonstrations resort to mathematical reasoning, and take material facts as their starting point in order to state certain problems, his thought remains essentially logical and dialectical in its inspiration. The theory's form, terminology, and conceptual framework remain strangely close to those of the sophistic method. *Mechanē* still has a meaning close to that of a trick or expedient; it is defined as an ingenious invention that enables a man to extricate himself from an embarrassing situation or *aporia* and assume the advantage over some natural force that is contrary and superior to him. This battle between *technē* and *phusis* and the methods that ensure victory for the former are conceived of in terms of a verbal jousting match in which the sophist attempts to win a difficult cause against his opponent. The sophists had developed what could be called a dynamics of logic. With their practice of *dissoi logoi*, antithetical speeches, they had accustomed men to believe that in any debate the arguments for and against can be drawn up in two lists, counted, and compared, and their relative strength and weight measured.[21] The *technē* of the sophist consists in mastering the procedures through which weaker arguments can counterbalance stronger ones, and defeat them, dominate them, *kratein*. In *Rhetoric*, Aristotle defines it as the art of turning the weaker of two arguments into the stronger.[22] Similarly, he defines mechanics as a sphere in which "the smaller dominates the greater" and as the body of methods by which heavy weights can be balanced and moved by smaller forces.[23] When with the help of a lever the puny strength of a man is able to overcome the much greater force of a heavy mass, this is, from a logical point of view, a strange phenomenon, *atopon*. There is something extraordinary (*thaumasion*) about the instruments that bring about such a veritable reversal of strength. The purpose of theory is to elucidate this mystery. It shows that all mechanical procedures can be reduced to the effects and interaction of five simple instruments, the properties of which are derived from the nature of the circle. It thus lays the foundations for a system of rational mechanics, but it also definitively limits its scope and establishes in advance the boundaries beyond which this *technē* must not venture. Just as in geometry it must be possible to construct every figure with a ruler and a compass, in mechanics every viable machine must be based on the combination of the simple instruments.

According to the theory of the five instruments, the principle (*archē*) of all their effects derives from the properties of the circle. It is tempting to liken the astonishing reversal of power produced by the simple machines as described by Aristotle to the key procedure of sophistry — turning an opponent's arguments against him: the stronger the argument, the more unfavorable it becomes to him when used against him. Aristotle holds that the movement of a circle presents an ambiguity that makes a similar reversal possible. In the same movement, the points situated at the two ends of the diameter are moved in opposite directions, so that if a circle transmits its rotation to a second circle that touches it at a given point, this second circle will also move, but in the opposite direction. The faster the movement of the first circle, the faster the second will be forced to turn in the reverse direction.[24] These analogies between what are for us two quite foreign domains — dialectical argument, on the one hand, and ways of affecting nature, on the other — do more than express a mere comparison or an affinity in terminology. They demonstrate how both these domains involve the same mental categories and use the same conceptual framework. This can be proved by the truly logical and dialectical character of the argument Aristotle uses to show that the circle is indeed the principle accounting for the fact that in machines what is smaller and weaker may be capable of dominating what is larger and stronger. The explanation for this is that the circle itself is contradictory, the most astonishing thing in the world, combining several opposites in one single nature. It moves in two directions at the same time; it is both concave and convex, mobile and immobile. To Aristotle it is therefore normal and reasonable that it should be the principle for the reversal of strength. It is not surprising that something extraordinary should result from something even more extraordinary.[25]

This line of reasoning may seem strange, but its very strangeness makes it all the more significant. It shows how, in the absence of any experimental physics, it was impossible for technological thought to establish its own conceptual apparatus. To formulate its problems, it had to turn not only to mathematics but also to the ideas already elaborated in theories of reasoning, discussion, and demonstration, in what I have referred to as a dynamics of logic. It imagined action on nature taking the same form and following the same models as action on men. It saw technical instruments as the means to dominate things in precisely the same way as the orator dominates the assembly through his mastery over language. For the orator, it is the *dunamis* of the word and the strength of arguments that he manipulates or increases with his methods of proof to achieve victory in the judiciary *agōn*. The mechanic also increases a *dunamis* with the artificial devices of his machines in order to dominate a more powerful force. Not everything in mechanics can be expressed in mathematical terms. The dynamism of natural forces, which could not yet be calculated in terms of the laws proper to physics, is made more intelligible by being transposed in this way into the sphere of dialectics, in which the logical strength of arguments can be weighed.[26]

Similar remarks apply to Archimedes's work on mechanics, although it was very different in inspiration. His theoretical research in this area is concerned exclusively with statics, that is to say, the problems of equilibrium that can be formulated and demonstrated following the rational method of exposition used by Euclid in the *Elements*. Arnold Reymond remarks: "It may seem surprising that, having invented or perfected so many ballistic machines, Archimedes made no attempt to study the theory behind them.... In my opinion his failure to do so can be explained by the logical difficulties raised by the idea of movement."[27] This would suggest that the arguments of Zeno of Elea prevented Archimedes from attempting to lay the foundations for rational dynamics. More light is shed on the problem by the treatises on ballistics left by the Alexandrian engineers. Philo stresses on several occasions that it is impossible to conduct this type of research by pure reasoning and rigorous demonstration.[28] In order to produce effective ballistic machines with the desired range, it was necessary to experiment, making the required empirical adjustments. As Schuhl points out, even the formula the engineer used to adapt the proportions of his machines according to the weights and range of the projectile (a formula for which Diels gives a mathematical expression) was arrived at not through theoretical demonstration but in an altogether empirical fashion, through successive adjustments and trial and error.[29] In his *Life of Marcellus*, Plutarch praises Archimedes for having wished to leave nothing in writing about the construction of these machines, which, after all, had done more to make him famous than any other part of his work. Archimedes's attitude should not be interpreted simply as aristocratic prejudice, a refusal to degrade his science by applying it to servile works. To his way of thinking, if a piece of research gave way to *empeiria* and was not entirely rational, it could not, strictly speaking, be considered subject matter for a true science.

Greek thought never succeeded in closing this gap between, on the one hand, science based on a logical ideal and, on the other, *empeiria* dependent on random procedures based on observation. This is why even the Alexandrian engineers, who — unlike Aristotle and Archimedes — pay considerable attention to technical applications in their treatises, still use not applied science but a compromise between theory and experiment, which are not properly integrated and whose demands ultimately prove to be conflicting.[30] In the sphere of mechanics, theory remains faithful to Aristotle's logical bias. In the case of Hero, the five simple instruments formed a coherent and self-enclosed system that excluded innovation or progress. The solution to all mechanical problems consisted in calculating how one could, with these instruments, balance unequal forces given in advance, of which one was human strength and the other some weight of varying magnitude. The very rationality of the system prescribes its limiting factors and its inability to develop further. In contrast, once mechanics was left behind, as in the case of ballistics or pneumatic machines, the power of *phusis* on which they relied was no longer measurable. The explanatory principles suggested by theory were too general and qualitative, and they fit the technical details of construction only approximately. Neither the machines nor the forces they manipulated nor their resulting effects were calculated. Thus the machine they produced harnessed physical forces in a way that eluded the rigorous control of reason. It made it possible to momentarily deflect these forces from their normal course, thus producing a phenomenon that was astonishing and exceptional but of limited scope. The element of the extraordinary is still the chief concern in the pneumatic machines of an engineer such as Philo. Like a conjuror explaining the secret of his tricks, Philo gives the public the key to the finest *thaumata* of tradition and his own invention.[31]

The figure of the archaic artisan, closely related to the magician and surrounded with the rather disturbing prestige of the exceptional powers conferred upon him by his *mētis*, is transposed, in the *mēchanopoios*, into the figure of the engineer at grips with nature who, with his clever devices, can force it to produce marvels. The forces of *phusis* that he manipulates and the control of which he explains contain a *dunamis*, a life force, that is intractable to logical analysis. For this reason, he is believed to operate on a plane as foreign to the rational science of the pure theorist as to the blind routine of the man who works at a craft. In the eyes of the ancient Greeks, the domain of his operations and research has a daemonic element, in the sense that Aristotle uses when, wishing to indicate that there is an irrational force for change in *phusis*, he writes that *phusikon* is *daimonion*. Plutarch noted the effect produced on spectators by Archimedes's war machines, which turned Syracuse at war into a gigantic monster whose movements were controlled by the engineer as if he were the the monster's *psuchē*, and he remarked that these war machines seemed to be the fruits of a knowledge that was not so much human as belonging to a daemon.[32] The expression seems all the more fitting since Archimedes was not able to give his art of constructing machines the form of a completely rational science.

Thus, once it escaped from the narrow framework in which it was confined by the requirements of logical theory and moved toward new inventions, Greek technological research found itself confronting the irrational. Just as in its methods it had to acknowledge the importance of *empeiria*, so in its works it was confronted with a living and animated nature on which it could not impose its laws entirely. This is why machines created by engineers continued to be regarded as exceptional successes, achievements that did not appear capable of being adapted generally. Technical reflection was caught between logical thought, from which it had great difficulty disentangling itself, and the art of the miracle worker, with which it tended to be confused where its boldest inventions were concerned, and it never managed to become clearly defined in itself. It was not experimental. Even when mechanical devices were used, it remained tied to a dynamic concept of the nature on which it operated. It never claimed that its devices had an indefinite power to transform nature. Machines had only the limited value of an expedient; they were traps set at points where nature allowed itself to be overcome. The machine was not yet considered a universal model of physical structures.

In the area of practical crafts, the impression of stagnation becomes even more striking. The artisans did not leave direct evidence concerning their work, but the writers of Antiquity are all in agreement in seeing these crafts as the very epitome of a routine activity.[33] The *technē* of the artisan is not a true knowledge.[34] The artisan does not understand his method or comprehend what he is doing. He is content to slavishly apply the rules he was taught during his apprenticeship.[57] His *technē* depends on fidelity to a tradition that is not scientific, and outside this tradition any attempt at innovation would leave him at the mercy of chance. Experience can teach him nothing, for in his position — caught in the gap between rational knowledge, on the one hand, and *tuchē* (chance), on the other — there is no question of theory or of facts able to verify theory; in fact, there is no experimentation, properly speaking. He obeys the strict rules of his art and blindly imitates the rigor and certainty of a rational procedure, but at the same time, using the kind of flair he has acquired by practicing his craft, he must adapt himself to the always more or less unpredictable and fortuitous nature of the material upon which he works.[36] In technological operations, time is not a stable, homogeneous quantity that can be grasped by the mind. Rather, it is active, a time that is defined by the opportunity that must be seized, the *kairos*, the point where human action meets a natural process developing according to its own rhythm. When intervening with his tools, the artisan must recognize and wait for the moment when the time is ripe and be able to adapt himself entirely to circumstances. He must never desert his post, according to Plato, for if he does, the *kairos* might pass and the work will be ruined.[37] The ability to sum things up at a glance, an essential part of the artisan's technical mastery, only emphasizes that he is slave to a *kairos* and is incapable of dominating through his intelligence.[38]

When they became secularized, the technical skills were not given the status of applications of science. They became established as a set of traditional methods and practical skills whose effectiveness was no longer considered anything but natural, but which lent themselves neither to critical reflection nor to innovation.

One might even wonder whether, in this development toward a more positive status, technological thought was not somehow degraded. It did not acquire any greater affinity with rational knowledge, and it appears to have forfeited the dynamism and boldness that belonged to it in more ancient times, when the memory of its affinities with magical knowledge had not yet completely died out. During the seventh century, there does appear to have been an upsurge in Asia Minor in technology, from which rich developments might have been expected but which was thwarted in continental Greece as soon as it became set in the molds imposed on it by the political organization of the city. The craftsman enjoys higher prestige in Homer than does the artisan of the classical period.[39] This decline in the artisan's status, which is confirmed by the way the relevant vocabulary developed, corresponds with a transformation in the nature and function of technological activity itself.[40] Originally the craftsmen, who were grouped into brotherhoods similar to certain religious *genē*, were itinerants summoned into the service of a noble clientele. They made luxury articles, precious works such as the *agalmata*, in which Louis Gernet has shown that a mythical notion of value was still present.[41] Through the choice of material, formal beauty, and perfect workmanship, the creation of the craftsman was seen by the person who commissioned it as a testimony of wealth, power, and success. It was not so much a utilitarian object or something to be bought and sold as it was a symbol of personal value and social superiority. The brotherhoods of craftsmen, which, like those of the diviners and of the bards, jealously guarded their knowledge and secrets, staked their reputations on a competition to produce the most prestigious articles. This *eris*, which is agonistic rather than commercially competitive in spirit, directs a stream of technological activity toward the production of extraordinary

314

works of a kind to arouse astonishment and admiration.[42] Psychologically, the ancient craftsman was close to the miracle worker, in that he strove for the exceptional work and for the exploit that would ensure his victory in a test of technical skill.

The attitude was quite different during the classical period. In the first place, the city condemned luxury and favored an ideal of austere severity, even in style of dress.[43] Ostentation and extravagant expenditure, which were the privilege of aristocratic families, were frowned upon in the name of civic equality. Furthermore, in the new social order the artisan was relegated to a position that corresponded to his function in the state, and confined to a subordinate role. The itinerant craftsman — a somewhat peripheral figure, disturbing but at the same time prestigious — became a sedentary workshop owner. His business was no longer to dazzle people with his marvelous productions but to bring articles for everyday use to sell in the agora, as a means of earning his living. His role was not craftsmanlike or creative, in the true sense of these terms, but concerned with commerce and exchange. He provides his fellow citizens with the useful articles they need. He is no longer expected to amaze or be inventive, but is required simply to do his job correctly by applying the rules of his craft.

In these circumstances, it is not surprising that the spirit of inventive craftsmanship and ingenuity, the resourceful *mētis* that used to be the most important feature of technological intelligence, appears to have forsaken the blacksmith's forge and the cobbler's workbench.[44] In the age of the city, *mētis* is the inspiration for the tricks, skills, and methods of other men. It serves the sophist, who is never at a loss for an argument, and always has an answer to everything, who sometimes, as Gorgias does, assumes the role of the miracle worker and word magician; it also serves the engineer, such as Philo, who takes over the traditions of *thaumata* from the craftsman.[45] As for the ordinary artisan, the *cheirotechnēs*, the manual laborer, who, unlike the *architektōn*, does not have the leisure to study mathematics, all that is now left to him is the routine of a craft.

Even within his professional activity, the essentials do not fall within his competence. The rules of his *technē* concern the manufacturing methods, the *poiēsis*; the creation itself, the *poiēma*, which is the goal of his work, is beyond him. In the Greeks's eyes, in fact, it had nothing to do with the strictly technological sphere. Whether it was a house, shoe, flute, or shield, the product answered a specific natural need. It was not seen as something artificial, in the true sense of the term.[46] It was an *eidos*, a Form laid down in advance, as was the case for natural objects. The artisan did not invent it, nor could he alter it. As an artisan, he was not even equipped to understand it. The user, not the producer, possessed the knowledge of the object's form.[47] Form is superior to the workman and to his *technē*, and it directs and controls the work that brings it into being. It gives this work its goal, fixes its limits, defines its framework and its means. In art, as in nature, the final cause is what determines and rules the productive process as a whole. The efficient cause — the artisan, his tools, and his *technē* — is nothing but the instrument with which a preexistent Form fashions matter.

With regard to the work of the artisans even more than to that of the engineers, Greek thought remained permeated by naturalistic images and dynamic concepts. The artisan was not seen, as he is in Descartes, as a mechanic whose product cannot contain anything more than what he has put into it, it being understood that all the perfection formally contained in the machine must exist eminently in the mind of the workman who conceived it. For the ancients, the artisan is a man who orders material impenetrable to mind by embodying in it a Form superior to his own mind. The work produced is more perfect than the producer; the man is dwarfed by his task. Outstripped by the very work that he produces, the artisan is not in command of nature; he submits to the requirements of the Form. His work demands from him neither initiative nor reflection. His function and his excellence are, as Aristotle puts it, to obey.[48]

I began my remarks by pointing out what appeared to be a paradox: there was a block in Greek technological thought at a point when it seemed to be taking shape and developing its own essential features thanks to the sophists' reflections on *technē*. Yet in the various contexts where we have been able to grasp its character, we have found it quite unlike technological thought today, different in both structure and emphasis. It had not yet acquired the features that, in our eyes, define technical intelligence and the basis for its dynamism. It was not integrated with science, or it was only partially so. The experimental method had no place in it. As it did not develop the concepts of natural law, physical mechanics, or the essentially artificial character of technology, it was not equipped with the conceptual framework that could have ensured its progress. Furthermore, only in the work of the Alexandrian engineers, especially Hero, is there any evidence of interest in the instruments and machines as such, and only here was their construction undertaken with an attitude that could be described as truly technological. Previously, theory had other preoccupations and remained an integral part of mathematical and logical thought.

With the sophists, in particular, there is no question of there being a genuinely technological framework to their thought. Their teaching paid no attention of artisan activities; it was not concerned with the methods of operating on matter.[49] Their domain was *praxis*, which they specifically opposed to the *poiēsis* of the artisan.[50] When they presented their purely human, positivist, and rational procedures as a replacement for blind chance and the supernatural inspiration of the oracles, their concerns involved the general conduct of life, political activity, and human relationships. Admittedly, they claimed to regulate and codify action and to teach techniques for success. But for the Greeks of the fifth century, acting did not mean making objects or transforming nature. It meant influencing men, overcoming them, dominating them. Within the framework of the city, speech was the instrument most necessary for action, and mastery of it meant power over others. The sophists' reflections on human *technē*, on the means of extending one's power and perfecting one's tools, led neither to technological thinking nor to a philosophy of technology. They led to rhetoric and established dialectics and logic.

Technological stagnation among the Greeks went hand in hand with the lack of any truly technological thought. Two parallel processes were required for technological progress to get under way: transformations in the political, social, and economic order, and the development of new structures of thought. Only after these obstacles were overcome did technology become established. By constructing machines, it formed its own intellectual equipment.

PART FIVE

The Psychological Category of the Double

CHAPTER FOURTEEN

The Figuration of the Invisible

and the Psychological Category

of the Double: The Kolossos

I would like to show, by taking one particular example, how the Greeks gave a visible form to certain powers of the beyond belonging to the realm of the invisible.

The nature of these sacred powers appears to be closely connected with the way they are represented. In religious symbolism, as in all kinds of symbolism, thought constructs its objects through and by means of forms.

The example I have chosen is the *kolossos*. Originally the word conveyed nothing about size. It did not refer to effigies of gigantic, "colossal" dimensions, as it later came to do for purely accidental reasons. In the terminology of Greek sculpture, which is varied and shifting, as Emile Benveniste has shown, the term "*kolossos*," a word of animate gender and with pre-Greek origins, is connected with the root *kol-*, which is associated with certain place names in Asia Minor (Kolossai, Colophon, Koloura) and retains the idea of something erected, something that has been set up.[1]

This is what appears to distinguish the *kolossos* from other archaic idols — the *bretas* and the *xoanon*, for instance — whose appearance is similar in many respects, with their rigid posture and their arms and legs welded to the body. But the *bretas* and *xoanon* seem to have been almost always movable. They were moved from place to place, carried in processions, even held directly in the arms of the priest or priestess; in fact, they could be called "portable" idols.[2] The fundamental characteristic of the *kolossos*, on the other hand, is that it is fixed to one spot, immobile.[3] It was made in two forms, as a pillar or a menhir, consisting of an upright stone or a stone slab planted in the earth, sometimes even buried in it.

The few extant texts on the *kolossoi* help throw light on the archaeological evidence that allows us to determine the function and symbolic meaning of these idols.

At Midea (present-day Dendra), a cenotaph dating from the thirteenth century BCE contained, instead of skeletons, two blocks of stone, lying on the ground, one larger than the other, both roughly hewn into quadrangular slabs tapering toward the top to indicate the necks and heads of human figures. One was a man, the other a woman.[4] Buried in a tomb alongside the objects belonging to the dead person, the *kolossos* functioned as a substitute for the absent corpse.

This practice of substitution was in keeping with beliefs that are by now familiar. When a man who has gone far away appears to have disappeared forever, or when he has perished without its being possible to bring back his body or perform funerary rites for him, the dead man — or rather his "double," his *psuchē* — is compelled to wander endlessly between the world of the living and that of the dead. He no longer belongs to the former, while he has not yet been relegated to the latter.[5] His ghost therefore harbors a dangerous power that manifests itself in mischief directed against the living.

When a *kolossos* is used in a tomb as a substitute for the corpse, it is not meant to reproduce the features of the dead man or to create the illusion of his physical presence. What it embodies in permanent form in stone is not the image of the dead man but his life in the beyond, the life that is opposed to that of living men as the world of night is opposed to the world of light. The *kolossos* is not an image; it is a "double," as the dead man is a double of his living self.

However, the *kolossos* is not always relegated to the darkness of the tomb. The naked stone may also stand erect in the daylight over an empty tomb, in some lonely and deserted spot that is so wild it is said to belong to the powers of the underworld. One example was at Phlius, on the cenotaph raised to Aras and his children. Another is at Lebadeia, where, in a forest untouched by human hands, a stone slab with neither inscription nor carved image was raised over the pit of Agamedes: Trophonios had been swallowed up in the opening of the *bothros* and had disappeared into the depths of the earth, and here rites for the evocation of the dead were celebrated. The prescribed libations and the blood of a black ram were poured over the stela; then those present called the dead man's name three times, gazing at the stone where it was believed he would reappear.[6]

Thus the same square stone used at Midea to separate the dead man from the living by relegating him forever to his underground resting place can, when it is erected above ground, make it possible to establish contact with him. Through the *kolossos*, the dead man returns to the light of day and manifests his presence in the sight of the living. It is a peculiar and ambiguous presence that is also the sign of an absence. By making himself visible in the stone, the dead man also reveals himself as being not of this world.

At Selinus a whole stretch of land beyond the walls was devoted to the powers of the beyond.[7] Within an enclosure, leaning against the *peribolos* of Zeus Meilichios, Zeus of the underworld, a large number of roughly hewn *cippi* with human faces, both male and female, were stuck into the ground.[8] Two inscriptions found at Cyrene explain these *kolossoi*: the people of Selinus planted them in their field of the dead, where they also left *tabulae defixionum* addressed to the subterranean deities and the meals that were due to the deceased.

The first is the text of the sacred law concerning the welcome to be given to suppliants arriving from abroad.[9] If the person the suppliant claims to have been sent by has died, whether in his own country or in some other place, and if the master of the house who takes the suppliant in and grants him protection in the future knows the name of the sender, the master of the house invokes him by name for three consecutive days. If he does not know the identity of the sender, he pronounces the formula "Human being, whether you be man or woman." He makes two *kolossoi* — a man and a woman — out of wood or earth, welcomes them to his table, and gives them a share of all the food served. Having thus set in order his relationship with the anonymous dead person who sent the suppliant to him, the master of the house sends the dead person away from his home, back to the world of the dead: once the rites of hospitality have been completed, he takes the *kolossoi* and the portions of food to a forest that has not been cut and plants the *kolossoi* in the ground.

The second inscription reproduces the text of the oath guaranteeing the reciprocal obligations between the colonists setting off for Cyrene in Africa and their fellow citizens remaining behind in the metropolis of Thera.[10] The method of taking the oath is as follows: *kolossoi* are made, this time of wax; they are thrown into a fire while the following formula is pronounced: "Let whoever breaks this oath be turned to liquid and disappear, himself, his descendants, and all his goods."

In both these rituals, the *kolossos* journeys between the world of the living and that of the dead. But the journey is made in one direction, in the first case and in the other in the second. In one case, the dead are made present in the world of the living; in the other, the living are projected into death. The ritual of the suppliants is meant to establish a link of hospitality with an unknown dead person, whether a man or a woman. As in the rites of evocation, the *psuchē*, responding to the thrice-repeated call, rises once more to the light of day and becomes present in the *kolossos*, which thus fixes it inside the house. When the communal meal is completed, the presence of the dead person is removed by setting up the *kolossoi* in the ground of an uncultivated forest, the symbol here on earth of the otherworld. In the second case, in contrast, the living irrevocably pledge themselves to death should they ever break their oath. Through the *kolossoi* who represent them in the form of doubles, those swearing the oath cast themselves into the fire; this act anticipates their own life and social existences liquefication and disappearance into the invisible.[11]

324

In both cases, however, the *kolossos* — as a double — appears to be associated with the *psuchē*. It is one of the forms that the *psuchē* — as a power from the beyond — can adopt when it makes itself visible to human beings.

For the Greeks, therefore, the *kolossos* and the *psuchē* are closely related. They fall within a category of very clearly defined phenomena to which the term *eidōla* was applied. As well as the *psuchē*, which is a shade, and the *kolossos*, which is a crudely formed idol, this category includes the dream-image (*oneiros*), the shade (*skia*), and the supernatural apparition (*phasma*).[12] These phenomena, which to us seem so disparate, are unified in the sense that within the cultural context of archaic Greece they are all apprehended in the same way by the mind and thus take on a similar significance. It is therefore justifiable, where they are concerned, to speak of a true psychological category — the double — which presupposes a different mental organization from our own. A double is completely different from an image. It is not a "natural" object, nor is it simply a product of the mind. It is not an imitation of a real object, an illusion of the mind, or a creation of thought. For the person who sees it, the double is an external reality, but one whose peculiar character, in its very appearance, sets it in opposition to familiar objects and to the ordinary surroundings of life. It exists simultaneously on two contrasting planes: just when it shows itself to be present, it also reveals itself as not of this world and as belonging to some other, inaccessible sphere.

This is the case with the *eidōlon* of Patroclus, for example. Achilles sees it rising up before him when he goes to sleep after a long night of mourning during which, as he kept watch alone, his soul overcome with *pothos* (the nostalgic desire for the absent one), he did not cease to keep the memory of his dead friend present in his mind. The *eidōlon* stands upright above the head of the recumbent Achilles, as happens in the case of a dream, an *oneiros*; but it really is the *psuchē* of Patroclus. What Achilles beholds before him is Patroclus himself, with his own bearing, his eyes, his voice, his body, and his clothing. Yet when he tries to embrace him, the *eidōlon* proves impossible to grasp: it is a wisp of smoke that vanishes beneath the ground with a little cry, like a bat.[13] The effect of the *eidōlon* is a kind of trickery, a deception or snare (*apatē*): it is the presence of his friend, but it is also his irremediable absence; it is Patroclus in person, yet at the same time it is simply a breath of air, a wisp of smoke, a shadow, or a bird taking wing.[14]

The archaeological and epigraphical evidence discussed above highlights the aspects of the *kolossos* as a double and its links with a reality like the *psuchē*, which has a somewhat ambiguous character since it belongs both to the visible world and to the beyond. A text from Aeschylus's *Agamemnon* confirms that the *kolossos* must be situated within the psychological context specific to the experience of the double and that the religious significance of the menhir is determined by the fact that the Greeks see it as belonging to this same category. The chorus is describing Menelaus's palace, now deserted by Helen, who has gone after her lover.[15] Never has the presence of this woman weighed so heavily on this house as it does after she has left it. Through the power of the *pothos*, Menelaus's longing for his absent wife, Helen's ghost constantly haunts it, in three forms of doubles, which the chorus mentions in turn. The first is the *phasma*, which now seems to reign over the palace in the place of the departed wife. Then there are the *kolossoi* — translated by Charles Picard as "replacement figurines," which are used in magic concerned with love to evoke the absent one and in funerary rites to evoke the person who has died.[16] Finally, there are the dream figures (*oneirophantoi*) that appear in sleep. The sole effect of all these doubles, which for Menelaus are substitutes for his wife, is to make her absence all the more poignant and unbearable. They lack the quality that makes Helen a real woman: *charis*, the dazzling brilliance of life. All these *eidōla* of Helen — the ghost, the *kolossos*, and the dream figure — bring her husband the disappointment of a constantly elusive presence that manifests itself only to take flight once again. Under the seductive mask of Aphrodite, the unattainable Persephone can be glimpsed in the loved woman's double.[17]

In relation to this text from Aeschylus, a passage in Euripides's *Alcestis* reads almost as a pastiche on the same theme. Alcestis is preparing to descend into the underworld. Her husband, Admetos, whose life she is ransoming at the cost of her own, swears to her that he will mourn her forever and will never love another woman. He will continue to be united with Alcestis each night, in his dreams, and he will have an effigy made of her, which he will place in his bed. He will lie down beside it and embrace it, calling the name of his beloved. Thus he may believe that he is holding in his arms his wife, who is present though absent: *kaiper ouk echōn echein.*[18]

In this rather odd intercourse, his soul (*psuchē*) will feel not warm pleasure but a cold (*psuchron*) delight — for what is the *psuchē* if not a cold shade?[19]

Admetos's words call to mind a legend that Euripides knew well and that inspired another tragedy, *Protesilaus*. Protesilaus meets his death near Troy, in a far-off land, and his body cannot be brought back to his fatherland. He leaves behind an inconsolable widow. In the version of the story given by Apollodorus, the wife, Laodameia, makes an *eidōlon* of her husband.[20] Each night she makes love with this double. The gods take pity on her and send Protesilaus's *psuchē* back to his loving wife for a moment. In the version given by Hyginus, the figurine fashioned by Laodameia is made of wax.[21] Her father finds out what his daughter is doing at night and orders the effigy cast into the fire. Laodameia throws herself in after it, in order to follow Protesilaus into the beyond. These two versions of the myth use the two different orientations of the *kolossoi* — depending on the material they were made of — as the rituals at Cyrene discussed above. But whether it is made of stone or wax, and whether it is used to bring the shades of the dead back to the light of day or to send the living down among the shades, the *kolossos*, as a double, always establishes a link between the living and the underworld.

There is, however, one problem. How could a stone, fashioned and set up by man's hand, have the significance of a double that would relate it to such uncontrollable and mysterious psychic phenomena as dream figures and supernatural apparitions? How is it that a rough–hewn slab of stone can in certain circumstances appear double and ambiguous, with one face turned toward the invisible? What is it about the *kolossos* that makes it stand in such contrast to the world of the living that it seems to introduce into the earthly landscape where it has been erected not simply a stone, a familiar object, but the very power of death, in all its uncanny strangeness and terror? In seeking an answer, we must turn to the religious representations that, through the play of correspondences and oppositions they establish among the different aspects of reality, give the Greek view of the world its specific features. Like every sign, the *kolossos* refers to a whole system of symbolism, from which it cannot be isolated. Only within the context of this overall conceptual framework can its a close affinity with death and the dead be understood.

Certain aspects of this affinity must first be emphasized. In Greece, the oath, which operates by pledging those swearing it to the powers of the underworld, can be made by simply touching an unhewn stone: the oath is sworn "by the stone."[22] Recall also that Persephone sends the head of the Gorgon to meet those who desire to enter as living men into the realm of the dead, and that the Gorgon is a magical instrument of death who changes anyone who looks upon her into stone.[23] A number of indications show that death was seen as a petrification of living beings. Pindar, for example, uses the expression *lithinos thanatos* (stony death).[24] These symbolic associations are easy to understand when one thinks of the transformation of the living body — supple, animated, warm — into a stiff, silent, icy corpse. But the features that, by setting life and death in opposition, term for term, define them in relation to each other, while also establishing the boundaries of their respective domains, must be pinpointed more precisely.

In contrast to the sonorous world of voices, cries, and songs, death is first of all a world of silence. Certain priestesses in charge of the funerary rites, in which all music was forbidden, were known as "the silent ones."[25] To fashion a statue out of stone or clay and breathe life into it — as in the case of Hermes waking

Pandora, or the living statues in the service of Hephaistos — is to give it a voice, a *phōnē*.[26] Thus Theognis writes that he will be *hōste lithos aphthoggos*, like a stone without a voice, when he is buried and lifeless in the earth.[27] Conversely, metallic stones that sound like bronze when struck, or pottery that makes a crackling noise in the kiln when it is fired, are considered animated and alive because they are not enshrouded in the silence common to dumb stones. The coldness of stones is also related to death. As opposed to the warmth of the living, the *psuchē* evokes coldness (*psuchron*).

In that it is hard, dry, and rigid, a stone may recall a desiccated living man, who is moist, supple, and full of sap as long as he is in the prime of life. For the Greeks, old age is already a kind of desiccation. The young man is like a plant, full of sap when green but becoming dry and faded in time. A gloss by Hesychius comments on the word *alibantes* by way of the terms *nekroi* and *kolossoi*, the "dried-up ones," or the dead.[28] Furthermore, the *psuchai* of the dead are parched with thirst. By being watered with the various liquids of the living, they can be drawn back to the light of day and a reflection of their former vitality, along with memory and thought, can be restored to them for a moment.

But the fundamental opposition is between the visible and the invisible. Death, or Hades, is precisely the invisible (*aidēs*), and what the Greeks call the "helmet of Hades," the *kunē*, makes the wearer invisible. The dead are figures "clothed in night." Through a sort of reciprocal relationship between the faculty of sight and the property of being visible, both of which are associated with the light of day, the disappearance of a living man from the world of light and his entrance into the world of night can also be expressed by the image of his transformation into an unseeing block of stone. In contrast to a precious stone, which is alive in that it shines and reflects the light or allows itself to be entirely flooded with light, the block of dull and opaque stone, the *kolossos* with "empty eyes" that Aeschylus refers to, can be seen as representing the world of night.[29] There is an affinity between the dead man's *psuchē*, which is an invisible mist or a dark shade, and the stone, which is visible but opaque and blind, that arises from the fact that both are opposed to the realm of light and life, which is characterized by two properties: seeing and being seen.[30]

Stone and the *psuchē* of a dead man are both also contrasted with the living man, the former by reason of its immobility, the latter by reason of its elusive mobility. The living man moves about upright on the surface of the ground, his feet remaining constantly in contact with the earth. The *kolossos*, sunk into the earth, rooted deep into the ground, remains fixed and immobile. Hesychius's gloss referred to above has sometimes been read by replacing the word *alibantes* with *abantes*: "who do not walk." In the true sense of the term, *kolossoi* are those who cannot move their legs in order to walk. As for the *psuchē*, it moves about without ever touching the earth; it flits beneath the surface of the ground, forever in motion and forever elusive. Thus the *kolossos* and the *psuchē* are opposed to the walk of a man, representing two extreme positions in relation to an intermediary one: being embedded in the earth (the *kolossos*), being in contact with the surface of the earth (the living man), having no contact with the earth (the *psuchē*); total immobility (the *kolossos*), moving about from one place to another, successively occupying a series of positions on the surface of the ground, the same individual being at each instant in one place and one place only (the living man), a ubiquitous presence throughout space (the *psuchē*). But where mobility is concerned, the link between the *kolossos* and the *psuchē* arises not only from the fact that they are, as extremes, closer in some respects to each other than to the intermediate position represented by the living man.[37] Their antithetical features appear to express the complementarity that the rite of the *kolossos* is meant to establish with the *psuchē*. By embedding the stone in the ground, one attempts to fix, immobilize, localize in one definite spot of the earth the elusive *psuchē*, which is at once everywhere and nowhere.

The story of Actaeon is pertinent here. When Actaeon died he was never buried. His *eidōlon*, his ghost, stirred up all sorts of mischief against the population. The oracle of Delphi was consulted.

It commanded that an effigy be made of Actaeon and that it be bound with iron chains to the very stone where the ghost appeared. The order was carried out and the statue duly erected and chained to the stone. Actaeon's soul, which was now fixed to one place, thereupon ceased to persecute the living.[32]

This example, which belongs to a period when a human likeness had replaced the uncarved stone, shows clearly what the original purpose of the *kolossos* was. It served to attract and pin down a double that found itself in abnormal circumstances. It made it possible to reestablish correct relations between the world of the dead and the world of the living. The *kolossos* has this power to pin down because it is itself ritually embedded in the ground. It is not, therefore, a merely figurative symbol. Its function is both to translate the power of the dead man into a visible form and to enable it to be integrated into the ordered world of the living. The material sign cannot be separated from the ritual. It can assume its full meaning only through the completion of the rituals.[33] The symbol is "activated" by men and itself contains an active force. It has an effective power. The *kolossos* brings together several complementary functions: the figuration of the power of the dead man, the active manifestations of this power, and the regulation of its relationship with the living.

One final point should be made. In its role as double and through its function as mediator between two opposed worlds, the *kolossos*, considered as a sign, sometimes reveals a tension and a kind of oscillation. At times the visible aspect comes into the foreground; at others, the invisible. The subsequent history of the *kolossos* is well known. It was not long before the Greeks forgot about the funerary stone's relationship with the dead, remaining conscious only of its visible form. In the stela raised over a cenotaph or tomb, they no longer saw anything more than simple *mnēma*, a sign whose purpose was to recall the dead to those still living. Yet a different attitude can sometimes be glimpsed. When the ritual libations have been made and the black ram sacrificed, and when those officiating have called the dead man's name three times, it is truly the double that is seen rising above the tomb.[34] In the form of an uncarved stone embedded in the ground in a wild landscape, the *kolossos* represents a manifestation of the power of the underworld in the eyes of the living. Here, perhaps, arises a problem that goes far beyond the case of the *kolossos* and concerns one of the essential characteristics of a religious sign. The religious sign is not simply an instrument of thought. Its purpose is not limited to evoking in men's minds the sacred power to which it refers. Its intention is always also to establish a true means of communication with this power and to really introduce its presence into the human world. But while it thus aims to establish a bridge with the divine, so to speak, it must at the same time emphasize the distance and the immeasurable difference between this sacred power and anything that attempts to manifest it, always inadequately, to the eyes of men. In this sense, the *kolossos* is a good example of the tension found at the very heart of the religious sign, which gives it its peculiar character. In its operative and effective function, the *kolossos* seeks to establish real contact with the beyond and to bring about its presence in this earthly world. Yet in the very attempt to do this it emphasizes all the elements of the inaccessible, the mysterious, and the fundamentally foreign that the world beyond death holds for the living.

CHAPTER FIFTEEN

From the "Presentification"
of the Invisible to the Imitation
# of Appearance

The Greek Example

If anyone wants to consider, not only the forms that images have assumed at a given moment in a given country, but also, perhaps more profoundly, the functions of the image as such and the social and cognitive status of imagery in the context of a particular civilization, then the Greek case is certainly a very special example.

First, for historical reasons. During the so-called Dark Ages, that is, broadly speaking, from the twelfth to the eighth centuries before our era, Greece, which as you know has no knowledge of writing, also has no knowledge of imagery in the proper sense of the term, nor does it use systems of figural representation. The same word, *graphein*, it should be noted, is used for writing, drawing, and painting.

The establishment, under the influence of Eastern models, of what can be called a repertory of figures, a palette of images, and the elaboration of a language of art in pottery, sculpture, and relief, comes about toward the eighth century, as though it is starting afresh from a blank tablet. In this as in other areas, we are witness to a kind of birth, or at least a renaissance, which authorizes us to speak of the advent of figuration in Greece. When the Greeks rediscover imagery, the form it takes amounts to a divestiture so absolute in comparison to the preceding period that, as Pierre Demargne observes, it can be regarded as a creation "*ex nihilo.*"[1]

That is not all. In surveying the extensive, diffuse, and uncertain semantics in Greek pertaining to statuary, Emile Benvenist claimed

333

that the Greeks did not have any specific word to designate the statue in our sense of the term. As he states: "The people who fixed the most refined canons and models of plastic art for the Western world had to borrow from others the notion itself of figural representation."[2] Furthermore, simply to analyze the terms used by the Greeks throughout their history to indicate "statue" shows that what Benveniste called "the notion of figural representation" is not a simple immediate fact that could in some way be defined once and for all. The notion of figural representation does not just come from itself. Neither univocal nor permanent, it is what might be called a historical category; a construct elaborated, not without difficulty, through very different routes in different civilizations.

There are about fifteen expressions in Greek to mean "divine idol" in the many forms it can take: an aniconic form as, for example, a brute stone (*baitulos*), beams (*dokana*), a pillar (*kiōn*), and a stela (*herma*): a theriomorphic or monstrous kind like the Gorgon, Sphinx, and Harpies. And there is the anthropomorphic figure in the great diversity of its types. These range from the small wooden archaic idol, poorly fashioned, with arms and legs welded to the body, like the *bretas*, the *xoanon*, and the *palladion*, to the archaic Kouroi and Korai, and finally includes the great cult statue, which is given a variety of names: it can be called *hedos* or *agalma* as well as *eikōn* and *mimēma*, the last, however, not used in this precise sense before the fifth century. Now, of all these terms, excluding the last two, there is no single one that has any relation whatsoever to the idea of resemblance or imitation, of figural representation in the strict sense.

In addition, it is not enough to say that late Greek archaism had to create a language of plastic forms for itself from scratch, without also adding that it developed these forms in a quite original way so that, starting from idols that functioned as symbolic actualizations of different models of the divine, it finally arrived at the image, properly speaking: that is, the image conceived as an imitative artifice reproducing in the form of a counterfeit the external appearance of real things.

At the pivotal point of the fifth and fourth centuries, the theory of *mimēsis*, sketched out by Xenophon, and elaborated in a fully systematic way by Plato, marks the moment when in Greek culture the turn is completed that leads from the "presentification," the making present, of the invisible to the imitation of appearance.[3] It is at this time that the category of figural representation emerges in its specific features and, at the same time, becomes attached to *mimēsis* — the great human fact of imitation, which gives it a solid foundation.

The symbol that actualizes, that makes present in this world below a power from the world beyond (a fundamentally invisible being) is now transformed into an image that is the product of an expert imitation, which, as a result of skillful technique and illusionist procedures, enters into the general category of the "fictitious" — that which we call art. From now on, the image derives from figurative illusionism all the more, because it does not belong to the domain of religious realities.

The Archaic Idol: The Xoanon

Another question, therefore, arises. As long as the image is not yet clearly attached to the peculiarly human faculty of creating works through imitation, works that have no reality other than their semblance, whose entire essence is a "faux-semblant," what then is the status of the image? How does it function? What is its relation to that very thing it represents or evokes? I will confine myself essentially in this essay to the issue of statuary and its role in the representation of the gods, allotting only brief remarks to the figuration of the dead on painted or carved steles, in relief, and in free-standing sculpture.

Figure of the gods, figure of the dead. In each case, the problem is the same: by means of localization in an exact form and a well-determined place, how is it possible to give visual presence to those powers that come from the invisible and do not belong to the space here below on earth? The task is to make the invisible visible, to assign a place in our world to entities from the other world. In the representational enterprise, it can be said that at the outset, this paradoxical aspiration exists in order to inscribe absence in presence, to insert the other, the elsewhere, into our familiar universe. Whatever the avatars of the image may have been, this impossible quest is one that perhaps continues to remain valid to a large degree — that of evoking absence in presence, revealing the elsewhere in what is given to view.

Let us begin with the gods.

First, a general remark. Besides the storytelling that occurs in myth and the organized progression of acts in ritual, every religious system includes a third facet — the phenomenon of representation. Yet for the mind of the spectator who regards it, a figure in a religious context is not simply intended to evoke the sacred power to which it refers, which in certain cases it "represents, as in the case of an anthropomorphic statue, and which in other cases it evokes symbolically. Its larger ambition is quite different.

However the sacred power is represented, the aim is to establish a true communication, an authentic contact, with it. The ambition is to make this power present *hic et nunc*, to make it available to human beings in the ritually required forms. But in its attempt to construct a bridge, as it were, that will reach toward the divine, the idol must also at the same time and in the same figure mark its distance from that domain in relation to the human world. It has to stress the incommensurability between the sacred power and everything that reveals it to the eyes of mortals in what can only be an inadequate and incomplete way. In the context of religious thought, every form of figuration must introduce an inevitable tension: the idea is to establish real contact with the world beyond, to actualize it, to make it present, and thereby to participate intimately in the divine; yet by the same move, it must also emphasize what is inaccessible and mysterious in divinity, its alien quality, its otherness.

To illustrate this far too general concept, I will take the example of a certain type of divine idol in the Greek world.

On numerous occasions Pausanias indicates the presence in some sanctuary or another of a form of idol he calls *xoanon*. This word, of Indo-European origin (by contrast to *bretas*, which has a similar meaning), is connected to *xeō*, to scrape or abrade, a word that belongs to the vocabulary of woodworking. The *xoanon*, as he describes it, is an idol of wood, more or less roughed out in a so-called pillar shape,[4] and of primitive workmanship.

For Pausanias, *xoana* are defined by three characteristics. As idols belonging to the most remote past, everything about them has an air of the archaic: their appearance, the cult whose object they are, and the legends about them. This "primitive" quality of *xoana* produces a marked effect of "strangeness" in the spectator, which Pausanias stresses by referring to these figures with terms like *atopos* and *xenos* (strange) as a way of indicating their distance from ordinary cultic images. Primitivity and strangeness. To these Pausanias adds a third feature, which is very directly connected to the other two. Because there is something disconcerting about them, something that is nonimaged in the usual sense of the term, *xoana* contain an aspect of the divine, *theion ti*, some supernatural quality.[5]

These archaic idols, which often play a fundamental role in the cultic worship of a god and concern that god very directly — even if they do not represent the deity in the canonical figural form — are not, in my opinion, images. Neither in their origins nor their functions have they crossed the threshold beyond which one is entitled to speak of images, *stricto sensu*.

Their origin. The most famous ones are not considered to have been made by the hand of a mortal artisan. Whether a god made them and offered them as a gift to one of his favorites, whether they fell from heaven or were carried in to shore by the waves of the sea, they are not human works.

Their form. To the degree that there is a form — since a simple piece of wood can take the place of an idol — their form counts less sometimes, on the plane of symbolic value, than the material of which they are made: a certain type of tree or even a particular tree the god has selected and with which he or she has a special communion. Additionally, the figure is most often clad in garments that cover and conceal it from top to toe.

Their functions. The idol is not made to be seen. To look at it is

337

to go mad. It is also often shut up in a chest, guarded in a dwelling forbidden to the public. Nevertheless, without being visible as an image is expected to be, the idol is still not invisible in the way a god is whom one cannot gaze at face-to-face.

The idol is caught in the game of hiding and revealing. Sometimes hidden, sometimes uncovered, the *xoanon* oscillates between the two extremes of being kept secret and being shown to the public. The sighting of the image takes place each time in relation to a preliminary hidden, which gives it its true significance by treating it as a privilege reserved for particular persons, at particular moments, under particular conditions. To see the idol presupposes a specific religious quality and yet also consecrates its eminent dignity. The sight of it, like that of the mysteries, acquires the value of an initiation. In other words, the contemplation of the divine idol seems like an unveiling of a mysterious and fearful reality. Instead of being the primary datum that it would be a question of imitating with an image, the visible becomes qualified as a revelation, both precious and precarious, of an invisible realm that constitutes the true and fundamental reality.

Figure and Ritual Action

The idol, however, is not simply brought into the game of hide and display. It is inseparable from the ritual operations that are worked on it. It is dressed and undressed, ritually bathed, and taken out for washing in a river or in the sea. The idol is offered fabrics or veils. It is taken outside and brought back within, where it is sometimes fastened with symbolic bonds, woollen yarn, or golden chains. This is because the idol is represented as mobile. Even if the *xoanon* has no feet or its legs are sealed together, it is always believed to be on the point of escaping, of deserting one place to go off elsewhere, to haunt another dwelling into which it will import the privileges and powers attached to its possession.

When a *xoanon* is involved, the plastic representation can never be wholly separated from ritual action. The idol is made *in order* to be shown and hidden, led forth and fixed in place, dressed and undressed, and given a bath. The figure has need of the rite if

338

it is to represent divine power and action. Still incapable in its immobile and fixed form of expressing any movement other than being turned and led about, it nevertheless conveys the god's action by symbolic gestures of animation and simulation.

In addition, the *xoanon* always makes its appearance at the center of a cycle of festivals that are organized around it and that form a coherent symbolic system with it in which all the elements — plastic sign and ritual actions — combine and correspond with one another. The problem of the *xoanon*'s efficacy outside this system is one that does not arise. It is through the succession of ceremonies of which it is the object that the idol manifests the power of the god. The idol represents divine action by miming it for the duration of the rite far more than it does in its capacity as a figure that locates this action in space.

Embedded within the ritual, the idol in its plastic form has not reached full autonomy. Yet this does not mean either that its status is comparable to that of a post, stake, pillar, or herm. To shackle a *xoanon* with a more or less symbolic bond does not have the same value as planting a post or stake in the ground. The idea of binding the idol implies a mobile image whose escape is arrested by fettering its legs with woollen yarn or a vegetal withy or, in a more precise symbolism, with golden chains. The rite does not fix the image in the soil with the idea of demarcating a center of religious force in that space. It aims at assuring a social group of the permanent preservation of a symbol that has talismanic value. The idol is not especially attached to a point in the earth and it does not localize a divine power. On the contrary, wherever it may be, it confers on its possessor the privilege and, as it were, the exclusivity of certain powers. It marks a "personal" closeness with the divinity, which can be transmitted through inheritance and can circulate in royal families or religious *genē* (clans). This idea of appropriating the idol, a complement of its mobility, is conveyed by the fact that it lodges, at least in the beginning, in the secret recesses of a human house — the dwelling of the king, chief, or priest. In any case, it is a private, privileged residence, not a public site. In the era of the city, when the temple — impersonal and collective — comes to shelter the divine image, the memory of the bond that joined the most ancient *xoana* to a particular house and lineage will still remain very vivid. Athena's *xoanon* sits in Erechtheus's residence at Athens, while in Thebes the *thalamos* of Semele in the palace of Kadmos keeps watch over the image of Dionysos. In the full classical period, the custom is preserved of lodging certain images of a mysterious character in private dwellings rather than in a temple. The priest offers hospitality to the statue in his own house for the duration of his sacerdotal function. Custody of the image consecrates the personal bond that from now on unites him with the divinity. The idol thus comes to function as a sign of investiture. It matters little, in this respect, whether it has some kind of human form or not. The boundary is still rather fluid between the *xoanon* and certain symbolic objects that also bestow a particular religious quality on their possessors.

Figures and Symbolic Objects

The function of this type of *sacra* consists in certifying and transmitting the powers the divinity accords as a privilege to its elect rather than in making a divine "form" known to the public, The symbol does not represent the god, abstractly conceived in and for itself. It does not attempt to instruct anyone about its nature. It expresses divine power insofar as it is handled and used by certain individuals as an instrument of social prestige, a means of getting a hold on and of acting on others.

The scepter of Agamemnon represents these two allied features of a divine symbol and an object of investiture. Charged with efficacious power, it imposes silence on the assembly, gives decision the value of execution, and acknowledges the king to be the offspring of Zeus. Held in the hands and transmitted by heredity, it objectives in some way the potency of sovereignty. It is a divine object, like the *xoanon*, having been fabricated by Hephaistos, given by Zeus to Hermes, and passed successively to Peleus, Atreus, Thyestes, and Agamemnon. Just like the *xoanon*, the scepter can function just as well as an "idol" of the god. At Chaironeia, it becomes the object of the principal cult by representing Zeus. But it preserves its ancient values as a talisman whose power must be appropriated and its privileges transmitted. Each year, a new priest takes charge of the divine symbol and carries it into his house to make daily sacrifices to it. The scepter's role at Chaironeia is taken by a crown for the priest of Zeus Panamaros, a trident among the Eteoboutades, and a shield in the royal family of Argos (or, just as well, a *xoanon*). At Argos, specifically in the ceremony of the Bath of Pallas, the *xoanon* of Athena was not taken out by itself alone; it was accompanied by the shield of Diomedes, which was also "carried" in the procession. In a social context in which divine powers and the symbols that express them do not yet have a fully public character, but still remain the property of privileged families, there is a reciprocal relation between the idol and the symbolic object that assumes the same function.

Two stories, whose parallels highlight this analogy between *xoanon* and *sacra*, help us grasp the turning point of social history which passes from private cult to public cult, and transforms the idol, an object of investiture, a more or less secret familial talisman, into an impersonal image of a divinity made to be seen. The first is told to us by Herodotus.[6] At Gela, in a period of unrest, the city becomes divided against itself. One group of inhabitants secedes and establishes itself on high ground from which it threatens the rest of the community. A man named Telines decides therefore to confront the rebels without any arms other than certain *sacra* he keeps in his possession. Relying on their supernatural power, he goes before the mutineers, calms their revolt, and leads them back to Gela in a renewal of concord and social order. He asked only one compensation in return for his exploit: henceforth his descendants will, like hierophants, provide the priests of the goddesses, probably Demeter and Kore. The *sacra* he used are precisely those of the cult of these goddesses. Would not this then be the inaugural moment when the cult became public and was adopted as the official cult of the city? Herodotus, it is true, indicates that he does not know how Telines could have obtained these *sacra*, whether he had received them from someone or had procured them himself. But the *Scholiast to Pindar's second Pythian ode*

341

makes clear that this cult had been brought as a family cult from Triopion by the ancestors of Telines when Gela was founded and that only much later had it been instituted as a public one.[7]

The same themes: popular revolt, pacification of sedition, not with violence but with *sacra*, talismans with both political and religious value, belonging to certain families, that by some sort of compromise became objects of public cult in the new social order of the city: all these can be found in the second tale that directly concerns the *xoanon* of Athena at Argos. The custom of carrying the shield of Diomedes, Callimachus tells us, is a very ancient rite instituted by Eumedes, the "favorite" priest of the goddess. Here are the conditions: the population is in revolt, but Eumedes escapes death by the same procedure Telines had used. In his flight he carries off the sacred image, the *palladion*, and no doubt the shield too, that object of royal investiture. He sets these on a rocky escarpment for his protection. Callimachus does not relate the sequel. One can imagine it. Eumedes institutes the rite that henceforth will benefit the entire city and all its citizens with the "favor" that Athena had previously reserved for her "protégé."

In the public cult, however, the value of ancient private *sacra* is also transformed at the same time as it is maintained. Since it ceases to incarnate the privilege of a family or of a closed group, the idol will have lost its more or less secret talismanic value in order to acquire the significance and structure of an image. In this sense, the appearance of the temple and the institution of a public cult not only mark a turning point in social history that is the age of the city but also imply the advent of a new form of representation of the gods, a decisive mutation in the nature of the divine symbol.

The Image, the Temple, and Publicity

More than a place of cult where the worshippers meet, the Greek temple is a residence. The god inhabits it, but it is a residence that has nothing markedly private about it. Instead of being enclosed like the human *oikos*, in a familial interior, the divine house is oriented toward the exterior, turned toward the public gaze. In the palace, a fresco decorated the inside of a room. In the temple, however, the sculpted frieze, projected on the facade, is shown to the spectator who looks at it from the outside. The god resides in the inmost part of the building. But this god is one who from now on belongs to the entire city. The city built the god a house, separated from the human dwelling place, but at the same time it left the Acropolis to the divinity and established itself instead in the lower town. Because the god too is public, the inside of the temple is no less impersonal than its exterior. In no longer being a sign of privilege for the one whose house it inhabits, the god reveals his or her presence in a directly visible way to the eyes of all: under the gaze of the city, the god becomes form and spectacle.

The advent of the great cult statue can only be understood in the frame of reference of the temple with its two aspects, as a house reserved for the god and as a fully socialized space. Constructed by the city, the temple is consecrated to the god as his or her residence. The temple is called *naos* (residence) and *hedos* (seat of divinity). And the word *hedos* also means the great divine statue. It is through this image that the divinity comes to live in its house. Thus there is complete reciprocity between the temple and the statue. The temple is made to lodge the statue of the god and the statue is created to exteriorize the presence of the god as a spectacle in the intimacy of his or her dwelling place.

Like the temple, the image has the quality of being fully public. We could characterize this statue by saying that henceforth all its *esse* consists in a *percipi*, all its being in a being perceived. It has no reality other than its appearance, no ritual function other than to be seen. Lodged in the temple in which the god is made to reside, it is no longer taken out and used. Expressive just in its form, it has no further need to be dressed or carried in a procession or bathed. The statue is no longer required to operate in the world as an efficacious force; rather its task is to act on the eyes of the spectators, to translate for them in a visible way the invisible presence of the god and communicate some lesson about divinity. The statue is representation in a really new sense. Liberated from ritual and placed under the impersonal gaze of the city, the divine symbol is transformed into an image of the god.

The Figure of the Body

This disengagement of the image, properly speaking, takes place through a discovery of the human body and a progressive conquest of its form. Yet we must still specify the import of these assertions. What is meant is evidently not a question of the human body as an organic and physiological reality on which the self relies for its support. If religious symbolism is directed toward the human body and reproduces its appearance, it is because it sees there the expression of certain aspects of the divine. The problem should therefore be posed in the following way: in the case of the *xoanon*, the human aspect is not yet felt to be essential, nor is the form of the body well executed. When monumental statuary turns to translate divinity into a form visible to all, why will it systematically and exclusively give the god the appearance of the human body? And what are the meaning and significance for religious thought of this valorization of the human figure, which appears at this time as the only one appropriate for representing the divine?

Jean Cuisenier has recalled here the interpretation proposed by Hegel to explain this anthropomorphism of divine images in classical Greek religion.[9] Yet what is the exact import of the term "anthropomorphism?" Does it mean that for the Greeks the gods were conceived of and represented in the image of human beings? To me it seems the opposite — that the human body became perceptible to Greek eyes when it was in the flower of its youth, when it was like an image or a reflection of the divine.

Athletic exercises must have greatly helped to valorize the human body. Nakedness is already an important fact. The first masculine statues in Greece are naked like the athlete in the field or palaestra. But the essential issue resides in the dual nature of the games, both spectacle and religious festival — national spectacle, one might say, which joins and opposes the diverse cities in a great public competition. Each city is engaged in a struggle in which the victor represents his community more than he does himself. Religious festival too: the contests are sacred ceremonies. In civic religion and in this Panhellenic religion the games helped shape and in

344

which they take pride of place, the memory of those ritual functions that the *agōn* might well have once had is doubtless lost and gone. But the contest retains its value as an ordeal. Victory *consecrates* the victor in the full sense of the word. It suffuses his person with sacred prestige. In the form of ritual scenario that is the contest, the triumph of the athlete, as seen in Pindar, evokes and extends the exploit accomplished by the hero and the gods; it raises man to the level of the divine. And those physical qualities — youth, force, swiftness, agility, skill, and beauty — that the victor must display in the course of the *agōn*, and which, in the eyes of the public, his naked body incarnates, are still eminently religious values.

But the contests do not put only physical qualities to the test. Other aspects of the body, which the games present in a religious light to the gaze of the spectators, are also affirmed. When the Ionians participated in boxing, in dance, and in song, when they celebrated the games, "any chance arrival would think them to be immortals and exempt forever from old age, for he would see the grace in all of them."[10] Grace, *charis*: all of a sudden, there shines through the beauty of the human body, like a reflection in a mirror, a value that belongs to the divine which is at the very opposite extreme from a monstrous sacredness. Fashioned in marble, bronze, or gold, the image of the human body must in turn make *charis* into something that can be seen: brightness, luminous brilliance, and the radiance of an unchanging youthfulness.

The horrible grimace of Gorgon symbolizes the powers of terror, chaos, and death. On the opposite side, but in as conventional a manner as the rictus of the mask, the smile on the human figure signifies *charis*-the brightness that divinity bestows in this world below on the body of a human being, when that person, in the flower of his or her youth, reflects the nature of those called the Fortunate Ones, of one such as Aphrodite, who is called the Smiling One.

At Lesbos, a public contest consecrated this religious value of corporeal beauty. During a festival called Kallisteia, a beauty contest, the seven most beautiful girls were chosen and grouped into a chorus resembling that of the Seven Muses, goddesses to whom the same city rendered a cult.[11] The Olympic victor also, Philip of Kroton, the most beautiful Greek of his time according to Herotodus tells us, was heroized after his death by the inhabitants of Segesta because of his beauty just as other athletes were honored for their strength or stature.[12]

What we call physical qualities can then appear to Greek religious consciousness as values that transcend the human, as powers of divine origin. in human existence they have only a precarious and inconstant reality, marked with the sign of evanescence. Only the gods possess these qualities in their plenitude as permanent assets inseparable from their nature.

The size, smile, and beauty of corporeal forms of the *kouros* and the *korē*, along with the movement their bodies suggest, express these powers of life — a life always present, always vivid. The image of the gods fixed by the anthropomorphic statue is that of the immortals, the Happy Ones, the forever young, those who in the purity of their existence are utterly alien to decline, corruption, and death.

The Figure of the Deceased

A second problem immediately follows. If the archaic statue uses the human figure to convey this set of "values" that in their plenitude only belong to divinity and appear like a fragile reflection when they gleam on the body of mortals, we can then understand how the same image, the votive *kouros*, can sometimes represent the god himself and sometimes a human person who, by virtue of his victory in the Games or through some other consecration, is revealed as "equal to the gods." But how does it happen that, when erected over a tomb or sculpted on a stela, this very same *kouros* can also have a funerary function and be capable of representing a dead person? I have treated this point at length in various articles and studies devoted to the relation between the archaic funerary figure and "beautiful death," *kalos thanatos*. This is the kind of demise that guarantees an imperishable glory for the young warrior fallen on the battlefield in the flower of his age by maintaining in the memory of successive generations the perpetual recollection of what he was: his name, exploits, career in life, and the heroic end that established him forever in his status as the "beautiful dead," the excellent man, *agathos anēr*, fully and definitively complete. A few words then will suffice to recall the essential points needed for our conclusions.

Until the end of the seventh century, Attica maintained a type of stela very close to that which Homeric epic describes: a stone, more or less squared off, that marks the place of the tomb. This stone already assumes a memorial function. In its upright position, fixed, permanent, and immutable, it evokes the dead person whose ashes repose underground by emphasizing that, despite his death — his absence — he remains and will remain always present in the memory of men. It is in the course of the sixth century, in a context both civic and aristocratic, that different types of representational steles and the series of funerary *kouroi* develop. Death is no longer evoked by the brute stone that has no inscription, but by the visible beauty of a corporeal form that the stone fixes forever with a name, as death fixed it on the corpse of the young heroic warrior whom all admire, because in him, even or especially when he is dead, as Homer and Tyrtaeus say, "everything is fitting, everything is beautiful," *panta kala*.

The figures on the stela or the funerary *kouros* are erected on the tomb "in place of" what the living person was, did, and merited. "In place of," *anti*, signifies that the figure is substituted for a person as his or her "equivalent," that, in a certain sense, it does the same thing the living person used to do (as in the inscription on the late fifth-century stela of Ampharete: "This is the dear child of my daughter whom I hold here, the one I held on my knees when we were alive and looked upon the light of the sun; and still I hold him now that we are both dead"),[12] and thus possesses the same beauty and the same value. Yet it implies simultaneously the inverse: a new mode of being, different than the old one, namely, the status of a dead person that the deceased has acquired by disappearing forever from the light of the sun.[13] "I am set up here in Parian marble, in place of a woman, *anti gunaikos*; in memory of Bitte, but for her mother, tears of mourning,"

347

proclaims a funerary inscription of Amorgos in the middle of the fifth century.[14] "In place of a woman": but the formula with its variants makes clear that the person, whose substitute takes her place, is not envisaged in anything other than the qualities she once had. It is "in place of her youth and beauty" that the spouse of the young Dionysia comes to adorn her funerary monument, "in place of her noble character" that the husband of Aspasia builds a *mnēma* for this exemplary woman (*esthlē*), "in place of his virtue and wisdom" that his father, Kleoboulos, erected a *sēma* for the dead Xenophantos.[15] In the figural representation of the dead person, the beauty of the deceased is perpetuated by the beauty of the image as its equivalent. "Your mother has set upon this marble tomb a young virgin who your height and your beauty, Theris," we read in a funerary epigram of the *Palatine Anthology*.[16] A stela at Athens that crowns the tomb of a young man recommends that the passerby weep that so beautiful a boy had died, *hōs kalos ōn ethane*. It is on the monument that this youthful beauty, preserved by death before it could fade, can continue to be seen throughout the succession of ages. On a *korē* of the middle of the sixth century, the work of Phaidimos, one can read: "He [the father] raised me here, the *sēma* of his daughter Phile, beautiful to look upon," and on an inscription of Thasos, at the end of the sixth: "Beautiful is the *mnēma* that her father built for the deceased Leorete, for we will never see her alive again."[17]

For the image to acquire the psychological significance of a copy that imitates a model and gives the spectator an illusion of reality, the human figure must have ceased to incarnate religious values; in its appearance, it must have become in and for itself the model to be reproduced. The whole development of sculptural technique orients the image in this direction. But as a result, the new form of plastic language challenges the ancient system of representation. By bringing out the body's properly human dimension, sculpture initiated a crisis for the divine image. The progressive advances in the making of statues must have also aroused a distrustful reaction, as evidenced by the work of Plato: nostalgia for ancient divine symbols, attachment to the most tra-

348

ditional forms of representing the gods, and reservations about all kinds of figuration of the divine. Once it ceases to incarnate the invisible, the beyond, and the divine, the image cannot be constituted as an imitation of appearance without having also aroused anxiety and criticism.

As for the status and destiny of the image in the West, it must be recalled again that by the third century of our era, Plotinus marks the start of another turning point. The image, instead of being defined as an imitation of appearance, will be interpreted philosophically and theologically and, at the same time, will be treated in its artistic form as an expression of essence. Once again and for a long time to come the image will be given the task of representing the invisible.

PART SIX
Personal Identity
and Religion

Chapter Sixteen

Some Aspects of Personal Identity

in Greek Religion

We call the great deities of the Greek pantheon "personal gods," and the expression does not appear to arouse objections. It implies, however, that the Greeks understood the "person" in the sense that we do today, and that they organized all or a large part of their religious experience around this idea. A characteristic feature of Greek religion is to give to the powers of the beyond a distinctive individual form and a fully human appearance. But does this make them "persons," and are the links that unite them in worship with the faithful "personal" relationships? Was the society of the gods, for the Greeks, really made up of individual and unique figures—individuals completely defined by their personalities, individuals possessing an inner existence, manifesting themselves as focus and source of action, as responsible agents? In short, we must ask to what extent the individualization and humanization of the supernatural powers imply a concept of personal identity. What aspects of the ego, of the inner man, did Greek religion help to define and form, and with what aspects was it quite unfamiliar?

In the context of public worship and the religion of the city, the answer is quite clear. Religious life was an integral part of the social and political life of which it is but one aspect. Between the priesthood and the magistracy, there are less difference and opposition than equivalence and reciprocity. The priesthood is a magistracy, and every magistracy has a religious side to it. There is no break, no discontinuity, between the gods and the city or between religious qualities and civic virtues. Impiety (*asebeia*), wronging the gods, is equally an affront to the social group, a crime against the city. In this context, the individual establishes a relationship with the divine through his membership in the community. The religious agent operates as the representative of the group, in the name of, within, and through this group. Society always acts as the mediating link between the faithful and the god. It is not a direct interaction between two individual personalities but the expression of the relationship that links a god to a human group — a particular household, a city, a type of activity, a certain place in the land. If the individual is banished from the domestic altars, excluded from the temples of his town, and exiled from his fatherland, he is thereby cut off from the world of the divine. He loses both his social identity and his religious essence: he is reduced to nothing. To regain his status as a man, he must present himself as a suppliant at other altars, sit at the hearths of other houses, and become integrated into new groups, so that, through participation in their worship, he can reestablish the links that anchor him to the divine.

This type of political religion is so familiar that we need not dwell on it here. But it does not exhaust the whole experience of Greek religion. One prominent aspect of this experience is the social integration of a civic religion whose function is to conse-crate the existing order, in both its human and its natural aspects, and to allow individuals to adjust to it. But this is contrasted with another aspect, which inverts and complements the first and which we can describe roughly by saying that it is expressed in Dionysianism. It is significant that the Dionysian religion makes its appeal principally to those who do not altogether fit into the institutional organization of the *polis*. It is first and foremost the province of women.[1] Women, as such, are excluded from political life. The religious quality that equips them to play the major role of the Bacchae in the Dionysian religion is the reverse of the infe-riority with which they are branded in the political sphere, and which prohibits them from participating on an equal footing with men in directing the city's affairs. In the worship of Dionysos, slaves too find the place they are normally denied.[2] Finally, the very terms *thiasoi* and *orgeones*, which are applied to the colleges of devotees associated with the orgies, recall the rural groups of the original demes. These were opposed to the noble *gēnē* who lived in the city and controlled the state, and they had a hard fight to gain admittance to the phratries of the historical period.[3] Therefore, at an early date, the Dionysian tendency in religion provided a group framework for those who found themselves on the periphery of the recognized social order. Some of the religious titles that applied to the god, such as *eleutherios* and *lusios*, testify to this convergence of the social and the religious within a shared aspiration for freedom and deliverance. Even during the classical period, when it was controlled by the state, the Dionysian cult offered its faithful a religious experience that was the inverse of official worship: not the consecration of an order into which one must become integrated, but liberation from this order and from the constraints on which, in certain respects, it was based. The Dionysian cult represented a quest for a radically different experience, far removed from everyday life, ordinary occupations, and imposed servitude. It attempted to abolish all restrictions, to do away with all the barriers by which the organized world was defined: boundaries between man and god, natural and supernatural, human, animal, and vegetable, social barriers, and the boundaries of the ego. The civic cult corresponded to an ideal of *sōphrosunē*, based on control and self-discipline; each creature was to remain in its place, within the limits assigned to it. In contrast, the Dionysian religion cultivated delirium and madness — divine madness, which meant being taken over and possessed by the god. Through this *mania*, man frees himself from the order that, according to the official religion, constitutes the proper domain of the sacred, the *hieron*. Through an experience of ecstasy and enthusiasm, this order is revealed as merely an illusion, having no religious value at all. What the devotee thereafter seeks to attain through intimate contact with the divine is a different state, a state of total sanctity and purity, to which the term *hosios* is applied, indicating complete consecration and meaning, in the strict sense, a freedom with respect to the sacred.[4]

But is this fusion with the god a personal communion? Clearly not. It is reached not in solitude, through meditation, prayer, and dialogue with an internal god, but in a group, in and through the *thiasos*, using techniques of collective hysteria that involve dancing, leaping, singing, yelling, and wanderings that plunge man into the depths of wildest nature. In any case, being possessed is not the same as communion.[5] The god who suddenly takes possession of a man in the midst of paroxysms of excitement makes him lose possession of himself, "overrides" him, and even when he has taken charge of him, remains inaccessible and incomprehensible. For Dionysos is a master of magic and illusion; a god of wonders, perplexing and disconcerting, never where he is nor what he is, essentially elusive, the only one of all the Greek deities, it has been said, that no form could contain, no definition encompass, because, both within man and in nature, he embodies what is radically Other.[6]

Therefore, a "personal" type of relationship between man and god will not be found in Dionysianism. The mystery religions may, however, prove more relevant to this inquiry, for in them, religious life may have taken on a more individual character. A mystery established a community that was not social but spiritual, in which each individual participated of his own free will, through free association, and regardless of his civic status. The mystery does not only address the individual as such; it also offers him an exceptional religious privilege, a spiritual election that removes him from the common destiny of man and assures him a better fate in the beyond. It is therefore not surprising to find that communion with the god plays a central part in the organization of the mystery religions. However, the symbolism through which this communion is expressed refers not to an exchange of love between two beings, a spiritual intimacy, but to social or familial relationships whereby the initiate becomes the deity's son, adopted child, or spouse. Do these formulas express, in traditional terms, a truly intimate bond? It is difficult to believe this. The "royal" legends feature the themes of adoption, filial relationships, and sexual unions with the gods. They are used to justify the sacred prerogatives of certain families and as the foundation for religious powers and privileges — blessed immortality in particular — that these families possess by reason of some special familiarity and individual connections with the deity. This divine "favor" was the prerogative of the noble *genē*, some of whom, such as the Eumolpidae and the Kerykes at Eleusis, retained control over the administration of the mysteries. The initiation cults now offered this favor to the public, thus operating a kind of popularization or democratization of what had originally been the exclusive prerogative of a religious aristocracy. The initiations do not appear to have involved the kinds of spiritual exercises or ascetic techniques transform a man from within. They operated almost automatically through formulas, rites, and spectacles. True, the initiate must have felt personally involved in the divine drama, parts of which were represented in mime before his eyes. There are descriptions of his being overwhelmed, passing from a state of tension and anxiety to a feeling of freedom and joy.[7] But there is no indication of any teaching or doctrine that would have been able to give this emotional moment of participation enough cohesion, consistency, and permanence to turn it into a religion of the soul. In fact, the mysteries, like the Dionysian religion, show no particular interest in the soul. They are not concerned with defining either its nature or its powers.[8] A doctrine of the *psuchē* was to develop in quite different circles, in connection with certain spiritual techniques.

Once again, then, the results are negative, although it is tempting to qualify them by taking into account certain pieces of literary evidence that are more engaged in concrete realities, such as those provided by Euripides's *Hippolytus*.[9] There is an element of personal affection in the young man's exclusive devotion to Artemis, and the goddess does not fail to respond to this. Between the deity and her worshipper there are bonds of friendship) *philia*, a passionate intimacy *homilia*, and constant exchange,

357

expressed by the verb *suneinai*. Although she is invisible, like all the gods, Artemis is present at Hippolytus's side: he hears her voice, he speaks to her, and she replies. However, Euripides is careful to stress the exceptional and unusual nature of this relationship with the divine. The very fact that Hippolytus enjoys such an intimacy with the goddess singles him out as a special case. He declares to Artemis: "I alone, of all mortals, enjoy the privilege of living at your side and of conversing with you."[10] It is a privilege that is not without its dangers. It implies a proud uniqueness in his behavior, a way of life that no Greek could approve of and that Theseus found easy to associate with the eccentricities of the followers of Orpheus.[11] Hippolytus wants to be pure, but with the purity of a god rather than that of a man. His virtue is too haughty and strained. He believes he can deny and despise a whole side of human nature.[12] One of Theseus's remarks underlines the extent of the opposition between normal Greek piety and the religious inspiration of Hippolytus. (It is not that normal Greek piety was unacquainted with such inspiration: it was familiar with it but saw it as a temptation to be refused; it was something that could only find fulfillment within the sects or be transposed into philosophy.) Theseus reproaches his son for practicing an *askēsis* that turns away from true piety, which involves submission to the traditional order of values, in particular with regard to the respect a son owes his parents.[13] He points out that this excessive and forced asceticism — the means whereby he achieves intimacy with the divine, according to Hippolytus — is in reality nothing but a cult devoted to himself: *sauton sebein*. Theseus interprets the "personal" aspect of his son's religious attitude as necessarily including an element of hubris. And indeed, this immoderation is punished by the anger of the gods, through the resentment of the insulted Aphrodite.[14] However familiar Hippolytus claims to have been with Artemis, the last word of the tragedy maintains and asserts the distance between gods and men. Hippolytus has just been brought back, wounded and bleeding. He sees the gates of Hades opening before him. Suddenly, Artemis appears at his side. The young man recognizes her and enters into a last loving and impassioned dialogue: "Oh, my mistress, do you see my wretched state?" And how does the goddess reply? "I see it, but tears are forbidden to my eyes."[15] *Ou themis*: it would be contrary to order for the eyes of a god to weep over the wretchedness of mortals. Soon the goddess leaves Hippolytus. She abandons him in the face of death: she has no right to defile her gaze with the spectacle of a dying man or a corpse.[16] Just when Hippolytus needs her divine presence at his side more than ever, Artemis leaves him and withdraws into the divine world, which has no knowledge of the all-too-human realities of suffering, sickness, and death. If such a thing as intimacy or communion with a god can exist, it cannot operate on the level of the individual's personal destiny, his status as a man. When the decisive moment comes, it is not Artemis but Theseus, repentant and forgiven, who cradles Hippolytus's head and receives his dying breath.[17]

The case of Hippolytus was a special one, an example of the direct link and loving intimacy that can unite a Greek deity and her devotee. Yet even in this case the relationship between the man and the deity seems circumscribed in a way that precludes certain essential personal elements. The relevance of expressions such as "personal gods" in reference to archaic and classical Greece is therefore called into question. The Greek pantheon was constituted during a period when the opposition between human beings and natural forces, the idea of a purely spiritual form of existence and an inner dimension to man, had not yet been formulated.[18] The Greek gods are powers, not persons. Religious thought is a response to the problems of organizing and classifying these powers. It distinguishes among various types of supernatural powers, each with its own dynamic and mode of action, its own sphere and limitations. It imagines the complex interplay of their relations in terms of hierarchy, balance, opposition, and complementarity. It is not concerned with their personal or nonpersonal aspects.[19] True, the divine world is composed not of vague and anonymous forces but of well-defined figures, each with its own name and status, its own attributes, and its own characteristic adventures. But that is not to say that this world is

359

composed of separate individuals, autonomous focuses of existence and action, ontological units — persons, in our sense of the
word. A divine power does not really have any existence of its
own. It exists only by virtue of the network of relationships that
makes it a part of the divine system as a whole. And within this
network, it is not necessarily a single entity but can equally well
be plural, either an indefinite plurality or a fixed number of figures. For us, a single person cannot be several: one term excludes
the other. But for the religious consciousness of the Greeks, there
is no radical incompatibility between them.[20] It has often been
noted that when describing a divine power Greek writers go from
the singular to the plural and vice versa without difficulty, even
within a single sentence.[21] Similarly, the Greeks can imagine
Charis as a single deity or the Charites in the plural, either as an
indivisible group without any distinction among the plurality of
powers within it, or as a set of three deities, each of which is individualized to some degree and has its own name. Even the most
individualized figures, such as Zeus and Hera, are not so unified
that one cannot speak of a double or triple Zeus or Hera.[22] On
occasion, depending on the demands of the situation, the same
divine power may be imagined as a unity, in the singular, or as a
multiplicity, in the plural. Similarly, even the collection of different supernatural powers that together make up the entire society
of the gods can be considered in the singular form, *ho theos*, the
divine power, the god, although this does not mean there is any
suggestion of monotheism here. Furthermore, in cultic practices,
there was not the one unique figure of Zeus that mythology has
made familiar but rather a whole series of Zeuses, each individualized by his particular cult title. These differed widely in their
religious significance, yet each certainly was, in some way, Zeus.[23]
The reason for this paradox is precisely that a god expresses the
different aspects and modes of action of a power, rather than of
any personal form of existence. From the point of view of a
power, the opposition between the particular and the universal,
or the concrete and the abstract, is irrelevant.[24] Aphrodite is a
beauty, a particular goddess, but at the same time she is beauty —

what we would call the essence of beauty — that is, the power that is present in all beautiful things and through which they are made beautiful. Erwin Rohde has pointed out that the Greeks conceived of not the divine person but rather the divine essence as a unity, and Leopold Schmidt very correctly wrote: "For anyone born a Greek and thinking like a Greek, the idea of a clear antithesis between unity and plurality is put aside where the supernatural beings are concerned. He has no difficulty in conceiving unity of action divorced from any unity of person."[25]

We should not be misled by the Greek god's anthropomorphism any more than by his apparent individuality, for the anthropomorphism, too, is strictly limited.[26] A divine power always represents a complex of cosmic, social, and human features that are not clearly distinguished. For the Greeks, Zeus is related, first, to various forms of sovereignty or power over others; second, to certain human attitudes and forms of behavior, such as the respect shown to suppliants and strangers, contracts, oaths, and marriage; third, to the sky, light, lightning, rain, mountaintops, and certain trees. These phenomena, which seem so diverse to us, are related to one another in Greek religious thought in that each, in its own way, is an expression of a different aspect of the same power. The figuration of the god in fully human form does not affect this fundamental fact, which is an element of religious symbolism that must be accurately interpreted in its precise context. The idol is not a portrait of the god: the gods have no bodies. Their essence is to be invisible, always beyond the forms in which they manifest themselves or in which they are made present in temples. The relationship between the deity and its cult symbol — whether it is anthropomorphic, zoomorphic, or aniconic — has nothing to do with the relationship between a man's body and his ego. Originally, in Greece, the great anthropomorphic cult statue was of the *kouros* or *korē* type: it represented not a particular subject, a divine or human individual, but an impersonal type, the young man or the young girl. It depicted and presented the form of the human body in general. This is because, from this perspective, the body is not linked to an ego, the incarnation of one person.

Rather, it is charged with religious significance and expresses certain powers: beauty, charm (*charis*), brilliance, youth, health, strength, life, movement, and so forth, which are really properties of the deity, and which the human body, more than any other, reflects when, in the flower of youth, it is as if lit up by a divine light. Thus the problems raised by the anthropomorphic representation of the gods in Greece remain, essentially, outside the sphere of personal identity.

There were, apart from the gods, other supernatural powers the Greeks worshipped. In the first place, there were the dead. To what extent did the cult of the dead concern the personal identities of those who had died? Was its function to ensure the permanence of each human individual, as a unique being, beyond death? Not at all.[27] Its purpose was quite different: to maintain the continuity of the family group and the city. In the beyond, the dead become faceless, losing their distinctive features; each one is lost in an undifferentiated mass that reflects not what each one was in his lifetime but a general mode of being both opposed to and linked with life, the reservoir of power from which life is drawn and to which it returns in its cyclical movement. To the slight extent that the cult of the dead depends upon a belief in immortality, this is an impersonal immortality. The epithet that Hesiod uses to describe the status of the dead in Hades is *nōnumnoi*: nameless.[28]

In addition, there are the heroes. In the classical period, these form a fairly well-defined religious category that is opposed both to the dead and to the gods. Unlike the dead, the hero keeps his own name and his individual appearance in the beyond; his individuality stands out from the anonymous mass of the deceased.[29] And, in contrast to the gods, he was seen by the Greeks as a man who had been alive and who was promoted to a quasi-divine status when consecrated at his death. The hero is a "special" individual; he is exceptional and more than human, but he must nevertheless embrace the human condition. He is familiar with human vicissitudes, trials, and limitations, and he must confront suffering and death. What distinguishes him, even in the midst of

362

his human destiny, is the actions he dares to undertake and successfully performs: his exploits. The heroic exploit epitomizes all the virtues and dangers involved in human action. In a way, it represents action in an exemplary form. Thus it encompasses actions that create, innovate, or initiate (as when the hero civilizes, invents, or founds cities or noble lineages); actions that, in critical conditions and at the crucial moment, ensure victory or restore the order that is threatened (as when the hero fights a monster); and actions that, by overcoming the normal limitations and ignoring all the normal prohibitions, transcend the human condition, and, like a river returning to its source, join the divine power once more (as in the cases of the sacrilegious hero, the descent to the underworld, or victory over death).

It would appear, then, that the Greeks used stories about the heroes to express problems connected with human action and its place in the order of the world. Indeed, during the short period when tragedy flourished in Greece, it used legends about the heroes to present certain aspects of man in action, at the crossroads of decision, grappling with the consequences of his actions. Even when it used stories from the heroic tradition, however, tragedy differed from the cults and the myths of the heroes. It transformed these stories for its own purposes, for at this stage in their history the Greeks posed questions about man himself, his place with regard to fate, his responsibility for actions whose beginning and end are beyond him, the ambiguous values of the things among which he must choose, and the need to decide nonetheless.

But outside the sphere of tragedy, on the more specifically religious level that is the object of the present study, the heroic stories appear in a very different light. In their cults, the heroes' individuality becomes blurred or disappears. Some heroes are totally anonymous and are referred to, as in the case of the hero of Marathon, by the name of the place where they are buried and which they are believed to protect.[30] There are many others whose individual personality is unknown in the cult, which sees them only in terms of the narrowly specialized function over which they preside.[31] Paradoxically, Hermann Usener finds more examples among the heroes than anywhere else to illustrate his theories about functional gods.[32] There are the doctor hero, the doorkeeper, the cook, the fly-catcher, the key holder, the heroes of the meal, of beans, and of saffron, and heroes to mix wine with water, to grind grain, to guard borders, to protect roofs, to scare horses, and so on.

As for the legends about the heroes, they make the heroes stand out as individual figures in that they are the protagonists of tales with a more or less consecutive story, but the exploits recorded are valid in themselves and on their own account, quite apart from the hero performing them. The myths are never narrated in such a way as to present the problems from the agent's point of view: the hero does not plan, prepare, or look ahead; he does not have to organize the temporal sequence of his actions. When his exploits follow one after another, it cannot even be claimed that they are in a linked sequence or any definite order. Each trial is complete in itself; there is no connection between it and those that precede it, which it may repeat but to which it makes no new contribution, nor is there any tie between it and those that follow it, for which it is neither a preparation nor a necessary precondition.[33] How could the hero be responsible for a success that he never has to win or deserve? The heroic exploit is characterized by its gratuitous nature.[34] The source and origin of the action and the reason for its success are found not within the hero but outside him. He does not perform the impossible because he is a hero; rather, he is a hero because he has performed the impossible. The exploit is not the outcome of his personal excellence but the sign of some divine grace, the manifestation of supernatural assistance. The heroic legends do not present man as a responsible agent, in control of his actions and of his personal destiny. They describe certain types of exploits, model trials that echo ancient initiation ceremonies and that use the medium of exemplary human deeds to illustrate the conditions necessary to acquire exceptional religious qualifications and social privileges. The myths of the heroes convey the possibility, under certain conditions, of establishing a bridge between the world of men and that of the gods and of revealing the presence of the divine in the hero, through some trial. The known cases from the historical period of men being made heroes are most significant in this respect. They always show a man visited by a power, transfigured thanks to some religious quality, and exhibiting this *numen* either in his attributes, usually physical ones, or in the particular circumstances of his life or death. A man could be made a hero for his extraordinary beauty, his gigantic stature, his superhuman strength, or even for the magnitude of the crimes he is thought to have committed, for his mysterious disappearance without a trace, or for the mischief attributed to his ghost after his death. None of this has anything even remotely to do with personal identity.

Must we, then, at the end of this study, conclude purely and simply that the notion of personal identity was completely absent? To do so would be to ignore a whole aspect of Greek religion, which, even though it was in certain respects atypical, nevertheless played a decisive role at the very origins of personal identity and its history in the development of western man. On the periphery of official religion, in the sects, there developed between the sixth and fifth centuries a new concept of the soul, which was to come into its own in philosophical thought and which — to borrow one of Louis Gernet's expressions — held out hitherto "unheard-of possibilities for the ascent of man."[35] The soul in man is seen as an element that is foreign to earthly life, a being from elsewhere, an exile related to the divine. Before there could be any realization of a truly internal dimension to human experience, it was necessary to discover a mysterious and supernatural power within man, the soul or *daimōn*. The magi, those extraordinary figures whose role at the origins of philosophical thought has often been stressed, claimed to hold some power of mastery and control over the daemonic soul. By means of their ascetic practices and exercises in mental concentration, possibly connected with physical techniques — in particular the suspension of breathing — they claimed to concentrate and unite psychic powers normally dispersed throughout the individual and to separate at will from the body the soul that they had thus isolated and concentrated. They restored it for an instant to its homeland, where it recovered its divine nature before being made to redescend and be chained once more to the body.[36] The *psuchē* is no longer, as it was for Homer, that insubstantial wisp of smoke, a ghost without body or strength, which leaves man as he breathes his last. It is a power that exists at the very heart of the living man, that he controls and that it is his duty to develop, purify, and liberate. Once the *psuchē* has become the daemonic being in man with which he seeks to identify, it acquires the consistency of a real object, a real being that can exist on its own, a "double." But at the same time, it is part of the man himself and represents a new dimension to him that he must master and understand ever more deeply by submitting himself to a demanding spiritual discipline. The *psuchē* was both an objective reality and a subjective inner experience, and it provided the first framework within which the subjective world could be considered objectively and allowed to develop; it was a starting point for the progressive construction of the category of the ego.[37]

The fact that the category of personal identity had this religious origin in Greek civilization had two consequences. In the first place, the soul acquired its objectivity and true form of existence by being set in opposition to the body or even excluded from it. The discovery of an inner life went with a belief in the dualism of body and soul. The soul is defined as being the opposite of the body. It is fettered to it, as in a prison, buried within it, as in a tomb. Thus, at first, the body was excluded from the person and had nothing to do with a man's individuality.[38]

Second, since the soul is divine, it cannot express what characterizes human beings. Its destiny is to go beyond, to surpass, the individual. It is significant, in this connection, that it should belong to the category of the "daemonic," that is, paradoxically enough, to the least individualized, the least "personal" element of the divine. For example, Aristotle was to say that nature (*phusis*) is not divine but daemonic.[39] Thus, for the ancient Greeks, what defines the internal dimension of the subject is related to the mysterious power of life that animates nature as a whole and sets it in motion. It is clear that at this stage in its development personal identity was not concerned with the single individual, with his irreplaceable and unique qualities, or with man as distinguished from the rest of nature in his specifically human aspects. On the contrary, it is oriented toward the search for a coincidence and a fusion of the particulars and the whole. Even in the current of thought most opposed to the religion of the city and its spirit, there is a similar marked attempt to fit the human individual into an order that surpasses him. Even when a man does not directly participate in the social order conceived of as something sacred, even when he eludes it, this is not to assert his own value as an individual but to reenter an ordered whole through another route by identifying himself to the fullest extent possible with the divine.

Part Seven
From Myth to Reason

CHAPTER SEVENTEEN

The Formation of Positivist Thought
in Archaic Greece

Rational thought has, as it were, its official identity papers: we know its date and place of birth. It was in the sixth century BCE, in the Greek cities of Asia Minor, that a new, positivist type of reflection concerning nature emerged. John Burnet was expressing the accepted opinion on this subject when he remarked, "The early Ionian teachers opened the road which science has simply had to follow along ever since."[1] In this view, the birth of philosophy in Greece was seen as the beginning of scientific thought — or one might even say, thought itself. It is said that in the Milesian school *logos* was for the first time freed from myth, just as the scales fall from the eyes of a blind man; it was not so much a change in intellectual attitude, a mental mutation, as a single decisive and definitive revelation: the discovery of the mind.[2] It would accordingly be futile to seek the origins of rational thought in the past: true thought could have no origin outside itself. It lies outside history, so history can only account for the successive obstacles, mistakes, and illusions encountered in the development of the mind. This is the meaning of the Greek "miracle": in the thought of the Ionian philosophers, a nontemporal reason was embodied in time. The arrival of the *logos* is thus held to have introduced a radical discontinuity into history. Philosophy is seen as a traveler without luggage, entering the world without a past, without antecedents, without affiliations; it was an absolute beginning.

From this point of view, the Greeks are inevitably raised above all other peoples and seen as predestined, for in them the *logos* was made flesh. Burnet argued that the Greeks invented philosophy because of their exceptional intellectual qualities, their observational ability, and their powers of reasoning.[3] And, beyond Greek philosophy, this quasi-providential superiority is transmitted to the whole of Western thought, the offspring of Hellenism.

In the course of the last fifty years, however, the West's confidence in this monopoly on reason has been undermined. The crisis in contemporary physics and science has shaken the foundations — hitherto believed definitive — of classical logic. Contact with great civilizations with spiritual traditions different from our own, such as China and India, has shattered the framework of traditional humanism. Today, the West can no longer assume that its thought is the only thought or hail the dawn of Greek philosophy as that of the mind itself. At a time when rational thought is anxious about its future and is questioning its basic principles, it turns back to examine its origins. It poses questions about its own past in order to situate and understand itself historically.

Two dates stand out as landmarks in this inquiry. In 1912, Francis Macdonald Cornford published *From Religion to Philosophy*, in which he tried for the first time to define the link between religious thought and the beginnings of rational knowledge. He did not return to the problem until much later, toward the end of his life. Thus it was not until 1952 — nine years after his death — that his studies establishing the mythical and ritual origins of the first Greek philosophy were published, under the title *Principium Sapientiae: The Origins of Greek Philosophical Thought*.[4]

In opposition to Burnet, Cornford shows that Ionian "physics" has nothing in common with what we today call science. It knew nothing at all of experimentation; nor was it the product of an intelligence directly observing nature. It transposed into a secular form, and onto a more abstract level of thought, the system of representaton elaborated by religion. The cosmological myths are taken up and extended by the cosmologies of the philosophers.

They provide an answer to the same type of question: how did an ordered world emerge from chaos? And they work with analogous concepts: behind the "elements" of the Ionians can be discerned the ancient deities of mythology. In becoming nature, the elements shed their aspect of individualized gods; but they remain active powers, animated and imperishable, and still felt to be divine. Homer's world was organized according to a distribution of honors and spheres of influence among the gods: for Zeus, the "ethereal" sky (*aithēr*, fire); for Hades, the "misty" shadow (*aēr*, air); for Poseidon, the sea; all three share Gaia, the earth, on which men live and die.[5] The cosmos of the Ionians is organized by dividing up the various provinces and by sharing out the seasons between opposed powers that counterbalance each other.

This is no vague analogy. Cornford shows that the philosophy of Anaximander and Hesiod's *Theogony* have such similar structures that even their details correspond.[6] Furthermore, the process of conceptual development that culminates in Anaximander's naturalistic system was already at work in Hesiod's religious hymn of praise to Zeus. The same mythical theme of setting the world in order is in fact expressed in two different ways, reflecting two different levels of abstraction.

In the first version, the myth recounts the adventures of divine figures.[7] Zeus fights for sovereignty against Typhon, the dragon with a thousand voices, the power of confusion and disorder. Zeus kills the monster, whose corpse gives birth to the winds that blow in the space separating sky from earth. The gods press Zeus to assume the power and throne of the immortals, and he apportions honors among them. In this form, the myth remains very close to the ritual drama that it illustrates, the model for which is found in the royal festival of the new year, in the month of Nisan, in Babylon.[8] At the end of a temporal cycle — a great year — the king must reaffirm his sovereign power, which is called into question by the revolution of time, by which the world returns to its point of departure.[9] The royal trial and victory, which are ritually mimed in a struggle against a dragon, stand for the recreation of the cosmic, seasonal, and social order.

373

The king is at the center of the world, just as he is at the center of his people. Each year he repeats the exploit accomplished by Marduk that is celebrated in a hymn, the *Enuma Elish*, sung on the fourth day of the festival: Marduk's victory over Tiamat, the female monster that embodies the powers of disorder, the return to the inchoate, in short, chaos. Marduk is proclaimed king of the gods and slays Tiamat with the help of the winds, which lodge themselves inside the monster. Once she is dead, Marduk splits her open like an oyster and throws one half up in the air, fixing it there to form the sky. He then sets the place and movement of the stars, fixes the year and the months, creates the human race, and apportions privileges and destinies. The thought expressed through the Babylonian rite and myth does not yet clearly distinguish between man, the world, and the gods. Divine power is concentrated in the person of the king. Setting the world in order and organizing the seasonal cycle appear to be integral parts of royal activity. They are aspects of the function of kingship. Nature and society are fused.

In contrast, in another passage from Hesiod's poem, the account of the creation of order is totally devoid of mythical imagery, and the protagonists' names are sufficiently transparent to reveal the "natural" character of the process that culminates in the organization of the cosmos.[10] In the beginning was chaos, the dark abyss, the airy void in which nothing is distinguished from anything else. *Chaos* must open up like a huge mouth (*chaos* is linked etymologically with *chasma*: the yawning chasm, *chainō*, *chaskō*, *chasmōmai* to open, to gape, to yawn) so that light (*aithēr*) and day, following night, can enter it, illuminating the space between Gaia (earth) and Ouranos (sky), which are henceforth set apart from each other. The emergence of the world proceeds with the appearance of Pontos (sea) which comes forth in turn from Gaia. Hesiod stresses that all these successive births come about without Ērōs (love), that is, not through union but through separation.[11] Ērōs is the principle that brings opposites together — the male and the female, for instance — and binds them to one another. But before this principle comes into operation, genesis comes about through separating elements that were previously united and fused (*Gaia* gives birth to *Ouranos* and *Pontos*).

In this second version of the myth can be seen the structure of thought that serves as a model for all Ionian physics. Cornford gives the following schematic analysis. First, there is an indistinct state where nothing appears. Second, from this primordial unity, through a process of separation, pairs of opposites — hot and cold, dry and wet — emerge that will differentiate four provinces in space, namely, the fiery sky, the cold air, the dry earth, and the wet sea. Third, the opposites unite and interact, each one in turn dominating the others, following a cycle that is renewed indefinitely, through meteorological phenomena, the sequence of the seasons, the birth and death of all that lives — plants, animals, and men.[12]

The fundamental concepts that the construction of Ionian philosophy is based on — the separation out from a primordial unity, the constant struggle and union of opposites, and an eternal cycle of change — reveal the ground of mythical thought in which the Ionians' cosmology is rooted.[13] The philosophers did not have to invent a system to explain the world: they found one ready-made. Cornford's work marks a turning point in the method of approaching the problem of the origins of philosophy and rational thought. Because he was obliged to counter the theory of the Greek miracle that presented Ionian physics as a sudden, spontaneous revelation of reason, Cornford was essentially concerned with reestablishing the thread of historical continuity between philosophy and the religious thought that had preceded it. This led him to look for aspects that persisted in both and to emphasize what could be recognized as common to both. His work sometimes even suggests that the philosophers were content to repeat in a different language what had already been expressed in myth. Now that, thanks to Cornford, the connection between them is known, the problem necessarily assumes a new form. What has to be done now is not simply to recognize the ancient elements that survive in philosophy but also to distinguish those that are truly new, in other words, what makes philosophy cease to be myth and become philosophy. The transformation of thought in the earliest Greek philosophy must be defined and its nature, scope, limitations, and historical conditions described.

Cornford was not unaware of this aspect of the question. It is reasonable to believe that he would have developed his ideas on it more fully had he been able to complete his last work. He expressed the view that myth is rationalized in philosophy.[14] But what does this mean? It means, in the first place, that it took the form of an explicitly formulated problem. Myths were accounts, not solutions to problems. They told of the sequence of actions by which the king or the god imposed order, as these actions were mimed out in ritual. The problem found its solution without ever having been posed. However, in Greece, where the new political forms had triumphed with the development of the city, only a few traces of the ancient royal rituals remained, and even their meaning had been lost.[15] The memory of the king as creator of order and maker of time had disappeared.[16] The connection is no longer apparent between the mythical exploit of the sovereign, symbolized by his victory over the monster, and the organization of cosmic phenomena. When the natural order and atmospheric phenomena (rains, winds, storms, and thunderbolts) become independent from the functions of the king, they cease to be intelligible in the language of myth in which they had been described hitherto. They are henceforth seen as questions open for discussion. These questions (the genesis of the cosmic order and the explanation for *meteōra*), in their new form as problems, constitute the subject matter for the earliest philosophical thought. Thus the philosopher takes over from the old king-magician, the master of time. He constructs a theory to explain the very phenomena that in times past the king had brought about.[17]

Hesiod dissociates the royal function from the cosmic order. Zeus's fight against Typhon for the title of king of the gods has lost its cosmogonic meaning. All of Cornford's learning was needed to discern that the winds born from Typhon's body are the same winds that are engulfed inside Tiamat and separate the heavens from the earth. Conversely, the account of the genesis of the world describes a natural process with no connection to ritual. Nevertheless, despite its attempts at conceptual clarification, Hesiod's thought remains mythic. True, *Ouranos*, *Gaia*, and *Pontos* are physical realities, in their concrete aspects of sky, earth, and sea; but they are also divine powers whose actions are analogous to those of men. Mythic logic rests on this ambiguity, operating on two levels at once: thus the same phenomenon — for example, the separation of earth from water — is understood simultaneously as a natural fact in the visible world and as a divine birth at the beginning of time. In contrast, for the Milesians — as Cornford remarks, following Werner Jaeger — Okeanos and Gaia have shed all their anthropomorphic features and have become purely and simply water and earth.[18] Expressed in this form, this remark seems rather hasty. The Milesian elements may not be mythic figures such as Gaia, but they are not concrete realities such as earth either. They are eternally active powers, at once divine and natural. What is new, conceptually, is that these powers are strictly delimited and abstractly conceived: they are restricted to producing a definite physical effect, and this effect is a general abstract quality. In place of earth and fire, or under those names, the Milesians postulate the qualities dry and hot, turning them into nouns by the new use of the article *to* — the hot — and thereby objectifying them and treating them as substances.[19] The hot is a reality wholly defined by the action of heating and no longer needs a mythic counterpart such as Hephaistos to convey its aspect as a "power." The forces that produced and that animate the cosmos thus operate on the same level and in the same manner as those that we see at work each day, when rain moistens the earth or when fire dries a wet garment. The original, the primordial, are stripped of their mystery and acquire the reassuring banality of everyday matters. The world of the Ionians, this world "full of gods," is at the same time fully natural.

In this respect, the revolution is so extensive and carries thought so far that philosophy's subsequent developments seem to reverse this process somewhat. With the physicists, a certain positivity suddenly invaded the totality of being, including man and the gods. There was nothing real that was not nature.[20] And, removed from its mythic background, nature itself became a problem, a subject for rational discussion. Nature, *phusis*, is the power of life and movement. As long as there was no distinction between the two meanings of *phuein*, "to produce" and "to give birth to," they remained fused, as did the two meanings of *genesis*, origin and birth; the explanation of becoming was thus based on the mythical image of sexual union.[21] Understanding meant finding the father and mother, tracing the genealogical tree. But for the Ionians, the natural elements, now conceived of as abstractions, can no longer be united by marriage, the way men can. Thus cosmology involves a change not only in language but also in content. Instead of telling of successive births, it describes first principles, the constituents of being. It changes from a historical account into a system that reveals the deep structure of reality. The problem of *genesis*, of becoming, is transformed into an inquiry seeking what lies beyond the changeable, that which is stable, permanent, and identical. At the same time, the concept of *phusis* is subjected to a critical appraisal that progressively strips it of all that it still borrowed from myth. In order to account for the changes in the cosmos, men increasingly appealed to the models provided by ingenious technical constructions, instead of referring to animal life or the growth of plants. Man understands better, and in a different way, what he himself has constructed. The movements of a machine are explained by the permanent structure of matter, not by changes produced by vital forces.[22] The old mythical concept of a struggle between qualitatively opposed powers that brings about the genesis of things gives way in Anaximenes to a mechanical sorting of the elements, which are now differentiated from each other only in quantitative terms. The sphere of *phusis* becomes more precise and limited. Once it is conceived of as a mechanism, the world gradually loses the divine element that animated it, according to the first physicists. By the same token, the problem of the origin of movement arises; the divine becomes concentrated outside nature, in opposition to nature, moving and controlling it from outside, as does Anaxagoras's *Nous*.[23]

At this point, Ionian physics joined a different current of

thought, one that was in many respects opposed to it.[24] One might almost say that it provides support for it, since these two emerging forms of philosophy, despite all their contrasts, seem to complement one another. In Italy, in Magna Graecia, philosophers emphasized not the unity of *phusis* but the duality of man, apprehended in an experience as much religious as philosophical. They claimed that there was a human soul that is different from the body, opposed to it, and that is the guiding force as the divine is for nature. The soul possesses a dimension that is not spatial, and a form of action and movement — namely, thought — that does not involve the movement of anything material.[25] Since it is related to the divine, the soul can, in certain conditions, apprehend it, be rejoined with it, unite with it, and gain an existence liberated from time and change.

Behind nature there is an invisible background, a reality that is more true, secret, and hidden, which the soul of the philosopher grasps by revelation and which is the opposite of *phusis*. Thus, with the very first step it takes, rational thought seems to return to myth.[26] But it only seems to do so; in adapting a structure of mythical thought to its own purposes, it in fact leaves its point of departure behind. The dual views of *phusis* and the resulting distinctions between several levels of reality emphasize and clarify the separation between nature, gods, and men, a separation that is the prior condition for rational thought. In myth, the diversity of levels of thought concealed an ambiguity that allowed these spheres to be confused. Philosophy distinguishes these spheres from one another in order to prevent confusion. As each of the concepts of the human, the natural, and the divine becomes more clearly separated in philosophy, this contributes to their mutual clarification and elaboration.

Nevertheless, what disqualified nature in the eyes of some philosophers, reducing it to the level of a mere appearance, was that the becoming of nature (*phusis*) was no more intelligible than the genesis of myth. The authentic being beyond nature that philosophy strives to reach and reveal has nothing to do with the supernatural of myth: it belongs to a quite different category; it is a pure abstraction, that which always remains identical, the very principle of rational thought, made objective in the form of the *logos*.[27] Among the Ionians, the new demand for positivity was from the start aimed at the absolute in the concept of *phusis*; in Parmenides, the new insistence on intelligibility is aimed at the absolute in the concept of Being, unchanging and identical. Rational thought is torn between these two contradictory demands, both of which represent a decisive break with myth. Thus, in one theory after another, it embarks on a dialectic whose development gives rise to the history of Greek philosophy.

The birth of philosophy, therefore, is connected with two major transformations of thought. The first is the emergence of a positivist thought that excludes all forms of the supernatural and rejects the implicit assimilation of physical phenomena with divine agents in myth; the second is the development of an abstract thought that strips reality of the power of change that myth ascribed to it and rejects the ancient image of the union of opposites in favor of a categorical formulation of the principle of identity.

Cornford does not venture to explain the conditions that made this twofold revolution possible in sixth-century Greece. However, in the course of the half-century that elapsed between the publication of his two works, other authors studied the problem. In *Essai sur la formation de la pensée grecque*, in the introduction to his discussion of the positivist philosophy of the Milesians, Pierre-Maxime Schuhl emphasizes the scale of the social and political transformations that took place before the sixth century. He notes that the introduction of institutions such as money, the calendar, and alphabetical writing must have helped liberate men's minds, and that navigation and commerce tended to give a new, practical orientation to thought.[28] For his part, Benjamin Farrington saw a connection between the rationalism of the first physicists of Ionia and the technical progress made in the wealthy cities of Asia Minor.[29] He suggests that in replacing the ancient anthropomorphic schemata with a mechanistic, instrumentalist interpretation of the universe, the philosophy of the Ionians reflected the increased importance of technology in the social life of the time. The problem was further examined by George Thomson, who raises a conclusive objection to Farrington's thesis. It is impossible to establish a direct link between rational thought and technological development. In terms of technology, Greece invented nothing and introduced no innovations. Greek technology was derived from that of the East, which it never truly surpassed. And despite all its technological knowledge, the East never extricated itself from myth to construct a rational philosophy.[30] Other explanations are therefore called for, and Thomson rightly draws attention to two major groups of factors: first, the absence in Greece of monarchies of the Eastern type, which had very early on been replaced by other political forms; second, the beginnings of a commercial economy with the introduction of currency, and the appearance of a merchant class for whom objects lose their qualitative differences (or use value) and retain only the abstract significance of a commodity like any other (exchange value). However, in order to delineate more precisely the concrete conditions in which the change from religious to rational thought became possible, we must approach the problem from yet another angle. Ionian physics has thrown some light on the content of the earliest philosophy. Cosmogonic myths were transposed into philosophy, which proposed a "theory" concerning phenomena that in ancient times the king had been held to control and effect. The other current of rational thought, the philosophy of Magna Graecia, will enable us to trace the origins of the figure of the philosopher and his antecedents.

At the dawn of the intellectual history of Greece can be glimpsed a whole series of strange figures, to whom Erwin Rohde has drawn attention.[31] These half-legendary figures, who belong to the category of ecstatic visionaries and purificatory magis, represent the most ancient model of the "sage." Some of them are closely associated with the legend of Pythagoras, the founder of the first philosophical sect. Their way of life, their studies, and their spiritual superiority situate them on the margins of the ordinary run of human beings. They are, in the strictest sense, "divine men"; indeed, they sometimes proclaim themselves gods.

W.R. Halliday saw an archaic form of enthusiastic prophecy in the existence of a category of public diviners or *dēmiourgoi* who combined certain characteristics of the inspired prophet, the poet, the musician — as both singer and dancer — and the doctor as both purifier and healer.[32] This type of diviner, who was very different from the priest and often stood in opposition to the king, permits a first glimmer of understanding about the line of figures that includes Aristeas, Abaris, Hermotimus, Epimenides, and Pherecydes. All these figures combine the associated functions of diviner, poet, and sage, all of which depend on the same mantic power.[33] The diviner, the poet, and the sage all have in common the exceptional faculty of seeing beyond sensible appearances. They possess a kind of sixth sense that allows them to enter a world normally prohibited to mortals.

The diviner is a man who can see the invisible. He knows, through direct contact, things and events from which he is separated by space and time. A quasi-ritualistic formula is used to define him: the man who knows all things past, present, and to come.[34] This formula is also applied to the inspired poet, but with the nuance that the poet tends to specialize in the exploration of things of the past.[35] In the case of serious poetry, whose purpose is instruction rather than entertainment, the things of the past that divine inspiration reveals to the singer consist not, as they did in Homer, of an exact catalog of human persons and happenings, but rather, as in Hesiod, of an authoritative account of origins, that is, divine genealogies, the genesis of the cosmos, the birth of the human race.[36] In divulging what lies hidden in the depths of time, the poet offers, in the form of a hymn, incantation, or oracle, the revelation of an essential truth that is at the same time a religious mystery and a doctrine of wisdom. It would be most surprising if a similar ambiguity were not also found in the teachings of the earliest philosophers. They too are concerned with a reality concealed behind appearances and eluding common knowledge. The form of the poem in which even a doctrine as abstract as that of

Parmenides is still presented reflects how much of the character of a religious revelation was retained in early philosophy.[37] Like the diviner and the poet, and still to some extent confused with them, the sage was originally defined as the exceptional being who has the power to see and reveal the invisible. When the philosopher seeks to describe his work, the nature of his spiritual activity, and the object of his inquiries, he employs the religious vocabulary of the sects and brotherhoods. He presents himself as one who is elect, a *theios anēr*, who enjoys divine grace. He undertakes a mystical journey into the beyond, following a path of inquiry that is reminiscent of the way of the mysteries and at the end of which he obtains, through a kind of *epopteia*, a vision that culminates the final stage of initiation.[38] He leaves the crowd of "senseless fools" and enters the tiny circle of initiates: those who have seen (*hoi eidotes*), who know (*sophoi*). The various degrees of initiation in the mystery religions correspond in the Pythagorean brotherhood to the hierarchy of members who are classified according to their stage of advancement.[39] They also correspond to Heraclitus's idea of the hierarchy of the three different types of human beings: those who understand the *logos* (who have had the *epopteia*), those who are hearing it for the first time but do not yet understand it (the *muēsis* of the new initiates), and those who have not heard it at all (the *amuētoi*).[40]

The prophetic vision of the inspired poet is placed under the sign of the goddess Mnēmosynē, Memory, the mother of the Muses. Memory does not confer the power of evoking personal recollections, of seeing the order of events that have faded into the past. She gives the poet — like the diviner — the privilege of beholding unchangeable and permanent reality; she brings him into contact with the originary being, a mere infinitesimal fraction of which is revealed to human beings in the march of time and immediately veiled once again. This function of revealing reality, attributed to a kind of memory that unlike ours, does not survey time but rather escapes from it, reappears in a modified form in philosophy's *anamnēsis*.[41] Platonic reminiscence makes it possible to recognize the eternal realities that the soul was able to contemplate in a journey that it made while liberated from the body. Plato makes quite clear the link between a particular concept of memory and a new doctrine of immortality that breaks away from the usual Greek conception of the soul, from Homer down to the Ionian thinkers.

To understand this innovation, which gives the whole mystical current of Greek philosophy its originality, is it enough to refer, as Rohde does, to the influence of the Dionysian movement and the experience of the soul's separation from the body and union with the divine that the Dionysian ecstasies were held to produce?[42] The Dionysian ecstasy, a collective delirium in which the god abruptly takes possession of the man, is an impersonal state that is undergone passively. The concept of the individual soul, possessing in and through itself the innate power of liberating itself from the body and traveling in the beyond, is of quite a different order.[43] Such a belief could not be rooted in the cult of Dionysos. Its origins lie in the practices of the *iatromanteis*, who were the precursors of the philosophers and whose legend suggests a comparison with the figure and conduct of the shaman of the civilizations of northern Asia.[44] The sages are individuals on the margins of the social group, distinguished by their asceticism, which might include retreats in the desert or in caves, vegetarianism, more or less total fasting, sexual abstinence, a rule of silence, and so on. Their souls possess the extraordinary power to leave the body and reenter it at will after a descent into the underworld, a journey through the ether or a voyage through space that enables them to appear a thousand miles from where they lie unconscious, in a kind of cataleptic sleep. Certain details underline the features of shamanism that the sages show, namely, the golden arrow that Abaris carries everywhere with him, the theme of flight through the air, the abstinence from food. In this very special religious context, a theory of metensomatosis is formulated, explicitly connected with the teaching of the earliest sages. This doctrine is a continuation of the archaic idea that life is renewed in death, with which it forms a cycle. But among the magi, the old idea of some kind of traffic between the dead and the living acquires a different

384

and more precise meaning. The mastery over the soul that makes it possible for the sage, after a period of strict asceticism, to journey in the other world gives him a new type of individual immortality. What makes him a god among men is that, thanks to a discipline of spiritual tension and concentration (whose connections with a technique of respiratory control have been pointed out by Gernet), he knows how to concentrate in itself the soul that is normally dispersed throughout the body.[45] Thus concentrated, the soul can detach itself the body, escape from the limitations of the life in which it is temporarily imprisoned, and retrieve the memory of the whole cycle of its previous incarnations. It is easier to understand the role of the "memory exercises" that Pythagoras had introduced as a rule to be followed in his brotherhood when one recalls what Empedocles called him: "That man who, through the tension of the forces of his mind, could easily see every single thing in ten, in twenty human lives."[46] The combination of the three ideas of mastery over the soul, its escape from the body, and the destruction of the flow of time through the recollection of previous lives is characteristic of what has been termed Greek shamanism, and it can still be clearly detected in ancient Pythagoreanism.

Nevertheless, the earliest philosopher was no longer a shaman. His role was to teach, to establish a school. What had been secrets for the shaman were divulged by the philosopher to a group of disciples. He extended what had been the privilege of one exceptional individual to all those who desired to enter his brotherhood. It hardly seems necessary to point out what the consequences of this innovation were. Once the secret practices were divulged and thrown open to a wider audience, they became subjects for instruction and discussion. They were organized into a doctrine. The personal experience of the shaman, who believes he is the reincarnation of a man of god, is now made general to all mankind, in the form of a theory of reincarnation.

The turning point that came when the philosopher emerged as distinct from the magus is characterized by this divulging of a religious secret, this extension of a reserved privilege to an open group, and the publicizing of a hitherto forbidden knowledge. A similar historical turning point is discernible in many other contexts during the period of social upheaval and religious ferment that paved the way for the appearance of the city between the eighth and the seventh century. During this time, religious prerogatives that had previously belonged to certain royal and noble *genē* were extended, popularized, and in some cases fully integrated as state institutions. The ancient priestly clans began to place all their sacred knowledge and their control of things divine at the service of the entire city. The holy idols, the old *xoana*, talismans that had been jealously guarded in the royal palace or the priest's house, were moved to the temple, a public place, and, in full sight of the city, became images made to be seen. Legal decisions, the *themistes*, that had been the privilege of the *eupatridai* were written down and made public. As private cults were thus diverted toward a public religion, new forms of religious groupings, centered around certain powerful personalities, emerged on the margins of the official city religion. *Thiasoi*, brotherhoods, and mysteries offered access to holy truths that had formerly been the prerogative of certain hereditary houses, without distinction as to rank or origin. The creation of religious sects, such as those that passed as Orphic, the founding of mystery religions, and the establishment of brotherhoods of "sages," such as that of Pythagoras, are all manifestations, in different conditions and circles, of the same great social movement of the expansion and popularization of what had been an aristocratic sacred tradition.

The development of philosophy took place within this movement and at its end, for it alone carried the movement to its ultimate conclusion. Despite their expansion, the sects and mysteries remained closed, secret groups. This was, in fact, their essential feature. So, despite sharing certain doctrinal theories with early philosophy, the revelations in the mysteries necessarily remained a privilege that was not subject to discussion. In contrast, as philosophy developed, it burst out of the framework of the brotherhood in which it had originated. Its message was no longer addressed to a single group or sect. Through the spoken and written word the philosopher addressed the whole city, and every city. He gave his revelations complete and total publicity. By carrying the "mystery" into the market place, right into the agora, he made it the subject of public and argumentative debate, in which dialectical discussion finally assumed more importance than supernatural enlightenment.[47]

These general remarks can be confirmed by more detailed observations. Thomson has pointed out that the founders of Milesian physics, Thales and Anaximander, belonged to a noble, priestly, clan, the Thelidai, descended from a Theban family of priest-kings, the Kadmeioi, who had come from Phoenicia.[48] Thus the astronomical and cosmological investigations of the earliest philosophers were able to transpose, by divulging them in the city, an old, sacred tradition originating in the East.

Heraclitus is an even more interesting example. Everything about his use of language — his contrasting, antithetical style, with its juxtaposition of opposed expressions, its use of puns, and its deliberately enigmatic form — is reminiscent of the liturgical language used in the mysteries, particularly at Eleusis. Heraclitus was descended from the founder of Ephesos, Androklos, who led the emigration to Ionia and whose father was Kodros, king of Athens. Heraclitus would have been king himself had he not renounced the title in favor of his brother. The Ephesian royal family had retained, along with the right to the purple robe and the scepter, the privileges of the priesthood of Demeter Eleusinia. However, even if the *logos* that Heraclitus reveals obscurely in his writings proceeds on from the *legomena* of Eleusis and the Orphic *hieroi logoi,* it is no longer exclusive. It is, on the contrary, common to all men, the "universal" upon which they must all rely equally "as the City does on the law."[49]

There is nothing surprising about the coinciding emergence of the philosopher and that of the citizen. Indeed, the city's social institutions established the separation between nature and society that is the conceptual prerequisite for the exercise of rational thought. With the coming of the city, the political order was separated from the organization of the cosmos. It was now seen as a human institution that was the subject of concerned inquiry and impassioned discussion. In this debate, which was not simply theoretical but engaged all the violent animosity of the hostile groups concerned, the emergent philosophy was, by its very nature, bound to play a part. The philosopher's "wisdom" qualified him to propose remedies for the upheaval caused by the beginnings of a commercial economy. He was expected to describe the new political equilibrium that would make it possible to recover the harmony that had been lost, and to re-establish social unity and stability by "harmonizing" the opposed elements that were tearing the city apart. In Greece, the names of the sages are associated with the earliest forms of legislation and the first attempts to provide a political constitution. Here again, the philosopher takes over functions that belonged to the priest-king in the days when nature and society were not distinguished and he was in charge of both at the same time. However, the transformation of thought is just as marked in the philosophers' political ideas as it is in their cosmologies. Once they were separated, both nature and society became subjects for a more positive, more abstract reflection. Theories about the social order, now conceived of as purely human, could be elaborated rationally, like those concerning the natural order now considered *phusis*. Solon expresses the social order in the concept of the *metron*, the just measure, which must be imposed on rival factions by the decision of the *nomothetēs*, who thereby limits their excessive ambitions. The Pythagoreans express it in the concept of the *homonoia*, the numerical agreement that brings about the harmony of the contraries, fusing them into a new unity.[50] The old idea of the social order was based on a distribution, a dividing up (*nomos*), of honors and privileges among different groups that were opposed within the political community, just as the elemental powers were opposed within the cosmos. After the sixth century, this idea was transformed into the abstract concept of *isonomia*, equality before the law for individuals who were all defined in the same way, in that they were citizens of the same city.[51]

Just as philosophy develops from myth and the philosopher from the magus, the city develops from the old social organization. It destroys it but at the same time retains its framework. It translates the tribal organization into a form that is the result of more positive and more abstract thinking. Consider, for example, the reforms of Cleisthenes: the four Ionian tribes of Attica, which Aristotle later claimed corresponded to the four seasons of the year, were replaced by an artificial structure that made it possible to resolve purely political problems.[52] Ten tribes were created, each consisting of three *trittyes* composed of several demes. The *trittyes* and the demes were established on a purely geographical basis. They consisted of the inhabitants of a certain area of land, not of blood relatives, as (in principle) in the *genē* and *phratrai*. These remained intact, but not as part of the tribal organization or of the political institutions of the city. Of the three *trittyes* that composed each tribe, the first was in the coastal region, the second in the interior heartlands, and the third in the urban zone. Being thus a deliberate amalgamation, the tribe brought about the political unification, the "mixture," as Aristotle calls it, of the diverse groups and activities of which the city was composed.[53] This artificial administrative organization had its counterpart in an artificial division of civil time. Religious life continued to be regulated according to the lunar calendar. But the administrative year was divided into ten periods of thirty-six or thirty-seven days each, each one corresponding to one of the ten tribes. The Council of the Four Hundred was increased to five hundred members — fifty from each tribe — so that over the ten periods of the year, each tribe in turn held office in the permanent committee of the council.

The coherence and clear-cut nature of Cleisthenes's reforms exhibit the characteristic features of the new type of thought that found expression in the political structure of the city. At another level, they are features comparable to those that, along with the emergence of philosophy, seem to me to define the transformation of myth into reason. The separation of society from nature is presupposed and at the same time strengthened by such developments as the introduction of a civil calendar which fulfills the purely human needs of administration and is entirely distinct from lunar time, and the abandonment of the correspondence between the number of tribes in the social group and the number of seasons in the cosmos. There is a new positivist spirit behind reforms that aim less to establish harmony between the city and the sacred order of the universe than to achieve certain precise political objectives. The tendency toward greater abstraction is detectable at every level: in the administrative divisions founded on precisely defined territorial sectors instead of blood ties; in the arbitrary system of numbers used to allocate social responsibilities fairly to particular groups of men for certain periods of time, on a mathematical basis; in the very definitions of city and citizen, for the city is no longer identified with any one privileged figure or with any activity or family in particular, but is whatever form the unified group consisting of all the citizens, without regard to identity, ancestry, or profession, takes. In the order of the city, social relationships, considered abstractly and apart from personal or family ties, are defined in terms of equality and similarity.

However, mental changes analogous to those which, when limited to the single domain of philosophy, seem to bring about the incomprehensible advent of a reason devoid of all history are not visible only in political structures. Quite apart from law and art, the development of an economic institution such as money is evidence of changes related to the birth of rational thought. It is necessary only to refer to Gernet's study on the mythical implications of value in the ancient premonetary symbols of Greece.[54] The *agalma* (a vase, jewel, tripod, or garment), the product of a luxury industry, had the role of an exchange commodity used in a kind of commerce among the nobility. This facilitated the circulation of movable wealth. But in this premonetary system, exchange had not yet emerged as an independent function that could be studied in positivist terms within a system of truly economic thought. The

value of the precious object remained bound up with the supernatural virtues it was believed to possess. The *agalma* was a means
for transmitting sacred powers, social prestige, and ties of dependence, all belonging to the same system of symbols for wealth.
When the *agalma* circulated in the form of gifts and exchanges,
and the ownership of goods was also transferred, individuals
acquired commitments and religious forces were mobilized.

Money in the true sense of the word — minted, stamped, and
guaranteed by the state — was invented by the Greeks in the seventh century.[55] Its effect was revolutionary on a whole series of
levels. It accelerated the process of which it was itself an effect:
the development in the Greek economy of a commercial sector
dealing in some of the articles that were commonly consumed. It
allowed the creation of a new type of wealth, radically different
from wealth in land or flocks, and a new class of wealthy men,
whose effect on the political reorganization of the city proved
decisive. On the psychological and moral levels, it had a shock
effect, the dramatic repercussions of which are apparent in the
poetry of writers such as Solon and Theognis.[56] If money makes
the man, if man is the epitome of an insatiable desire for wealth,
the entire traditional image of *aretē*, human excellence, is called
into question. Furthermore, money, in the strictest sense of the
word, is no longer — as in the East — simply an ingot of precious
metal that can be swapped for any kind of merchandise because it
has the advantage of being easily preserved and exchanged; money
has become a social symbol, the equivalent and universal measure
of value. The general use of minted money helps give rise to a
new, positivist, quantifiable, and abstract concept of value.

To appreciate the full extent of this mental innovation, we
need only compare two extreme attitudes. First, the term *tokos*,
which denotes the interest from money, is connected with the
root *tek-* (to give birth to, to beget) and thereby assimilates the
product of capital to the increase of livestock by natural reproduction according to the seasons and following the order of *phusis*.[57] But in Aristotle's theory, the increase of money through
interest and usury is the very epitome of a phenomenon contrary

to nature: money is a human artifact that, in order to make the process of exchange more convenient, establishes the appearance of a common measure between values that are, in themselves, all quite different. In this new form of money, even more than in the new institutions of the city, there is a rationality that makes it possible to define the domain of *nomos* at the level of a purely human artifice.

Is it justifiable to even further and, like Thomson, assume there is a direct link between the most important concepts of philosophy — being, essence, and substance — and if not money itself, then at least the abstract character of merchandise that it confers on all the diverse material commodities exchanged on the market through the process of buying and selling?[58] A theoretical position such as Aristotle's should warn against the temptation of transposing concepts too mechanically from one level of thought to another.[59]

For Aristotle, the essence of a particular thing, natural or artificial, is defined by its use value, the end for which it has been produced. Its commercial value has nothing to do with its reality (*ousia*) but depends on a mere social illusion.[60] Only a sophist like Protagoras could assimilate the reality of things with the conventional value, expressed in terms of money, ascribed to them by the judgment of men. Protagoras's relativism, which can be summed up in an expression such as "man is the measure of all things," reflects the idea that money, a pure *nomos*, a human convention, is the measure of all values. But it is significant that for Plato, whose philosophy carries on the line of thought of Pythagoras and Parmenides, the figure of the sophist symbolizes precisely the man who remains on the level of nonbeing even as he is defined as a dealer engaged in commercial transactions.[61]

True, the term *ousia*, which in philosophical terminology means being, substance, also means patrimony or wealth. But as Gernet has pointed out, this connection serves only to underline the opposite directions taken by philosophy, on the one hand, and legal and economic thought, on the other.[62] The economic meaning of *ousia* is first and foremost the *klēros* (land), the patrimony,

which for a long time remained inalienable and which represented a family's visible wealth. This type of visible possession
(*ousia phanera*) is contrasted, in a common but somewhat vague
distinction, with the category of the *ousia aphanēs*, the invisible
asset. The latter sometimes includes ready money as well as cred-
its and securities. The two terms of this dichotomy reflect the
important difference that money suffers a devaluation in comparison with land, which is a visible possession, stable, permanent,
and substantial — the only kind of wealth that is truly real and
whose "price" is inflected by a religious and affective value. At
this level of social thought, Being and Value are associated with
the visible, while that which cannot be seen, the abstract, seems
to introduce some purely human and illusory element, if not disorder. In contrast, in philosophical thought, the very concept of
ousia is developed in opposition to the visible world. Reality, permanence, and substantiality become attributes of what cannot be
seen; the visible becomes a mere appearance in opposition to true
reality, to *ousia*.

Another term reflects the attempts at abstraction made in the
context of commerce and the use of money. *Ta chrēmata* means
things, reality in general, and goods, especially in the form of
ready money. Aristotle writes: "We call goods, *chrēmata*, all things
whose value is measured by money."[63] This is an example of the
way the use of money substituted an abstract, quantitative, and
economic concept of the thing as a commercial commodity for
the ancient qualitative and dynamic concept of the thing as *phusis*.
But two caveats are necessary at this point. The first concerns a
point of chronology: this example of commercial rationalism comes
from the fourth century, not from the period of the earliest philosophical thought. It clarifies the thought of some of the sophists,
not that of Pythagoras, Heraclitus, and Parmenides.[64] Second,
these *chrēmata* belong to this earthly world, the world here below,
to use a religious expression that is not out of place in this philosophical context. *Ousia*, which constitutes reality for the philosopher, is of a different order. It is on a different level from nature,
as well as from the abstract notion of money. It is associated with

the invisible world revealed by religious thought — with that stable and permanent reality that has more being than *phusis*, rather than less, as currency does.

Does this mean that, in the last analysis, philosophy applies a form of rational and positivist thought acquired through the use of money to the concept of imperishable and invisible being that it took from religion? That would still be an oversimplification. According to Parmenides, being is not the reflection of the concept of commercial value; it does not purely and simply transpose the abstraction of the monetary sign into the domain of the real. Parmenides's being is One; this unity, which is one of its essential features, sets it in opposition to money no less than to sensible reality.

In the language of the Ionians, reality is still expressed by a plural, *ta onta*, the things that exist, as they are given to us in their concrete multiplicity. As Werner Jaeger remarks, the physicists are interested in natural realities, in their actuality and presence, and they seek the foundation of these realities.[65] Whatever its origin and principle, Being for them takes on the visible form of a plurality of things. Parmenides, however, expresses Being for the first time with a singular, *to on*: it is a question not of particular beings but of Being in general, total and unique. This change of vocabulary registers the emergence of a new concept of being. It is now no longer seen as the diversity of things apprehended through human experience; it is seen, rather, as the intelligible subject of *logos*, of reason, expressed through language in accordance with its own principles of noncontradiction. This abstract notion of a purely intelligible being that excludes plurality, division, and change is conceived of in opposition to sensible reality and its perpetual becoming. But it also contrasts with a reality such as money, which not only involves multiplicity, the way natural things do, but furthermore implies the principle of the possibility of indefinite multiplication. Parmenides's being can no more be "converted into cash" than it can be subjected to becoming.

This means that the philosophical concept of Being cannot

have originated in the use of money or in commercial activity. It expresses the same aspiration toward unity, the same quest for a principle of stability and permanence, that is manifested in social and political thought at the time of birth of the city and found in certain currents of religious thought, such as Orphism. But this aspiration toward the One and the Identical is now expressed in the context of new and properly philosophical problems that arise when the old question "How does order emerge out of chaos?" is transformed into a different set of aporias: What is immutable in nature? What is the principle (*archē*) of reality? How can we attain it and express it? The set of mythical notions that the Ionian "physicists" had inherited from religion — genesis, love, hate, and the union of and strife between opposites — no longer answered the needs of an inquiry that sought to define, in an entirely profane language, that which constitutes the permanent foundation of Being. Parmenides's doctrine marks the moment when a contradiction is declared between, on the one hand, the becoming of the sensible world — that Ionian world of *phusis* and *genesis* — and, on the other, the logical requirements of thought. Mathematical thinking played a decisive role in this respect. With its method of demonstration and because of the ideal character of its objects, it acquired the value of a model. In striving to number the expanse it came up against the problem, within its own domain, of the relationship between the one and the many, the identical and the different, and it formulated this problem rigorously in logical terms. It led to the denunciation of movement and plurality as irrational and to the clear formulation of the theoretical difficulties concerning assertion and attribution. In this way, philosophical thought found it possible to disengage itself from the spontaneous forms of language in which it had been expressing itself, and to subject them to a preliminary critical analysis. According to Parmenides, beyond words (*epea*) as employed by men in general, there is a *logos*, a reason that is immanent in speech; this consists in an absolute insistence on noncontradiction: being is, nonbeing is not.[66] In this categorical form, the new principle underlying rational thought finalizes the break with the old logic of myth. But at the same time, thought finds itself quite cut off from physical reality, for reason can have as its object nothing but immutable and identical being. After Parmenides, the task of Greek philosophy was to reestablish the link between the rational universe of speech and the sensible world of nature by means of a more precise and nuanced definition of the principle of contradiction.[67]

I have pointed out the two features that characterize the new type of thought that developed in Greek philosophy: first, the rejection of the supernatural and "marvelous" in the explanations of phenomena; second, the break with the logic of ambivalence and the quest for internal coherence in speech, based on a rigorous definition of concepts, the establishment of clear distinctions among the various levels of reality, and a strict observance of the principle of identity. These innovations, which constituted a first form of rationality, are not the result of a miracle. There was no immaculate conception of reason. The emergence of philosophy was, as Cornford has shown, a historical fact, growing out of the past as well as in opposition to it. This mental change was an integral part of transformations that occurred at every level in the Greek societies — in the political institutions of the city, in law, in economic life, in money — between the seventh and the sixth century. This is not to suggest that philosophy simply reflected these other developments. While it may be an expression of general aspirations, philosophy raises problems that concern it alone, such as the nature of Being and the relationship between Being and thought. To resolve these problems, it had to develop its own concepts and construct its own rationality. In doing this, it relied very little on sensible reality; it did not borrow much from the observation of natural phenomena; it did not carry out experiments. The very idea of experimentation remained quite foreign to it. Its reason was not yet the same as our reason, the experimental reason of contemporary science, directed toward facts and their theoretical systematization. True, it established a mathematics, the first formalization of sensible experience, but it made no attempt to use this to explore physical reality. Between mathematics and

physics, or between calculus and experience, there was no connection. Mathematics remained a part of logic.[68] In Greek thought,
nature represents the domain of the "more-or-less," to which neither exact measurement nor rigorous reason can be applied.[69]
Reason is not to be discovered in nature; it is immanent in language. It did not originate in techniques for operating on things.
It was developed from the organization and analysis of the various
means of influencing men, of all the techniques for which language is the common instrument, namely, the arts of the lawyer,
the professor, the orator, and the politician.[70] Greek reason is the
type of reason that makes it possible to act in a positive, deliberate, and methodical manner upon men, but not to transform
nature. In its limitations, as well as in the innovations it brought
about, it was truly the product of the city.

CHAPTER EIGHTEEN

The Origins of Philosophy

Where does philosophy begin? There are two ways to interpret this question. First, one can ask where to locate the borders of philosophy, the margins that separate it from what is not yet or not completely philosophy. Or one can ask where it appeared for the first time, where it emerged — and why it happened there rather than somewhere else. There are thus the questions of identity and of origin, and these are bound together inseparably, even though, according to a logic that is too neat or too simple, the second seems to assume that the first has been resolved. It could be said that in order to establish the date and place of philosophy's birth, we must also know what it is; we must have a definition of it that would allow us to distinguish it from nonphilosophical forms of thought. But, conversely, how could we not recognize that it is impossible to define philosophy in the abstract, as if it were an eternal essence? To know what it is, we must examine the conditions under which it came into the world; we must follow the movement by which it came to be constituted historically when, within the horizon of Greek culture, new problems were posed and the new conceptual tools required for their solution were elaborated, thus delineating a space of knowledge that did not previously exist. It was in this space that philosophy established itself in order to undertake a systematic exploration of its dimensions. And it was through the elaboration of a form of rationality and a type of discourse, hitherto unknown, that both philosophical practice and the figure of the philosopher emerged and acquired their proper status, demarcating themselves socially and intellectually from professional activities such as the political or religious functions in place in the city, and inaugurating an original intellectual tradition that, despite all its transformations, has never ceased to be rooted in its origins.

Everything began in the early sixth century BCE, in the Greek city of Miletos, on the coast of Asia Minor, where the Ionians had established rich and prosperous colonies. Within fifty years, three men — Thales, Anaximander, and Anaximenes — appeared in quick succession. The nature of the problems they addressed and the orientation of their thinking were similar enough for them that they were already grouped together as a single school in Antiquity. As for modern historians, some have seen the emergence of this school as the thunderclap announcing the "Greek miracle." In the work of the three Milesians, it is said, Reason suddenly became incarnate. Descending from the sky to the earth, it burst onto the scene of history, there in Miletos, for the first time; its light, revealed for all time — as if the scales had finally fallen from the eyes of a blind humanity — has not ceased to illuminate the progress of knowledge. "The early Ionian teachers," John Burnet writes, "opened the road which science has simply had to follow along ever since."[1]

How do matters stand in reality? Are the Milesians already philosophers, in the full sense of the term? To what extent do their works (which even in the best cases are known only through very rare fragments) constitute a decisive break from the past? In what sense do their innovations justify their reputation as inventors of the new mode of reflection and investigation that we call philosophizing? There is no simple answer to these questions. But it is precisely by confronting them directly, by taking them up in all their complexity, that we can situate the various aspects of the problem of philosophy's origins.

First, a word on vocabulary. In the sixth century, the words "philosopher" and "philosophy" did not yet exist. The first known use of *philosophos* occurs in a fragment from the beginning of the fifth century attributed to Heraclitus. In fact, it is only with Plato and Aristotle that these terms became established, by taking on a sense that is precise, technical, and in some respects polemical. To call oneself a "philosopher" is to distinguish oneself from one's predecessors as much as, or even more than, to associate oneself with them: it means *not being* a "physicist," like the Milesians, who limited themselves to an investigation into nature (*historia peri phuseōs*). It also means not being one of those men who, still in the sixth and fifth centuries, were referred to with the term *sophos* (sage) — such as the Seven Sages, among whom Thales was included — or one of the *sophistēs*, those skilled in knowledge, such as the experts in the art of speech, the masters of persuasion who claimed authority in all domains. These latter were renowned throughout the fifth century; Plato used them as foils for the authentic philosopher, the better to establish his own discipline.

Phusiologos, sophos, sophistēs, or even, taking into account certain statements by Plato, *muthologos*, the teller of fables or old wives' tales — these are all ways of saying that from the viewpoint of a philosophy that has been fully constituted, established, and institutionalized (with the founding of schools like the Academy and the Lyceum, where one is taught to become a philosopher), Thales the sage, although he initiated the investigations of the Milesians, still did not cross the threshold into the new dwelling.[2] But however resolute the assertion of difference may be, it does not exclude an awareness of filiation. Referring to the "ancient" thinkers who "lived long ago" and whose "materialism" he rejects, Aristotle observes that Thales is rightly considered "the founder of this type of philosophy."[3]

Given the hesitations concerning the vocabulary used to describe them and the classical Greek philosophers' uncertainties about them, the Milesians' status cannot be taken for granted.

To evaluate their contribution to the origins of philosophy most precisely, we must begin by situating them within the context of Greek culture in the Archaic period. This was a fundamentally oral culture. Education was based not on reading written

texts but on listening to poetic songs transmitted from generation to generation. The whole of knowledge was thus stored in
vast epic compositions, legendary stories that functioned as the
group's collective memory and as an encyclopedia of knowledge
held in common. These songs contained everything a Greek had
to know about man and his past — the exploits of heroes long past;
about the gods, their families, and their genealogies, and about
the world, its form, and its origins. In this respect, the work of the
Milesians is indeed a radical innovation. Neither singers nor poets
nor storytellers, they express themselves in prose, in written texts
whose aim is not to unravel a narrative thread in the long line of a
tradition but to present an explanatory theory concerning certain
natural phenomena and the organization of the cosmos. In this
shift from the oral to the written, from the poetic song to prose,
from narration to explanation, the change of register corresponds
to an entirely new type of investigation — new both in terms of its
object (nature, *phusis*) and in terms of the entirely positive form
of thought manifested in it.

To be sure, the ancient myths, particularly Hesiod's *Theogony*,
also recount the world's emergence out of chaos, the differentiation of its various parts, the constitution and establishment of its
architecture as a whole. But the process of genesis in these narratives takes the form of a genealogical picture; it unfolds according
to the order of filiation among the gods, the rhythm of successive
births, marriages, and intrigues that mingle and oppose divine
beings of different generations. The goddess Gaia (Earth) engenders Ouranos (Sky) and Pontos (Sea) from herself; coupled with
Ouranos, whom she has just created, she gives birth to the Titans,
the first masters of the sky, who rebel against their father and who
in turn will be fought and deposed by their children, the Olympians; these latter then confer on Zeus, the youngest among them
and the new sovereign, the task of imposing a definitive order on
the universe.

This dramatic imagery is no longer found in the work of the
Milesians, and its disappearance marks the arrival of another
mode of intelligibility. Giving an account of a phenomenon will

no longer consist in naming its father and mother or establishing its filiation. If the realities of nature follow a regular order, this is not because one day a sovereign god, after all his fighting was done, imposed it on other divinities like a monarch dividing up the duties, functions, and domains of his kingdom. To be intelligible, this order must be thought of as a law immanent to nature and governing it from the beginning. Myth recounted the genesis of the world by singing the glory of the prince whose reign founded and maintains a hierarchical order among the sacred powers. The Milesians sought abiding principles behind the apparent flux of things, and these principles were the basis for a proper balance of the various elements that make up the universe. Even if they preserve certain fundamental themes from the old myths — such as the reference to a primordial state of indistinction from which the world developed — and even if, like Thales, they affirm that "everything is full of gods," the Milesians do not include any sort of supernatural being in their explanatory schemas. For the Milesians, nature in its positivity has taken over the entire field of reality; nothing exists, nothing happens or will ever happen, that does not have its foundation and its reason in *phusis*, which can be observed every day. The force of *phusis*, in its permanence and in the diversity of its manifestations, that takes the place of the ancient gods; through the power of life and the principle of order that it harbors, *phusis* takes on all the characteristics of the divine.

Therefore, three features, taken together, mark the innovative character of Milesian physics. First, a field of inquiry is constituted in which nature is apprehended in terms that are at once positive, general, and abstract: water, air, and the limitless (*apeiron*), as well as earthquake, lightning, eclipse, and so on, are all referred to as abstract generalities. Second, the Milesians believe that cosmic order is based not on a sovereign deity, on his *basileia* or royal power, but on a law of justice (*dikē*) inscribed in nature, a rule of division (*nomos*) that implies an egalitarian order for all the constitutive elements of the world, such that none can dominate or prevail over the others. Third, this physics is oriented toward geometry, insofar as it does not retrace a narrative plot as it unfolds, but proposes a *theōria* and confers a shape on the world, that is, shows how things happen by projecting them into a spatial framework. But these three features did not spring forth in the sixth century like a miraculous advent of a Reason unknown to history. On the contrary, they appear to be intimately bound up with the transformations that had occurred at every level of the Greek societies, transformations that, after the collapse of the Mycaenean kingdoms, led these societies toward the development of the city-state, the *polis*. From this perspective, it is worth noting the affinities between a man like Thales and his contemporary in Athens, Solon, the poet and legislator. Both were included among the Seven Sages, who, in the Greeks' eyes, embodied the first kind of *sophia* to have appeared among men: a wisdom permeated with moral reflection and political preoccupations. This wisdom defines the foundations of a new human order that would replace the absolute power of the monarch or the prerogatives of a small minority with a written, public, common law that is equal for all. Over the course of the sixth century, from Solon to Cleisthenes, the city increasingly takes the form of a circular cosmos centered on the *agora*, the public square, a cosmos in which all citizens, take turns obeying and ruling and must, over time, occupy and then cede all the symmetrical positions that make up the civic space. This image of a social world regulated by *isonomia*, equality under the law, is projected onto the physical universe in Anaximander. The ancient theogonies were integrated into myths of sovereignty rooted in royal rituals. In its positivity, its conception of an egalitarian order, and its geometric framework, the new model of the world elaborated by the physicists of Miletos is of a piece with the institutional forms and mental structures specific to the *polis*.

"Astonishment," declares Socrates in the *Theaetetus*, "is the very origin of philosophy."[4] In Greek, "to be astonished" is *thaumazein*, and this term, because it indicates the reversal in relation to myth carried out by the Milesian investigations, places these investigations at the very point where philosophy has its origin. In myth, *thauma* is "the marvelous"; the stupor it provokes is the sign that the supernatural is present in it. For the Milesians, the strangeness of a phenomenon does not impose a feeling of the divine but rather presents it to the mind as a problem. The strange no longer fascinates; it mobilizes the intelligence. Astonishment changes from mute veneration into curiosity and questioning. When *thauma* is reintegrated into the ordinariness of nature at the end of the investigation, what remains of the marvelous is only the ingenuity of the proposed solution. This change of attitude has a series of consequences. To attain its goal, an explanatory discourse must be exposed—not only stated in a form and in terms that can be understood, but also given over entirely to publicity, placed before the eyes of all, just as, in the city, the writing of laws makes them an equally shared, common good for each citizen. Taken out of the realm of the secret, the physicist's *theōria* thus becomes a subject of debate; it is obliged to justify itself; it must account for its claims and lay itself open to critique and controversy. The rules of the political game—open discussion, contentious debate, the confrontation of opposing arguments—become the rules of the intellectual game. Alongside religious revelation, which, in the form of the mystery, remains the privilege of a restricted circle of initiates, and alongside the mass of common beliefs that everyone shares without question, a new notion of truth takes shape and is affirmed: open truth, accessible to all, and justified by its own demonstrative force.

The path that the Milesians layout, however, leads to a horizon that is different from theirs. After them, and in a manner that breaks with them, a mode of reflection will be established whose demands and ambitions go beyond what they undertook to achieve. Called to appear before the court of *logos*, demonstrative reason, the entire apparatus of notions on which the physicists based their inquiries—nature, genesis, change, the emergence of the multiple and the mobile from a single permanent element—is denounced as illusory and inconsistent. At the beginning of the fifth century, various currents of thought arose that, both continued and contradicted the Milesians, that "pushed back" at them in order to constitute something like the other side of the arch on which philosophy would build its edifice: against the full positivity of the Ionian physicists, the ideal of complete and perfect intelligibility was affirmed. To prevent the human discourse on nature from collapsing, ruined from within like the ancient myths, it is not enough to leave out the gods; argumentation must be completely transparent and must not contain the slightest incoherence or the shadow of an internal contradiction.[5] Its truth value is established by the formal rigor of its demonstration, its identity to itself in all its parts, its congruence even in its most distant implications, and not by its apparent agreement with natural givens, that is, its false sensory evidence, which is always vague and uncertain, relative and contradictory.

The effort to construct interlinking series of propositions that follow one another with such necessity that each one implies all the others took on multiple aspects during the fifth century. Parmenides gave it its first extreme form by laying out with uncompromising rigor the foundation of the concept of being. The logical imperatives of thought dispel any illusion that the multiplicity of beings could have been produced by any genesis. Being excludes generation. From what could being have been engendered? If it was from itself, then there was no generation. If it was from nonbeing, this leads to a contradictory conclusion: before generation, what we call being was nonbeing. We therefore cannot not say or think that being has become, only that it is. The truth of this statement is not empirically observed; on the contrary, despite the appearance of movement and change, the dispersion of things in space and their variability over time, the obviousness of this truth imposes itself absolutely on the mind, the result of an indirect demonstration by which it becomes manifest that the contrary statement is logically impossible. Governed from within by this demonstrative order, thought has no object other than what properly belongs to it, namely, the *logos*, the intelligible.

The progress of mathematics — in which the Milesians' geometric orientation led to a privileging of the study of figures —

confers an exemplary solidity and precision on this search for
intelligibility through demonstrative rigor. As presented in Euclid's *Elements*, geometry, with its apodictic character, becomes a
model for true thought. This discipline can take the form of a
body of propositions entirely and exactly deduced from a limited
number of postulates and axioms because it does not deal with
concrete realities, or even with the figures that the geometer uses
in his demonstrations. It bears on pure concepts, which it itself
defines and whose ideality — that is, to use Maurice Caveing's
phrase, whose perfection, objectivity, and full intelligibility —
depends on their not belonging to the sensible world.[6]

Behind nature and beyond appearances, an invisible background is formed, a truer reality, secret and hidden, which the
philosopher seeks to attain and which he makes the proper object
of his meditation. By insisting on this invisible being against the
visible, the authentic against the illusory, the permanent against
the fleeting, the certain against the uncertain, philosophy takes
over, in its way, from religious thought. It locates itself within the
very framework established by religion when it posited the sacred
powers that provide the foundation of this world beyond the
world of nature and in an invisible realm, and thus established a
complete contrast between gods and men, immortals and mortals, the plenitude of being and the limitations of a fleeting, vain,
phantom-like existence. However, even in this common aspiration to go beyond the plane of mere appearances and to accede to
the hidden principles that reinforce and support them, philosophy
is opposed to religion. To be sure, the truth which it is the philosopher's privilege of attaining and revealing is secret, concealed
in the invisible and hidden from the common man; its transmission, through the teaching of the master to the disciple, preserves
in some respects the character of an initiation. But philosophy
brings the mystery into the public square. It makes this mystery
no longer the matter of an ineffable vision but the object of an
inquiry carried out in broad daylight. Through free dialogue,
argued debate, or didactic statements, the mystery is transformed
into a knowledge whose vocation is to be universally shared. The

authentic being aimed at by the philosopher thus appears to be as much the contrary of as the heir to the mythic and the super-natural; the object of the *logos* is rationality itself, the order presiding over deduction, the principle of identity from which all true knowledge draws its legitimacy. With the physicists of Miletos, the new demand for positivity was for the first time taken to its absolute in the concept of *phusis*; in the work of Parmenides and his Eleatic successors, the new demand for intelligibility is taken to its absolute in the concept of *being* — one, immutable, and identical. Between these two demands, which are in some ways conjoined, in some ways in conflict, but both of which mark a decisive rupture with myth, rational thought is engaged, system after system, in a dialectic whose movement engenders the history of Greek philosophy.

Notes

PREFACE TO THE 1985 EDITION

1. See Chapters Three, Fifteen, and Eighteen.

2. Jean-Pierre Vernant, *Myth and Society in Ancient Greece*, trans. Janet Lloyd (New York: Zone Books, 1988); Marcel Detienne and Jean-Pierre Vernant, *The Cuisine of Sacrifice among the Greeks*, trans. Paula Wissing (Chicago: University of Chicago Press, 1989).

3. Vernant, *Religions, histoires, raisons* (Paris: Maspero, 1979).

4. Jean-Pierre Vernant and Pierre Vidal-Naquet, *Myth and Tragedy in Ancient Greece*, trans. Janet Lloyd (New York: Zone Books, 1988).

INTRODUCTION

1. Ignace Meyerson, *Les fonctions psychologiques et les oeuvres* (Paris: Vrin, 1948).

2. Zevedei Barbu, *Problems of Historical Psychology* (London: Routledge & Kegan Paul, 1960).

3. *Ibid.*, pp. 69–144.

4. See Meyerson, *Les fonctions psychologiques*, ch. 3 ("L'histoire des fonctions"), especially pp. 151–85, on the history of personality.

CHAPTER ONE: HESIOD'S MYTH OF THE RACES

This essay first appeared as "Le Mythe hésiodique des races: Essai d'analyse structurale," *Revue de l'histoire des religions* 157 (1960), pp. 21–54.

1. Hesiod, *Works and Days*, 213. On the place and meaning of the two myths

in the poem as a whole, see Paul Mazon, "Hésiode: La composition des Travaux et des Jours," *Revue des études anciennes* 14 (1912), pp. 328–57.

2. This is the case of the race of silver; see Hesiod, *Works and Days*, 1.143.

3. See René Schaerer, *L'homme antique et la structure du monde intérieur d'Homère à Socrate* (Paris: Payot, 1958), pp. 77–80.

4. Hesiod, *Works and Days*, 158.

5. Erwin Rohde, *Psyche: The Cult of Souls and Belief in Immortality among the Greeks*, 8th ed., trans. W.B. Hills (New York: Harper and Row, 1966), pp. 67–78.

6. Victor Goldschmidt, "Theologia," *Revue des études grecques* 63 (1950), pp. 33–39.

7. On this classification, see Armand Delatte, *Etudes sur la littérature pythagoricienne* (Paris: Champion, 1915), p. 48; Goldschmidt, "Theologia," p. 30ff.

8. Goldschmidt, "Theologia," p. 37, n.1.

9. It is generally agreed that the myth originally included three or four races. See, however, the reservations expressed by Mazon, who believes that Hesiod's work is entirely original ("Hesiode," p. 339), and Martin P. Nilsson, *Geschichte der griechischen Religion*, vol. 1 (Munich: Beck, 1955), p. 622. The themes of an age of gold and of successive human races destroyed by the gods appear to have an Eastern origin. On this point, see the exchange between J. Gwyn Griffiths and H.C. Baldry in the *Journal of the History of Ideas*: J. Gwyn Griffiths, "Archaeology and Hesiod's Five Ages," *Journal of the History of Ideas* 17 (1956), pp. 109–19; H.C. Baldry, "Hesiod's Five Ages," *Journal of the History of Ideas* 17 (1956), pp. 553–54; and Griffiths, "Did Hesiod Invent the 'Golden Age'?" *Journal of the History of Ideas* 19 (1958), pp. 91–93.

10. In Hesiod's *Theogony*, genealogies of the gods and cosmological myths provide a basis for the organization of the cosmos. They explain how the different cosmic levels (the heavenly, the subterranean, and the earthly worlds) came to be separated, and they account for the distribution and harmony of the various elements that compose the universe.

11. The ages do not differ only with respect to how long they last; their experience of time, the rhythm of the lapse of time, and the direction in which time flows are not the same either. See p. 45ff.

12. On this idea of continuous decline in the myth, see Friedrich Solmsen, *Hesiod and Aeschylus* (Ithaca: Cornell University Press, 1949), p. 83 n.27.

13. Plato, *Statesman*, 269cff. Several features in the myth in the *Statesman* recall the myth of the races.

14. Hesiod, *Works and Days*, 175.

15. Contrary to Solmsen: "The third generation ... has traveled much farther on the road of *hybris* than the second" (*Hesiod and Aeschylus*, p. 84). Despite the reference to lines 143–47, this claim is unsubstantiated.

16. Compare Hesiod, *Works and Days*, 134ff. and 145–46.

17. *Ibid.*, 127.

18. *Ibid.*, 158.

19. *Ibid.*, 144.

20. Eduard Meyer noticed the link between the races of gold and silver, on the one hand, and the race of bronze and the heroes, on the other. But he interpreted it as one of consanguinity, with a process of decline in the first case and improvement in the second. *Hesiods Erga und das Gedicht von den fünf Menschengeschlechtern* (Berlin: Weidmann, 1910), pp. 131–65.

21. See Hesiod, *Works and Days*, 123 and 141: *epichthonioi, hupochthonioi*.

22. *Ibid.*, 154: *nōnumnoi*.

23. The symmetry between the posthumous destiny of the men of bronze and that of the heroes is just as marked as in the case of the men of gold and the men of silver. The men of bronze disappear in death, leaving no name; the heroes live on in the Islands of the Blessed, and their names, celebrated by the poets, live on forever in men's memories. The former fade away in night and oblivion, while the latter belong to the domain of light and memory (see Pindar, *Olympians*, 2.109ff.).

24. Rohde, *Psyche*, p. 77.

25. See Hesiod, *Works and Days*, 184: Nothing will ever again be as it was in the past, *hōs to paros per*.

26. *Ibid.*, 119.

27. *Ibid.*, 118–19; note the expression: *automatē*. Compare the picture of human life in the age of iron, in 176–78, with that presented in the myth of Prometheus, in 42–48 and 94–105.

28. See François Daumas, "La valeur de l'or dans la pensée egyptienne," *Revue de l'histoire des religions* 149 (1956), pp. 1–18; Elena Cassin, "Le Pesant d'or," *Rivista degli studi orientali* 32 (1957), pp. 3–11. On the correspondences among gold, the sun, and the king, see Pindar, *Olympians*, 1.1ff.

29. Plato, *Republic*, 413cff.

30. Hesiod, *Works and Days*, 111.

31. Pausanias, *Description of Greece*, 6.20.1.

32. Hesiod, *Works and Days*, 126.

33. *Ibid.*, 123 and 126. On *phulakes*, see Callimachus, *Hymn to Zeus*, 79–81: The kings come from Zeus, who sets them up as the "guardians of the towns." In Plato (*Republic*, 413cff.), the men of gold who are born to rule are called *phulakes*. The term "guardian," in Plato, refers sometimes to the category of men who govern in the widest sense and sometimes, more specifically, to those who are entrusted with the military function. This specialization is understandable: the kings are *phulakes* inasmuch as they watch over their people in the name of Zeus; the warriors fulfill the same function in the name of the king. The epichthonian daemons who are linked with the function of royalty here assume a role normally reserved for female divinities, such as the Charites. But these divinities, on whom depends the fertility or, alternatively, the sterility of the earth, are ambivalent powers. In their white aspect, they manifest themselves as Charites, while in their black aspect, they become the Erīnyes (see Aeschylus, *Eumenides*, and Pausanias, *Description of Greece*, 8.34.1ff.). The same ambiguity is revealed in the relationship between the epichthonian and hypochthonian daemons. They appear to represent the two aspects, one positive and the other negative, of the effect of the king on the fertility of the soil. The powers that can encourage or impede fertility manifest themselves on two planes. They operate in the third functional domain (agriculture) as female divinities, but they also operate on the first (kingship) insofar as it affects the third, and here they take the form of male daemons.

34. Hesiod, *Works and Days*, 112; *Theogony*, 91.

35. Hesiod, *Works and Days*, 114ff. and 225ff.

36. *Ibid.*, 238ff. The same theme appears in the *Iliad*, 16.386. On the relationship between Zeus, the *skēptron*, and the kings "who hand out justice," see Homer, *Iliad*, 1.234 and 9.98.

37. Hesiod, *Works and Days*, 252 and 122.

38. See Hipponax, frag. 38 (O. Masson) = 34–35 (Diehl). "Father Zeus, king of the gods (*theōn palmu*), why have you given me no gold, king of silver (*argurou palmu*)?"

39. Hesiod, *Works and Days*, 134.

40. Referring to a course of lectures given by Georges Dumézil at the Ecole des Hautes Etudes in 1946–47, Francis Vian writes, in a note, on the subject of Hesiod's second race: "It is characterized by immoderation and impiety as seen from a theological, not military, point of view." *La guerre des Géants: Le mythe avant l'époque hellénistique* (Paris: Klincksieck, 1952), p. 183, n.2.

41. Hesiod, *Works and Days*, 251.

42. See Mazon, "Hesiode," p. 339, n.3.

43. Hesiod, *Theogony*, 209; compare *Works and Days*, 134, and *Theogony*, 719.

44. Hesiod, *Theogony*, 881–85; Apollodorus, *The Library*, 2.1.

45. Hesiod, *Theogony*, 717; see also 697.

46. Hesiod, *Works and Days*, 144–46.

47. *Ibid.*, 146–47.

48. See, for example, Homer, *Iliad*, 7.146.

49. *Ibid.*, 2.578; Homer, *Odyssey*, 24.467; *Iliad*, 20.156; Euripides, *Phoenician Women*, 110; Homer, *Iliad*, 19.362.

50. This "panoply" is also found in the *palladion* and *tropaion*.

51. Homer, *Iliad*, 16.140; 19.361 and 390; 22.225; *Palatine Anthology*, 6.52; see also Hesychius: *meliai*, either *dorata* (trees) or *logchai* (lances).

52. Hesiod, *Works and Days*, 145.

53. Vian, *La guerre des Géants*, especially p. 280 ff.

54. Hesiod, *Theogony*, 185–87.

55. Callimachus, *Hymn to Zeus*, 47.

56. Clement, *Stromateis*, 1.21.

57. Scholium on Euripides, *Phoenician Women*.

58. Sophocles, *Women of Trachis*, 1058–59.

59. Homer, *Iliad*, 2.604 and 611; 7.134; scholia to Aeschylus, *Prometheus*, 438.

60. Apollodorus, *Library*, 3.4.1.

61. Euripides, *Phoenician Women*, 931 and 935; Pausanias, *Description of Greece*, 9.10.1.

62. Apollodorus, *Library*, 1.9.23; Apollonius Rhodius, *Argonautica*, 3.401ff and 1026ff.

63. Apollonius Rhodius, *Argonautica*, 1356–64.

64. Hesiod, *Works and Days*, 146 and 150–51. It does not seem feasible to take this, as some have, to mean "they worked in bronze." Karl Kerényi, *La mythologie des Grecs: Histoires des dieux et de l'humanité*, trans. Henriette de Roguin (Paris: Payot, 1952), p. 225.

65. Aristotle, *Poetics*, 16.1454, B22; Plutarch, *On the Delays of Divine Vengeance*, 268; Dio Chrysotomus, *Orationes*, 4.23; Julian, *Orations*, 2.81c.

66. Apollonius Rhodius, *Argonautica*, 1.57–64; Apollodorus, *Epitome*, 1.22.

67. Scholiast to *Iliad*, 1.264, and to Apollonius Rhodius, *Argonautica*, 1.57.

68. Aeschylus, *Seven against Thebes*, 529ff. Note that this warrior has a name that evokes a young girl (*parthenos*). Kaineus acquired invulnerability when he changed sex; Achilles, the warrior who was invulnerable except in his heel, was brought up with girls and dressed like a girl. Warrior initiation rites involve transvestism.

69. We know that Gē tried to procure for the Giants a *pharmakon* for immortality, which would protect them from the attacks of Herakles and the gods; Apollodorus, *The Library*, 1.6.1.

70. Hesiod, *Works and Days*, 158.

71. Hesiod, *Theogony*, 385ff. Note the exact parallelism between the episode of the hundred-handed and that of Kratos and Bia. Like the Hekatoncheires, Kratos and Bia take the side of Zeus against the Titans at the decisive moment. This ensures victory for the Olympians, and Kratos and Bia, again like the Hekatoncheires, receive as a reward certain privileges they had not hitherto enjoyed.

72. Compare Hesiod, *Theogony*, 149ff, and *Works and Days*, 145ff.

73. Hesiod, *Theogony*, 617–64.

74. *Ibid.*, 649.

75. *Ibid.*, 651.

76. *Ibid.*, 656–58.

77. *Ibid.*, 661.

78. *Ibid.*, 735.

79. *Ibid.*, 639–40.

80. There are a number of intermediary stages between the mortality of the "ephemeral ones" and the immortality of the gods, in particular the series of beings known as *makrobioi*, among which must be classed the nymphs, such as the *meliai*, and the Giants.

81. Hesiod, *Works and Days*, 57–58.

82. *Ibid.*, 90ff.

83. *Ibid.*, 179.

84. Hesiod, *Theogony*, 585.

85. Pandora is the name of a goddess of the earth and fertility. Like her double, Anesidora, she is represented in illustrations as emerging from the earth, in accordance with the theme of the *anodos* of a chthonian and agricultural power.

86. Hesiod, *Works and Days*, 705, and *Theogony*, 599.

87. Hesiod, *Works and Days*, 309.

88. *Ibid.*, 14.

89. *Ibid.*, 193–94.

90. *Ibid.*, 113ff. Their end resembles sleep more than death. The children of the night, Thanatos and Hypnos, are twins, but opposites; see Hesiod, *Theogony*, 763ff: Hypnos is quiet and gentle toward men, while Thanatos has a heart of iron and an implacable spirit.

91. Hesiod, *Works and Days*, 130–31.

92. *Ibid.*, 132–33.

93. On the positive aspect of the old man as a synonym of wisdom and justice, see Hesiod, *Theogony*, 234–36.

94. See Xenophon, *Constitution of the Lacedaemonians*, 4.1: Lycurgus was particularly concerned with the *Hēbōntes* or *kouroi*.

95. Vian, *La guerre des Géants*, p. 280.

96. Hesiod, *Works and Days*, 181.

97. Georges Dumézil, who read this essay in manuscript, points out that in *Jupiter, Mars, Quirinus: Essai sur la conception indo-européene de la société et sur les origines de Rome* (Paris: Gallimard, 1941), he suggested a trifunctional interpretation of the myth of races. He wrote: "[I]t seems clear that, just as in the corresponding Indian myth, the myth of races in Hesiod associates each of the Ages (or rather each of the three 'pairs' of Ages), in the course of which humanity is renewed only to decline, with a 'functional' conception of the differences in the species — the three functions being religion, war and labor (p. 259). Subsequently, Dumézil came to accept as satisfactory the interpretation proposed by Goldschmidt. (See Dumézil, "Triades de calamités et triades de délits à valeur fonctionelle chez divers peuples indo-européens," *Latomus* 14 (1955), p. 179 n.3.) He remarked that the present study seems to support and confirm his first hypothesis.

98. See Edouard Will, "Aux origines du régime foncier grec: Homère, Hésiode et l'arrière-plan mycénien," *Revue des études anciennes* 59 (1957), pp. 5–50. This article contains illuminating remarks concerning the changes in the status of landowner to which Hesiod's work bears witness (shared inheritance, the division of land into small plots, different ways of handing on the *klēros*, credit and debt, the process of dispossession of small landowners, and the seizure of vacant holdings by the powerful). Louis Gernet notes that at the time when the term *polis* was introduced to describe an already organized society, the judicial function was transformed, as can be seen by comparing Homer and

Hesiod. Gernet, *Recherches sur le développement de la pensée juridique et morale en Grèce* (Paris: Leroux, 1917), pp. 14–15.

99. It is well known that at an early stage in the development of the city-state, the warrior disappeared as a particular social category and also as a type of man embodying specific virtues. The transformation of the warrior of the epics into the hoplite fighting in a close formation not only was a revolution in military technique but also represented a decisive social, religious, and psychological change. See, in particular, Henri Jeanmaire, *Couroi et Courètes: Essai sur l'éducation spartiate et sur les rites d'adolescence dans l'antiquité hellénique* (Lille: Bibliothèque universitaire, 1939), pp. 115ff.

100. On the dispute between the two brothers and the basis for and vicissitudes of the lawsuit, see Bernard Abraham van Groningen, "Hesiode et Persès" (Amsterdam: Noord-Hollandsche, 1957).

101. Hesiod, *Works and Days*, 264. Gernet writes: "Hesiod's *dikē* [unlike Homer's more homogeneous *dikē*] is multiple and contradictory because it is in keeping with a new and critical state of society: *dikē* as custom will sometimes be the force behind the law (189, 192); *dikē* as sentence is frequently considered unjust (39, 219, 221, 262, 264; cf. 254, 269, 271). These two forms of *dikē* are opposed to divine Dikē (219–20 and 258ff.): in these two passages, *dikē* is the formal antithesis of the two *dikai*" (*Recherches sur le développement de la pensée*, p. 16). See also the author's remarks on the becoming divine of Aidōs in Hesiod, *Works and Days*, 75.

102. Hesiod, *Works and Days*, 238ff.

103. This common interest is made explicit in Aratus's poem, in the passage where, following Hesiod, he gives an account of the races of metal. The reign of *dikē* here appears to be inseparable from agricultural activity. The men of gold know nothing of discord and strife. For them, "the oxen, the plough and Dikē herself, who is the dispenser of rightful blessings, provide for everything in great abundance." When the men of bronze forge the sword of war and crime, they kill and devour the oxen used for ploughing (*Phenomena*, 110ff).

104. Hesiod, *Works and Days*, 214; the opposition is very marked.

105. *Ibid.*, 14.

CHAPTER TWO: HESIOD'S MYTH OF THE RACES
This essay first appeared as "Le mythe hésiodique des races: Sur un essai de mise au point," *Revue de philologie* 40 (1966), pp. 247–76.

1. Jean Defradas, "Le mythe hésiodique des races: Essai de mise au point," *L'information littéraire* 4 (1965), pp. 152–56; Jean-Pierre Vernant, "Le mythe hésiodique des races: Essai d'analyse structurale," *Revue de l'histoire des religions* 157 (1960), pp. 21–54. See Chapter One.

2. Defradas, "Le mythe hésiodique des races."

3. Hesiod, *Works and Days*, 127 and 174.

4. Defradas, "Le mythe hésiodique des races."

5. *Ibid.*

6. *Ibid.*

7. For instance, I wrote: "Thus each pair of ages is defined not only by its position in the sequence (the first two, the next two, and the last two) but also by a specific temporal quality that is closely linked to the type of activity with which it is associated" (see p. 45).

8. Hesiod, *Works and Days*, 448–500.

9. *Ibid.*, 614–17.

10. Jean-Pierre Vernant, "Genèse et structure dans le mythe hésiodique des races," in Maurice de Gandillac, Lucien Goldmann, and Jean Piaget (ed.), *Entretiens sur les notions de genèse et de structure* (Paris: Mouton, 1965), p. 121.

11. See p. 120. See also Jean-Pierre Vernant, "Aspects mythiques de la mémoire en Grèce," *Journal de Psychologie* 56 (1959), pp. 1–29.

12. See p. 120 and n.21.

13. Ignace Meyerson, "Le temps, la mémoire, l'histoire," *Journal de Psychologie* 53 (1956), special number titled "La construction du temps humain," p. 340. See Jacqueline de Romilly, *Histoire et raison chez Thucydide* (Paris: Belles Lettres, 1956).

14. See p. 32.

15. I am speaking here of the myth of origins and structural divisions, not, as Defradas says, a chronological schema and a structural schema.

16. See p. 28.

17. Defradas, "Le mythe hésiodique des races," p. 156; Victor Goldschmidt, "Theologia," *Revue des études grecques* 63 (1950), pp. 20–42.

18. Defradas, "Le mythe hésiodique des races."

19. See p. 32.

20. See Erwin Rohde, *Psyche: The Cult of Souls and Belief in Immortality among the Greeks*, 8th ed., trans. W.B. Hills (New York: Harper and Row, 1966), pp. 69–70.

21. Hesiod, *Theogony*, 211–33.

22. See Clémence Ramnoux, *La nuit et les enfants de la nuit dans la tradition grecque* (Paris: Flammarion, 1959), p. 66ff.

23. In *Works and Days*, 14, Hesiod mentions the *eris* that makes *polemon kai dērin* (war and fighting) increase. The meaning of *dēris* is defined in the following passage, in which the poet exhorts his brother to stop stirring up *neikea kai dērin* (quarrels and disagreements) in the agora in order to seize someone else's possessions (33). See also 30 (*neikeōn t'agoreōn*) and 29 (*neikea...agorēs*). Perses, a poor wretch (*deilos*) (214), cannot hope to acquire the possessions of others in the form of war booty; since he is incapable of using the *eris* of his arm, he must fall back on the *eris* of his tongue: "Wealth should not be seized; god-given wealth is much better. One can steal great wealth by violence, with the strength of one's arm; one can also steal it through one's tongue, as often happens when gain deceives men's sense" (320–24). On the other *eris*, see *Works and Days*, 12, 13, 19.

24. *Ibid.*, 21–22.

25. *Ibid.*, 28.

26. *Ibid.*, 42.

27. See Hesiod, *Works and Days*, 48, and *Theogony*, 537 and 565.

28. See Hesiod, *Theogony*, 585 (*kalon kakon ant'agathoio*) and 602 (*heteron de poren kakon ant'agathoio*).

29. Hesiod, *Works and Days*, 57–58, *kakon, hōi ken hapantes terpōntai kata thumon heon kakon amphagapōntes.*

30. *Dolos* and *doliē technē* of Prometheus: Hesiod, *Theogony*, 540, 547, 550, 551, 555, 560, 562; Pandora as *dolos*, Hesiod, *Theogony*, 589, and *Works and Days*, 83.

31. Hesiod, *Works and Days*, 65–68 and 73–78.

32. *Ibid.*, 90ff. The *gēras* of 92 is usually corrected to *kēras*. The correction is not necessary. The meaning is perfectly clear. It is the sense specified in 93, an interpolation borrowed from the *Odyssey*: "For in poverty men grow old quickly." It should not be forgotten that *Gēras* appears among the other powers of evil as one of the children of Night.

33. Hesiod, *Theogony*, 591.

34. *Ibid.*, 603 and 605: *ho g' ou biotou epideuēs sōei.*

35. *Ibid.*, 609–10: *tōi de t'ap' aiōnos kakon esthlōi antipherisei emmenai.* A comparison with Hesiod, *Works and Days*, 179 shows how Pandora can symbolize life in the age of iron.

36. Hesiod, *Works and Days*, 373–75: *teēn diphōsa kaliēn*. Note the theme of *apatē* and *peithō*.

37. Hesiod, *Theogony*, 593–602.

38. Hesiod, *Works and Days*, 705: *euei atep daloio*. For Hesiod, the young man in the flowering of his youth is full of sap. Old age is a progressive process of drying up. The role played by women in the desiccation caused by old age can be better understood if we bear in mind the information given in lines 586–87: in the heart of the dry season, when Sirius burns men's heads and knees *gounata*, women are *machlotatai* (more lascivious), and men are *aphaurotatoi* (weaker). In contrast, during the autumn rains, when the sun's heat slackens and Sirius spends only a little while over the men's heads each day, men's bodies become *pollon elaphroteros*, much more vigorous (414–16).

39. *Ibid.*, 705: *ōmōi gērai dōken*.

40. Thus there appears to be a symmetry between the theme of Pandora in Hesiod and that of Helen in the *Cypria* and, later, in the tragedies. The series of Night's children continues after Nemesis with Apatē, Philotēs, Gēras, and Eris. In the *Cypria,* to make men expiate their impiety and to put an end to their teeming reproduction, Nemesis, or divine vengeance, brings forth a "femme fatale" who is a mixture of Apatē and Philotēs and whose arrival provokes *eris,* war, and death. According to Athenaeus 334c-d (= frag. 7, Allen), the author of the *Cypria* wrote that Nemesis, having been united in *philotēs* with Zeus, gave birth to Helen (*thauma brotoisi*) (the same expression is used for Pandora in Hesiod, *Theogony*, 575, 584, 588). But this "marvel" is at the same time a *dolos,* a trap. (The aspect of *apatē* is reinforced in the figure of Helen by the theme of the double, the *eidōlon*, which can be compared to *Theogony*, 572 and 584, and *Works and Days*, 62–63 and 71, where *thauma* is associated with *eidos*, and *eikōn*. Seductive as she is, Helen is an *eris* who brings about the *boulē Dios*. On Helen as *eris*, see Aeschylus, *Agamemnon*, 1468–74; Euripides, *Helen*, 36, *Electra*, 1282 (Zeus has sent to Ilium an *eidōlon* of Helen so that *eris* and *phonos* will appear among mortals), and *Orestes*, 1639–42 (the gods have used this "beautiful one" *kallisteuma* to bring about conflict between the Greeks and the Phrygians; they have caused many deaths in order to purge the world of the insolence *hubrisma* of mortals whose fertility was filling it).

41. Hesiod, *Works and Days*, 105.

42. On Hesiod's methods, see Peter Walcot, "The Problem of the Proemium of Hesiod's *Theogony*," *Symbolae osloenses* 33 (1957), pp. 37–47, and "The

Composition of the Works and Days," *Revue des études grecques* (1961), pp. 1–19. See also the account of my lectures devoted to the composition of the proemium of the *Theogony* in the *Annuaire de l'Ecole pratique des Hautes-Etudes* 6 (1962–63), p. 142ff.

43. Hesiod, *Theogony*, 93ff.

44. *Ibid.*, 29ff.

45. Hesiod, *Works and Days*, 118–19.

46. See *ibid.*, 117–18: *automatē, karpon pollon te kai aphthonon*. Plato provides the best commentary on this picture at the beginning of the third book of the *Laws*, where he describes the state of humanity after the flood, when neither iron nor bronze was yet used (678d1). Men are still few in number and take pleasure in each other's company (678c5); they are fond of each other and look upon each other with affection; they do not have to vie with each other for food, for there is no fear that there will not be enough (678d9ff.). They are therefore unacquainted with both discord (*statis*) and war (*polemos*) (678d6). They have a generous disposition: *oute gar hubris out' adikia, zēloi te au kai phthonoi ouk eggignontai* (679c), for neither immoderation nor injustice nor jealousy nor rivalry arises.

47. Hesiod, *Works and Days*, 200–201.

48. *Ibid.*, 195–96; see also 28: *Eris kakochartos*.

49. *Ibid.*, 183–85.

50. *Ibid.*, 176–79.

51. *Ibid.*, 107.

52. *Ibid.*, 202: *Nun d' ainon basileusi ereō*.

53. *Ibid.*, 213: *ō Persē, su d' akoue dikēs, mēd' hubrin ophelle*.

54. Note the opposition in *ibid.*, 214, between *deilōi brotōi* (Perses) and *esthlos* (the king, whom Hesiod addressed in the previous short parenthesis).

55. *Ibid.*, 127 and 158.

56. *Ibid.*, 144.

57. *Ibid.*, 134 and 146.

58. *Ibid.*, 145–46.

59. *Ibid.*, 158.

60. See above, p. 40.

61. See above, p. 30.

62. See above, p. 39.

63. Hesiod, *Works and Days*, 126 and 142.

64. *Ibid.*, 154: *nōnumnoi: thanatos* [...] *heile melas* .

65. *Ibid.*, 161 and 166: *Tous men thanatou telos amphekalupse.*

66. *Ibid.*, 167: *tois de dich' anthrōpōn bioton kai ēthe' opassas.*

67. Rohde, *Psyche*, pp. 76–77.

68. Hesiod, *Works and Days*, 141–42: *hupochthonioi makares thnētois kaleontai, deuteroi, all' empēs timē kai toisin opēdei.*

69. *Ibid.*, 252–53.

70. See p. 45.

71. Hesiod, *Works and Days*, 114: *oude ti deilon gēras epēn*; 131: *mega nēpios.*

72. Defradas, "Le mythe hésiodique des races," p. 155.

73. See p. 31

74. See p. 32.

75. See pp. 32 and 44.

76. The only possible exception is the men of silver, who live for a hundred years as children, then commit follies and die forthwith. But it is clear that such a comparison would be misleading. Only the *individual* members of the race of silver are portrayed as progressing toward death, through a century-long childhood, just as Hesiod and Perses are moving toward death in the process of progressive aging. There is no question of a change in the conditions of life of the race of silver *as a whole*. It is not the case that after several generations the men of silver, instead of remaining young until they die, are born adult or old. It is therefore not correct to claim, as Defradas does, that "Hesiod does not treat the age of iron any differently from the preceding races" ("Le mythe hésiodique des races").

77. Hesiod, *Works and Days*, 179: *all' empēs kai toisi memeizetai esthla kakoisin.*

78. *Ibid.*, 180–201.

79. *Ibid.*, 200–201.

80. *Ibid.*, 114.

81. *Ibid.*, 181.

82. *Ibid.*, 118–19.

83. *Ibid.*, 191: *kai hubrin anera timēsousi.*

84. *Ibid.*, 194.

85. Compare *ibid.*, 195–96 with 21–26. Beggar is jealous (*phthoneei*) of beggar, singer of singer. Neighbor is envious (*zēloi*) of his richer neighbor and therefore sets himself to work harder in order to become richer in his turn. Envy (*zēlos*) is thus, like *eris*, double and ambiguous. Just as there is a good *eris* along-

side the *kakochartos eris* — which takes pleasure in evil — there is a good *zēlos* as well as a *kakochartos zēlos*. This is a remarkable example of the interplay of ambiguous concepts in Hesiod. The good *eris*, the praiseworthy one, which is profitable for mortals and is allied to *dikē*, possesses elements of *phthonos* and *zelos*, powers usually associated with war (see, for example, Lysias 2.48: war broke out among the Greeks: *dia zēlon kai phthonon*). The wicked *eris*, the warlike one, implies *zelos* and *phthonos* in the bad sense, but it also includes a measure of emulation in the good sense — whatever urges the warrior to prove himself "better" (*areiōn*) than his adversary and to conquer him through his own superior valor. This positive aspect of warlike *zelos* appears in Hesiod's *Theogony*, 384: Zelos associated with Nike, and Kratos associated with Bia, are grouped around the sovereign Zeus's throne. In contrast, at the end of the age of iron, the wicked *zelos* urges the bad man, the villain (*kakos*), to attack the more valorous and nobler man (*areiona*), not with equal weapons in a fair fight where the best man wins but "with deceitful words, backed up by a false oath" (Hesiod, *Works and Days*, 193–95).

86. *Ibid.*, 184.

87. See, for example, *ibid.*, 342ff. and 349.

88. *Ibid.*, 396.

89. *Ibid.*, 228ff.

90. *Ibid.*, 235 and 182.

91. This suggests that in the context of mythical imagery we already have a foreshadowing of what will be the important philosophical concept of "mixture" (*mixis*).

92. *Ibid.*, 112. As Bernhard Abraham van Groningen suggests, this appears to be the meaning of line 108, which was condemned by Mazon: "that gods and men have the same origins." *La composition littéraire archaïque grecque: Procédés et réalisations*, 2nd ed. (Amsterdam, Noord-Hollandsche, 1960), p. 228 n.3. Defradas suggests another interpretation: "If the hierarchy of the different classes of men explains the hierarchy of divine beings that are the objects of cults, the suspect phrase must be the true introduction to this" ("Le mythe hésiodique des races"). There is a decisive objection to this hypothesis. The hierarchy of divine beings that the myth has to account for includes all supernatural beings except the *theoi*. If the myth does indeed have the function that is attributed to it, the word *theos* should be taken in its technical sense, to mark the difference between the gods strictly speaking and daemons or heroes.

93. Hesiod, *Theogony*, 535ff.

94. Hesiod, *Works and Days*, 197–200: is it necessary to point out that in the world of Hesiod, Aidōs and Nemesis are still present? The *nun* of the present life (176) is contrasted to *tote* (197), which marks the final point of the cycle, the departure of all that remained of the divine in this world.

95. Defradas, "Le mythe hésiodique des races," p. 155.

96. Maurice Halbwachs, *Les cadres sociaux de la mémoire* (Paris: Presses Universitaires de France, 1962).

97. On the Hesiodic calendar, see Martin P. Nilsson, *Primitive Time-Reckoning* (Lund: Gleerup, 1920).

98. Homer, *Iliad*, 6.146ff. See also p. 132: "The clearer conception elaborated in lyric poetry of a human time fleeing, never to return, along an irreversible line calls into question the idea of an entirely cyclical order and of a periodic and regular renewal of the universe." On the conception of a sequence of days, months, and seasons succeeding each other within the framework of an annual circular cycle, see the *Homeric Hymn to Apollo*, 249–50: "But when the days and months reached their end and the Hours came with the circling of the year, *aps peritellomenou eteos kai epēluthon Hōrai.*" See also Hesiod, *Works and Days*, 386: *autis de periplomenou eniautou.*

99. Plato, *Statesman*, 268eff.

100. *Ibid.*, 272a. See Hesiod, *Works and Days*, 117–18 (*arousa automatē*).

101. Plato, *Statesman*, 270d-e.

102. Mazon, quoted by Defradas, "Le mythe hésiodique des races," p. 153.

103. Sophocles, *Antigone*, 1108, and *Electra*, 305–306.

104. Apart from line 127, *epeita* in line 137, and the final *tote* in line 197, when Aidōs and Nemesis leave earth for the heavens.

105. Defradas, "Le mythe hésiodique des races"; Goldschmidt, "Theologia."

106. Goldschmidt, "Theologia," p. 36.

107. *Ibid.*, p. 35.

108. *Ibid.*, p. 31.

109. *Ibid.*, p. 37.

110. This is why this text presents the historian of Greek religion with a very important problem with regard to the cult of the heroes. We know that in Homer the term *hērōs* has no precise religious significance. In Hesiod, the term appears for the first time with a religious meaning in the context of the

classification of supernatural powers. But there is still no question of a *timē*, a cult, or at least a public cult extending beyond the family circle, within which rituals connected with honoring the dead normally remain. By contrast, in the organization of religion in the city-state, the public cult of the heroes has a very definite place and character. How and when did this cult become established with the particular features we know it had in the classical period? This is a difficult problem. Let us note, simply, that the category of the heroes comprises elements that clearly had diverse origins. Neither of the two traditional theories is successful in accounting for all the facts: both the theory that the cult of the heroes is connected with the cult of the dead and the theory that sees the heroes as ancient, outdated gods fail in this respect. In addition to the heroes who are clearly former deities or famous dead whose cult is connected with a particular tomb, there are deities of the earth, who are very close to Hesiod's subterranean daemons, and deities connected with particular functions of every kind. It seems very likely that the unification of these various elements into a single homogeneous and well-defined category with an appointed place in worship and in the hierarchy of divine beings must have been related to certain social needs connected with the founding of the city. Here again Hesiod seems situated between the Homeric world and the world of the *polis*. From a theological point of view, he truly seems to be a precursor, given his terminology and his classification of divine beings into gods, daemons, the dead, and heroes. This was apparently the opinion of Plato (*Cratylus*, 397eff.) and of Plutarch (*Moralia*, 415B); for Homer neither classes the heroes in a religious category nor distinguishes clearly between the *theoi* and the *daimones*. Plutarch is therefore quite correct when he writes that Hesiod was the first to distinguish between the two kinds: *katharōs kai diōrismenōs*.

111. These two principles of interpretation are more fully developed in the conclusion of my first study (see pp. 46–48).

112. Defradas, "Le mythe hésiodique des races," p. 155.

CHAPTER THREE: STRUCTURAL METHOD AND THE MYTH OF THE RACES
This essay originally appeared as "Méthode structurale et mythe des races," Jacques Brunschwig, Claude Imbert, and Alain Roger (eds.) *Histoire et Structure: A la mémoire de Victor Goldschmidt* (Paris: Vrin, 1985).

1. Victor Goldschmidt, "Theologia" and "Addendum," in *Questions platoniciennes* (Paris: Vrin, 1970), pp. 141–59 and 159–72, and "Remarques sur la méth-

ode structurale en histoire de la philosophie," in Fernand Brunner and Gilbert Boss, *Métaphysique, histoire de la philosophie: Recueil d'études offert à Fernand Brunner* (Neuchâtel: Baconnière, 1981), pp. 213–40; Peter Walcot, "The Composition of the *Works and Days*," *Revue des études grecques*, 74 (1961), pp. 4–7.

2. See above, "Hesiod's Myth of the Races: A Reassessment," pp. 86–87.

3. Goldschmidt, "Remarques sur la méthode structurale," pp. 219–20; see also pp. 217–18.

4. On this point, see Pietro Pucci, "Lévi-Strauss and Classical Culture," *Arethusa* 4, no. 2 (1971), pp. 103–17.

5. Goldschmidt, "Theologia," p. 167.

6. Goldschmidt, *Questions platoniciennes*, pp. 169–70.

7. *Ibid.*, p. 169; see also p. 155.

8. *Ibid.*, p. 169.

9. See the commentary on line 108 by M.L. West, in Hesiod, *Works and Days* (Oxford: Clarendon, 1978), p. 178.

10. Goldschmidt, *Questions platoniciennes*, pp. 168–69.

11. Hesiod, *Works and Days*, 731.

12. On the relationship and the differences between the story of the races and the myth of Prometheus with respect to the theme of the separation of men and gods, see Helen King, "Hesiod and Hippocrates: The Myth of the Five Ages and the Origin of Medicine," unpublished paper, and "Tithonos and Tethix," in Thomas M. Falkner and Judith de Luce (eds.), *Old Age in Greek and Latin Literature* (Albany, NY: State University of New York Press, 1990), pp. 15–35.

13. See Jean Rudhardt, "Le mythe hésiodique des races et celui de Prométhée: Recherche des structures et des significations," in *Du mythe, de la religion grecque et de la compréhension d'autrui* (Geneva: Droz, 1981), pp. 255–57. Rudhardt's analysis presents the most thorough attempt to harmonize the story of the races with the myth of Prometheus and to integrate them both into the "chronological" framework implied by the succession of divine generations and the replacement of Kronos's reign with that of Zeus. According to this perspective, the separation becomes more pronounced between the races of gold and silver, on the one hand, and the series that follows, on the other. Between the race of heroes and the race of iron, there is, on the contrary, a sort of continuity. The race of iron perpetuates the race of heroes in a perverted form. In fact, Hesiod does not say explicitly that the race of heroes was annihilated like the others. He does not apply the formula "when the earth covered them over" to

them or say that the race of iron was created by Zeus or the gods. In this sense, even if two different races are designated by the two distinct names, there is indeed a particular proximity in the succession from the race of heroes to the race of iron.

14. On the shared existence of the gods and the heroes, see Hesiod, frag. 1.5ff., in Reinhold Merkelbach and M.L. West (eds.), *Fragmenta Hesiodea* (Oxford: Clarendon, 1967).

15. Homer, *Odyssey*, 9.105-15, 187-89, 274-76. On Homer's Cyclopes as figures of an earlier and primitive state of humanity, see Plato, *Laws*, 3, 680b-e.

16. Hesiod, *Works and Days*, 225-47.

17. *Ibid.*, 249-55.

18. Hesiod, *Works and Days*, 171 and 549.

19. M.L. West, *Works and Days* (Oxford: Clarendon Press, 1978), p. 186.

20. *Ibid.* For tragedy: Aeschylus, *Persians*, 634; Euripides, *Alcestis*, 1003. For Dioscuri: Homer, *Odyssey*, 11.301-304.

21. Euripides, *Rhesos*, 970ff.

22. Isocrates, *Euagoras*, 70-71.

23. Gregory Nagy, *The Best of the Achaeans: Concepts of the Hero in Archaic Greek Poetry* (Baltimore: Johns Hopkins Press, 1979), p. 191.

24. Hesiod, *Theogony*, 987 and 991.

25. In Euripides's *Alcestis*, Alcestis dies for her husband and is a *makaira daimōn* in the afterlife. Her tomb is honored as divine (1003ff.). See also Aeschylus, *Persians*, which contains the expressions *chthonioi daimones hagnoi* (628) and *isodaimōn basileus* (633).

26. Marie Delcourt, *Légendes et cultes des héros en Grèce* (Paris: Presses Universitaires de France, 1942), p. 39, quoted in Goldschmidt, *Questions platoniciennes*, p. 165.

27. See p. 423 n.110.

28. J.N. Coldstream, "Hero-Cults in the Age of Homer," *Journal of Hellenic Studies* 96 (1976), pp. 8-17; Anthony M. Snodgrass, *Archaeology and the Rise of the Greek State: An Inaugural Lecture* (Cambridge: Cambridge University Press, 1977), p. 31, and "Les origines du culte des héros dans la Grèce antique," in Gherardo Gnoli and Jean-Pierre Vernant (eds.), (Cambridge: Cambridge University Press, 1982), pp. 107-19; Claude Bérard, "Récupérer la mort du prince: Héroïsation et formation de la cité," in Gnoli and Vernant, *La Mort, les morts*, pp. 89-105.

29. See Theodora Hadzisteliou Price, "Hero-Cult and Homer," *Historia* 22 (1973), pp. 129–44.

30. Homer, *Iliad*, 10.414, 11.166 and 371, 24.349. For the tomb of Aipytos in Arcadia, see 3.604; for Erechtheus in the Athenian acropolis, see 2.547.

31. Homer, *Iliad*, 12.22–23.

32. Nagy, *Best of the Achaeans*, p. 160.

33. Hesiod, *Works and Days*, 166 and 167.

34. Nagy, *Best of the Achaeans*, pp. 151–73.

35. See Chapter Two n.110.

36. Goldschmidt, *Questions platoniciennes*, pp. 162 and 172.

CHAPTER FOUR: MYTHICAL ASPECTS OF MEMORY

This essay originally appeared as "Aspects mythiques de la mémoire en Grèce," *Journal de Psychologie* 56 (1959), pp. 1–29.

1. Ignace Meyerson, "Le temps, la mémoire, l'histoire," *Journal de Psychologie* 53 (1956), p. 335.

2. The cult of Ērōs is widespread; for that of Aidōs, at Sparta and Athens, see Pausanias 3.20.10 and 1.17.1, and Hesiod, *Works and Days*, 200; for that of Phobos, at Sparta, see Plutarch, *Life of Kleomenes*, 8 and 9; at Athens, Plutarch, *Life of Theseus*, 27; for Pistis, in Attica, see L. R. Farnell, *The Cults of the Greek States* (Oxford: Clarendon, 1896), vol.5, 481, n.248. For the deification of Mētis, see Hesiod, *Theogony*, 358 and 886ff.; for Atē, see Homer, *Iliad*, 9.503ff., 10.391, 19.85ff.; Apollodorus, *The Library*, 3.12.3, and the tragedians; for Lyssa, see Euripides, *Bacchae*, 880ff.

3. As Louis Gernet has noted, before writing was available, the institution of the *mnēmōn* (the figure who is responsible for the remembering the past for the sake of legal decisions) was based on trust in the individual memory of a living "recorder." Only later did the term come to refer to magistrates responsible for the preservation of written records. But the role of the *mnēmōn* was not restricted to the legal context. Gernet points out that it derived from a religious practice. According to legend, the *mnēmōn* acts as a servant to a hero. His function is to remind his master constantly of a divine task, the forgetting of which would lead to death (Plutarch, *Greek Questions*, 28). The *mnēmōn* may also have a technical function (Homer, *Odyssey*, 8.163), a politico-religious one (Plutarch, *Greek Questions*, 4), or one that involves the organization of the religious calendar (Aristophanes, *Clouds*, 615–26). Gernet's remark proves valid on every level: "One may

well wonder whether at the stage when writing was introduced, the function of memory was not already somewhat in decline." Louis Gernet, "Les temps dans les formes archaïques du droit," *Journal de Psychologie* 53 (1956), p. 404.

4. Hesiod, *Theogony*, 54ff., 135, 915ff.

5. See Pindar, frag. 32, in Aimé Puech, *Pindare* (Paris: Belles Lettres, 1923), vol. 4: *Manteueo, Moisa, prophateusō d' egō* ("Give forth your oracles, O Muse, and I will be your prophet"). See also Plato, *Ion*, 534e.

6. See, in particular, Francis Macdonald Cornford, *Principium Sapientiae: The Origins of Greek Philosophical Thought* (Cambridge: Cambridge University Press, 1952), p. 89ff.

7. On poetry as *sophia*, see Jacqueline Duchemin, *Pindare, poète et prophète* (Paris: Belles Lettres, 1955), p. 23ff. The poet refers to himself by the names of *sophos anēr* and *sophistēs*. Pindar, *Isthmians*, 5.28.

8. Homer, *Iliad*, 1.70; Hesiod, *Theogony*, 32 and 38.

9. Homer, *Iliad*, 2.484ff., and *Odyssey*, 8.491; Pindar, *Paeans*, 10 and 6.50–58, in Puech, *Pindare*, vol. 4, and *Olympians*, 2.94ff.

10. Plato, *Ion*, 535bc.

11. The poet asks the Muses to take up the story from a particular point and then to follow the sequence of events as faithfully as possible; see Homer, *Iliad*, 1.6: "Start from the day when first a quarrel divided the son of Atreus and divine Achilles." Note also the phrase "And now tell me, Muse, who was the first..." *Ibid.*, 11.218, 14.508, and elsewhere.

12. See Arnold van Gennep and A.J. Reinach, *La question d'Homère: Les poèms homériques, l'archéologie et la poésie populaire* (Paris: Merevre de France, 1909), pp. 50ff.; Milman Parry, "The Traditional Epithet in Homer" and "Homeric Formulae and Homeric Metre," in *The Making of Homeric Verse: The Collected Papers of Milman Parry*, ed. Adam Parry (Oxford: Clarendon, 1971), pp. 1–191 and 191–239; A. Severyns, "Le poète et son oeuvre," in *Homère* (Brussels: Office de publicité, 1946).

13. The facts about Celtic bards are better known. The Welsh bard and the Irish fili pass through a series of stages, tested by trials that include magic practices and divinatory exercises. J. Vendryes writes: "Their studies lasted for several years, during which time the apprentice poet was initiated into the knowledge of the historical, genealogical, and topographical traditions of the country, and also into the use of meter and all the poetic skills." The master taught in places of retreat and silence. The pupil was trained in the art of

composition in low rooms with no windows, in total darkness. It is because of this habit of composing in the dark that one poet describes himself: "with his eyelids drawn like a curtain to protect him from the light of day." Vendryes, *Choix d'études linguistiques et celtiques* (Paris: Klincksieck, 1952), p. 216ff.

14. Parry writes that for Homer, as for all bards, versifying meant remembering. Fernand Robert notes, "The bard is a reciter, and his entire poetic language, sprinkled with often very ancient phrases, may well be considered, as may meter itself, a technique of memorization." Robert, *Homère* (Paris: Presses Universitaires de Paris, 1950), p. 14. On the relationship between recitation and improvisation, see Raphaël Sealey, "From Phemios to Ion," *Revue des études grecques* 70 (1957), pp. 312–55. It will be noted that in Plato (*Ion*, 535b and 536c), the rhapsodist Ion, who is purely a reciter, is nonetheless presented as a man inspired, possessed by the divine *mania*. On the role of rhythm as an aid to memory in oral composition, see Marcel Jousse, "Etudes de psychologie linguistique: Le style oral rythmique et mnémotechnique chez les verbo-moteurs," *Archives de Philosophie*, 2, no. 4 (1925).

15. Homer, *Iliad*, 2.484ff.

16. Even if, as has been suggested, Homer's fondness for inventories is to be compared with that of the scribes of the Mycenaean tablets, he is modifying, not merely continuing, a tradition; see T.B.L. Webster, "Homer and the Mycenaean Tablets," *Antiquity*, 29, no. 113 (1955), pp. 10–14.

17. Herodotus 2.53.

18. See H. Munro Chadwick and N. Kershaw Chadwick, *The Growth of Literature*, vol. 1, *The Ancient Literatures of Europe* (Cambridge: Cambridge University Press, 1932), p. 270ff.

19. Hesiod, *Theogony*, 28.

20. *Ibid.*, 45 and 115.

21. The race of gold lives forever young and dies abruptly; the race of silver remains in childhood for a hundred years and grows old all of a sudden, once it has crossed the threshold of adolescence. The men of the age of iron, before being destroyed, will be born old, with their hair already white; Hesiod, *Works and Days*, 109ff.

22. See Hesiod, *Theogony*, 100: *kleea proterōn anthrōpōn*.

23. *Ibid.*, 713ff. and 868.

24. Hesiod, *Works and Days*, 120ff., 140ff., 152ff., 168ff.

25. The gods are the *genos* of those who exist forever, *aien eontōn*.

26. Homer, *Odyssey*, 10.515ff. and 11.23ff.

27. René Schaerer rightly saw that in the *Theogony* time runs toward order and finally reaches stability for the gods, but the time of men runs in the opposite direction and, in the end, tends to tip over into death. This disparity is one of the poem's lessons. "La représentation mythique de la chute et du mal," *Diogènes* 11 (1955), pp. 58ff.

28. Hesiod, *Works and Days*, 176ff.

29. Hesiod, *Theogony*, 55 and 102ff.

30. Pausanias 9.39. It should be noted that at Lebadeia the ritual bears all the marks of an initiation ceremony. This is halfway between the consultation of an oracle and revelation in a mystery.

31. See Erwin Rohde, *Psyche: The Cult of Souls and the Belief in Immortality among the Greeks* (New York: Harper and Row, 1966), p. 543.

32. Hesiod, *Theogony*, 1216; Aristophanes, *Frogs*, 186.

33. Apollionius Rhodius, *Argonautica*, 1.643ff.

34. Teiresias: Homer, *Odyssey*, 10.493–95; Amphiaraos: Sophocles, *Electra*, 841.

35. This is why, in Plutarch, consulting Trophonios is presented not as if he were an ordinary oracle but as revealing the fate of souls after death. In the cave, Timarchos receives instruction, through images, in the eschatological doctrines and the myths of reincarnation. *Genius of Socrates*, 590ff.

36. See Robert Turcan, "La catabase orphique du papyrus de Bologne," *Revue de l'histoire des religions*, 150 (1956), pp. 136–72. The author notes the use of *krueros*, which normally applies to Hades (Hesiod, *Works and Days*, 1153), to indicate the earthly world.

37. See Pindar, frag. 131: the soul (the image of our being, our "double," *aiōnos eidōlon* sleeps while our limbs are active, but when they sleep it reveals the future to us. See also Aeschylus, *Eumenides*, 104: during sleep the soul is illuminated by eyes to which the gift of sight is denied when the day comes. See also Cicero, *De Divinatione*, 1.63, and *Tusculan Disputations*, 1.29.

38. Plato, *Phaedrus*, 248c.

39. See Gilbert Murray, *Four Stages of Greek Religion: Studies Based on a Course of Lectures* (New York: Columbia University Press, 1912), pp. 45–46; Richard Broxton Onians, *The Origins of European Thought about the Body, the Mind, the Soul, the World, Time, and Fate* (Cambridge: Cambridge University Press, 1954), p. 427ff.

40. In his commentary on Plato's *Timaeus*, 42c, Proclus writes of the soul's being "led to the blessed life, ceasing its peregrinations in the sphere of becoming...a life that is deliverance from the cycle and rest far from evil." See Otto Kern, *Orphicorum Fragmenta*, vol. 2 (Berlin, 1963) frag. 229. On the "circle of necessity," Diogenes Laertius (*Life of Pythagoras*, 8.14) says: "The soul is said to revolve following the changing wheel of necessity, *kuklon anagkēs ameibousan*, now united to one animal and now to another." See Jane Harrison, *Prolegomena to the Study of Greek Religion*, 3rd ed., (New York: Meridian, 1957), p. 589. On the wheel of birth and death, Simplicius (Aristotle, *On the Heavens*, 2.1. 284a14) writes: "The soul is chained to the wheel of necessity and of birth, *en tōi tēs eimarmenēs te kai geneseōs trochōi*, from which, according to Orpheus, it is impossible to escape except by winning the approval of the gods to whom Zeus has entrusted the power of liberating a soul from this cycle *kuklou t' allēxai*, and of granting rest far from evil" (Kern, *Orphicorum Fragmenta*, frag. 230). The texts of Proclus and Simplicius are quoted and discussed in Onians, *Origins of European Thought*, p. 452, and W.K.C. Guthrie, *Orpheus and Greek Religion: A Study of the Orphic Movement* (New York: Norton, 1966), p. 166. For Plato's comparison to forgetfulness, see *Gorgias*, 493c. In Plato, the unfortunate drawers of water have not yet joined the Danaides. He treats them as uninitiated, *amuētoi*, or *atelestoi*. It is in Plato's *Axiochus* that the expression *Danaidōn hudreiai ateleis* occurs (371e).

41. See the text of the plates, published in Hermann Diels and Walther Kranz, *Die Fragmente der Vorsokratiker, Griechisch und Deutsch*. 7th ed. (Berlin: Weidmann, 1951) vol. 1, pp. 17–22; Kern, *Orphicorum Fragmenta*, 104–109; see also Gilbert Murray, "Critical Appendix on the Orphic Tablets," in Harrison, *Prolegomena to the Study of Greek Religions*, p. 659ff.; Pierre-Maxime Schuhl, *Essai sur la formation de la pensée grecque: Introduction historique à une étude de la philosophie platonicieune*, 2nd ed. (Paris: Presses Universitaires de France, 1949), p. 239ff.; Guthrie, *Orpheus and Greek Religion*, p. 193ff.

42. Plato, *Republic*, 613bff.

43. See Alister A. Cameron, *The Pythagorean Background of the Theory of Recollection* (Menasha, Wis.: Banta, 1938).

44. Jane Harrison, *Prolegomena to the Study of Greek Religion* (Cambridge: Cambridge University Press, 1908), p. 659.

45. This idea that the soul has paid the price of injustice — *poinan d' antapeteis* (= Diel-Kranz, *Fragmente*, vol. 1, pp. 16 and 23) — can be compared to the

Pythagorean definition of justice: *to antipeponthos*, that is to say: *ha tis epoiēse, taut' antipathein*; Aristotle, *Nichomachean Ethics*, 1132b21ff.; see Rohde, *Psyche*, p. 397 n.44.

46. See Plutarch, *Lives of the Noble Romans*, 28, and *On the Obsolescence of Oracles*, 414bc: human souls rise from mortal men to heroes, then from heroes to daemons, and finally, when they are totally purified and consecrated, from daemons to gods; see Harrison, *Prolegomena to the Study of Greek Religion*, p. 504.

47. The notion of an "ancient sin" may operate in three ways that are not always easy to distinguish clearly: (1) the crime of an ancestor that continues to weigh like a curse on the whole line of descendants; (2) a crime committed in a previous life by an individual; (3) a crime committed against the gods by the human race, for which each man must pay the price. Unifying these different cases is the central theme of a sacrilege seen as a contagious source of defilement passed from generation to generation, from which men gain deliverance either by purificatory rites or by adopting a particular rule of life.

48. *Poinan palaiou pentheos* (literally: the price of blood, the ransom that pays for an ancient bereavement) seems to refer to the murder of Dionysos Zagreus, committed by the Titans, for which human beings must pay the price to Persephone, the mother of Dionysos Zagreus. If this is so, it represents the first example of the myth of Dionysos's dismemberment by the Titans, the ancestors of the human race; see Herbert J. Rose, "The Ancient Grief," in Gilbert Murray, *Greek Poetry and Life: Essays Presented to Gilbert Murray on his Seventieth Birthday* (Oxford: Clarendon, 1936), and "The Grief of Persephone," *Harvard Theological Review* 36 (1943), p. 247ff. For the opposite view, see, in particular, Ivan M. Linforth, *The Arts of Orpheus* (Berkeley: University of California Press, 1941), pp. 345–50.

49. This fragment of Pindar is known from Plato, *Meno*, 81b.

50. Empedocles, *Expiation*, frag. 115, in *The Extant Fragments*, ed. M.R. Wright (New Haven, CT: Yale University Press, 1981), p. 270.

51. *Ibid.*, frag. 146–47.

52. *Ibid.*, frag. 112; see Rohde, *Psyche*, p. 412 n.4, and Schuhl, *Essai sur la formation*, p. 300ff.

53. Empedocles, *On Nature*, frags. 2, 8, 9, 15, 17, 29.

54. Empedocles, *Purifications*, frag. 117.

55. *Ibid.*, frag. 129.

56. See Rohde, *Psyche*, p. 406 n.96, and Louis Gernet, "Les origines de la philosophie," *Bulletin de l'enseignement public du Maroc* 183 (1945), p. 8.

57. See Rohde, *Psyche*, p. 375, and, in appendix, Excursus 10, on the previous births of Pythagoras, pp. 598–601.

58. See Schuhl, *Essai sur la formation*, p. 251; Gernet, "Les origines de la philosophie," p. 8.

59. See Armand Delatte, *Etudes sur la littérature pythagoricienne* (Paris: Champion, 1915), p. 67; Schuhl, *Essai sur la formation*, p. 251.

60. Proclus on Plato, *Timaeus*, 1.124.4, quoted by Delatte, *Etudes sur la littérature*, p. 67.

61. Empedocles, *Purifications*, frag. 129; Plato, *Phaedo*, 65c, 67c, 70a; see also *Republic*, 9.572aff.

62. Gernet, "Les origines de la philosophie," p. 8.

63. *Ibid.*, p. 8. See Aristotle, *On the Soul*, A5, 410b28; compare *De Spiritu*, 482a33ff.; Iamblichus in *Stobaeus*, 1.49.32, vol. 1, p. 366, w.; Porphyry, *Letter to Marcella*, 10; Diogenes Laertius 8.28–32. Note the parallelism between the phrasing of the *Phaedo* and that of Diogenes Laertius, who reproduces the *Pythagorean Memoirs* after Alexander Polyhistor. Having stated that the veins, arteries, and nerves are the bonds of the soul, he adds: "When the soul grows strong and rests, collected into itself, its own words and actions become its bonds." The soul is conceived as a *pneuma* that can circulate through the channels of the arteries, veins, and nerves. When withdrawn into itself instead of being united with the body, it is enclosed in its own words, the *logoi*, which we are earlier told are breaths (*anemoi*); see A.J. Festugière, "Les 'Mémoires pythagoriques' cités par Alexandre Polyhistor," *Revue des études grecques* 58 (1945), pp. 1–65, and "L'âme et la musique," *Transactions and Proceedings of the American Philological Association* 85 (1954), p. 73.

64. See Rohde, *Psyche*, p. 299ff.; Schuhl, *Essai sur la formation*, p. 244ff.

65. Aristotle, *Rhetoric*, 3.17.10.

66. Aristotle, *Problems*, 916a33. See Augusto Rostagni, *Il verbo di Pitagora* (Turin: Bocca, 1924), pp. 96–99, 132–42, 153ff.; Gernet, "Les origines de la philosophie," p. 8. Gernet has pointed out an interesting remark made by Aristotle in *Physics*, 4.218b24–6. Aristotle explains, in his own way — that is, from a rationalist point of view — the phenomenon of the arrest or abolition of time at the oracle of Sardes, when the consultants stretch themselves out to sleep next to the tombs of the heroes: it seems to them that no time has passed from the

433

moment they lie down to the moment they wake up: "In fact they link together (*sunaptousi*) the instant before and the instant after and make them into one (*hen poiousin*)." For a purely physiological interpretation of the Alcmaeon text, see Charles Mugler, "Alcméon et les cycles physiologiques de Platon," *Revue des études grecques* 71 (1958), pp. 42–50. The same interpretation had already been proposed by Cameron, *Pythagorean Background*, pp. 39 and 58. In my opinion, however, Alcmaeon's expression should be compared with Plato, *Timaeus*, 90b–c.

67. Aristotle, *Physics*, 4.13.222b17. See Schuhl, *Essai sur la formation de la pensée grecque*, p. 251.

68. I am here making very direct use of material from Gernet's unpublished lectures on Orphism, given at the Ecoles des Hautes Etudes in February 1957.

69. Diels-Kranz, *Fragmente*, vol. 1, p. 47 n.2.

70. See Guthrie, *Orpheus and Greek Religion*, pp. 79 and 84ff.; Schuhl, *Essai sur la formation de la pensée grecque*, p. 232ff.

71. On androgyny as a symbol of primeval unity, see Marie Delcourt, *Hermaphrodite: Mythes et rites de la bisexualité dans l'antiquité classique* (Paris: Presses Universitaires de France, 1958), p. 105ff.

72. On Okeanos, see Aeschylus, *Prometheus Bound*, 137ff.; compare Hesiod, *Theogony*, 790; Homer, *Iliad*, 14. 200; Porphyry, *Scholium on the Iliad*, 18.490. The relationships between Okeanos and Kronos are well described in Onians, *Origins of European Thought*, p. 250ff. Compare Aeschylus, *Prometheus Bound*, 137ff., with Euripides, frag. 594 (August Nauck, *Tragicorum graecorum fragmenta*: in aedibus B.G. Teubneri, 1884–85), and with Plutarch, *Platonicae questones*, 8.4.

73. Bruno Snell, *The Discovery of the Mind: The Greek Origins of European Thought*, trans. T.G. Rosenmayer (New York: Harper and Row, 1970). On the subject of lyric poetry and the image of man expressed in it, Snell believes it feasible to speak of a "rise of the individual." See also Schuhl, *Essai sur la formation de la pensée grecque*, p. 160.

74. In the famous passage on human life in the *Iliad*, 6.146ff., the context in which his pessimism is expressed is still cyclical: "Just as are the generations of leaves, so are those of men. With the leaves there are some that are cast to the ground by the wind, but the luxuriant woods bring forth more, and the season of spring returns; similarly with the generations of men: one grows while the other is dying." When Simonides and Mimnermus take up the same theme, it strikes a

434

different note, because it is focused not on the sequence of the generations but on what the inexorable flow of time means for each individual.

75. Alongside time in lyric poetry we must consider tragic time. Victor Goldschmidt writes: "Tragic time is linear; everything that takes place within it involves the future, and whatever action is completed within it, whether despairing or happy, usurps eternity." "Le problème de la tragédie d'après Platon," *Revue des études grecques* 61(1948), p. 58. On the general problem of the relationships between the cyclical and the linear images of time among the Greeks, see Charles Mugler, *Deux thèmes de la cosmologie grecque: Devenir cyclique et pluralité des mondes* (Paris: Klincksieck, 1953).

76. See Emile Benveniste, "Expression indo-européenne de l'éternité," *Bulletin de la Société de Linguistique* 38 (1937), pp. 103–12.

77. See Rohde, *Psyche*, p. 398 n.50.

78. See Harrison, *Prolegomena to the Study of Greek Religion*, p. 599ff.; Guthrie, *Orpheus and Greek Religion*, p. 208ff.; Onians, *Origins of European Thought*, p. 452.

79. According to one Pythagorean tradition, the monad and the decad, as principles of unity and totality presiding over the organization of the cosmos, were identified with Mnēme and Mnēmosynē; Iamblichus, *Theologumena Arithmeticae*, 81.15; Porphyry, *Life of Pythagoras*, 31. See also Cameron, *Pythagorean Background*, p. 52; Franz Cumont, "Un mythe pythagoricien chez Posidonius et Philon," *Revue de philologie de littérature et d'histoire anciennes* 43 (1919), pp. 78–85.

80. See Delatte, *Etudes sur la littérature*, p. 69; Schuhl, *Essai sur la formation*, p. 251.

81. See Rohde, *Psyche*, p. 382ff.; Rostagni, *Il verbo di Pitagora*, p. 100ff.

82. Léon Robin has successfully shown that in Plato the theory of *anamnēsis* provides the answer to new problems of a strictly philosophical nature. "Sur la doctrine de la réminiscence," *Revue des études grecques* 32 (1919), pp. 451–61.

83. While it is true that *anamnēsis* takes place in time (*ibid.*, p. 459, and Plato, *Symposium*, 208a), it nevertheless has as its object an atemporal reality, which the soul is able to contemplate outside the time of human life (Plato, *Meno*, 86ab; *Phaedo*, 72e, 75bff., 76a). There may be a *mnēme* of the sequence of events that constitute our present life, but this is no longer a true knowledge (*Republic*, 7.516cd; *Gorgias*, 501a). However, see *Philebus*, 34b, where *mnēme* and *anamnēsis* seem rather to oppose each other, as the virtual does the actual; and

Laws, 5.732b. Both passages give *anamnēsis* a more psychological than ontological meaning.

84. Plato, *Republic*, 589a and *Alcibiades*, 130c. See Victor Goldschmidt, *La religion de Platon* (Paris: Presses Universitaires de France, 1949), p. 68.

85. Plato, *Phaedo*, 115cff.

86. Maurice Halbwachs, "La représentation de l'âme chez les Grecs: Le double corporel et le double spirituel," *Revue de métaphysique et de morale* 35 (1930), pp. 493–534.

87. Plato, *Timaeus*, 90a and 90c.

88. *Ibid.*, 41d–e; Plato, *Phaedrus*, 248a–c and 249a.

89. Plato, *Republic*, 611a, and *Timaeus*, 41d.

90. Plato, *Phaedo*, 72ab.

91. The living, Plato says, come from the dead no less than the dead from the living. If this perpetual circular compensation did not exist and "if, on the contrary, generation followed a straight line going from one contrary only to the one situated directly opposite [that is to say, going exclusively in the direction of life towards death], if it did not then turn back towards the other and execute this reversal," the world would continue toward chaos and death. *Phaedo*, 72bc.

92. Plato, *Laws*, 737c ff. and 740c ff. See Goldschmidt, *La Religion de Platon*, pp. 117–19.

93. Owing to our lack of documentation, we can do no more than pose the problem concerning the place of the techniques of memorization in Hippias's teaching. Nevertheless, the connection between the sophist's methods of memorization and his encyclopedic ideal of polymathy, his claim to universal knowledge, should be recognized (see Plato, *Hippias Minor*, 368bff.). For this reason, it might be tempting to see in Hippias's mnemotechnics the transposition and secularization of the power of omniscience traditionally connected with Mnēmosynē. Hippias boasts that he possesses and can procure for his pupils the omniscience that the deity used to bring to the bard in the form of an inspired vision. He claims to be able to do this thanks to techniques of memorization, which for him have a purely positive character and can be taught to others (*Hippias Major*, 285d). Actually, Hippias is only following in the footsteps of a poet. The Greeks in fact attributed the origin of the *technē mnēmonikē* to the lyric poet Simonides (*Suda Lexicon*: Simonides; Longinus, *Rhetoric*, 1.2.201; Cicero, *On Moral Ends*, 2.32). Two things about Simonides can throw

light on this secularization of the techniques of memorization and on the moment when this took place: first, Simonides may have perfected the alphabet and invented new letters, making a better written notation possible; second, he may have been the first to practice poetry as a profession and be paid for his poems.

94. Aristotle, *On Memory and Reminiscence*, 449b6 and 451a20.

95. *Ibid.*, 449b14 and b27, 450a20, 451a29, 452b8ff.

96. *Ibid.*, 449b29.

97. *Ibid.*, 450a13ff.

CHAPTER FIVE: THE RIVER OF AMELĒS AND THE MELETĒ THANATOU
This essay first appeared as "Le fleuve 'amélès' et la 'mélétè thanatou,'" *Revue philosophique* (1960), pp. 163–79.

1. See Hermann Diels and Walther Kranz, *Die Fragmente der Vorsokratiker: Griechisch und deutsch*, 7th ed. (Berlin: Weidmann, 1951) vol. 1, p. 15ff.

2. Léon Robin refers to "moral anxiety or intellectual anxiety which provokes remembrance, and a sense of inferiority which gives rise to love," in Plato, *Oeuvres complètes*, vol. 1 (Paris: Editions de la pléiade, 1940), p. 1376.

3. On these myths, see Pierre Maxime Schuhl, *Essai sur la formation de la penseé grecque: Introduction historique à une étude de la philosophie platonicienne* (Paris: Alcan, 1934), vol. 2, p. 241ff. See also pp. 56–82 above.

4. Pausanias 9.29.2–3. I would like to thank Marcel Detienne for calling my attention to this text. See Bernhard Abraham van Groningen, "Les trois Muses de l'Hélicon," *L'Antiquité classique* 17 (1948), pp. 287–96.

5. See p. 115ff.

6. See Pierre Boyancé, *Le Culte des Muses chez les philosophes grecs: Etudes d'histoire et de psychologie religieuses* (Paris: Boccard, 1936).

7. There is a striking similarity of themes between the religious thought of the sects and philosophical reflection. There is, however, one essential difference: the "wisdom" of the philosopher aims to establish an order within the city, whereas all considerations of political organization remain totally foreign to the spirit of the sects. On this collective training, see Thucydides 2.39; Plato, *Laws*, 865a.

8. Thucydides writes that in the Spartan *paideia*, the *andreion* obtained among the *neoi* through a *epiponōi askēsei*, a *ponōn meletēi* (Thucydides 2.39).

9. On the opposition, within a decidedly military concept of virtue,

between *ameleia* and the *meletē* associated with *epimeleia*, see Xenophon, *Oeconomicus*, especially 12.6ff. and 20.3ff.

10. See Charles Picard, "Nouvelles remarques sur l'apologue dit de Prodicos," *Revue archéologique* 42 (1953), pp. 10–41. *Ameleia* is associated with *malachia* in Thucydides 1.122.4, and with *argia* in Plato, *Republic*, 421d.

11. Iamblichus, *On the Pythagorean Life*, 164.

12. *Ibid.*, 63.

13. *Ibid.*, 164 and 165.

14. *Mēd' hupnon malakoisin ep' ommasi prodexasthai prin tōn hēmerinōn ergōn tris hekaston epelthein*: lines 40–41, Pieter Cornelius van der Horst, *Les vers d'or pythagoriciens* (Leiden: Brill, 1932).

15. *Tēs theiēs aretēs eis ichnia*; see Proclus, *Hymn to the Muses*, 6–7; the Muses teach us to make haste to find the trace (*ichnos*) on the deep stream of oblivion (*huper bathucheumona lēthēn*).

16. Plutarch, *The Education of Children*, 2a–e.

17. *Kai ta men rhadia tous amelountas pheugei, ta de chalepa tais epimeleiais halisketai.*

18. Diels-Kranz, *Fragmente*, vol. 1, 203.10.

19. *Ibid.*, 203.18–21 and 204.16ff.

20. Plutarch, *Education of Children*, 5d.

21. Iamblichus, *Pythagorean Life*, 42–43.

22. Plutarch, *Education of Children*, 9c.

23. *Olbios, hōs theiōn prapidōn ektēsato plouton.* Diels-Kranz, *Fragmente*, vol. 1, p. 365.5ff.

24. *Kadiskos aggeion esti en hōi ktēsious Dias egkathidruousin....* On Zeus's epithets, see Lewis Richard Farnell, *The Cults of the Greek States* (Oxford: Clarendon, 1896), vol. 1, p. 55. On his enshrinement, *Harpocration*, s.v. *ktēsiou Dios*, quoting Hyperides and Menander (184–85, Dindorf): *ktēsion Dia en tois tamieiois idruonto.*

25. Diels-Kranz, *Fragmente*, vol. 1, p. 364.4: *Hoppote gar pasēisin orexaito prapidessin.* See Iamblichus, *Pythagorean Life*, 67 and Diogenes Laertius 8.54.

26. Louis Gernet, "Les origines de la philosophie, *Bulletin de l'enseignement public du Maroc* 183 (1945), p. 8. See also p. 70 above.

27. Plato, *Phaedo*, 67c, 81a, 673; see also 65c, 70a, 81c and e, 83a. This exercise in concentration, in the true sense of the term, is also found in Porphyry, *Letter to Marcella*, 10: "If you practice withdrawing into yourself, gathering together apart from the body all your spiritual parts that are dispersed through it

and reduced to a multitude of particles separated out from a unity that until that moment had enjoyed its strength to the full." The Greek text says: *ei meteōēs eis heautēn avabainen, sullegousa apo tou sōmatos panta ta diaskedathenta melē kai eis plēthos katakermatisthenta apo tēs teōs en megethai dunamōs ischousēs enōseoōs.* See also Porphyry, *Sententiae,* 34.

28. Plato, *Phaedrus,* 275a. See also *Theaetetus,* 153b.

29. Proclus, *Comments on the Republic,* 349, Kroll.

30. See Harold W. Miller, "The Flux of the Body in Plato's *Timaeus,*" *Transactions and Proceedings of the American Philological Association* 88 (1957), pp. 103–13.

31. Proclus, *Comments on the Republic,* 122. See also 51: it is clear that the plain of Lēthē signifies generation, *tēn genesin,* and the river of forgetfulness, *pasan tēn rhusin tōn enulōn kai to phothion kutos hēmōn,* both of which constantly fill our souls with forgetfulness about realities that are forever unchanging.

32. Aristotle, *Physics* A. 13, 222b 17 (Diels-Kranz, *Fragmente,* vol. 1, p. 217.10ff; see also Schuhl, *Essai sur la formation,* p. 251).

33. Plato, *Gorgias,* 493aff.

34. *Ibid.,* 493e: *meta pollōn ponōn kai chalepōn.*

35. See *ibid.,* 493a: *anapeithesthai kai metapiptein anō katō,* and Aphrodite-Peithō. On the ambiguity of *peithō* and its relationship to *pistis,* see Mario Untersteiner, *The Sophists,* trans. Kathleen Freeman (Oxford: Blackwell, 1954), p. 102ff.; Alessandro Setti, "La memoria e il canto: Saggio di poetica arcaica greca," *Studi italiani di filologia classica* 30, no.2 (1958), pp. 129–71; and above all a stimulating article by Augusto Rostagni, "Un nuovo capitolo nella storia della retorica e della sofistica," *Studi italiani di filologia classical,* n.s., 2 (1922), pp. 148–201.

36. Diels-Kranz, *Fragmente,* vol. 1, p. 309.5.

37. *Ibid.,* 310.9ff.: *guiōn pistin eruke.*

38. *Ibid.,* 311.6: *alla kakois men karta melei krateousin apistein.* According to Clement, *Stromata,* 5.18, for Empedocles the characteristic of the wicked is the desire *kratein tōn alēthōn dia tou apistein.* The desire to command those who rule over us, and refusing one's *pistis* to whoever holds the truth — this, for the wicked soul, is the point where it turns upside down the *anō katō* of Plato's *Gorgias.*

39. Diels-Kranz, *Fragmente,* vol. 1, p. 311.7.

40. *Ibid.,* 311.13: *stegasai phrenos ellopos eisō.*

41. *Ibid.,* 353.1–2 (compare with 309.2) and 353.3: *ē s' aphar ekleipsousi periplomenoio chronoio.*

42. *Ibid.*, 352.20–21 and 352.22–23; *di' aiōnos paresontai, alla te poll' apo tōnd' ektēsai: auta gar auxei.*

43. See Jane Harrison, *Prolegomena to the Study of Greek Religion*, (Cambridge: Cambridge University Press, 1903), pp. 613–23, and Charles Picard, "L'éleusinisme et la disgrâce des Danaïdes," *Revue de l'histoire des religions* (1929), pp. 57–59.

44. Proclus points out this similarity in his commentary on *Timaeus*, where he writes: "Plato calls 'river of Lēthē' the whole of nature in which there is generation, and in which oblivion and, following Empedocles, the meadow of Atē are found" (339b).

45. It will be noted that the landscape of the underworld as Plutarch has Thespesios describe it on his return from Hades in *On the Delay of the Divine Justice* is different from that of the *Republic*. Here Lēthē appears neither as a river nor as a plain: it is a deep cavern like the caves of Dionysos. This cavern symbolizes the damp world of generation, the sweetness and lazy softness of pleasure. Before this cavern, Thespesios's soul feels its strength deserting it, while remembrance of the body and the desire for generation grow in it. So it is Hēdonē who is present in the dark cavern of Lēthē. In another text, Plutarch emphasizes that Hēdonē was hurled down to earth in the company of Atē (*Oracles at Delphi No Longer Given in Verse*, 397). On Alētheia, see Marcel Detienne, "La notion mythique d'*Alétheia*," *Revue des études grecques* 73 (1960), pp. 27–35. On Lēthē and Alētheia in Plato, see Proclus, *Commentary on the Republic*, 2.346.19, Kroll.

46. Hesiod, *Theogony*, 227 and 230. See, for example, Pindar, *Olympians*, 7.45–47: however, sometimes the cloud of oblivion creeps up unnoticed and conceals the right path from the spirit.

47. On Ātē and *hamartēma*, see Louis Gernet, *Recherches sur le développement de la pensée juridique et morale en Grèce: Etude Semantique* (Paris: Leroux, 1917), pp. 310–30.

48. Diels-Kranz, *Fragmente*, vol. 1, p. 357.15ff.

49. *Ibid.*, 358.6: *stugeousi pantes.*

50. *Ibid.*, 358.8: *neikei mainomenōi pisunos.*

51. Hesiod, *Theogony*, 226ff.

52. *Ibid.*, 775ff.

53. *Ibid.*, 795ff.: *keitai nēutmos, anapnustos, . . . kakon de he kōma kaluptei.*

54. Plato, *Republic*, 621b.

55. Pausanias 8.17.6, and 8.18.4–6.

56. For example, in the mythical representation of Empousa, a monster of the underworld, one of her feet is bronze, while the other is a horse's hoof.

57. Pausanias 8.18.7–8 and 8.19.2–3.

58. In a long passage from the dialogue *The E of Delphi*, directly inspired by the texts of Epicharmus, Plutarch draws a contrast between the permanent nature of the divine and the constant change within man (frag. 1 and 2), and, adopting the same expressions as the *Republic*, he writes on "the subject of time: "*Pheon aei kai mē stegon, hōsper aggeion phthoras kai geneseōs.*" Time is fully identified with the leaking *pithos* of the Danaides. Plutarch adds that immutable existence is called Apollo; the flux of becoming, Pluto. The former is accompanied by the Muses and Mnēmosynē, the latter by Lēthē and Siōpē (Silence) (392ff.).

59. Heraclitus criticizes Pythagoras's wisdom as being an *historia*, a *polumatheia* (frag. 129). Proclus draws a parallel between the Pythagoreans' *anamnēsis* of previous lives, through which the soul can accomplish itself (*telos*), and the *historia* of Egyptian priests who scrupulously preserve the memory of everything to do with the past of their people and of other peoples as a precaution against the oblivion which time brings. Proclus adds that such research imitates the permanence of the immutable principles of nature and makes assimilation into the order of the Whole possible. (*Timaeus*, 38B.) The insistence on complete and total knowledge (and on tracing the recollection of every event of the day and of every component of ten or twenty lives of a man) recalls the obligation in religious ritual to omit *nothing*.

CHAPTER SIX: HESTIA-HERMES

This essay originally appeared as "Hestia-Hermes: Sur l'expression religieuse de l'espace et du mouvement chez les Grecs," *L'Homme: Revue française d'anthropologie* 3 (1963), pp. 12–50.

1. Pausanias 5.11.8.

2. On the Sosibios Vase, Hermes follows Hestia; see Pierre Raingeard, *Hermès psychagogue: Essai sur les origines du culte d'Hermès* (Paris: Belles Lettres, 1934), p. 500. On bicephalic columns with masculine and feminine heads of Hermes and Hestia, Wilhelm Froehner, *Notice de la sculpture antique du Musée National du Louvre* (Paris: Mourgues Frères, 1874), vol. 1, p. 220 nn.198 and 199); On Hermes habitually associated with Hestia as a couple among the twelve gods, (see Arthur Bernard Cook, *Zeus: A Study in Ancient Religion* (Cambridge: Cambridge University Press, 1914–40), vol. 3, part 2, p. 1057ff.).

3. *Homeric Hymn to Hestia*, 1.11ff.; see also lines 1–2: "in high dwellings of

all who walk on earth (*chamai*)." In his *Interpretation of Dreams*, Artemidorus classes Hestia and Hermes among the epichthonian deities, in contrast to the celestial and subterranean gods.

4. *Homeric Hymn to Aphrodite*, 29–30.

5. Plato, *Phaedrus*, 247a.

6. Euripides frag. 983N2. See Macrobius 1.23: "If Hestia remains alone in the house of the gods, it means that the earth remains motionless at the center of the universe." See also Philolaos: "That One who remains in the middle of the sphere is named Hestia," Hermann Diels and Walther Kranz (eds.), *Die Fragmente der Vorsokratiker, griechisch und deutsch*, 7th ed., (Berlin: Weidmann, 1951), vol. 1, pp. 410 and 412. Note also the expression in the *Homeric Hymn to Hestia*, 3: "Hestia's status in the home is immutable (*hedrēn aidion*)."

7. Homer, *Iliad*, 24.334–35.

8. Aristophanes, *Peace*, 392.

9. *Homeric Hymn to Hermes*, 14–15.

10. *Ibid.*, 146–47.

11. The triple or quadruple representation of the face of the god was precisely what enabled him to control all directions in space simultaneously.

12. Lewis Richard Farnell, *The Cults of the Greek States*, vol. 5 (Oxford: Clarendon, 1896), p. 62, n.2; Aeschylus, *Choephoroi*, 124ff.

13. Plutarch, *Concerning Talkativeness*, 502.

14. See also J. Orgogozo, "L'Hermès des Achéens," *Revue de l'histoire des religions* 136 (1949), pp. 10–30 and 139–79.

15. See Louis Deroy, "Le culte du foyer dans la Grèce mycénienne," *Revue de l'histoire des religions* 137 (1950), p. 32 n.1.

16. See Louis Gernet, "Sur le symbolisme politique en Grèce ancienne: Le foyer commun," *Cahiers internationaux de sociologie* 11 (1951), p. 29. In *Life of Numa*, 9–11, Plutarch remarks that in Greece there was a tradition of a female priesthood that tended the sacred fires. The responsibility fell not on virgins, as in Rome, but on women abstaining from all sexual relations. During the city period, the ministry of the communal hearth became essentially political and was for this reason reserved for men. It should be noted that in Homer the cult of Hestia was already relegated to the background.

17. Deroy, "Le culte du foyer," pp. 26–43.

18. On "generating" fire, see Plutarch, *Life of Camillus*, 20.4, and *Table Talk*, 17.4.3.

19. *Homeric Hymn to Aphrodite*, 20–30.

20. Concerning the rites that mark the renunciation of the previous state on the eve of marriage, see Euripides, *Iphigenia in Tauris*, 372–75, and Louis Séchan, "La légende d'Hippolyte dans l'antiquité," *Revue des études grecques* 24 (1911), p. 115ff. On the rite of cutting hair for marriage as for mourning a relative, see *Palatine Anthology*, 6.276, 277, 280, 281. In Sparta, the young bride's head was shaved, Plutarch, *Life of Lycurgus*, 15.5.

21. On the *katachusmata*, the rites concerning the integration of the wife into her husband's household, see Ernst Samter, *Familienfeste der Griechen und Römer* (Berlin: Reimer, 1901), p. 159. The bride was led to the hearth, perhaps even seated beside it (in the crouching attitude of the suppliant), and her head was covered with sweetmeats (*tragēmata*), particularly dried fruit, dates, nuts, and figs. The same ritual was followed when a new slave first entered the house to which he was to belong. In that case, the mistress of the house (*despoina*) officiated as the representative of the hearth.

22. Plutarch, *Dialogue on Love*, 751d. On Charis's presiding over free exchange and gift giving, see Aristotle, *Nicomachean Ethics*, 1133a2, ed. René Antoine Gauthier and Jean Yves Jolif, vol. 2 (Louvain: Publications Universitaires de Louvain, 1959), Gauthier and Jolif, in their commentary on this work, do not seem to have appreciated the significance of this passage (p. 375).

23. On Hermes's association with Aphrodite in her role as *peithō*, see the inscription of Mytilene to Aphrodite Peithō and, among others, Hermes, *Inscriptiones Graecae* 12.2.73; Plutarch, *Advice to Bride and Groom*, 138c. On his association with Aphrodite in her role as the "schemer" (*machanitis*), see Pausanias 8.31.6; when she is *psithuros*, "of the seductive murmurings," see Harpocration s.v. *psithuristēs*: the Athenians worshipped Hermes under this name, in association with Aphrodite and Ērōs. On Hermes Peisinous at Cnidous, see Farnell, *Cults of the Greek States*, p. 70 n.43.

24. "You leave the bounds, ma'am, proper to a married; namely, the foyer of the house. For the front door is decreed as the limit for the life of a free woman. To chase and run into the street is the province of a barking dog, O Rhode," Menander frag. 546, in J.M. Edmonds (ed. and trans.), *The Fragments of Attic Comedy after Meineke, Bergk, and Kock* (Leiden: Brill, 1957–61).

25. Xenophon, *Oeconomicus* 7.30; see Hierocles in Stobaeus 4.1.502h. "Man's job is in the fields, in the *agora*, the affairs of the city; women's work is spinning wool, baking bread, keeping house." In *Apollodorus Against Neaera*, 122, Demosthenes, defining the married state (*to sunoikein*), gives special emphasis to

the domestic vocation of the wife as the guardian of her husband's hearth, in contrast to the functions of courtesans and concubines: "Mistresses we keep for the sake of pleasure, concubines for the daily care of our persons, but wives to bear us legitimate children and to be faithful guardians of our households, (*tōn endon phulaka pistēn*)."

26. Aeschylus, *Eumenides*, 658–61; see also Euripides, *Orestes*, 552–55, and *Hippolytus*, 616ff.

27. Aristotle, *Generation of Animals*, 1.20.729a. "A theory of this type, lacking all contact with its object, is pure myth," remarks Marie Delcourt in *Oreste et Alcméon: Etude sur la projection légendaire du matricide en Grèce* (Paris: Belles lettres, 1959), p. 85.

28. On Meleagros, see Apollodorus 1.8.2, and Aeschylus, *Choephoroi* 607ff. The brand (*dalos*) in the hearth is a kind of "double" or the external soul of Meleagros. The child dies when the brand, placed in a casket (*larnax*) by his mother, is consumed by fire. This was decided by the *moirai* seven days after his birth — a date that corresponds, as we shall see, with the celebration of the Amphidromia, the rites that integrate the newborn child into its father's home. On Demophoon, see *Homeric Hymn to Demeter*, 239ff. The goddess, nurse to the royal baby, hides it in the fire like a brand (*dalos*). The relevant Latin legends are those of Caeculus and Servius Tullus. The comparison is made by Gernet, "Sur le symbolisme politique," p. 27.

29. *Ibid.*, p. 27.

30. See André Aymard, "L'idée de travail dans la Grèce archaïque," *Journal de Psychologie* 41 (1948), pp. 29–45.

31. See Sophocles, *Electra*, 1088ff.: Clytaemnestra brought the palace of Agamemnon to Aegisthus as the price of her new marriage.

32. Aeschylus, *Agamemnon*, 1587 and 1435.

33. See the very perceptive and careful study by R.P. Winnington-Ingram, "Clytaemnestra and the Vote of Athena," *Journal of Hellenic Studies* 68 (1948), pp. 130–47.

34. The three tragic poets handled the same theme: Aeschylus, *Agamemnon*, 1224, 1259, 1625ff., 1635, 1665, 1671, and *Choephoroi*, 304; Sophocles, *Electra*, 299–302; Euripides, *Electra*, 917, 930, 950.

35. Aeschylus, *Agamemnon*, 10–11, 258, 1251, 1258, 1377ff., and see the irony of 483 and 592ff.; *Choephoroi*, 664ff.; Sophocles, *Electra*, 650ff. and 1243; Euripides, *Electra*, 930ff.

36. Winnington-Ingram, "Clytaemnestra."

37. Sophocles, *Electra*, 416ff.

38. On the similarities and differences between the *rhabdos*, Hermes's magic wand, and the *skēptron*, with which the former was eventually merged, see Jane Harrison, *Prolegomena to the Study of Greek Religion* (Cambridge: Cambridge University Press, 1903), p. 44ff. The *rhabdos* is a stick held in the air, used for hitting (Homer, *Odyssey*, 10.236); it is waved (*ibid.*, 24.1–9); it is never held still (Pindar, *Olympians*, 9.33). In contrast, one normally leans on the *skēptron*, which is like a walking stick (*baktron*) held upright, with one end placed on the ground. Thus, to throw the *skēptron* down during a meeting of the assembly, as Achilles did (Homer, *Iliad*, 1.245), takes on the meaning of a rejection of the royal authority and a rupture of solidarity with the group.

39. Aeschylus, *Agamemnon*, 966–70; *Choephoroi*, 204, 236, 503; Orestes is the root (*rhiza*), the seed (*sperma*), of the house of the Atridae; the same image is found in Sophocles, *Electra*, 764–65.

40. Euripides, *Electra*, 1052–54.

41. Aeschylus, *Agamemnon*, 1251–52, 1604–10, 1633, 1643; Sophocles, *Electra*, 561. In Greece, as among the German tribes, the woman, because of her sex, could not herself exact a bloody vengeance: *sidērophorein* was an exclusively masculine prerogative. See Gustave Glotz, *La solidarité de la famille dans le droit criminel en Grèce* (Paris: Fontemoing, 1904), p. 82.

42. Aeschylus, *Agamemnon*, 1379, 1672–73; Sophocles, *Electra*, 651.

43. Aeschylus, *Agamemnon*, 1435; Sophocles, *Electra*, 97 and 587; Euripides, *Electra*, 1035ff.

44. Sophocles, *Electra*, 533.

45. Aeschylus, *Agamemnon*, 1225.

46. Euripides, *Electra*, 930ff.; Sophocles, *Electra*, 365.

47. Euripides, *Orestes*, 1045–1148.

48. Sophocles, *Electra*, 1145–48.

49. Aeschylus, *Choephoroi*, 264.

50. On Electra's masculine nature, see Sophocles, *Electra*, 351, 397, 401, 983, 997, 1019–20, which stresses her similarity to Clytaemnestra; and Euripides, *Electra*, 982, and *Orestes*, 1204. On Electra's nature as authoritative and passionate like her mother, see Sophocles, *Electra*, 605ff. and 621.

51. Sophocles, *Electra*, 962.

52. On Electra as "virgin," see Aeschylus, *Choephoroi*, 140, 486; Sophocles,

Electra, 1183; Euripides, *Electra*, 23, 42, 98, 255, 270, 311, 945, and *Orestes*, 26, 72, 206, 251.

53. Sophocles, *Electra*, 341ff. and 365; Euripides, *Electra*, 1102–1104.

54. Aeschylus, *Eumenides*, 736ff.

55. Aeschylus, *Agamemnon*, 62 and 1231.

56. Aeschylus, *Eumenides*, 213ff.

57. Sophocles, *Electra*, 97; Euripides, *Electra*, 1035: in taking Aegisthus as her lover, Clytaemnestra is only following the example Agamemnon set by bringing Cassandra back as a concubine.

58. The marriage of a brother and a sister born *of the same father* is not completely forbidden, but that of a brother and a sister born *of the same mother* is strictly prohibited. It should be remembered that the term *adelphos* (brother) is related to female consanguinity: it originally meant issue from the same womb.

59. On the woman offered in wedlock as *poinē* of the vendetta, see Glotz, *La solidarité de la famille*, p. 130.

60. The ritual bears witness to the persistence of the aspect of abduction in marriage; see Plutarch, *Life of Lycurgus*, 15.5, and *Roman Questions*, 271d29.

61. For the tragic poets, see Aeschylus, *Seven against Thebes*, 754; Sophocles, *Oedipus Rex*, 1257, and *Antigone*, 569; Euripides, *Orestes*, 553, *Medea*, 1281, and *Ion*, 1095; see also Albrecht Dieterich, *Mutter Erde* (Leipzig: Teubner, 1905), p. 47. For the prose writers, see Plato, *Cratylus*, 406b, and *Laws*, 839a.

62. Menander, *The Rape of the Locks*, 435–36, frag. 720, Edmonds: *Tautēn gnēsiōn paidōn ep' arotō soi didōmi*. See Emile Benveniste, "Liber et liberi," *Revue des etudes latines* 14 (1936), pp. 51–58.

63. Plutarch, *Advice to the Bride and Groom*, 144b.

64. Sophocles, *Electra*, 421–23; Aeschylus, *Agamemnon*, 966.

65. Hesiod, *Works and Days*, 232ff.

66. Hesiod, *Theogony*, 969–71.

67. *Homeric Hymn to Hestia*, 1.5ff.; see Cicero, *The Nature of the Gods*: "In ea dea, omnis et precatio et sacrificatio extrema est." Cornutus c. 28: Hestia is at once *prōtē* and *eschatē*; she is the beginning and the end.

68. Aristotle, *Politics*, 1252b15.

69. Zenobius 4.44; Diogenianus 2.40.

70. As Odysseus did in the palace of Alcinous: Homer, *Odyssey*, 7.153–54.

71. Pindar, *Nemean Odes*, 11.1ff.

72. See Gernet, "Sur le symbolisme politique."

73. On the *katachusmata* rites, see p. 427 n.29. The bonds between the man and his wife are the same as those which unite two antagonistic groups who have become guests and allies after a truce. The same word, *philotēs*, denotes the intimacy between spouses and the contract that establishes a fictitious kinship between recent antagonists with a view to binding them by reciprocal obligations. See Glotz, "La solidarité de la famille," p. 22. No doubt there is some romanticizing in the stories of Aphrodite and Ares, but they mainly demonstrate institutional realities, with all the behavior patterns and psychological attitudes that they require. On the ties uniting the wife to her husband's home, see Euripides, *Alcestis*, 162ff. Before dying, Alcestis invokes Hestia, the domestic goddess of the conjugal hearth. She addresses her as *despoina* (mistress) and entrusts her children to her.

74. Euripides, frag. 928N2; see also Menander, *peri epideiktikōn*, in *Rhetorici graeci*: 3.275, Spengel: "The young husband about to have sexual relations should be urged to pray to Ērōs, to Hestia, and the deities of procreation."

75. Porphyry in Eusebius, *Preparation for the Gospel*, 3.11.7.

76. See Ludovic Beauchet, *Histoire du droit privé de la République athénienne* (Paris: Libraire Marescq aîné, 1897), vol. 1, p. 399ff.

77. Manu, *The Laws of Manu*, 9.127ff.

78. Plato, *Laws*, 924eff. For the same regulations for degrees of affinity in inheritance, see Isaeus, *On the Estate of Hagnias*, 1–2 and 11; Demosthenes, *Against Macartatus*, 51.

79. The question even arises whether the son of the *epiklēros* may assume the functions of his mother's *kurios*, thus taking on the legal role of the brother. A practice such as that of the *epiklēros* could, it seems, shed some light on the psychological relationship between Electra and Orestes. In relation to Orestes, Electra is as much a mother as a sister. In relation to her son, the *epiklēros*, is as much a sister as a mother.

80. It is now the husband's turn to be "neutralized," in that he represents a home that is not his father's. His kinship with his wife's father is at once the sign and the instrument of this neutralization. In fact, in the case of a man, the mere *sunoikēsis* would not suffice, since the man, unlike the woman, has no domestic vocation and cannot assume the attributes of the home. The man is bound to the house by blood, by race, or, if that be lacking, by an act of adoption that also establishes a direct link, an agnatic relationship, between father and son. Beauchet, *Histoire du droit privé*, vol. 2, p. 7.

81. On Hestia sitting on the *omphalos*, see Pierre Roussel, "L'Hestia à l'Omphalos," *Revue archéologique* (1911), pp. 86–91. On Hestia and Delphi, see Aeschylus, *Eumenides*, 165 and 168; and Jean Audiat, "L'hymne d'Aristonos à Hestia," *Bulletin de correspondance hellénique* 52 (1932), pp. 299–317.

82. See Gernet, "Sur le symbolisme politique," p. 22.

83. Marie Delcourt, *L'oracle de Delphes* (Paris: Payot, 1955), 144–49.

84. The *omphalos* is "the principle for the rootedness and growth of the embryo (*rhizōsios kai anaphusios tou prōtou*), Philolaos, in Diels-Kranz, *Fragmente*, vol. 1, p. 413.6–7.

85. Artemidorus, *Oneirocritica* 1.43, quoted in Delcourt, *L'oracle*, p. 145). As regards the expression *epi xenēs*, the parallelism with Hestia should be noted, in 4.34 and 5.27.

86. Artemidorus, *Oneirocritica* 1.74 and 2.10. On the relationship between the oven and the female abdomen, see Herodotus 5.92.5ff.: to put bread in a cold oven meant to be joined with a woman when she was dead.

87. On Hermes Tetragonos, see Heraclitus, *Homeric Questions*, 72.6.

88. Hippocrates, On *Diet and Hyglene*, 4.92 comes to mind: "For from the dead come nourishment, growth and seed."

89. See Fernand Robert, *Thymélè: Recherches sur la signification et la destination des monuments circulaires dans l'architecture religieuse de la Grèce* (Paris: Boccard, 1939).

90. Gernet, "Sur le symbolisme politique," p. 24.

91. Pausanias 8.9.5; see also Jean Charbonneaux, "Tholos et Prytanée," *Bulletin de correspondance hellénique* 49 (1925), pp. 159–75.

92. Sophocles, *Electra*, 416ff. This text should be compared with the Aeschylus, *Agamemnon*, 965ff. In both cases, the man is the root (*rhiza*) implanted in the earth, which, developing into a tree protecting the house, confers on the hearth (*hestia*) its "shadowed" character. Aeschylus makes Clytaemnestra say, when she is pretending to welcome Agamemnon joyously on his return: "For if the root still lives, leafage comes again to the house and spreads its over-reaching shade against the scorching dog-star; so, now that thou hast come to hearth and home, thou showest that warmth hath come in winter-time; aye, and when Zeus maketh wine from the bitter grape, then forthwith there is coolness (*psuchos*)."

93. Xenophon, *Oeconomicus*, 4.2.

94. Plato, *Phaedrus*, 239c. Agesilāos, wishing to persuade his soldiers that their Asian adversaries would be women rather than men, had the prisoners he

had captured stripped naked. Their bodies, soft and white from a lifetime spent in the shade of the house, never removing their clothes for physical exercise in the palaestra, aroused the contempt and derision of the Spartans; Xenophon, *Hellenica*, 3.4.19; Plutarch, *Life of Agesilaos*, 600e, *Sayings of Spartan Women*, 209c, and *Roman Questions*, 28. In vase paintings, female figures were conventionally pictured as white-skinned, in contrast to brown-skinned men.

95. *Homeric Hymn to Demeter*, 98ff.

96. *Ibid*, 113–17.

97. Aeschylus, *Eumenides*, 665; compare the expression used by Aristophanes, *The Birds*, 694: in the bottomless matrix of obscurity, *Erebous d' en apeirosi kolpois*.

98. See Homer, *Odyssey*, 23.41ff.: while the slaughter of the suitors is taking place in the *megaron*, all the women of the palace hide themselves in the depths of their chambers (*muchō thalamōn*), behind heavy walls and bolted doors.

99. See Xenophon, *Oeconomicus*, 9.3. On the relationship between *muchos* (cavern, aboveground pit) and *thalamos*, see A.J. Festugière, "Les mystères de Dionysos," *Revue biblique* 44 (1935), p. 382; and Leonard Robert Palmer, "The Homeric and the Indo-European House," *Transactions of the Philological Society* (1947), pp. 92–120. The term *muchos* can also denote the low altar-hearth (*eschara*). See Euripides, *Medea*, 397: *muchois hestias*, the depths of the hearth. Danae's prison: Sophocles, *Antigone*, 947. Trophonios's cavern: Euripides, *Ion*, 394. The tomb: Euripides, The *Suppliants*, 980.

100. The girl's room before her wedding: Homer, *Odyssey*, 7.7. The nuptial couch: Homer, *Iliad*, 18.492; Pindar, *Pythian Odes*, 2.60. Pollux defines the *thalamos* as the place of conjugal union (*topos tou gamou*). The definition of thalamos: Heliodorus 4.6.

101. Homer, *Odyssey*, 21.8–9. The expression *thalamon eschaton* should be remembered from and compared with Hesychius's glossary: Hestia: *eschatē* (the ultimate, at the end). According to Cornutus, *Compendium of Greek Theology*, 28, Hestia is both *prōtē* and *eschatē*, the first and the last.

102. The woman as mistress of the keys to the treasure: Aeschylus, *Agamemnon*, 609–10; the virgin daughter as holder of the same privilege: Aeschylus, *Eumenides*, 827–28.

103. Xenophon, *Oeconomicus*, 7. 20–21, 25, 33, 35–36; in 39, the wife says to her husband, "For my care of the goods indoors (*endon*) and my management would look rather ridiculous, I fancy, if you did not see that something is gath-

ered in from outside (exōthen ti eispheroito)." To which the husband replies: "And my ingathering would look ridiculous if there were not someone to keep what is gathered in." Note that safeguarding and distribution (phulake and dianomē) are specifically the functions of Hestia Tamia.

104. Hesiod, Theogony, 598–99: in this antifemale attack, which identifies the domestic thalamos with the feminine gastēr, two complementary activities — acquisition (man, Hermes) and gathering in (woman, Hestia) — are transformed into a conflict of two oppositions: labor (masculine) and expenditure (feminine). Further, for Hesiod, the woman is not content with "squeezing her husband dry" through her appetite for food and by devouring the fruits of his toil (Works and Days, 705); she also squeezes him dry with her sexual appetite, which the midsummer heat only serves to increase (Works and Days, 586–87).

105. On the contrast between totalitarian and distributive economies, see Georges Dumézil, Mitra-Varuna: An Essay on Two Indo-European Representations of Sovereignty, trans. Derek Coltman (New York: Zone Books, 1988), pp. 131–34.

106. A full study has yet to be made of the figure and functions of the Homeric tamia and her relations with Hestia. Some points should be stressed: in Odysseus's palace, Eurykleia is the attendant, the nurse, and the one who tends the fires. Laertes obtained her in his youth in exchange for twenty cows, from her father, Ops (the Eye), son of Pisenor. The heralds in Ithaca were recruited from this family (Homer, Odyssey, 2.38). Laertes honored Eurykleia on an equal footing with his wife but refrained from any intimate relations with her (ibid., 1.431). She suckled Odysseus, whom she calls her child. It is on her suggestion that Autolykos, the boy's maternal grandfather, is asked to choose a name for the newborn child (ibid., 9.403). Her role is to watch unceasingly over all the goods of the house. Her vigilance, care, and foresight are much praised. She is an accomplished phulax. These are the qualities that Xenophon insists should belong to the tamia (Oeconomicus, 9.11). She should have no weaknesses, whether for food, drink, sleep, or men; she must have a perfect memory. But the true tamia, the best phulax of the house should be the wife herself (ibid., 9.14–15).

107. Artemidorus 2.37; see Gernet, "Sur le symbolisme politique," p. 38.

108. On the Kos ritual, Johannes van Prott, Fasti Sacri (Leipzig: Teubner, 1893); Farnell, Cults of the Greek States, p. 349ff.; Martin P. Nilsson, Griechische Feste von religiöser Bedeutung (Leipzig: Teubner, 1906), p. 17ff.; Cook, Zeus, vol. 1, p. 564; Gernet, "Sur le symbolisme politique," p. 33.

109. Pausanias 8.53.9.

110. Aristotle, *Politics*, 1322bff, and *Constitution of Athens*, 3.5 and 56.2.

111. On the historical relations between the royal Mycenaean hearth and the communal hearth of the city, see Farnell, *Cults of the Greek States*, p. 350ff.

112. Homer, *Odyssey*, 21.8ff.

113. Recall the formula *keimēlia keitai* (Homer, *Iliad*, 6.47, and *Odyssey*, 11.9). In the first book of the *Odyssey*, Telemachos offers his guest a gift, saying: "Thou mayest go to thy ship glad in spirit and bearing a gift costly and very beautiful, which shall be to thee a *keimēlion*, even such a gift as dear friends give to friends." Again, in the "*Iliad*," Achilles gives Nestor a cup: "Take this now, old sire, and let it be a *keimēlion* for thee, a memorial of Patroclus' burying" (23.618). See also Plato, *Laws*, 913a.

114. The presence among the herds of Atreus of a lamb with gold or purple fleece is the sign that Pelops's son is born to be king. Occasionally Hermes is presented as having engendered the golden lamb, the symbol of royal investiture (Euripides, *Orestes*, 995). In any case, it is he who intervenes to reestablish the legitimate sovereignty when Thyestes, in his contest with Atreus, fraudulently presents the royal beast, which belongs to his brother. Hermes has the same relationship to the ram, the symbol of royalty, as to the *skēptron*, the mobile symbol of sovereignty: the god of exchange transmits both from Zeus to the House of Atreus. Orgogozo, "L'Hermès des Achéens," makes some interesting remarks on Hermes's place in the myths of the golden fleece and his associations with the function of royalty.

115. On the significance of the agros, see Pierre Chantraine, *Etudes sur le vocabulaire grec* (Paris: Klincksieck, 1956), pp. 34–35.

116. Xenophon, *Oeconomicus*, 7.19.

117. On the significance of probaton and the opposition *keimēlia-probasis*, see Emile Benveniste, "Noms d'animaux en indo-européen," *Bulletin de la Société de linguistique* 45 (1949), pp. 91–100. The double aspect of wealth could also be expressed as Hesiod does: "Through work men grow rich in flocks and substance, *polumēloi t'aphneioi te*." (*Works and Days*, 308). Aphneios is in fact related to a type of riches other than herds. It is wealth that is stored in houses or cities. In Homer, *Odyssey*, 1.392, the term refers to a house; in Homer, *Iliad*, 2.570, it refers to a town, Corinth. On Corinth (aphneios), see Thucydides 1.13.5. See also *Odyssey*, 1.165, which emphasizes the contrast between "light-footed" men (*elaphroteroi podas*) and men weighed down with possessions, the kind of riches made up of gold and precious cloths (*aphneioteroi*).

118. On Hermes Agrotēr, see Euripides, *Electra*, 463; on Hermes Nomios, see Aristophanes, *Thesmophoriae*, 977.

119. See Simonides of Amorgus, frag. 18, Diels-Kranz: Hermes, patron of shepherds. This recalls the importance in the religious plastic arts of the figure of Hermes Kriophoros bearing a ram on his shoulders. On Hestia, see Scholia to Aristophanes, *Plutus*, 395

120. *Homeric Hymn to Hermes*, 569–71.

121. On Hermes Epimēlios, see Pausanias 9.34.3; on Hermes Polumēlos, see Homer, *Iliad*, 14.490.

122. Hesiod, *Theogony*, 444ff.

123. See Aristotle, *Politics*, 1258b.

124. In Athens, the two feasts were separate. The naming of the child took place on the tenth day after birth (*dekatē*).

125. On running around the hearth: Scholia to Plato *Theaetetus*, 160e; Hesychius s.v. *Dromiamphion hēmar*. On laying the baby on the groung: Scholia to Aristophanes, *Lysistrata*, 758.

126. *Homeric Hymn to Demeter*, 231–63.

127. Apollonius Rhodius, *Argonautica*, 4.869ff.

128. Pausanias, 2.3.11. On the *katakrupteia*, see Charles Picard, "L'Héraion de Perachora et les enfants de Médée," *Revue archéologique* (1932), pp. 218ff.; and Edouard Will, *Korinthiaka: Recherches sur l'histoire et la civilisation de Corinthe des origines aux guerres médiques* (Paris: Boccard, 1955), p. 88ff.

129. I use the word "return" deliberately. Born of the hearth as he is born of the earth, man always returns in death to the world from which he issued.

130. Apollodorus 3.6.3. Walking on the ground is quite a different matter from lying on the ground. The upright position does not carry the same risks as the prone position, which delivers people into the hands of the chthonic powers. So the newborn child, even when left exposed, was never put in direct contact with the soil. The tales of exposure always mention a chest (*larnax*), a basket (*liknon*), or a pot (*chutra*).

131. Pausanias 6.20.3–6.

132. The *Suda Lexicon*'s *peristiarchos* article explains the significance that this ring traced round the hearth can assume in an entirely different context. Pigs, used in Athens to purify the assembly, were first driven around the hearth; see Farnell, *Cults of the Greek States*, p. 363.

133. The *apo* and *ek* of *apothesis* and *ekthesis* both indicate a gap, distance.

These two terms do not appear to have the exactly opposite meaning that has sometimes been attributed to them with regard to the procedure of exposure. See Marie Delcourt, *Stérilités mystérieuses et naissances maléfiques dans l'antiquité classique* (Paris: Belles lettres, 1938), p. 37ff.; and for the other side, Pierre Roussel, "L'exposition des enfants à Sparte," *Revue des études anciennes* 45 (1943), pp. 5–17). To be convinced that the *ekthesis* is not necessarily the depositing of the child in a frequented area in the hope that it will survive — an exposure decided on by the father for social reasons, whereas *apothesis* would mean abandoning the child in a deserted place for properly religious reasons and to ensure its death — one need only consult Euripides, *Ion*, and Longus, *Pastorals* in which it is precisely the term *ekthesis* that is used. The newborn Ion is left in a deserted cave (*antron erēmon*) from which Hermes will fetch him (1494); he is exposed to wild animals (*thērsin ektetheis*, 951) and birds of prey (504–505), exposed to death (*hōs thanoumenon*, 18 and 27), and doomed to Hades (*eis Haidan ekballē*, 1496). Longus's *Pastorals* are built entirely around the opposition between the world of the *agros* and the world of the city (*polis* and *astu*). Exposed *en agrō* (1.2.1, 4.1, 5.1, 4.21.3), far from the town where their parents dwell, in areas frequented solely by shepherds searching for their lost animals, the two children always remain pure "rustics," even when they grow up and find their family, (4.39.1). On the opposition *agros-astu*, see 4.11.1–2, 15.4, 17.1, 1.9.1, 38.3.4.

134. Plato, *Theaetetus* 150b–c. On the "alternative implications": "When a child is born, the question the father has to answer is whether to raise him or expose him. Exposure of the child resulted from failure to celebrate the Amphidromia, or, in other words, from the disavowal of paternity in consequence of this. "Beauchet, *Histoire du droit privé*, vol. 2, p. 87. See also Glotz, *La solidarité de la famille*, p. 41, and *Etudes sociales et juridiques sur l'antiquité grecque* (Paris: Hachette, 1906), p. 192.

135. This could also be translated — and Glotz seems to have read the text in this way — as "of good constitution and legitimate birth." *Gonimos* and *alēthēs* could have both meanings. On *gonimos*, in the sense of the legitimate son, opposed to *nothos*, bastard, see *Palatine Anthology*, 9.277.

136. Plato, *Theaetetus*, 160e–61a.

137. Plutarch, *Life of Lycurgus*, 16.1–4.

138. Plutarch, *Table Talk*, 693F.

139. "*Exo boulimon, hesō de plouton kai hugieian!*" It is hardly necessary to recall that the *rhabdos* is an attribute of Hermes that gives him patronage of cer-

tain "expulsion" rituals, especially those that Eustathius calls *pompaia*, escorts (Eustathius, commentary on Homer, *Odyssey* 22.481). "When the *pompaia* are celebrated and the sullied are expelled to the crossroads, a *pompos* is held in the hands, which is said to be nothing other than the *kērukeion*, the wand of Hermes (*sebas Hermou*): from this *pompos* and the word *dios* comes the word *to diopompein*, sacred expulsion."

140. Immanuel Bekker, *Anecdota Graeca*, vol. 1 (Berlin: Nauckium, 1814), p. 278.4; Margaret de Gaudrion Verrall and Jane Harrison, *Mythology and Monuments of Ancient Athens* (London: Macmillan, 1890), p. 168.

141. On the relationship between this type of sacrilege and "devouring hunger," see the story of Erysichthon in Callimachus, *Hymn to Demeter*, 30ff.

142. Plutarch, *Advice to Bride and Groom*, 144a–b.

143. Thomas Gaisford, *Paroemiographi Graeci, quorum pars nunc primum ex codicibus manuscriptis vulgatur* (Osnabrück: Biblio Verlag, 1836), p. 25: *bouzugēs*; see Farnell, *Cults of the Greek States*, vol. 3, p. 315 n.17. On the domestic symbolism of fire and water, see Plutarch, *Roman Questions*, 1: in Rome, the new bride has to "touch fire and water." This was doubtless a rite of integration in her husband's home, like the *katachusmata* in Greece.

144. Pausanias 7.22.1ff.

145. Euripides frag. 781, 55 N². Porphyry, in Eusebius, *Preparation for the Gospel*, 3.11, also associates Hestia with the subterranean deities.

146. Deroy, "Le culte du foyer," pp. 32 and 43.

147. Hesychius, *Lexicon iota*, 1016.

148. Plato, *Republic*, 616ff.; see Pierre-Maxime Schuhl, "Le joug du Bien, les liens de la Nécessité et la fonction d'Hestia," in *Mélanges d'archéologie et d'histoire offerts à Charles Picard à l'occasion de son 65e anniversaire* (Paris: Presses Universitaires de France, 1949), vol. 2, p. 965ff. On Hestia as immobile at home: Plato, *Phaedrus*, 247a.

149. Plato, *Cratylus*, 401c–e.

CHAPTER SEVEN: GEOMETRY AND SPHERICAL ASTRONOMY IN EARLY GREEK COSMOLOGY
This essay originally appeared as "Géometrie et astronomie sphérique dans la première cosmologie grecque," *La Pensée* 109 (1963), pp. 82–92. It was the text of a lecture given at l'Université Nouvelle de Paris in a series on the history of scientific thought.

1. See G.S. Kirk and J.E. Raven, *The Presocratic Philosophers* (Cambridge: Cambridge University Press, 1960), pp. 10–19.

2. Xenophanes, in Hermann Diels and Walther Kranz, *Die Fragmente der Vorsokratiker, griechisch und deutsch*, 7th ed. (Berlin: Weidmann, 1951), vol. 1, pp. 135.16–17.

3. Hesiod, *Theogony*, 726ff.

4. See Charles H. Kahn, *Anaximander and the Origins of Greek Cosmology* (New York: Columbia University Press, 1960).

5. *Ibid.*, p. 56.

6. *Ibid.*, pp. 84–85.

7. Diogenes Laertius 1.1.15.

8. Aristophanes, *Birds*, 1004–1005.

9. The fact that the expression *kratoumenē* not only means being supported but also has a direct connection with the idea of power is proved by the use of the verb *kratein* in cosmological, medical, and technical writings. See Kahn, *Anaximander*, pp. 80 and 130.

10. Herodotus 3.142.

CHAPTER EIGHT: GEOMETRIC STRUCTURE AND POLITICAL IDEAS IN THE COSMOLOGY OF ANAXIMANDER

This essay originally appeared as "Structure géometrique et notions politiques dans la cosmologie d'Anaximandre," *Eirene* 7 (1968), pp. 5–23.

1. Gregory Vlastos, "Equality and Justice in Early Greek Cosmologies," *Classical Philology* 42 (1947), pp. 156–78; Charles H. Kahn, *Anaximander and the Origins of Greek Cosmology* (New York: Columbia University Press, 1960); Jean-Pierre Vernant, *The Origins of Greek Thought* (Ithaca: Cornell University Press, 1982), pp. 119–29. See also Pierre Lévêque and Pierre Vidal-Naquet, *Cleisthenes the Athenian: An Essay on the Representation of Space and Time in Greek Political Thought from the End of the Sixth Century to the Death of Plato*, trans. David Ames Curtis (Atlantic Highlands, NJ: Humanities Press, 1996), pp. 81–97; and Marcel Detienne, "En Grèce archaïque: Géométrie, politique et société," *Annales-Economies/Sociétés/Civilisations* (1965), pp. 425–41.

2. *Inscriptiones Graecae* 12. 5. 872, 27; 31, 38; quoted in Detienne, "En Grèce archaïque," p. 428. On the opposition *meson-idion*, see Herodotus 7.8.

3. Herodotus 3.142: the same expression occurs in connection with Kadmos of Kos (Herodotus 7.164) and with Demonax, who, in Cyrene in about

550 BCE, "set down in the middle" all that the kings had previously possessed, *panta ta proteron eichon hoi basilees es meson tōi dēmōi ethēke* (Herodotus 4.161).

4. See Plato, *Timaeus*, 63a: "Let us suppose that in the center of the universe there is a solid body which is in equilibrium. Such a solid would never move towards any of the extremities of the world since they are everywhere alike. Furthermore, if anyone were to move in a circle around this solid, whenever he stopped and happened to be at the antipodes he could call this same point in the world now 'below' and now 'above.'"

5. Aristotle, *On the Heavens*, 295b10–16; Hermann Diels and Walther Kranz, *Die Fragmente der Vorsokratiker, griechisch und deutsch*, 7th ed. (Berlin: Weidmann, 1951), 80.1.5.

6. Hippolytus, *The Refutation of All Heresies*, 1.6, Diels-Kranz, *Fragmente*, vol. 1, p. 84.7–8.

7. Kahn, *Anaximander*, p. 76.

8. *Ibid.*, pp. 80 and 130.

9. Jan Janda, "Review of Les Origines le la Pensée Grecque," *Eirene* 5 (1966), p. 205.

10. Demosthenes, *Against Lacritus*, 24.

11. Hippocrates, *On Ancient Medicine* 14.3 and 4.

12. *Ibid.*, 14.

13. *Ibid.*, 5.

14. Hippocrates, *De Arte*, 8.

15. Aristotle, *Rhetoric*, 2.1402a and *Mechanics*, 847a.22.

16. Homer, *Odyssey*, 23.46. Perhaps the *krateutai* (Homer, *Iliad*, 9.214), the firedogs made for supporting spits, should also be mentioned. The word was connected with *krateō* and *kradē*. On *krataipedos* opposed to the Mycenaean word *sarapudos* (meaning soft, inconsistent, referring to a type of soil), just as *krataipous* (an animal with a firm, stable gait) would be opposed to *sarapous* (meaning with uncertain feet, a wavering gait), see Louis Deroy and Monique Gérard, *Le cadastre mycénien de Pylos* (Rome: Atenco, 1965), pp. 75–76. On their relationships as confrontations of strength, see Aristotle, *On Generation and Corruption*, 331a28–35 and 331b1–12; and Plato, *Timaeus*, 56e–57c.

17. Homer, *Odyssey*, 11.597.

18. *Homeric Hymn to Gaia*, 1.

19. Hesiod *Theogony*, 117. On Chaos, the bottomless abyss without direction, compare *ibid.*, 740–43: *mega chasma*.

20. *Ibid.*, 114.

21. *Ibid.*, 885.

22. *Ibid.*, 868ff.; Pherecydes of Syros in Origen, *Against Celsus*, 6.42, Diels-Kranz, *Fragmente*, vol. 1, p. 49.23–26; Pindar, *Pythians*, 1.26–55; Aeschylus, *Prometheus Bound*, 364ff.; Valerius Flaccus, *Argonautica*, 4.515ff.

23. Hesiod, *Theogony*, 609.

24. *Ibid.*, 730–33.

25. *Ibid.*, 811–13.

26. See Gregory Vlastos, Review of *Principium Sapientae*, by Francis Macdonald Cornford, *Gnomon* 27 (1955), p. 74ff.; Hermann Ferdinand Fränkel, *Early Greek Poetry and Philosophy: A History of Greek Epic, Lyric and Prose to the Middle of the Fifth Century*, trans. Moses Hadas and James Willis (New York: Harcourt Brace Jovanovich, 1975), pp. 125–36.

27. Hesiod, *Theogony*, 383 and 403.

28. Hippolytus, *Refutation*, 1.1.

29. Aristotle, *Metaphysics*, 1091a33b7.

30. Hesiod, *Theogony*, 115–16; 49: Zeus is *phertatos theōn kratei te megistos*; 71 and 73: Zeus *embasileuei…kartei nikēsas*. See also 465, 490, 496, 506, 837, 883, 892, 897.

31. Homer, *Iliad*, 14.246 and 14.200 and 301.

32. *Ibid.*, 8.17ff., 15.108 and 164–65, 21.190.

33. On the significance of *periechein*, meaning simultaneously to envelop and to nourish, to govern, to dominate, see Eduard Zeller and Rodolfo Mondolfo, *La filosofia dei Greci nel suo sviluppo storico*, 2nd ed. (Florence: Nuova Italia, 1950), vol. 1, pp. 2.62 and 4.179.

34. Xenophanes in Aristotle, *On Melissos, Xenophanes, and Gorgias*, 977a27; Bekker, in Diels-Kranz, *Fragmente*, vol. 1, p. 117.27–28.

35. Aristotle, *Metaphysics*, 1074b3.

36. Aëtius 1.3.4; Diels-Kranz, *Fragmente*, vol. 1, p. 95.17–19; Aristotle, *Physics*, 203b11, Diels-Kranz, *Fragmente*, vol. 1, p. 85.14–19. On the equivalence of *kratein* and *kubernan*, see Diogenes of Apollonia, frag. 5. Zafiropulo, *Fragmente der Vorsokratiker*, 2: 61, 5–6: "It seems to me that through the air *pantas pai kubernasthai kai pantōn kratein*." And similarly in Hippocrates, *On diet*, 1.10.21ff.: *to thermotaton kai ischurotaton pur, hoper pantōn epikrateetai, diepon hapanta kata phusin* […] *touto panta dia pantos kubernai.*

37. Diogenes Laertius 1.35, Diels-Kranz, *Fragmente*, vol. 1, p. 71.12–13;

Aetius 1.25.2; Parmenides, frag. 8.31–32, Diels-Kranz, *Fragmente*, vol. 1, p. 237.10–11.

38. See Homer, *Iliad*, 15.189ff.

39. Aristotle, *Physics*, 203b7ff.

40. Melissos 4, in Simplicius, *On Aristotle's Physics*, 110.2.

41. *Ibid.*, 110.51. See also Melissos 6: "If Being is *apeiron*, it must be one. For if there were two they could not be limitless but would each have a limit in relation to the other."

42. Melissos 8 in Simplicius, *On Aristotle's "On the Heavens,"* 558.19.5.

43. In Simplicius, *Physics*, 164.24ff., Diels-Kranz, *Fragmente*, vol. 2, p. 37.18ff. Compare Plato, *Cratylus*, 413c: The *nous* of Anaxagoras, which does not mix with anything and orders everything, is undominated, independent *autokratōr*. On the meaning of *autos ep' eōutou*, see A.J. Festugière's remarks in his edition of Hippocrates, *L'Ancienne médicine* (Paris: Klincksieck, 1948), p. 47ff.

44. Aristotle, *Physics*, 205b.

45. Hippolytus, *Refutation*, 1.8.

46. *Ibid.*, 1.9; Diogenes Laertius 2.17. Diels-Kranz, *Fragmente*, vol. 2, p. 46.1.10–11.

47. Hippolytus, *Refutation*, 4.8.

48. Diels-Kranz, *Fragmente*, vol. 1, p. 77.38 and 78.2.

49. Hippolytus, *Refutation*, 1.7, Diels-Kranz, *Fragmente*, vol. 1, p. 92.11–13.

50. Hippolytus, *Refutation*, 1.8, Diels-Kranz, *Fragmente*, vol. 2, p. 16.9–11.

51. Diogenes Laertius 2.17, Diels-Kranz, *Fragmente*, vol. 1, p. 45.10–11.

52. Diogenes of Apollonia, Frag. 5, *ibid.*, vol. 2, p. 61.5–7.

53. Diogenes of Apollonia, Frag. 8, *ibid.*, vol. 2, p. 66.4–5; frag. 3, *ibid.*, vol. 2, p. 60.13.

54. Diogenes Laertius 9.57, Diels-Kranz, *Fragmente*, vol. 2, p. 52.6.

55. Diels-Kranz, *Fragmente*, vol. 2, p. 54.9.

56. Aristophanes, *Clouds*, 264.

57. Euripides, *The Trojan Women*, 884ff.

58. Diogenes of Apollonia, *On Nature*, 3. See also the beginning of 4.

59. Hippolytus, *Refutation*, 1.14, Diels-Kranz, *Fragmente*, vol. 1, p. 122.36.

60. Frag. B28, Diels-Kranz, *Fragmente*, vol. 1, p. 135.16–17.

61. Diogenes Laertius 2.17, Diels-Kranz, *Fragmente*, vol. 2, p. 45.10.

62. As Michael C. Stokes has rightly pointed out, what "surrounds" the earth in Anaximander is not the *apeiron* but the air, and air does not possess

kratos over the universe or dominate the other elements any more than any other element. The *apeiron* does not directly envelop the earth, with which it is not in immediate proximity. The *apeiron* envelops the cosmos as a whole, as a totality composed of all the various elements: The Unlimited "does not surround the earth in close proximity to it, but surrounds the whole universe — and the other universes if there are any. It is outside our cosmos, and does not persist as an entity within it.... So though the Unlimited probably persists after the process of cosmogony is over, it does not do so within the world, and does not surround earth like Air in the cosmology of Anaximenes." "Hesiodic and Milesian Cosmogonies II," *Phronesis* 8 (1963), pp. 30–31.

63. Aristotle, *Meteorology*, 340a16. See Kahn, *Anaximander*, p. 187.

64. Aristotle, *Physics*, 204b13–19 and 24–29.

65. The collected texts can be found in Kahn, *Anaximander*, p. 36, and are discussed on p. 44.

66. Aristotle, *Physics*, 205a27.

67. Aristotle, *Generation*, 332a19–25.

68. Plato, *Phaedo*, 108a–109a.

69. Hippolytus, *Refutation*, 1.9.

CHAPTER NINE: SPACE AND POLITICAL ORGANIZATION IN ANCIENT GREECE

1. Pierre Lévêque and Pierre Vidal-Naquet, *Cleisthenes the Athenian: An Essay on the Representation of Space and Time in Greek Political Thought from the End of the Sixth Century to the Death of Plato*, trans. David Ames Curtis (Atlantic Highlands, NJ: Humanities Press 1996).

2. Gustave Glotz, *Histoire grecque*, 4th ed. (Paris: Presses Universitaires de France, 1948), p. 469.

3. Jean-Pierre Vernant, *The Origins of Greek Thought* (Ithaca, NY: Cornell University Press, 1982); Chapter 7 above.

4. See Louis Gernet, "Sur le symbolisme politique en Grèce ancienne: Le foyer commun," *Cahiers internationaux de sociologie* 11 (1951), pp. 21–43.

5. See Jean-Pierre Vernant, "Hestia-Hermès, sur l'expression religieuse de l'espace et du mouvement chez les Grecs," *Revue française d'anthropologie* 3 (1963), pp. 12–50; and Chapter 6 above.

6. See Roland Crahay, "Structure politique de l'anthropologie religieuse dans la Grèce classique," *Diogène* 41 (1963), pp. 53–71.

7. Lévêque and Vidal-Naquet, *Cleisthenes the Athenian*, p. XXV.

8. Gernet, "Sur le symbolisme politique," p. 42.

9. *Ibid.*, p. 43. Moses I. Finley notes, quite rightly: "Whereas in the Near East government and politics were a function of the religious organisation, Greek and Roman religion was a function of the political organisation." "Between Slavery and Freedom," *Comparative Studies in Society and History* 6 (1964), p. 246.

10. Lévêque and Vidal-Naquet, *Cleisthenes the Athenian*, p. 15.

11. Herodotus 5.66; see Lévêque and Vidal-Naquet, *Cleisthenes the Athenian*, p. 28.

12. Herodotus 1.170; Vernant, *Origins of Greek Thought*, p. 127.

13. Herodotus 3.142; Vernant, *Origins of Greek Thought*, p. 126.

14. Lévêque and Vidal-Naquet, *Cleisthenes the Athenian*, p. 53.

15. Herodotus 1.170.

16. Herodotus 4.161. As Lévêque and Vidal-Naquet note, Aristotle himself makes the comparison between the reforms introduced by Cleisthenes and the establishment of the democracy at Cyrene. Aristotle, *Politics*, 7.1319b18–22; Lévêque and Vidal-Naquet, *Cleisthenes the Athenian*, p. 46.

17. Aelian, *Various Histories*, 3.17.

18. Etienne Lapalus, *Le fronton sculpté en Grèce, des origines à la fin du IV siècle: Etude sur les origines, l'évolution, la technique et les thèmes du décor tympanal* (Paris: Boccard, 1947), p. 145; quoted in Lévêque and Vidal-Naquet, *Cleisthenes the Athenian*, p. 61.

19. Lapalus, *Le fronton sculpté*, p. 148.

20. Lévêque and Vidal-Naquet, *Cleisthenes the Athenian*, p. 97.

21. Aristotle, *Politics*, 2.1267b28; Hesychius and Photius later called Hippodamos a "*meteōrologos*," a specialist in celestial phenomena.

22. See Victor Ehrenberg, *The Greek State* (Oxford: Blackwell, 1960), p. 89.

23. Aristotle, *Politics*, 1261a18 and 24.

24. *Ibid.*, 1261b1–5.

25. *Ibid.*, 1263b35–37.

26. Plato, *Laws*, 745b–e.

Chapter Ten: Prometheus and the Technological Function
This essay originally appeared as "Prométhée et la function technique," *Journal de psychologie* 43 (1952), pp. 419–29.

1. Louis Séchan, *Le mythe de Prométhée* (Paris: Presses Universitaires de France, 1951).

2. Georg Curtius, *Principles of Greek Etymology*, trans. Augustus S. Wilkins and Edwin B. England (London: Murray, 1886).

3. Phoroneus, the king of Argos, is the only hero to appear in connection with fire technology (Pausanias 2.19.5).

4. See Séchan, *Le mythe de Promethée*, p. 4, with the corresponding notes, and ch. 1, n.59.

5. *Ibid.*, pp. 13 and 14.

6. Georges Dumézil, *Le festin d'immortalité: Etude de mythologie comparée indo-européenne* (Paris: Geuthner, 1924), ch. 4.

7. Hesiod, *Theogony*, 567, and *Works and Days*, 52.

8. It is true that Hesiod suggests a different etymology for Pandora: the gift of all the gods (*Works and Days*, 81–82). However, the connection with Anesidora can leave no doubt about the true meaning of the name.

9. Hesiod, *Works and Days*, 11–17.

10. *Ibid.*, 300. Hesiod also describes fertility as depending on the just exercise of royal sovereignty. But this is fertility in its most collective form: Hesiod, *Works and Days*, 225ff. The prosperity that work ensures is, in contrast, a divine favor granted to the individual. This aspect of individualization comes up again in Prometheus's role as the distributor of shares.

11. Dumézil, *Le festin*, p. 94.

12. In this sense, Prometheus, the one with foresight, and his twin brother, Epimetheus, the thoughtless one, constitute two sides of a single character.

13. Aeschylus, *Prometheus Bound*, 228ff.

14. Plato, *Protagoras*, 320Dff.

15. *Ibid.*, 324c.

16. See n.10 above.

17. Plato, *Republic*, 428aff.

18. Even *andreia* ends up losing all its specific attributes in a generalized conception of virtue. This is possibly a third example to add to the "similar modifications to two parallel traditions" that Dumézil emphasizes in Zoroastrianism and in Cicero: "Les archanges de Zoroastre et les rois romains de Cicéron: Retouches homologues de deux traditions parallèles," *Journal de Psychologie* (1950), p. 449. But for Plato, there are more obvious social and political reasons for the change.

19. Attention has been drawn to the bias toward technological research among the Ionians in a whole current of Greek medicine and in a contemporary of Plato's such as Archytas. See Pierre Maxime Schuhl, *Essai sur la formation de la*

pensée grecque: Introduction historique à une étude de la philosophie platonicienne, 2nd ed. (Paris: Presses Universitaires de France, 1949), pp. xx and xxi. The importance of technology also finds expression in religion, both through the ritualization of certain techniques and through the myths, which, by connecting the origin of the technical skills with the gods or the heroes, bestow a certain value upon man's inventive faculties.

20. Aeschylus, *Prometheus Bound*, 506.

21. *Ibid.*, 447ff.

22. In addition to *Prometheus Bound*, the trilogy included *Prometheus Unbound* (Luomenos), and *Prometheus, the Fire-Giver* (Purphoros).

Chapter Eleven: Work and Nature in Ancient Greece
This essay originally appeared as "Travail et nature dans la Gréce ancienne," *Journal de psychologie* 52 (1955), pp. 1–29.

1. See Pierre Maxime Schuhl, *Machinisme et philosophie*, 2nd ed. (Paris: Presses Universitaires de France, 1947), pp. 1–22; André Aymard, "Hiérarchie du travail et autarcie individuelle dans la Grèce archaïque," *Revue d'histoire de la philosophie et d'histoire générale de la civilisation* (1943), pp. 124–46, and "L'idée de travail dans la Grèce archaïque," *Journal de psychologie* 41 (1948), pp. 29–45; Alexandre Koyré, "Les philosophes et la machine," *Critique* 23 (1948), pp. 124–33 and 610–29, and "Du monde de l' 'à-peu-près' a l'univers de la précision," *Critique* 28 (1948), pp. 806–23, repr. in *Etudes d'histoire de la pensée philosophique* (Paris: Colin, 1961), pp. 279–329).

2. Ignace Meyerson, "Le travail: Une conduite," *Journal de psychologie* 41 (1948), pp. 7–16.

3. Aristotle, *Politics*, 7.1325b15ff.: action — *bios praktikos* — does not imply any exterior object; compare Aristotle, *Nicomachaean Ethics*, Z41140a: *tēs men gar poiēseōs heteron to telos, tēs de praxeōs ouk an eiē gar autē hē eupraxia telos* (production has an end other than itself, action has not, for the completed action is itself the end), and *Metaphysics*, 6.1048b18ff. and 8.1050a23ff.

4. Plato, *Charmides*, 163b–d.

5. See Eugène Dupréel, *Les Sophistes: Protagoras, Gorgias, Prodicus, Hippias* (Neuchâtel: Griffon, 1948), p. 133.

6. Possibly it referred even to beggars, according to Aymard, "L'idée de travail," p. 39.

7. Henri Jeanmaire, *Dionysos: Histoire du culte de Bacchus; L'orgiasme dans*

l'antiquité et les temps modernes, origine du théâtre on Grèce, orphisme et mystique dionysiaque, èvolution du dionysisme après Alexandre (Paris: Payot, 1951), pp. 30–33.

8. In figural representations, Pandora and her double, Anesidora, "who makes gifts come forth," are deities of the earth and of fertility.

9. The comparison between Hesiod, *Theogony*, 595, and *Works and Days*, 305, is revealing; compare also *Works and Days*, 704: woman is *deipnolochēs*, always on the lookout for festivity and pleasure. She consumes her husband's wealth as well as his sexual vigor.

10. On the different levels in the representation of the deities presiding over agriculture, see Jean Bayet, "Les feriae sementivae et les indigitations dans le culte de Cérès et de Tellus," *Revue de l'histoire des religions* 137 (1950), pp. 172–206.

11. On grain for threshing: Hesiod, *Works and Days*, 597 and 805; Homer, *Iliad*, 5.500; Theocritus, *Idyll*, 7.30 and 155. On grain for grinding: Homer, *Iliad*, 13.322, and *Odyssey*, 2.355.

12. Hesiod, *Works and Days*, 780ff.

13. *Ibid.*, 826–28.

14. *Ibid.*, 309.

15. *Ibid.*, 493.

16. See John V.A. Fine, "Studies in Mortgage, Real Security, and Land Tenure in Ancient Athens," *Hesperia*, supp. 9 (1951), pp. 16–22; Louis Gernet in Luisa Banti (ed.), "Horai," *Studi in onore di Ugo Enrico Paoli* (Florence: Monnier, 1955), pp. 345–53.

17. On these religious aspects of real estate, see Aristotle, *Constitution of Athens*, 11.4, where Solon praises the freeing of "the venerable mother of the Olympians, the black Earth ... once enslaved but now free."

18. Comedy provides a glimpse of what life must have been like for the peasant of Attica, working his land with the help of a few slaves. Dikaiopolis, from the rural deme of Acharnae, is confined to Athens on account of the war and has a horror of the city. He pines for his village, "which does not know the word 'to buy' and provides him with everything, all on its own": Aristophanes, *Acharnians*, 35ff. See also Aristophanes, *Plutus*, especially the praise given by poverty to the peasant life, one long round of work and frugality. The peasant of Menander's *Geōrgos* who is entirely devoted to his land is also a true brother of Hesiod's farmer.

19. Hesiod, *Works and Days*, 289f; Xenophon, *Oeconomicus*, 1.16 and 1.8.5. In the same sense, see Aristotle, *Politics*, 7.1325a32.

20. Xenophon, *Oeconomicus*, 1.21 and 4.2.

21. The farmers who work in the fields "receive a strong and manly education"; they have the "right kind of mind and body." *Ibid.*, 5.13. On the life of the farmer as a hard training for the warrior life, *ibid.*, 5.4ff.

22. *Ibid.*, 4.24.

23. *Ibid.*, 6.7.The same opposition appears in Pseudo-Aristotle, *Oeconomica*, 1.1343.25ff. Agriculture leads to courage, *andreia*. In contrast to the artisans' trades, which render bodies unsuited to service (*achreia*), it makes men able to bear a life of hard labor in the open air: *thuralein kai ponein*.

24. Some people have been shocked by this application of the procedures of Socratic maieutics to agricultural knowledge. See, for example, Marcel Caster, "Sur l'économique de Xénophon," in Alexandre Marie Desrousseaux (ed.), *Mélanges offerts à A.M. Desrousseaux* (Paris, Hachette, 1937), p. 49 n.2. But Xenophon's intention is to make clear the spontaneous, natural aspect of agriculture, as opposed to technical skills that have to be learnd (*Oeconomicus*, 19.15, 16, 17). The deity itself teaches the rules of agriculture (17. 3).

25. Xenophon, *Oeconomicus*, 15.10, 18.10, 15.4, 6.9.

26. *Ibid.,* 15.11.

27. *Ibid.,* 20.14.

28. *Ibid.,* 19.18.

29. *Ibid.,* 20.2 and 4.

30. *Ibid.,* 20.14.

31. *Ibid.,* 5.19.

32. *Ibid.,* 5.20.

33. *Ibid.,* 5.12; see also 20.14: the land treats well whoever treats it well. See also Xenophon, *The Education of Cyrus*, 8.3.38: the land respects justice above all; it gives a true and just yield for the seed it has received. The same idea appears, in an ironic form, in Menander frag. 92A35 and 96, Edmonds: "Nobody cultivates a more pious land, *agron eusebesteron*. When I sow it with barley in its justice it returns to me all that I have sown in it." In *Oeconomica*, Pseudo-Aristotle notes that of all the occupations agriculture is ranked first in order of "justice" (1.1343a30).

34. The Greek festivals and religious calendar are evidence of how agriculture is integrated with religion.

35. Eugène Dupréel, *Sociologie générale* (Paris: Presses Universitaires de France, 1948), p. 207ff.

36. If to cultivate the land (in both the literal and the religious senses) is normally considered active participation in the natural and divine order, certain human operations may appear to be in contradiction with this order. Demeter's wrath against Erysichthon, who used his axe in her wood, is well known. It was a sacred wood. But one interpretation of the story can be compared with the story of Lycurgus, who kills his son, Dryas, or — in other versions — cuts off his own foot thinking he is cutting a vine, and with the story of Phylacus, who renders his son impotent while cutting down a tree or — in another version — while castrating animals.

37. The theme of virtue's choosing the path of painful effort (*ponos*) runs from Hesiod through Herodotus (7.102), Xenophon, and Prodicus. See Charles Picard, "Nouvelles remarques sur l'apologue dit de Prodicos," *Revue archéologique* 42 (1953), pp. 10–41.

38. On this ideal of self-sufficiency, see Aymard, "L'idée de travail."

39. In agriculture, men draw their sustenance *apo tēs gēs*, just as all creatures draw it naturally from their mothers. But agriculture draws nothing from man *ap' anthrōpōn*, in contrast to commerce and paid work: Pseudo-Aristotle, *Oeconomica*, 1343b.

40. It is important to recall the development of slavery in the country districts from the Hellenistic period onward, and the concentration of real estate. In a revealing text, Pliny contrasts the time when the land, worked by the generals and the great personages of Rome, rejoiced beneath garlanded ploughshares and triumphal ploughs, and the time when, delivered over to the hands of slaves and to feet that wear chains, it still consents to yield its fruits (*Natural History*, 18.4). In mythology, images of war chariots, triumphal teams of oxen, and ploughs are often interchangeable.

41. Compare, for instance, Pseudo-Aristotle, *Oeconomica*, 1343a25ff., and Aristotle, *Politics*, 1330a25ff. The inconsistency in the works written by or attributed to Aristotle can be explained by the fact that in the Greek world there were two very different forms of farms and farming that conferred contrasting social statuses on the individuals involved. On the one hand, there were small farms, personally farmed by free peasant citizens, as in Athens; on the other, there were "tenant farmers" who were excluded from citizenship, as in the warrior-type Dorian cities.

42. Gernet, who drew my attention to the figure of Margites and his importance in connection with one particular representation of technical activity, sug-

gests a comparison with the Celtic god Lug. The exact opposite concept is found in the two texts of Exodus cited by Pierre Maxime Schuhl, "Labeur et contemplation," *Efforts et réalisations* (1952). The eternal inspires Betsabel with a "universal" skill so that he can do every type of work and make every kind of artistic product (Exodus 31.1.11 and 35.30ff.). Technical skill is used here to refer to artisan trades as a whole.

43. Georges Dumézil, *Tarpeia: Essais de philologie comparative indo-européenne* (Paris: Gallimard, 1947), pp. 208–46.

44. Hesiod, *Theogony*, 639ff.; Apollodorus, *The Library*, 1.2.1; see Dumézil, *Tarpeia*, p. 222.

45. According to Callimachus, *Hymn to Delos*, 4.31, the Telchines were held to have made Poseidon's trident. The Telchines and the Daktyloi are the first metalworkers.

46. On this aspect of nomadism see Plutarch, *Life of Numa*, 15. On the relationship between metallurgy to *oribasie* (mountain dancing), see Jeanmaire, *Dionysos*, p. 182.

47. I am referring to the classical period. It is well known that in Homer craftsmen had still not lost their "itinerant" character.

48. Fritz Schachermeyr notes the contrast, in this respect, between the Greek *polis*, which was based on personal bonds, and the towns of the East, which had a territorial basis. In order to express the idea of the Babylonians, one is obliged to say "the people of the territory of the town of Babylon." "La formation de la cité grècque," *Diogène* 4 (1953), pp. 33.

49. The Cynics go against the entirety of ancient political thought in their support of an ideal of self-sufficiency. See Aristotle, *Politics*, 1.1253a25ff.

50. Plato, *Protagoras*, 320dff.

51. *Ibid.*, 324c–d.

52. Plato, *Republic*, 369bff.

53. *Ibid.*, 371b.

54. In Sparta, the citizens are called *homoioi*. They are forbidden to exercise professional activities.

55. *Philia* is essentially a political sentiment. Professional feelings are different — envy or rivalry, for instance. As Hesiod says: "And potter is angry with potter, and craftsman with craftsman, and beggar is jealous of beggars and, minstrel of minstrel." Activities connected with a trade entail *eris* (Hesiod, *Works and Days*, p. 25). Elsewhere, I have indicated the opposition between, on the

466

one hand, the technological deities — Athena, Hephaistos, Prometheus — and, on the other, Zeus, who is political and the sovereign ruler; I have also discussed the relationship between the technological deities and the function of distributing lots (see above, pp. 186–87). In Aeschylus, *Prometheus Bound*, 45–50, Hephaistos complains about his trade, calling it a "lot" that fell to him. He is told that all the other gods also received their lots as he did, except Zeus, who is above specialization.

56. Aristotle, *Politics*, 2.1261a35.

57. *Ibid.*, 7.1329a35.

58. *Ibid.*, 3.1280b20ff.

59. Plato, *Protagoras*, 324e–325a.

60. In *Capital*, Karl Marx points out that this conception indicates an economic stage where an article's use value is still regarded as more important than its commercial value. *Capital: A Critique of Political Economy*, vol. 1, *The Process of Production of Capital* (London: Lawrence and Wishart, 1954), p. 365.

61. Homer, *Odyssey*, 14.228. Plato says: "Each of us is not, by nature, exactly like everyone else; on the contrary, our own nature distinguishes us from others; different men are suited to different tasks" (*Republic*, 370bc). Aristotle writes: "Nature is not niggardly, like the smith who fashions the Delphian knife for many uses; she makes each thing for a single use, and every instrument is best when intended for one and not for many uses" (*Politics*, 1252b1–5).

62. Xenophon, *The Education of Cyrus*, 3.2.

63. See Pierre Maxime Schuhl, "Remarques sur Platon et la technologie," *Revue des etudes grècques* 66 (1953), pp. 465–72.

64. Xenophon, *Oeconimicus*, 1.22. It is understandable that artisans would lack the manly virtues: like women, they work indoors. The same attitude toward the natural division of tasks between men and women appears in the Pseudo-Aristotle, *Oeconomica*, 1343b28ff.

65. Aristotle, *Politics*, 1252a30ff. It is well known that the opposition between the free man and the slave was not always accepted as natural.

66. Plato, *Republic*, 374b. But Aristotle notes that nature does not make men cobblers in the same way that it makes them slaves (*Politics*, 1260b1).

67. What Agatharchides says about the organization of work in the gold mines of Nubia is highly revealing: the workforce — composed of several thousand workers — was divided up to perform different tasks in the following manner: for the hewing, the strongest men (in the prime of life); for collecting,

children; for breaking up the ore, men over thirty years of age; for grinding with a millstone, women and old men; for purifying the gold and for truly metallurgical operations, the *technitai*. Technical abilities find their place in the hierarchy of task distribution founded essentially upon natural differences, that is, groups divided according to age and sex (Diodorus of Sicily 3.12.14).

68. Antiphon the Sophist, 1.2.

69. No technical work ever consisted simply in applying learned rules (Plato, *Statesman*, 299d–300a). The skill consists in knowing when to use them at the favorable moment (*kairōi*) and in a suitable manner (*en tōi deonti*). As Plato remarks, if the artisan misses the right moment for doing his task, the task will be ruined. For this reason, the artisan can never leave his work (*Republic*, 2.370b). On this use of the *kairos*, see Aristotle, *Nichomachaean Ethics*, 2.1104a9.

70. Hippocrates, *On Art*, and *On the Places in Man*, 34.

71. Aristotle, *Politics*, 1.1256b34: Every skill is limited; there is none whose instruments are infinite in number and size; 1.1257b28: For every skill, the means to the end are not infinite, and this end (*telos*) necessarily acts as a limit (*peras*).

72. See Plato, *Republic*, 373aff. The techniques of imitation that produce pleasure can be endlessly multiplied, since pleasure belongs to the sphere of what is unlimited. Conversely, techniques that claim to be universal, like those of the sophists, also necessarily produce illusions, not realities; Plato, *Sophist*, 233e.

73. Alfred Victor Espinas, *Les origines de la technologie* (Paris: Alcan, 1897), pp. 157–214.

74. This "naturalization" of the techniques of artisans is strikingly expressed in the texts where Democritus systematically assimilates them to natural processes. Similarly, in Hippocrates's "Heraclitean" treatise, *On Diet*, all technical skills are assimilated to the natural processes in the human body and in the world. For example, the weavers "proceed in a circular movement, they continue weaving from one end to the other: this is like the circulation in the body." The goldsmiths wash and melt the gold over a gentle flame "just as seed, being kept gently warm, becomes established in the body." Thus "all the arts share in human nature" (*On Diet*, 24). For Plato, at the opposite pole of ancient thought, human and "mortal" *technē* is no more than a reproduction of a divine *technē* (*Laws*, 889cff. and 892b).

75. For Aristotle, moneymaking is *ou kata phusin*, in that it is not aimed at satisfying a need but seeks money for its own sake. Making a shoe has a natural

end — the use of the shoe — but it can have another end that is not natural: the sale of the shoe (*Politics*, 1257a6ff.). Every *technē* can in this way be deflected away from its natural function toward moneymaking (*ibid.*, 1258a10). Insofar as it remains within the bounds of natural needs, exchange is *kata phusin*. But, in contrast to the nature of a true *technē*, moneymaking is "unlimited," as if the art of acquiring wealth — usury, for example — had the power to generate money from money indefinitely. The fact is that it does not generate anything at all: money is only an illusion, "having no value except by convention and not by nature since a change in the conventions of those who use it can render it incapable of satisfying our needs" (*ibid.*, 1257b11–15).

76. Plato, *Republic*, 601d. On manufactured objects, see Victor Goldschmidt, *Essai sur le "Cratyle": Contribution à l'histoire de la pensée de Platon* (Paris: Champion, 1940), p. 69ff.; and W.D. Ross, *Plato's Theory of Ideas* (Oxford: Clarendon, 1951), p. 170ff.

77. Aristotle, *Politics*, 3.1282a17ff. and 7.1328a27–33.

78. *Ibid.*, 3.1277b28–30.

79. Plato, *Republic*, 601cff.

80. Aristotle, *Politics*, 1.1254a.

81. The social history of work confirms that this system of thought is a true reflection of the way the *polis* was organized. The place of slaves in artisan activities continued to increase: in order to take part in political life, citizens increasingly left the responsibility of producing riches to them and to metics. However important artisans may have been in the life of commercial cities such as Athens or Corinth, economic activities always remain in the background in the city's institutions and the conceptions they express. The *polis* continues and extends traditions of an aristocratic nature: it is not "bourgeois" like the town of the Middle Ages.

CHAPTER TWELVE: SOME PSYCHOLOGICAL ASPECTS OF WORK IN ANCIENT GREECE
This essay originally appeared as "Aspects psychologiques du travail dans la Grèce ancienue," *La Pensée* 66 (1956), pp. 80–84.

1. See Ignace Meyerson, "Travail, fonction psychologique," *Journal de psychologie* 52 (1955), pp. 3–17.

2. "While labor which creates exchange-values is abstract, universal, and homogeneous, labor which produces use-values is concrete and special and is

made up of an endless variety of kinds of labor according to the way in which and the material to which it is applied." Karl Marx, *A Contribution to the Critique of Political Economy* (Chicago: Kerr, 1904), p. 33.

3. See above, p. 279ff.

4. Karl Marx, *Capital: A Critique of Political Economy*, vol. 1, *The Process of Production of Capital* (London: Lawrence and Wishart, 1954) p. 365: "In most striking contrast with this accentuation of quantity and exchange-value, is the attitude of the writers of classical antiquity, who hold exclusively by quality and use-value."

5. See above, p. 285.

6. Of course, Aristotle is not unaware of exchange value, since he defines it in the *Politics* (a definition that Marx quotes at the beginning of *Contribution to the Critique of Political Economy*). However, as Marx points out, Aristotle cannot "as an ancient Greek" understand what it is that constitutes the unity of salable commodities and makes it possible for them to be interchangeable as exchange values. Like other ancient writers, he sees a product only in terms of its use value (ch. 2, note to pp. 78 and 79).

7. Marx remarks, strikingly, that in terms of their exchange value salable commodities are no longer regarded "as to the service which [they] render, but as to the service which [they] have been rendered in (their) production." *Ibid.*, p. 34.

8. This point of view remained current until the capitalist system of production was introduced. "Had we inquired under what circumstances all, or even the majority of products, take the form of commodities, we should have found that this can only happen with production of a very specific kind, capitalist production.... It is only from this moment [when labor power takes the form of a commodity] that the commodity form of products becomes the dominant social form" (Marx, *Capital*, vol. 1, pp. 169 and 170 n.1). Similarly, "Stenart knew very well that products took on the form of commodities and commodities the form of money in pre-capitalistic epochs as well; but he proves conclusively that it is only in the capitalistic period of production that the commodity becomes the elementary and fundamental form of wealth, and alienation [of commodities] the ruling form of acquisition and that, consequently, *labour creating exchange-value is specifically capitalistic in its character*" (Marx, *Contribution to the Critique*).

9. This view of craftsmen's activities in Plato and Aristotle is strikingly analyzed by Victor Goldschmidt, *Le système stoïcien et l'idée de temps* (Paris: Vrin, 1953), p. 146ff.

10. Aristotle, *Metaphysics*, 26.9.1034a30ff.

11. See above, p. 193.

12. "When of two related things one is a means and the other an end, in their case there is nothing in common except for the one to act and the other to receive the action. I mean for instance instrument or artificer and the work that they produce: between a house and a builder there is nothing that is produced in common, but the builder's craft exists for the sake of the house" (Aristotle, *Politics*, 7.1328a219ff). The slave exists for the master in the same way. He belongs to him and is part of him. But the master is in no way "attached" to the slave (*ibid.*, 1.1254a9ff).

13. See, for example, Plato, *Euthydemus*, 289cff.

14. Aristotle states that every artisan is a slave in the sphere of his trade. Naturally the reason for this alienation is that the product of his work is not intended for the artisan himself. It may be sold; it is a salable commodity. But in this society, the same product may be something other than a salable commodity, because of the presence of domestic labor and the existence of certain forms of servile labor. So, within the framework of a social system where the category of the salable commodity is not yet of paramount importance, exchange value is only appreciated in the form of "a value in use destined for another man." This is made particularly clear in Aristotle's analyses of exchange values. It is hardly necessary to note that for Marx, "the production of commodities does not become the normal, dominant type of production until capitalist production serves as its basis." Karl Marx, *Capital: A Critique of Political Economy*, vol. 2, *The Process of Circulation of Capital*, p. 31.

15. Aristotle, *Politics*, 1.1254a.

16. *Ibid.*, 3.1282a17ff. and 1277b28–30; Plato, *Republic*, 601cff.; *Cratylus* 390bff.

17. Aristotle, *Metaphysics*, 1050a30–35.

CHAPTER THIRTEEN: SOME REMARKS ON THE FORMS AND LIMITATIONS OF TECHNOLOGICAL THOUGHT AMONG THE GREEKS
This essay originally appeared as "Remarques sur les formes et les limites de la pensée technique chez les Grecs," *Revue d'histoire des sciences* (1957), pp. 205–25.

1. Using the term for the work of the carpenter: Homer, *Iliad*, 3.61; for work with metals: Homer, *Odyssey*, 6.232, 11.614, 3.433; for weaving: *Odyssey*, 6.110 and 235.

2. The magic fetters that imprison Ares and Aphrodite are the *desmoi tech-nēntes poluphronos Hēphaistoio*; the Old Man of the Sea uses the resources of a *doliēs technēs* when he changes shape (Homer, *Odyssey*, 8.296 and 4.455).

3. On *mētis* as practical intelligence at work in the skill of the artisan as well as in magic spells, see Henri Jeanmaire, "La naissance d'Athèna et la royauté magique de Zeus," *Revue archéologique* 48 (1956), pp. 12–39.

4. On the history of the concept of *technē*, see René Schaerer, *Episteme et Techne: Etude sur les notions de connaissance et d'art d'Homère à Platon* (Macon: Protat Frères, 1930).

5. In the fourth century, Aristotle classifies technical production as a part of *metablētikē*. In this sense, it is not so much the manufacture or transformation of things but rather an aspect of exchange. The work of the artisan falls into the category of *mistharnia*, working for wages (*Politics*, 1.1258b25).

6. Alfred Victor Espinas, *Les origines de la technologie* (Paris: Alcan, 1897). On the transition in Greece from un-self-conscious technical skill to technology, see especially pp. 6–7 and n.1.

7. Pierre Maxime Schuhl, *Machinisme et philosophie*, 2nd ed. (Paris: Presses Universitaires de France, 1947), p. xiii and ch. 1.

8. See R.J. Forbes, *Man the Maker: A History of Technology and Engineering* (London: Constable, 1950), vol. 2, p. 589ff. The introduction of the water mill around the third century CE begins a new age of technology, in which motive power is supplied by machines. On the Greek contributions and inventions in the technical sphere, see Emile Meyerson, *Essais* (Paris: Vrin, 1936), p. 246ff.

9. On the technology of the *organon*: Espinas, *Les origines*, pp. 75–156; on the age of the tool: Schuhl, "Machinisme," p. viii; on eteotechnology: Lewis Mumford, *Technics and Civilization* (London: Routledge, 1946); on man's techniques in adapting to things: Alexandre Koyré, "Du monde de l' 'à-peu-près' à l'univers de la précision," *Critique* 28 (1948), p. 611.

10. Homer, *Iliad*, 18.373ff. and 417ff., and *Odyssey*, 8.555–65.

11. Espinas, *Les origines*, p. 45ff.

12. See Georges Friedmann, *Où va le travail humain?* (Paris: Gallimard, 1950), p. 28.

13. Herodotus 3.60. On the aqueduct of Samos, see Forbes, *Man the Maker*, vol. 2, pp. 667–68, and Arnold Reymond, *History of the Sciences in Greco-Roman Antiquity* (New York: Biblio and Tannen, 1965), p. 179.

14. Plato, *Statesman*, 259e: the *architektōn* is opposed to the *ergastikos* and is superior to him because he contributes to the piece of work a theoretical knowledge, based upon calculations. The same opposition is found in Aristotle, *Metaphysics*, 981b30.

15. Aulus Gellius 10.12.

16. Hero, *Baroulkos*, 4. The author mentions a number of methodological rules: one proposition cannot contradict another that has previously been demonstrated; investigations must take as their starting point that which is evident and that of which the cause is evident; anyone who desires to make progress in the discovery of causes start with one or several physical principles and relate to them all the questions that arise. He also gives perfectly clear and precise information of a quite remarkable technical ingenuity on how to secure blocks of stone to be lifted by cranes and on safety measures for avoiding accidents.

17. Ctesibius invented the fire engine, the hydraulic organ, and a number of war machines. He perfected the waterclock. Hero was familiar with the screw press. A.G. Drachmann, *Ktesibios, Philon and Heron: A Study in Ancient Pneumatics* (Copenhagen: Munksgaard, 1948).

18. See Espinas, *Les origines*, p. 86; Albert de Rochas d'Aiglun, *La science des philosophes et l'art des thaumaturges dans l'antiquité* (Paris: Masson, 1882); Schuhl, "Machinisme," p. 8.

19. See Meyerson, *Essais*; Schuhl, "Machinisme"; Victor Chapot, "Sentiment des anciens sur le machinisme," *Revue des études anciennes* 40 (1938); R.J. Forbes, "The Ancients and the Machine," *Archives internationales d'histoire des sciences* 8 (1949), pp. 919–33.

20. Koyré, "Du monde de l' 'à-peu-près,'" pp. 806–23.

21. See Eugène Dupréel, *Les sophistes: Protagoras, Gorgias, Prodicus, Hippias* (Neuchâtel: Griffon, 1948), pp. 38–45; Jacqueline de Romilly, *Histoire et raison chez Thucydide* (Paris: Belles Lettres, 1956), pp. 180–86.

22. Aristotle, *Rhetoric*, 2.1402a; see also Aristophanes, *Clouds*, 112ff. (quoted in Romilly, *Histoire et raison*, p. 184).

23. *En ois ta te elattonta kratei tōn meizonōn* (Aristotle, *Mechanics*, 847a22).

24. Aristotle remarks that craftsmen use this property of the circle when, in order to produce a *thaumaston*, they place in temples series of iron discs turning on one another by means of friction, some of the discs being kept invisible from the public (*ibid.*, 848a30).

25. *Kai touto eulogōs sumbebēken: ek men gar thaumasiōterou sumbainein ti thaumaston ouden atopon, thaumasiōtaton de to tanantia ginesthai met' allēlōn.*

26. Historical thought among the Greeks, like their technological thought, owes a debt to logic and dialectics. Ignace Meyerson writes: "The succession of events is logical in Thucydides.... For Thucydides time is not chronological; it is, so to speak, logical." He refers to remarks made by Romilly, according to whom the account of a battle in Thucydides is a theory and the victory a verified conclusion, and adds: "The world of Thucydides is a world rethought, and his history is an enacted dialectic." Ignace Meyerson, "Le temps, la mémoire, l'histoire," *Journal de Psychologie* 53 (1956), p. 340. Even medical thought, although it was very highly developed, did not entirely break free from the limitations imposed on it by oral discussion and confrontation. Louis Bourgey notes that the practice of making speeches on medical subjects was general, and that on this account eloquence originally exerted considerable power over medicine: "It was not just that they had to compose fine eloquent speeches, but they had also to confront their adversaries successfully. Very often, after a particular thesis had been presented, another doctor took the floor in support of the opposite thesis, or else the orator was directly cross-examined and was obliged to answer a host of detailed questions." *Observation et expérience chez les médecins de la Collection hippocratique* (Paris: Vrin, 1953), p. 114ff. This primacy of the speech was of course especially marked in the thought of sophistic doctors. It was justified, for them, by the theory that the principle of disease cannot be seen by the eye and is only visible to reasoning (*logismos*). The empirical strain in Greek medicine maintained, in contrast, that the true criterion of medical truth lay in grasping indications directly through the eyes, for all that exists must be able to be seen and known (see Bourgey, *Observation*, p. 117). Here again is the opposition, traditional to Greek thought, between *phanera* and *adēla*, things visible and things invisible — the former arising directly from *empeiria*, while the latter call for a different exercise of the mind, whether it be a question of inspired guesswork or of pure reasoning. See, on this, Pierre-Maxime Schuhl, "Adèla," *Annales de la faculté des lettres de Toulouse* 1 (1953), pp. 86–94, and Louis Gernet, "Choses visibles et choses invisibles," *Revue philosophique* 46 (1956), pp. 79–86. In *Baroulkos*, Hero emphasizes that at the base of all the difficulties in mechanical problems and of the obscurity that surrounds the investigation of causes in this science lies the fact that one cannot actually see the forces at work in heavy bodies, or how they are distributed. Since these forces belong to the sphere of

the invisible, it is inevitable that *logismos* (reasoning), is the dominating force in mechanics.

27. Reymond, *Histoire des sciences*, p. 204.

28. Philo, *Mechanics*, 4.3. It is not possible to understand everything in such matters, *logōi kai methodois*.

29. Schuhl, "Adèla," p. 16.

30. Drachmann rightly notes the eclectic nature of the theoretical considerations in Hero's *Pneumatics*. In Hero's work, the machines are no more used to illustrate the interplay of natural laws than natural laws (with a few exceptions) are used to explain how the instruments work. Theory provides principles of explanation that have a general application. There is no concept of precise physical laws or of an experimental apparatus for verifying them. This is not a treatise on applied physics but a collection of ingenious techniques (*Ktesibios*, p. 161).

31. Hero's attitude is already different in this respect. Unlike Philo, only once (at 1.9) does he refer to the surprise quality of his construction. He is struck not so much by the "marvelous" character of the machine as by the ingenuity it displays and by its aspect as a solution to a technical problem, without reference to its possible utility. See Drachmann, *Ktesibios*, p. 161.

32. Plutarch, *Life of Marcellus*, 17.

33. See Koyré, "Du monde de l' 'à-peu-près,'" pp. 627–68.

34. This apprenticeship was, at the most, a *doxa*. It was a form of knowledge only by virtue of the place it accorded to calculation, measurement, and weight; see Plato, *Philebus*, 55e, and *Theaetetus*, 176c. The term *technē*, which was originally applied to scientific knowledge as well as to the experience of the artisan, could, after Plato, be used in opposition to true science: *epistēmē*.

35. This was a purely practical apprenticeship of a still secret nature, which the artisan imparted to his son or to the son of a friend; it was quite different from a theoretical education. See Plato, *Protagoras*, 328a and 323d; Xenophon, *Oeconomicus*, 15.11.

36. Aristotle, *Politics*, 1258b36 and *Nichomachaean Ethics*, 2.1104a9.

37. Plato, *Republic*, 2.370b and 374c.

38. The sophist, whose teaching concerns *praxis* (the general conduct of life), not *poiēsis* (making), could claim to recognize the opportune moment and to teach the art of using it. He presents himself as the master of the *kairos*, while the artisan is its slave.

39. See André Aymard, "L'idée de travail dans la Grèce archaïque, 41 *Journal de psychologie* (1948), pp. 29–45.

40. In a lecture delivered at the Ecole Pratique des Hautes Etudes, Gernet pointed out that the use of the term *cheirōnax*, which retained the idea of a mastery in reference to the artisan, had died out by the middle of the fifth century. In the classical period, the word seldom retains a favorable meaning. It tends increasingly to be associated with the idea of a subordinate, contemptible craft. It is naturally linked with the term *cheirotechnēs*, which evokes the use of a purely physical force, in its crudest form. See Plato, *Republic*, 405a and 490c; Aristotle, *Politics*, 1277b.

41. Louis Gernet, "La notion mythique de la valeur en Grèce," *Journal de psychologie* 41 (1948), pp. 415–62.

42. During the age of the city, *eris* still existed in the arts of aesthetic as well as utilitarian character, such as the ornamentation on luxury vases.

43. See Thucydides 1.5.3 and 4.

44. Jeanmaire has shown how the portraits of Ērōs in Plato, *Symposium*, 203d, made it possible to pinpoint the form of intelligence that characterized *mētis* ("La naissance," pp. 24 and 25). From his father, *Porus*, son of Mētis, Ērōs inherits a resourceful mind and an inventive intelligence: "a famous hunter, always weaving some stratagem; desirous and competent of wisdom, throughout life ensuing the truth; a master of jugglery, witchcraft and artful speech." But is *mētis* still an "artisan virtue" to Plato? It seems not. In *Symposium*, 203a, Plato specifically contrasts the kind of men who are called "daemonic" because they are inhabited by daemons such as Ērōs and thus have access to the knowledge of things divine, with those whose knowledge is connected with a special science or a manual skill and who are merely artisans.

45. Gorgias, *Encomium of Helen*, 32ff.

46. See p. 208ff.

47. Plato, *Republic*, 601c; Aristotle, *Politics*, 1282a17.

48. The man who possesses *phronēsis* gives the orders; the artisan who has no *phronēsis* is bound to obedience; Aristotle, *Politics*, 1277b29.

49. Even in the case of Hippias, who appears to represent the ideal of polymathy, teaching was not held to have anything to do with artisan crafts. When he boasted of having made everything he was wearing, including his clothes and shoes, with his own hands, he was proclaiming his *autarkeia*, his self-sufficiency, in the manner of the Cynics, rather than declaring an interest in technical matters.

50. See Plato, *Charmides*, 163b–d; Dupréel, *Les sophistes*, p. 133.

CHAPTER FOURTEEN: THE FIGURATION OF THE INVISIBLE AND THE
PSYCHOLOGICAL CATEGORY OF THE DOUBLE

This essay originally appeared as "Figuration de l'invisible et catêgorie psychologique du double: le colossos," talk given at "Le signe et les systèmes de
signes," conference organized by the Centre de Recherches de Psychologie comparative in Royaumont, 12–15 April 1962.

1. Emile Benveniste, "Le sens du mot *kolossos* et les noms grecs de la
statue," *Revue de philologie* 5 (1931), pp. 118–35; see also Paul Chantraine, "Grec
kolossos," *Bulletin de l'Institut français d'archéologie orientale* 30 (1930), pp.
449–55. On the history of the term, see Georges Roux, "Qu'est-ce qu'un *kolossos?*," *Revue des études anciennes* (1960), pp. 5–40.

2. The *xoanon* of Artemis *Orthia*, in Sparta, was held in the hands of the
priestess during the ceremony of the flagellation of youths; the idol was small
and light (Pausanias 3.16.10–11). The *xoanon* of Thetis, which her priestess Kleo
secretly carried on her person from Messenia to Sparta, can have been no larger
or heavier (Pausanias 3.14.4). The same goes for the *bretas* of Hera, at Samos,
whose abduction and discovery in a willow bush near the river bank was enacted
each year (Athenaeus 15.672ff.).

3. See Georges Roux, "Qu-est-ce qu'un *kolossos*," and S. Broc, "L'Hermès
d'Hiéron à Delphes et le nom de l'hermès en grec," *Revue des études grecques* 70
(1963), pp. 39–51.

4. Axel Persson, *The Royal Tombs at Dendra near Midea* (Lund: Gleerup,
1931), pp. 73–108; Martin P. Nilsson, *The Minoan-Mycenaean Religion and its
Survival in Greek Religion*, 2nd ed. (Lund: Gleerup, 1950), p. 600ff.; and espe-
cially Charles Picard, "Le cénotaphe de Midéa et les colosses de Ménélas," *Revue
de philologie* 9 (1933), pp. 343–54, and *Les religions préhelléniques: (Crète et
Mycènes)* (Paris: Presses Universitaires de France, 1948), pp. 269ff. and 291.
Menhirs similar to those of Midea have been found at Thera, in a tomb, and at
Atchana, near one of the town gates.

5. See Homer, *Iliad*, 23.70ff.

6. See Pierre Guillon, "La stèle d'Agmédès," *Revue de philologie* 62 (1936),
pp. 209–35. More generally, on the connections between the funerary stela and
the *kolossos*, see Elise van Hall, *Over den oorsprong van de grieksche grafstele* (Amsterdam: Noord-hollandsche uitgevers-mij., 1942). On the ritual significance of
the *epiklēsis*, the three calls addressing the dead man by name in a case where the
corpse of the dead man has not been recovered, Erwin Rohde writes: "The souls

of the dead who have fallen in foreign lands must be 'called'. They will then, if this is properly done, follow the caller to their distant home where an 'empty grave' awaits them." *Psyche: The Cult of Souls and Belief in Immortality among the Greeks* (New York: Harper and Row, 1966), p. 42.

7. See Charles Picard, "Le rituel des suppliants trouvé à Cyrène et le champ des 'colossoi' à Selinonte," *Revue archéologique* 8 (1936), pp. 206–207.

8. At Lebadeia, dedications to Zeus Meilichios have been found on hermae topped with omphaloid cones that can be compared with the *cippi* of Selinus. The Zeus Meilichios of Sikyon was represented by an unhewn stone in the shape of a pyramid (Pausanias 2.9.6). On the symbolism of Zeus Meilichios, see Charles Picard, "Sanctuaires et symboles de Zeus Meilichios," *Revue de l'histoire des religions* (1943), pp. 97–127.

9. *Supplematum Epigraphicum Graecum* 9. 72; Franciszek Sokolowski, *Lois sacrées des cités grecques* (Paris: Boccard, 1962); see the French translation and commentary by Jean Servais, "Les suppliants dans la loi de Cyrène," *Bulletin de correspondance héllénique* (1960), pp. 112–47.

10. *Supplematum Epigraphicum Graecum* 9. 3; see François Chamoux, *Cyrène sous la monarchie des Battiades* (Paris: Boccard, 1953), p. 105ff.; Louis Gernet, "Droit et prédroit en Grèce ancienne," *L'année sociologique*, 3rd ser. (1948–49), pp. 65–66.

11. Gernet writes: "If, with the *colossos* catching fire, something happens immediately, the person making the oath is immediately committed by his 'double'" ("Droit et prédroit," p. 66). The ritual of burning wax figurines is also found in an Aramean treaty of vassalage that can be dated to 754 BCE; see André. Dupont-Sommer, "Trois stèles araméennes provenant de Sfiré: un traité de vassalité du VIIIe siècle avant J.C.," *Les Annales Archéologiques de Syrie*. 10 (1960), pp. 21–54. The comparison of the Greek and the Aramean texts, which are mutually illuminating, is made by Charles Picard, "Le rite magique des *eidōla* de cire brulés, attesté sur trois stèles araméennes de Sfiré," *Revue archéologique* (1961), pp. 85–87.

12. Thaddaeus Zielinski, "De Helenae simulacro," *Eos* 30 (1927), pp. 54–88, recognized this. On other forms of the *eidōla*, see Eugène Monseur, "L'âme pupilline," *Revue de l'histoire des religions* 51 (1905), pp. 1–23; W. Déonna, L'âme pupilline et quelques monuments figurés, *L'antiquité classique* 26 (1957), pp. 59–90; Jean Bayet, "Idéologie et plastique: L'expression des énergies divines dans le monnayage des Grecs," *Mélanges d'archéologie et d'histoire* (1959), pp. 65–106.

13. Homer, *Iliad*, 23.59–107.

14. The *psuchē* is sometimes called smoke (*kapnos*), shade (*skia*), or dream (*oneiros*).

15. Aeschylus, *Agamemnon*, 410–26.

16. "Figurines de remplacement": Charles Picard, "Le cénotaphe de Midéa et les colosses de Ménélas," *Revue de philologie* 59 (1933), pp. 343–54. Georges Roux in "Sur quelques passages obscurs de l'Agamemnon." proposes a quite different interpretation of this passage of *Agamemnon* that, in my view, does not take into account the context where the theme of the double reappears again and again almost obsessively. Moreover, it hardly seems necessary to point out that in the eyes of the Greeks the figure of Helen was naturally associated with the theme of the double. It is well known that there were not one but two Helens. The one that Paris abducted and for whom the war was fought at Troy was not the real Helen but her ghost, an *eidōlon* fashioned by Zeus, Hera, or Proteus. According to Stesichorus, the true Helen had been spirited away to Egypt (Plato, *Republic*, 586b, and *Phaedrus*, 243a). But it was also said that she was on the white island, living forever amid feasting and rejoicing in the abode of the Blessed; see Vittore Pisani, "Elena e l' *eidōlon*," *Rivista di filologia e di istruzione classica* 56 (1928), p. 481ff.

17. Helen's absence, manifested by vain phantoms in the palace, is matched by the absence of the Greek warriors, manifested in each stricken household by the urns filled with useless ashes in place of the men who were known there when they were alive: "But in every house from which warriors have departed, overwhelming grief reigns. Every heart is pierced with one unremitting thought. They remember the faces of those whom they saw depart; but to each house urns and ashes return in the place of men" (Aeschylus, *Agamemnon*, 429–35).

18. Euripides, *Alcestis*, 342ff.

19. *Ibid.*, 353–54. The story of Alcestis's *eidōlon* takes the form of an entirely profane narrative, but it perhaps reflects the memory of pre-Hellenic funerary rites, such as the practice of placing in the tombs female figurines, similar to the *kolossoi*, who in the beyond played the role of "concubines to the dead man," recorded in Egypt by Herodotus (2.129–32). See Charles Picard, "Les 'colossoi' de Dorak (Anatolie du Nord)," *Revue archéologique* (1960), pp. 106–108; Edouard Dhorme, "Rituel funéraire assyrien," *Revue d'archéologie orientale* 38 (1941), pp. 57–66: M. Rutten, "Idole ou substitut" *Archiv orientální* (1949), pp. 307–309; Christiane Desroches-Noblecourt, "'Concubines du mort'

et mères de famille au Moyen Empire," *Bulletin de l'Institut français d'Archéologie Orientale du Caire* 53 (1953), pp. 7–47.

20. Apollodorus 3.30.

21. Hyginus, *Fables*, 104.

22. Pausanias 8.15.2; Aristotle, *The Constitution of Athens*, 7.1 and 55.5. See also Gernet, "*Droit et prédroit*," p. 68.

23. Homer, *Odyssey*, 11.634–35. There is also a stone at the confluence of the two rivers of the underworld, marking the entrance to the house of Hades (*ibid.*, 10.515).

24. Pindar, *Pythian Odes*, 10.75. Stones are also sometimes referred to as the bones of the earth: Ovid, *Metamorphoses*, 1.383; Scholia to Apollonius Rhodius, 3.1086. See also Pausanias 9.16.7 and Pherecydes, *Fragments*, 1.82, Muller.

25. The cult of the *semnai* in Athens had to be carried out in silence. It was entrusted to a body of priestesses, the Hesuchides, named after the founder of the cult, Hesuchos, the silent one; "Scholia to Sophocles, Oedipus at Colonus" 489; Jane Harrison, *Prolegomena to the Study of Greek Religion* (New York: Meridian, 1957), p. 243ff.

26. Hesiod, *Works and Days*, 79; Homer, *Iliad*, 18.419.

27. Theognis, 569.

28. See Roux, "Qu'est-ce qu'un kolossos?"; John C. Lawson, "*Peri alibantōn*," *Classical Review* (1926), pp. 52–58; Giovanni Pugliese Carratelli, "*Tarchuō*," *Archivio glottologico italiano* 39 (1954), pp. 78–82.

29. For the Greeks, *charis* emanates not only from women, or any human being whose youthful beauty makes the body "shine" (especially the eyes) with a splendor that provokes love, but also from cut jewels, worked gems, and certain precious fabrics: The glitter of metal, the flash of stones in various waters, the variety of colors of a woven cloth, the medley of designs representing, in a more or less stylized form, a scene of plants and animals directly suggesting the powers of life — all these combine to make the work of the goldsmiths and weavers a sort of concentration of living light from which *charis* shines out. On the *kolossos*'s "empty eyes": Aeschylus, *Agamemnon*, 418. The "emptiness of the eyes" mentioned by Aeschylus in reference to Helen's *kolossos* tallies with Kallimachos's phrase describing Teiresias, who is blinded by Athena for having seen what no man should see: "Night took his eyes" (*The Bath of Pallas*, 82). There is perhaps an even closer connection. At the moment when the goddess deprives him of his sight and the sun's light, Teiresias " *estathē d' aphthoggos, ekollasan gar aniai gōnata, kai phō-*

nan eschen amēchania." Standing there without sight, speech, or movement (his legs are riveted together), Teiresias himself becomes a kind of *kolossos*, an image of death among the living. But he has his revenge later, among the dead: amid their inconsistent shades, he is the only one to retain his *phrenes* and *noos*, the sense and knowledge that belong to the living (Homer, *Odyssey*, 10.493). Like the *kolossos*, the diviner belongs both to the world of the living and to the world of the dead. This is the ambiguity represented by the image of the "blind visionary."

30. A passage from the *Iliad* gives a striking illustration of this dialectic between the visible and the invisible. At Aulis, before their departure, the Greeks make their sacrifices at the foot of a plane tree. A terrible omen suddenly appears: Zeus summons into the light of day a snake, which emerges from underneath the altar; it falls upon a clutch of sparrows and devours them and their mother: "Immediately, the god who made it appear hid it from their eyes [literally: made it invisible]; indeed the son of Kronos had suddenly changed it into stone" (Homer, *Iliad*, 2.318–19). The associations of the snake, a chthonian animal, with the world of the dead and especially the *psuchē* are well known. By turning it to stone after summoning it for a moment into the light of day, Zeus restores it to the realm of the invisible.

31. A comparison in the *Iliad* emphasizes this link between the aerial mobility of the *psuchē* and the immobility of the funerary stela. Achilles's horses, beasts from the underworld as swift as the wind, suddenly become as still as death, mourning Patroclus: "They are like a stela, forever immovable once it is set up over the tomb of a dead woman or man. There they remain, just as motionless, heads bowed to the ground" (Homer, *Iliad*, 17.434ff.; see also 19.405). Achilles' horses, born of a union between the god Zephyr and the harpy Podargē, ("the swift one"), belong to the group of daemon abductors who spirit away the living, leaving no trace of them (Rohde, *Psyche*, pp. 59–60). Once these spirits of the wind, elusive and invisible, who move about without touching the earth become still and root themselves to the ground, they become images of the stela, just as, conversely, the stela is their immovable counterpart.

32. Pausanias 9.38.5.

33. The inseparability of the material sign and the ritual action is demonstrated most strikingly in the case of the *kolossoi* of Midea. On one of the surfaces of these two quadrangular slabs, there is a series of hollows made to hold food for the dead, probably the *panspermia*. These "idols" are also tables on which offerings are received.

34. For example, when evoked according to ritual, the shade of Darius appears to the queen and the Persians "above the top of his tombstone" (Aeschylus, *Persians*, 659).

CHAPTER FIFTEEN: FROM THE "PRESENTIFICATION" OF THE INVISIBLE TO THE IMITATION OF EXPERIENCE

This essay originally appeared as "De la présentification de l'invisible à l'imitation de l'apparence," in Ecole du Louvre, *Image et signification* (Paris: Documentation française, 1983), pp. 25–37. This translation by Froma I. Zeitlin, in Jean-Pierre Vernant, *Mortals and Immortals: Collected Essays*, ed. and trans. Froma I. Zeitlin (Princeton, NJ: Princeton University Press, 1991), pp. 151–63. Reprinted by permission of Princeton University Press.

1. Pierre Demargner, *The Birth of Greek Art*, trans. Stuart Gilbert and James Emmons (New York: Golden Press, 1964), p. 402.

2. Emile Benveniste, "Le sens du mot *kolossos* et les noms grecs de la statue," *Revue de Philologie* 5 (1932), pp. 118–35.

3. Jean-Pierre Vernant, in Froma I. Zeitlin, ed. and trans. *Mortals and Immortals*, pp. 164–85.

4. For a fuller discussion of *xoana* and the multiple forms they may take outside of Pausanias's descriptions, see Alice A. Donohue, *Xoana and the Origins of Greek Sculpture* (Atlanta: Scholars Press, 1988) – ED.

5. Pausanias, 2.4.5, 10.19.3.

6. Herodotus 7.153.7–16.

7. Scholiast to Pindar's second Pythian ode, 2.30.

8. Callimachus, *Hymus in lavacrum Palladis*, 35–42.

9. Jean Cuisenier, "Tradition de l'image en Europe," *Image et Signification* (1983) p. 13.

10. *Homeric Hymn to Apollo*, I, pp. 146ff.

11. *Scholium on the Iliad*, 7.118.

12. Herodotus, 5.47.

13. On Ampharete's stela, see Werner Peek, *Griechische Grabgedichte, griechische und deutsch* (Berlin: Akademie, 1960), no. 96.

14. *Ibid.*, no. 54.

15. *Ibid.*, nos. 92, 78, 34.

16. *Palatine Anthology* 7.649.

17. Peek, *Griechische Grabgedichte*, nos. 52 and 40.

CHAPTER SIXTEEN: SOME ASPECTS OF PERSONAL IDENTITY
IN GREEK RELIGION

This essay originally appeared as "Aspects de la personne dans la religion grecque," lecture given at the conference "Problèmes de la personne" organized by the Centre de Recherches de Psychologie Comparative Lu Royaumont, 29 September – 3 October 1960.

1. At least it is so in one of its fundamental aspects, maenadism, to which I refer here; see Henri Jeanmaire, *Dionysos: Histoire du culte de Bacchus; L'orgiasme dans l'antiquité et les temps modernes, origine du théâtre en Grèce, orphisme et mystique dionysiaque, èvolution du dionysisme après Alexandre* (Paris: Payot, 1951), p. 158ff.; Louis Gernet, "Dionysos et la religion dionysiaque: Eléments hérités et traits originaux," *Revue des études grecques* (1953), pp. 377–95, especially p. 383: "Le ménadisme est chose féminine."

2. See Louis Gernet and André Boulanger, *Le génie grec dans la religion* (Paris: Renaissance du livre, 1932), p. 124.

3. *Ibid.*, p. 123. On the *orgeones*, see W.S. Ferguson, "The Attic Orgeones," *The Harvard Theological Review* 37 (1944), pp. 61–140.

4. Gernet and Boulanger, *Le génie grec*, p. 125. For an analysis of the Greek vocabulary used to express the sacred, and in particular the meanings of *hieros*, see Jean Rudhardt, *Notions fondamentales de la pensée religieuse et actes constitutifs du culte dans la Grèce classique* (Geneva: Droz, 1958); on the meaning of *hosios* (as opposed to *hieros*), where *hosios* has the sense of liberated from the sacred, deconsecrated and consequently free, permitted, profane, see Henri Jeanmaire, "Le substantif hosia et sa signification comme terme technique dans le vocabulaire religieux," *Revue des études grecques* 58 (1945), pp. 66–89. On the use of the same term for the Bacchae who minister to Dionysos, and its use in the circles of the sects with the meaning not of deconsecrated and lawful but of consecrated, sanctified, see Jane Harrison, *Prolegomena to the Study of Greek Religion* (New York: Meridian, 1957), p. 503ff. Being freed with regard to the *hieros* can take place downward, toward what is profane, or upward, in the direction of an identification with the divine.

5. See Dodds, *The Greeks and the Irrational*, (Berkeley: University of California Press, 1963), p. 135ff.

6. See Gernet, "Dionysos et la religion dionysiac," p. 393.

7. Plutarch, on Stobaeus, *Florilegium*, 4.107.

8. See Louis Gernet, "L'anthropologie dans la religion grecque," in Claas

Jouco Bleeker (ed.), *Anthropologie religieuse: L'homme et sa destinée à la lumière de l'histoire des religions* (Leiden: Brill, 1955), vol. 2, p. 52: "It is striking that not even the Dionysian religion as such or the mysteries of Eleusis were concerned with it [the soul]." See also Gernet and Boulanger, *Le Génie grec*, p. 287: "The thought of the Mystery religions remains so undeveloped that the Homeric representation of the fate of the souls (which has survived, down to modern times) predominates: it perpetuates 'impersonal' concepts of the most primitive type."

9. See J. Festugière, *Personal Religion among the Greeks* (Berkeley: University of California Press, 1954) and André Bonnard, *La tragédie et l'homme: Etudes sur le drame antique* (Neuchâtel: Baconnière, 1951), pp. 153–87.

10. Euripides, *Hippolytus*, 84.

11. *Ibid.*, 953–54.

12. For Hippolytus's self-confidence and the trenchant declaration of his own superiority or even perfection, see *ibid.*, 654ff., 995, 1007, 1365. *Aidōs*, the virtue that is associated especially with youth and that Hippolytus embodies is, through excess, transformed in his case into its opposite, arrogance: *to semnon*; see 93 and 1064.

13. *Ibid.*, 1080.

14. See *ibid.*, 19–21 (lines pronounced by Aphrodite) and 730–31, at the climax of the drama, when Phaedra makes the decision to kill herself and bring ruin upon Hippolytus.

15. *Ibid.*, 1396.

16. *Ibid.*, 1437ff.

17. One aspect of Greek tragedy is the solitude in which man finds himself when faced with death and, more generally, when confronted with anything that marks human existence with the seal of deprivation and nonbeing. Amid his failures and trials or on the threshold of death, man feels himself observed by a deity that is defined by its perfect fullness of being and cannot be related to or participate in the world of passion. Thus any human destiny may at the same time be seen from two opposite perspectives: from man's point of view, as a drama, and, from the point of view of the gods, as a distant and futile spectacle.

18. Suffice it to refer here to Bruno Snell, *The Discovery of the Mind in Greek Philosophy and Literature*, trans. T.G. Rosenmayer (New York: Harper and Row, 1970). Richard Broxton Onians, *The Origins of European Thought about the Body, the Mind, the Soul, the World, Time, and Fate*, 2nd ed., (Cambridge: Cambridge University Press, 1951); of Hermann Ferdinand Fränkel, *Dichtung und Philoso-*

phie des frühens Griechentums: Eine Geschichte der griechischen Epik, Lyrik und Prosa bis zur Mitte des fünften Jahrhunderts, 2nd ed. (Munich: Beck, 1962), and *Wege und Formen frühgriechischen Denkens: Literarische und philosophiegeschichtliche Studien*, 2nd ed. (Munich: Beck, 1960); and Clemence Ramnoux, *Vocabulaire et structures de pensée archaïque chez Héraclite* (Paris: Belles Lettres, 1959). See also the stimulating study by Louis Graz, "L'Iliade et la personne," *Esprit* (1960), pp. 1390–1403.

19. To take just one example: the problems of the god as a responsible agent and of his internal liberty are never considered. A deity's actions know no limits other than those that are imposed from outside by other powers whose privileges and spheres of influence must be respected. A god's liberty is measured in terms of the extent of his power, his dominion over others. Walter F. Otto rightly comments that nothing about the Greek gods calls attention to a "self" or refers to an "ego" with its own will, feelings, and individual destiny. *The Homeric Gods: The Spiritual Significance of Greek Religion*, trans. Moses Hadas (London: Thames and Hudson, 1954), p. 236.

20. "It is a fact, and one of great significance, that Greek thought never distinguished between *theos* and *theoi*, between god and gods." A.J. Festugière, "Remarques sur les dieux grecs," *La vie intellectuelle* (1932), p. 385.

21. See Gilbert François, *Le Polythéisme et l'emploi au singulier des mots Theós, Daímon dans la littérature grecque d'Homère à Platon* (Paris: Belles Lettres, 1957).

22. The concept of a divine power that is both one and threefold presents no difficulty or problem for the Greeks. One has only to reflect on the bitterness of the arguments about the trinity in Christianity to appreciate how much thought about the divine has changed.

23. The best illustration is possibly that provided by Xenophon in the *Anabasis*. Throughout this campaign, Xenophon places himself under the special protection of Zeus the king, as the oracle of Delphi had ordered him to do (3.1.6–12; 6.1.22). This deity manifests his particular favors to him through dreams; on several occasions, Xenophon offers sacrifices to him, as, on other occasions, he also does to Zeus the savior. But being in the good graces of Zeus the king and Zeus the savior does not prevent Xenophon from being on bad terms with Zeus Meilichios, and from finding himself entirely impoverished for this reason. Being far away from home, Xenophon forgot to make sacrifices to Zeus Meilichios, as he did when at home, on the day of the Diasia. Zeus the king

is concerned with the problems of authority and command, Zeus the savior presides over the hazards of war, but Xenophon's personal fortune and the state of his finances depend on Zeus Meilichios (7.8.1–7). Another significant fact is that among the epithets addressed to him in the course of his cult, a god may also have the proper name of another so-called "personal" deity. There are, for example, instances of a Zeus-Hades and a Hera-Aphrodite.

24. See Pierre Chantraine on the absence of this opposition on the linguistic level, in "Réflexions sur les noms des dieux helléniques," *Antiquité classique* 22 (1953), pp. 65–78.

25. Erwin Rohde, "Die Religion der Griechen," in *Kleine Schriften* (Tübingen: Mohr, 1901), vol. 2, p. 320; Leopold Schmidt, *Die Ethik der alten Griechen* (Berlin: Hertz, 1882), vol. 1, p. 52; quoted in François, "Le polythéisme," pp. 11 and 14.

26. See Rudhardt, *Notions fondamentales*, p. 80ff.

27. See Gernet and Boulanger, *Le génie grec*, p. 287: "When Socrates remarks in the 'Republic' that the individual possesses his own immortal soul this is greeted by an educated Athenian as a strange novelty." See also Rudhardt, *Notions fondamentales*, pp. 113 and 125.

28. Hesiod, *Works and Days*, 154.

29. This opposition is very clear in Hesiod's myth of the races, where the anonymous dead and the glorious heroes form a contrasting pair. The former disappear into the world of night, silence, and oblivion. The latter belong to the world of light, and their glory, celebrated by the voice of the poets, lives forever in men's memories.

30. Gernet and Boulanger, *Le génie grec*, p. 255.

31. See Paul François Foucart, *Le culte des héros chez les Grecs* (Paris: Imprimerie Nationale, 1918), p. 22ff.; Marie Delcourt, *Légendes et cultes de héros en Grèce* (Paris: Presses Universitaires de France, 1942), p. 62ff.

32. Hermann Usener, *Götternamen: Versuch einer Lehre von der religiösen Begriffsbildung* (Bonn: Cohen, 1896). On the Greek heroes as "Sondergötter," see pp. 247–73.

33. The labors of Herakles illustrate this. The myth of Perseus appears to present an example where the actions are already organized in a more complex and systematic way. In order to be successful, Perseus has first to persuade the Graiae to reveal to him the secret of the abode of the nymphs, obtain the magic instruments of victory from the nymphs, slay Medusa with Athena's help, and

finally escape from the pursuit of the two surviving Gorgons. However, each phase is really a repetition of one single mythical theme, expressing the same initiatory trial: to see without being seen, to make oneself invisible to a vigilant enemy. Perseus must kill Medusa, the eye of death, seeing her but not exchanging glances with her. He must escape from the Gorgons by means of the magic instruments of invisibility and take the Graiai by surprise by stealing their only eye at the precise moment when, being passed from hand to hand, the eye is not actually in the possession of any one of them.

34. Gernet, "L'anthropologie dans la religion grecque," p. 53.

35. *Ibid.*, p. 58.

36. On these exercises in mental concentration, similar to those used in yoga, and their relationship with memory exercises in the philosophical sects and Pythagorean brotherhoods, see *ibid.*, pp. 96 and 114, and Marcel Detienne, *La notion de daïmōn dans le pythagorisme ancien: De la pensée religieuse à la pensée philosophique* (Paris: Belles Lettres, 1963), pp. 69–85.

37. This conquest of the subject by himself and the progressive elaboration of the world of inner experience over and against the external world were achieved in different ways, with lyric poetry, moral thought, tragedy, medicine, and philosophy all playing their part. On the meaning of *psuchē* and other psychological terms and their semantic development in the various sectors of Greek thought, see the excellent study by T.B.L. Webster, "Some Psychological Terms in Greek tragedy," *Journal of Hellenic Studies* 77 (1957), pp. 149–54.

38. For this reason, it would later be necessary to recover the body and integrate it with the ego, so as to establish the person both in his concrete uniqueness and as an expression of the total man.

39. Aristotle, *On Prophesying by Dreams*, 46312–15.

CHAPTER SEVENTEEN: THE FORMATION OF POSITIVIST THOUGHT IN ARCHAIC GREECE

This essay originally appeared as "La formation de la pensée positive dans la Grèce archaïque," *Annales* 12 (1957), pp. 183–206.

1. John Burnet, *Early Greek Philosophy*, 2nd ed. (London: Black, 1920), p. v.

2. This interpretation can still be found in the work of Bruno Snell, although his point of view is historical. See *Die Entdeckung des Geistes: Studien zur Entstehung des europäischen Denkens bei den Griechen*, 3rd ed. (Hamburg: Claassen, 1955).

3. Burnet, *Early Greek Philosophy*, p. 10. As Clémence Ramnoux writes, according to Burnet, Ionian physics saves Europe from the religious spirit of the East; it represents the Marathon of intellectual life. "Sur quelques interprétations modernes d'Anaximandre," *Revue de métaphysique et de morale* 59 (1954), pp. 232–52.

4. Francis Macdonald Cornford, *From Religion to Philosophy: A Study in the Origins of Western Speculation* (London: Arnold, 1912), and *Principium Sapientiae: The Origins of Greek Philosophical Thought* (Cambridge: Cambridge University Press, 1952).

5. Homer, *Iliad*, 15.189–94.

6. Cornford, *Principium*, pp. 159–224.

7. George Thomson takes up the same demonstration in *Studies in Ancient Greek Society* (London: Lawrence and Wishart, 1954), vol. 2, pp. 140–72. Hesiod, *Theogony*, 820–71.

8. As W.K.C. Guthrie, who revised and published Cornford's manuscript, has noted, the hypothesis of a link between the cosmological myths in Hesiod's *Theogony* and a complex of Babylonian myths and rituals is supported by a Hittite text, the epic of Kumarbi, which establishes a connection between the Babylonian story and the Greek adaptation (Cornford, *Principium*, p. 249 n.1). Thomson also stresses the intermediary role that may have been played by a Phoenician version of the myth, which is later echoed in Philo of Byblos (*Studies*, pp. 141 and 153).

9. In Babylon, the rite was celebrated every year, during the eleven days that were added to the end of a lunar year and made it coincide with the solar year. With accurate knowledge of the seasons, it was possible to foresee and organize the timetable for agricultural work. The moment chosen to insert the eleven extra days was the spring equinox, before the ploughing. Thomson provides interesting information on the relationship between the function of the king, the development of agriculture, and the control of time, defined by the seasons through the intervention of the solar or lunar calendar. *Ibid.*, pp. 105–30.

10. Hesiod, *Theogony*, p. 116ff.

11. *Ibid.*, 132. See Cornford, *Principium*, p. 194ff.; Thomson, *Studies*, p. 151.

12. The year is composed of four seasons, just as the cosmos is made of four regions. The summer corresponds to the hot, the winter to the cold, the spring to the dry, and the autumn to the wet. In the course of the annual cycle,

each power predominates for a time and then, in accordance with the order of
time, has to pay the price for its "unjust aggression" (Anaximander, frag. 1) by
in its turn relinquishing its place to the opposite principle. The year thus
comes periodically back to its starting point, passing through alternating movements of expansion and contraction. In the same way, the human body is composed of four humors (Hippocrates, *De Natural Hominis*, 7) which dominate
according to the seasons. See Cornford, *Principium*, p. 168ff.; Thomson, *Studies*,
p. 126.

13. The strife between opposites, which is represented in Heraclitus by
Polemos and in Empedocles by Neikos, is expressed in Anaximander by the
injustices (*adikia*), that they commit in turn toward one another. The attraction
and union between the opposites, represented in Hesiod by Ērōs, and in Empedocles by Philia, appear in Anaximander as the interaction of the four principles,
once they have been separated out. This interaction that gives birth to the first
living creatures, when the heat of the sun warms the damp mud of the earth. For
Thomson, this type of thought, which could be called a logic of opposition and
complementarity, should be connected with the earliest social structure: the
complementary organization of the tribe into two opposed clans which are
exogamous and which intermarry. Thomson remarks that the tribe is a unity of
opposites (Thomson, *Studies*, pp. 45, 91, 126). Cornford shows that the cyclical
conception also persists among the Milesians. The cosmos, like the year, returns
to its starting point, the primordial unity. The unlimited (*apeiron*) is not only the
origin but also the end of the ordered and differentiated world. It is the principle, *archē*, the infinite, inexhaustible, eternal source from which all proceeds and
to which all returns. The unlimited is a "cycle" in space and time.

14. Cornford, *Principium*, pp. 187–88.

15. One of the most interesting passages in Thomson's book establishes a
connection between the cycle of the *octaeteris*, which made the lunar and solar
years coincide in Greece, and the archaic forms of royalty. Every nine years,
Zeus renewed Minos's royal power, just as in Sparta every nine years the ephores
study the stars for confirmation of the power of their kings. It has been suggested that the eight-year festivals of the Daphnephoria, at Thebes and the
Septerion at Delphi have a direct connection with both the introduction of the
calendar (at a much earlier date than is supposed by Martin Nilsson) and with
the institution of kingship.

16. It is still alive in Homer (*Odyssey*, 19.109), but in the story of Salmoneus

the figure of the magician-king, the creator of time, is used only to illustrate the theme of human hubris and the way it is punished by the gods.

17. And sometimes he too brings them about: Empedocles knows the art of stopping the winds and changing the rain into dry weather. See Louis Gernet, "Les origines de la philosophie," *Bulletin de l'enseignement public du Maroc* 183 (1945), p. 9.

18. Werner Jaeger, *The Theology of the Early Greek Philosophers* (Oxford: Clarendon, 1947), pp. 20–21; Cornford, *Principium*, p. 259. The example of Gaia that Cornford also uses is not the most apposite. Aristotle remarks that the Milesians do not in general give earth a role of first importance in their physics (see *Metaphysics*, A.8.989ff., where Aristotle explains the reasons for this). Furthermore, Gaia, as a divine power, has few human characteristics.

19. See Snell, *Discovery of the Mind*, p. 227ff.

20. The human soul is a part of nature, made of the stuff of the elements. The divine is what underlies nature, the inexhaustible material, the ever-moving tapestry on which, in a ceaseless process, forms are depicted and fade away.

21. Cornford, *Principium*, 180–81.

22. The use of a technical model does not, in itself, constitute a mental transformation. Myth uses technical images just as rational thought does, as is shown by the place given to the operations of binding, weaving, spinning, and modeling, the wheel, the balance, and so forth. But at this level of thought, the technical model is used to characterize a type of activity or the function of an agent: the gods spin destiny and weigh the fates the way women spin wool and housekeepers weigh it. In rational thought, the technical image assumes a new function, related to structures rather than activities. It explains how a mechanism works, rather than defining the operation of an agent. See Snell, *Discovery of the Mind*, p. 214ff. Snell emphasizes the difference between comparisons with the *technai* as used by Homer and their use in, for example, Empedocles. Empedocles seeks to describe not vital activities but the properties and permanent structure of an object.

23. See Jaeger, *Theology*, p. 160ff.

24. Pierre Maxime Schuhl has shown that these two currents corresponded to the two opposed tendencies in Greek religion and culture, and that the tension between them stimulated the development of philosophy. *Essai sur la formation de la pensée grecque: Introduction historique a une étude de la philosophie platonicienne*, 2nd ed. (Paris: Presses Universitaires de France, 1949).

25. Snell has traced through ancient Greek lyric poetry the discovery of the truly spiritual aspects of the human soul, that is, its connection with inner experience, its intensity, and subjectivity. He notes the innovation represented by the idea of the "depth" of thought. Homer is not familiar with expressions such as *bathumētēs, bathuphrōn*, with deep thoughts. What he says is *polumētis, poluphrōn*, with many-sided thoughts. The idea of intellectual and spiritual things (such as feeling, reflection, and knowledge) having "depth" is expressed in archaic poetry before it appears in, for example, Heraclitus (*Discovery of the Mind*, pp. 17–18).

26. The antithesis between the *phanera* (visible things) and the *adēla* (invisible things) that is fundamental in Greek religious thought is found transposed in philosophy, science, and the legal distinction between visible and nonvisible possessions. See Pierre Maxime Schuhl, "Adèla," *Homo* 1 (1953), pp. 86–94; Louis Gernet, "Choses visibles et choses invisibles," *Revue philosophique* 46 (1956), pp. 79–87.

27. In religion, myth expresses an essential truth; it is authentic knowledge, a model of reality. In rational thought, the reverse is the case. The myth becomes no more than the image of authentic knowledge, and its object, genesis, is simply an imitation of the model provided by immutable and eternal being. Myth thus comes to be associated with the domain of the probable, of belief, *pistis*, as opposed to the certainty of scientific knowledge. Although it is in keeping with mythical schemata, the doubling of reality in terms of model and image nevertheless has the effect of undermining myth, which is reduced to the level of imagery. See, in particular, Plato, *Timaeus*, 29ff.

28. Schuhl, *Essai sur la formation*, pp. 151–75.

29. Benjamin Farrington, *Greek Science, Its Meaning for Us* (New York: Penguin, 1944), vol. 1, p. 36ff.

30. Thomson, *Studies*, pp. 171–72.

31. Erwin Rohde, *Psyche: The Cult of Souls and Belief in Immortality among the Greeks*, 8th ed., trans. W.B. Hills (New York: Harper and Row, 1966), p. 299ff.

32. W.R. Halliday, *Greek Divination: A Study of Its Methods and Principles* (London: Macmillan, 1913).

33. Cornford, *Principium*, p. 89ff.

34. Homer, *Iliad* 1.70. See Cornford, *Principium*, p. 73ff.

35. This is also the definition Hesiod uses in the *Theogony*, 32: the Muses have inspired him to sing of things that have been and that will be; and 38: they

speak of things that are, that will be, and that have been. Furthermore, divination is, in principle, concerned with the past as much as with the future. The purificatory prophet Epimenides was later even to restrict his divinatory talents exclusively to discovering the facts of the past that had remained unknown (Aristotle, *Rhetoric*, 3.17.141824).

36. Hesiod, *Theogony*, 43ff. See Cornford, *Principium*, p. 77.

37. See Gernet, "Les origines de la philosophie," p. 2.

38. On the relationship between the vocabulary, imagery, and themes of a writer such as Parmenides and those used in the tradition of the mystic sects, see *ibid.*, pp. 2–6, and Thomson, *Studies*, p. 274.

39. Gernet, "Les origines de la philosophie," p. 4. Gernet stresses the religious meaning of the term *beatus* (*eudaimon*), the highest degree of the hierarchy, and points out that it is broken down into *doctus*, *perfectus*, and *sapiens*. See also Cornford, *Principium*, p. 110.

40. Heraclitus, frag. 1. See Cornford, *Principium*, p. 113; and Thomson, *Studies*, p. 247.

41. Gernet, "Les origines de la philosophie," p. 7; Cornford, *Principium*, pp. 45–61 and 76ff. See also p. 78.

42. Rohde, *Psyche*, pp. 259–60.

43. The difference is strongly stressed by E.R. Dodds, *The Greeks and the Irrational* (Berkeley: University of California Press, 1951), p. 140ff.

44. The connection is mentioned in passing by Rohde, *Psyche*, p. 283. The thesis concerning Greek shamanism has been developed by Karl Meuli, "Scythica," *Hermes* 70 (1935), pp. 121–77. See also Gernet, "Les origines de la philosophie," p. 8; Dodds, "Greek Shamans and Puritanism," in *Greeks and the Irrational*; Cornford, "Shamanism," in *Principium*. Cornford suggests, as does Nora Kershaw Chadwick, that Thrace, through its contacts with the Germans to the north and the Celts to the west, may have constituted the intermediary linking Greece to the mantic system related to the shamanism of northern Asia. Nora Kershaw Chadwick, *Poetry and Prophecy* (Cambridge: Cambridge University Press, 1942), p. 12. Meuli and Dodds also mention Scythia, with which Greece was brought into contact through the colonization of the shore of the Black Sea. The northern origins of the magi, Aristeas, Abaris, and Hermotimus and their close relationship with the hyperborean world may also be noted. True, Epimenides himself was a Cretan. But after his death, his corpse was found to be tattooed; according to Herodotus, tattooing was current among the Thracian aristocracy

(5.6.3). Furthermore, it is known that Crete held an important place in hyperborean legends. For my part, I would be inclined to establish a connection with techniques like yoga, rather than with shamanism.

45. See Gernet, "Les origines de la philosophie," p. 8. Ernst Bickel has stressed the connection between one archaic concept of the soul and our breath: *Homerischer Seelenglaube: Geschichtliche Grundzüge menschlicher Seelenvorstellungen* (Berlin: Deutsche Verlagsgesellschaft für Politik und Geschichte, 1926). See also Richard Broxton Onians, *The Origins of European Thought about the Body, the Mind, the Soul, the World, Time, and Fate* (Cambridge: Cambridge University Press, 1951).

46. See Gernet, "Les origines de la philosophie," p. 8.

47. Gernet writes: "True, the Pythagoreans have no 'mysteries,' but the fact is that, for them 'philosophy' is truly a mystery" (*ibid.*, p. 4). Philosophy becomes established as a specific intellectual discipline through discussion and controversy, through the need to reply to an opponent's objections. Even when the philosopher is not actually engaged in polemic, he reflects on the problems posed by his predecessors and contemporaries; his thinking is in relation to theirs. Ethical thought takes a rational form from the moment Socrates engages in public discussion with all the Athenians, in the agora, on the nature of courage, justice, piety, and so forth.

48. George Thomson, "From Religion to Philosophy," *Journal of Hellenic Studies* 73 (1953), pp. 77–84, and *Studies*, pp. 131–37.

49. "To speak with understanding one must hold fast to what is common to all as a city holds fast to its law" (Heraclitus, frag. 128, Burnet).

50. See Thomson, *Studies*, p. 228ff.

51. See Louis Gernet, *Recherches sur le développement de la pensée juridique et morale en Grèce* (Paris: Leroux, 1917) pp. 6 and 26, with reference to Rudolf Hirzel, *Themis, Dike, und Verwandtes: Ein Beitrag zur Geschichte der Rechtsidee bei den Griechen* (Leipzig, S. Hirzel, 1907). Emmanuel Laroche has shown that *nomos* originally had a religious and moral meaning that was fairly close to that of *kosmos*, implying order, arrangement, just distribution: *Histoire de la racine nem- en grec ancien (nemo, nemesis, nomos, nomizo)* (Paris: Klincksieck, 1950). In Athens, after the Peisistratids, it acquired the meaning of political law, replacing *thesmos*, owing to its association with the democratic ideal of *isonomia*. Whether it is based on absolute or proportional equality, the law (*nomos*) retains an aspect of distribution. Another sense of *nomos*, albeit one that is weaker than the primary

meaning "rule," is found, for example, in Herodotus: "custom" or "usage," without any normative overtones. There can be a slippage between the senses "political law" and "custom," and this is exploited in philosophical thought, especially by the sophists.

52. See Thomson, *Studies*, p. 224ff.

53. Aristotle, *Constitution of Athens*, 21.3.

54. Louis Gernet, "La notion mythique de la valeur en Grece," *Journal de psychologie* 41 (1948), pp. 415–62.

55. According to Herodotus 1.94, money was first minted by the kings of Lydia. See Schuhl, "Adèla," pp. 157–58, and Thomson, *Studies*, p. 194.

56. Gernet, "Recherches," p. 21ff.; Thomson, *Studies*, p. 195.

57. See Louis Gernet, "Le temps dans les formes archaïques du droit," *Journal de psychologie* 53 (1956), p. 401. Gernet notes that the payment of interest had to be made at each lunation (compare Aristophanes, *Clouds*, 1659).

58. Thomson, *Studies*, pp. 297, 300, 315. He writes of Parmenides: "Just as his universe of pure being, stripped of everything qualitative, is a mental reflection of the abstract labor embodied in commodities, so his pure reason, which rejects everything qualitative, is a fetish concept reflecting the money form of value."

59. On the specific character of various types of work and of intellectual activities, see Ignace Meyerson, "Discontinuités et cheminements autonomes dans l'histoire de l'esprit," *Journal de psychologie* 41 (1948), p. 28ff., and "Problèmes d'histoire psychologique des oeuvres: Spécificité, variation, expérience," in *Éventail de l'histoire vivante: Hommage à Lucien Febvre* (Paris: Colin, 1953), vol. 1, pp. 207–18.

60. Marx stressed that use value remained the dominant perspective throughout classical Antiquity. Speaking from the Marxist perspective he adopts, Thomson seems to fall into an anachronism: it is only when free and salaried work itself becomes a commodity that the "produce of labour universally becomes a commodity" (Karl Marx, *Capital: A Critique of Political Economy*, vol. 1, *The Process of Production of Capital* [London: Lawrence and Wishart, 1954], p. 170 n.1) and an abstract notion of work is developed (Marx, *A Contribution to the Critique of Political Economy* [Chicago: Kerr, 1904], pp. 66–67).

61. See Gernet, "Choses visibles."

62. *Ibid.*, pp. 79–87.

63. Aristotle, *Nichomachaean Ethics*, 4.1119b26; see Gernet, "Choses visibles," p. 82.

64. Heraclitus's famous pronouncement "The Whole is transmuted into fire, and fire into all things, just as goods (*chrēmata*) are exchanged for gold, and gold for goods" (Plutarch, *On the E at Delphi* = Hermann Diels and Walther Krantz, *Die Fragmente der Vorsokratiker, griechisch und deutsch*, 7th ed. [Berlin: Weidmann, 1956], vol. 1, p. 171), should not, in my opinion, be interpreted in terms of this sort of commercial rationality. See Clémence Ramnoux, *Héraclite, ou L'homme entre les choses et les mots* (Paris: Belles Lettres, 1959), pp. 404–405.

65. Jaeger, *Theology*, p. 197 n.2.

66. See Parmenides on Diels-Kranz, *Fragmente*, vol. 1, pp. 238.7ff. and 239.6ff.; on the relationship between words and the *logos* in Parmenides, see Schuhl, "Adèla," pp. 283 and 290 and p. 290 n.3.

67. *Ibid.*, p. 293ff.

68. See Léon Brunschvicg's preface to Arnold Reymond, *History of the Sciences in Greco-Roman Antiquity*, trans. Ruth Gheury de Bray (New York: Biblo and Tannen, 1965), pp. vi and vii. Plato's theory of the form-numbers illustrates how mathematics was integrated with logic. Developing an idea from Julius Stenzel, Albert Lautman notes that the form-numbers represent the principles that both give the arithmetical units their place within the system and account for the varying degrees of progressive division of the forms: "The schemata of the divisions of the Forms in the 'Sophist' are thus organized in the same way as the schemata of the generation of numbers." *Essai sur les notions de structure et d'existence en mathématiques* (Paris: Hermann, 1937, p. 152).

69. See Alexandre Koyré, "Du monde de 'l'à-peu-près' à l'univers de la précision," *Critique* 28 (1948), pp. 806–83.

70. On the transition from rhetoric and sophistry to logic, see Jacqueline de Romilly, *Histoire et raison chez Thucydide* (Paris: Belles Lettres, 1956), pp. 181–239. The practice of antithetical speeches or *antilogoi* led, via the establishment of "commonplaces" of speech, to the analysis of the structures of demonstration, the assessment and measure of opposite arguments, and a science of pure reasoning.

CHAPTER EIGHTEEN: THE ORIGINS OF PHILOSOPHY
This essay originally appeared as "Les origines de la philosophie," in Christian Delacampagne and Robert Maggiori (eds.), *Philosopher: Les interrogations contemporaines* (Paris: Fayard, 1980), pp. 463–71.

1. John Burnet, *Early Greek Philosophy*, 3 ed. (London: A. and C. Black, 1920), p. v.

2. See Plato, *Sophist*, 242c–d.

3. Aristotle, *Metaphysics*, 983b20.

4. Plato, *Theaetetus*, 155d.

5. See Plato, *Philebus*, 14a: "As if our thesis (*logos*) were lost and destroyed in the manner of a fable (*muthos*) and we could only escape through some absurdity in the argument (*alogia*)."

6. Maurice Caveing, "Les mathématiques dans la culture classique de la Grèce d'après les recherches récentes," *Revue de synthèse* 100 (1979), pp. 37–47.

Index

Zone Books series design by Bruce Mau
Typesetting by Archetype
Printed and bound by Maple-Vail on Sebago acid-free paper